Anna Pompei, Lunella Mereu and Valentina Piunno (Eds.)
Light Verb Constructions as Complex Verbs

Trends in Linguistics
Studies and Monographs

Editors
Chiara Gianollo
Daniël Van Olmen

Editorial Board
Walter Bisang
Tine Breban
Volker Gast
Hans Henrich Hock
Karen Lahousse
Natalia Levshina
Caterina Mauri
Heiko Narrog
Salvador Pons
Niina Ning Zhang
Amir Zeldes

Editor responsible for this volume
Daniël Van Olmen

Volume 364

Light Verb Constructions as Complex Verbs

Features, Typology and Function

Edited by
Anna Pompei, Lunella Mereu and Valentina Piunno

DE GRUYTER
MOUTON

ISBN 978-3-11-221389-6
e-ISBN (PDF) 978-3-11-074799-7
e-ISBN (EPUB) 978-3-11-074811-6
ISSN 1861-4302

Library of Congress Control Number: 2023939233

Bibliographic information published by the Deutsche Nationalbibliothek
The Deutsche Nationalbibliothek lists this publication in the Deutsche Nationalbibliografie;
detailed bibliographic data are available on the internet at http://dnb.dnb.de.

© 2025 Walter de Gruyter GmbH, Berlin/Boston
This volume is text- and page-identical with the hardback published in 2023.
Typesetting: Integra Software Services Pvt. Ltd.
Printing and binding: CPI books GmbH, Leck

www.degruyter.com

Contents

Anna Pompei, Lunella Mereu and Valentina Piunno
Introduction —— 1

Section 1: Argument structure sharing

Václava Kettnerová
1 Valency structure of complex predicates with Light Verbs.
 The case of Czech —— 19

Lars Hellan
2 Unification and selection in Light Verb Constructions.
 A study of Norwegian —— 45

Section 2: Event structure sharing

Mahdie Eshaghi and Gholamhossein Karimi-Doostan
3 Persian Light Verbs as event determiners —— 73

Anna Pompei and Valentina Piunno
4 Light Verb Constructions in Romance languages. An attempt to explain systematic irregularity —— 99

Anna Pompei
5 How light is 'give' as a Light Verb? A case study on the actionality of Latin Light Verb Constructions (with some references to Romance languages) —— 149

Roberta Mastrofini
6 When lightness meets lexical aspect. A corpus-based account of English Light Verb Extensions —— 201

Section 3: The verb fullness

Elisabetta Ježek
7 Semantic Co-composition in Light Verb Constructions —— 221

Marcos García Salido and Marcos Garcia
8   On the unpredictability of Support Verbs. A distributional study of Spanish *tomar* —— 239

Noemi De Pasquale
9   *Making a move* towards Ancient Greek Light Verb Constructions —— 257

Section 4: **The verb emptiness**

Johanna Mattissen
10   Light Verbs and 'light nouns' in polysynthetic languages —— 275

Lu Lu and Chu-Ren Huang
11   A diachronic insight into the aspectual meaning in Light Verb Constructions. A case study in Mandarin Chinese —— 305

Francesca Di Salvo
12   Light Verb Constructions in Latin. A study on (*in*) *memoria* and (*in*) *animo habeo* —— 337

Index —— 361

Index of languages —— 371

Anna Pompei, Lunella Mereu and Valentina Piunno
Introduction

1 State of art

This volume focuses on Light Verb Constructions (henceforth LVCs) as instances of complex verbs and takes into account their features, their typology and their function.

LVCs are traditionally considered as structures composed of a predicative noun and a Light Verb (henceforth LV) – as happens in English *take a walk*, French *faire une promenade*, Italian *fare una passeggiata*, Spanish *dar un paseo* and German *einen Spaziergang machen* –, which are equivalent to synthetic verb forms – i.e. English *walk*, French *se promener*, Italian *passeggiare* and German *spazierengehen* –, when the form exists (for instance, only the analytic form is realized in Spanish).

The notion of LVC dates back to Jespersen (1942: 117), who speaks about English deverbal nouns co-occurring with an 'insignificant verb', such as *have* or *give*, as for instance in *have a wash* or *give a look*, respectively. So, the idea of lightness concerning a verb refers to its supposed semantic bleaching with regard to its full meaning (e.g. *have a new dress*, *give a present to someone*), as if the predication were effectively conveyed only by the noun.

Since the 1960s, the phenomenon of LVs has been the object of great interest, mainly in German and in French linguistics. In the German tradition, the notion of *Funktionsverb* was introduced by Polenz (1963) to refer to a functional verb with a very general meaning (and on the path towards grammaticalization, according to Heringer 1968) joining a noun to form a lexicalized predicative unit (see also Engelen 1968; Helbig 1984). On the other hand, in the French tradition the notion of 'verbe support' originates as the development of the concept of 'operator' introduced by Zellig Harris (cf. Ibrahim 1996: 4 ff),[1] within the *Lexique-Grammaire* created by the *Laboratoire d'Automatique Documentaire et Linguistique* (LADL), under the direction of Maurice Gross. The main goal of LADL consists of building a database describing the syntactic properties of the verbal lexical units of a language (Vivès 1988). This model also develops the notion of 'support verb extension', namely a verb which is less semantically empty and can substitute the support verbs, thus adding different nuances of meaning (mainly aspectual values) to the whole con-

---

[1] The term *operator* refers to the fundamental relation which ties together a syntactic unit; the operator cannot be eliminated without dissolving the syntactic unit (e.g. *the* (*letter) *of Max to Tom*; *Hugh* (*crumpled) *the napkin*) (La Fauci 2000: 14–15).

struction (e.g. *to lose influence ~ to have influence*). Lexico-Grammatical works on French still represent an inexhaustible source of material built on a solid empirical basis (Bustos Plaza 2005): indeed, the systematic study of all the predicative nouns combined with a given support verb has produced a number of grids representing the verbs' distributional, structural and transformational properties. Although employing a different empirical and methodological approach, in the 1990s Gaston Gross developed the model of *classes d'objets* in line with the *Lexique-Grammaire* theoretical perspective as part of the work of the *Laboratoire de Linguistique Informatique* (LLI) at Paris XIII University. This model is aimed at the definition of a general typology of the nominal predicates by defining a list of semantic classes of predicative nouns and verbs typically co-occurring with each one of them, from the neutral support verb for a specific class (*verbe basique*) to aspectual, diathetic, 'eventive' support verbs, as well as several appropriate support verbs, which are peculiar of a class (Gross 2004b: 357). According to these two perspectives, the support verb only provides the grammatical information, and the whole predicative content is on the noun (*prédicat nominal*): the verb only 'actualizes' the predicative element by conveying the features of person, number, tense and aspect – which cannot be expressed by the noun –, as endings in synthetic verbal predicates do; on the other hand, it does not participate in the selection of arguments (Gross 2004a: 167). Two tests[2] in particular have been elaborated within the French school to evaluate noun predicativeness and verb lightness, i.e. the reduction test (Gross 1981: 39; Giry-Schneider 1987: 28) and the coreference one (Giry-Schneider 1987: 27–28; Gross 1989: 38).

After the seminal work of the German and French schools, LVCs have also been analyzed according to other theoretical perspectives. Among the most relevant for the purpose of this volume, Meaning-Text theory and the Generative Lexicon perspective provide important results in the analysis of these constructions.

The framework of Meaning-Text theory (cf. at least Žolkovskij and Mel'čuk 1965, 1967; Mel'čuk 1973, 1981, 1988, 1996, 2003) employs the term support verb like the French school and describes the support verb constructions as collocations composed of a predicative noun (the base) selecting a semantically empty verb (the collocate). This framework provides a formal representation by means of so-called Lexical Functions, which explain the paradigmatic and syntagmatic relations between linguistic items and distinguish their syntactic role in a word combination. According to this perspective, three types of 'pure' support verbs can be distinguished based on the syntactic role fulfilled by the noun they combine with. As a matter of fact, the Meaning-Text theory considers as predicative ele-

---

2 On this, see for instance Pompei and Piunno (this volume); Pompei (this volume).

ments of a support verb construction not only noun phrases – either as the subject (Lexical function 'Func') or the object (Lexical function 'Oper') of the verb – but also prepositional phrases (Lexical function 'Labor') (cf. Mel'čuk et al. 1995: 138; Alonso Ramos 1998: 7). Furthermore, complex Lexical Functions can be formed by the addition of phasic ('begin', 'stop', 'continue') and causative meanings to the support verb (Mel'čuk 2004: 206–207). In this perspective, the function of the support verb is only that of (a) expressing mood, tense and person markers, and (b) providing the syntactic positions needed for the noun actants to appear within a clausal contexte (Alonso Ramos 1998: 7). Hence, the predicative noun confers not only the semantic content to the support verb construction, but also the arguments involved in the predication. Furthermore, Meaning-Text theory also takes into consideration the so-called 'realization verbs', i.e. a set of lexically full verbs which may show the same syntactic behavior as Light Verbs, but with a heavier semantic content. This means that, *mutatis mutandis*, 'extensions' of support verbs are also present in this model. This theoretical framework has been specifically applied to French (cf. works by Mel'čuk and the lexicographical works by Mel'čuk et al. 1999 and Mel'čuk and Polguère 2007) and Spanish (cf. work by Alonso Ramos 1998, 2004, and her research group at La Coruña). It is worth noting that this perspective explicitly excludes the possibility of considering support verb constructions as complex verbs, since a semantic unit is postulated, whereas the syntactic unit is not admitted. Semantic unit means that the support verb construction has a unique meaning, i.e. the meaning of the predicative noun, the verb being semantically empty. On the other hand, syntactic unit in this model means a single 'node' (i.e. a single word form), while the support verb construction is considered as a collocation composed of two word forms constituting a phrase (Alonso Ramos 2001a, b).[3]

An approach considering the LV as not an empty form comes from the Generative Lexicon (Pustejovsky 1995). This model conceives of the lexicon as generative in the sense that a finite number of words may generate a potentially infinite number of meanings. The approach applies a system of representation of the meaning of

---

[3] In this perspective, the notion of complex verb is assimilated to a simple verb. Alonso Ramos (2001a: 80) points out that this interpretation is already present in the Lexico-Grammar framework (Leclère, 1971: 69, 74), and even in Bally (1950), who considers the inflectional suffix of the verb as an infix (e.g. *-ait* in *il prenait peur*, considering *prendre-peur* as a word unit). The notion of complex verb is also reconducted to the more recent one of syntactic incorporation (cf. Alonso Ramos 2001a: 80 and references therein), which is considered as a sort of derivation of a simple predicate having one argument less than the base predicate. On the other hand, rather than the syntactic incorporation of the object, Alonso Ramos (2001a: 99–101) prefers the notion of 'semantic object', which is related to a minor transitivity of the verb, due to a minor individuation of the entity in object position, as happens for instance in the Spanish support verb construction *hacer campaña* 'campaign', with respect to the use of the verb with a noun preceded by a definite/indefinite article.

lexical entries which consists of four levels, namely, the argument, event, *qualia*, and lexical inheritance structures (cf. Pustejovsky 1995). Furthermore, words are considered as underspecified: their meaning emerges from the interaction between lexical entries by means of some specific mechanisms of the lexicon. This model has inspired several works on LVCs (*inter alia*, De Miguel 2006, 2008; Ježek 2011; Mastrofini 2004). In particular, among the generative mechanisms of the lexicon, the co-compositional principle has been applied to LVCs to prove that their argument and predicate are in "a bidirectional relation, wherein both [...] are mutually influenced" (De Miguel and Batiukova 2017: 104). This is similar to a conception of predicativity as 'diffused' throughout the LVC.

In some non-transformational syntactic approaches, both the noun and the verb contribute to forming the predicate in LVCs. The acknowledgement of the presence of two predicates leads to the application of the notion of 'complex predicate' to LVCs. This has been done, for example, in theoretical perspectives such as Lexical-Functional Grammar and Relational Grammar.

In the Lexical-Functional Grammar framework (Bresnan 1982, 2001) in particular, a rich literature concerning LVCs has been produced (Mohanan 1990, 1994, 1997; Butt 1995, 1998, 2003, 2010). Thus, Mohanan (1997: 431) attributes the use of the term 'complex predicate' for LVCs such as *make the claim* to Cattell (1984), who highlighted that this complex expression is perceived as a single unit of some sort, also having a semantically equivalent simple expression, i.e. the verb *claim*. According to Mohanan (1997: 432), who deals with Hindi Noun+Verb LVCs as complex predicates, "a complex predicate construction is one in which two semantically predicative elements jointly determine the structure of a single syntactic clause". In this perspective, the notion of complex predicate is applied to different kinds of LVCs, such as Verb+Noun/Adjective/Verb. Next to LVCs, scholars have included several types of multi-headed predicates in the notion of complex predicates, such as periphrastic causatives, verb particle combinations, resultatives, auxiliation, serialization, co-verbs, as well as control and raising structures (Alsina et al. 1997; Amberber et al. 2010). Nevertheless, according to Butt (2010), mono-clausality is the distinctive feature of complex predicates. From this point of view, control and raising structures cannot be included in the set of complex predicates, since they imply two distinct syntactic domains, even though some arguments are shared across them (see *inter alia* Huang 1992, Hook 1993, Abeillé et al. 1998, Wurmbrand 2001 for different positions). Mono-clausality can be determined on the basis of language dependent tests, such as clitic climbing (Aissen and Perlmutter 1983 on Spanish and Italian), passivization and reflexivization (Rosen 1989 about French and Italian), and the scope of negation (Choi 2005 for Korean). The fact that the different heads of a complex predicate contribute to the joint predication also means that "their arguments map onto a monoclausal syntactic structure" (Butt 2010: 49), where there is a single subject.

This creates a challenging mismatch between argument structure (*a-structure*) and syntax. The multidimensional architecture of Lexical-Functional Grammar allows to solve this issue including the "notion of argument structure composition, by which a complex, bi- or multiclausal a-structure corresponds to a mono-clausal f-structure", where *f-structure* stands for the functional information, which corresponds to an overt categorial (*c-structure*) realization of the syntactic functions of subject, object and predicate (Butt 2019: 2). Several hypotheses have been proposed in the Lexical-Functional Grammar perspective about the mechanism which allows argument structure composition, e.g. Argument Merger (Mohanan 1994), Argument Fusion (Butt 1995), Predicate Composition (Alsina 1996). On this, Butt (2019) provides the most recent proposal within the Lexical-Functional Grammar approach, also reviewing the developments in some other theoretical frameworks, such as LTAG (Lexicalized Feature-based Tree-Adjoining Grammar), HPSG (Head-Driven Phrase Structure Grammar) or CCG (Combinatory Categorial Grammar). Furthermore, Butt (2010) points out that, in the perspective of complex predicates, LVs have been sometimes analyzed as auxiliaries. However, Butt and Geuder (2013) point out that LVs differ from auxiliaries on a semantic level, as they are always identical to a full verb, whereas auxiliaries may also correspond to a full verb just at the beginning of the grammaticalization process that produces them (Butt and Lahiri 2013). In this perspective, LVs are not only functional elements licensing the predication (as Grimshaw and Mester 1988 state for the Argument Transfer analysis of Japanese LV *suru* 'do'). From a diachronic point of view, Butt and Lahiri (2013) show that in Urdu LVs have not been subject to semantic bleaching and consequent grammaticalization, since their forms were the same thousands of years ago; they are not even simply aspectual markers (Hook 1991, 1993). They are instead considered as lexically defective and convey a "special type of lexical meaning which consists in a modulation of the event description" expressed by the predicative element (Butt and Geuder 2013: 326). Their relationship with the full verb equivalent can be seen in terms of lexical polysemy. These features characterize LVs as semi-lexical heads. The mixed nature of LVs also led to analyses of LVs in the perspective of the Minimalist Program (Butt and Ramchand 2005), where v may constitute both a lexical and a functional category, as well as a mixture of both.[4]

In the framework of Relational Grammar (Perlmutter and Postal 1974), the notion of complex predication has been introduced with a specific focus on causatives (Davies and Rosen 1988). In this perspective, different predicates may exist in a single clause (clause union), as long as they are placed in successive strata (rather than in the same stratum) in a multistratal structure. This idea has been exploited to

---

[4] In generative syntax LVs can be considered as instantiations of v (Adger 2003: 134).

analyze LVCs in Japanese and Telugu (Dubinsky 1989 and Davies 1989 respectively; see also Kim 2003). In this approach, the predicative noun is the initiator-Predicate of the construct (the so-called 'initiator-P') in the lowest stratum (La Fauci and Mirto 2003: 45–59). In order to license the subject of a proposition, the initiator-P needs the aid of a non-initiator-P which is located in the successive stratum. This predicate can be represented by an LV or by an equivalent verb (e.g. the Italian LV *fare* 'do' in *fare un peccato* lit. 'do a sin' vs the equivalent LV extension *commettere* 'commit' in *commettere un peccato* 'commit a sin'), which are considered as 'supplementary' predicates. The supplementary predicate inherits the subject of the initiator-P ('1' in the Relational Grammar's terms); this means that the subject that is legitimated by the initiator-P is also the subject of the construct (La Fauci and Mirto 2003: 46). The initiator-P has also an argument function (the function of '2' in the terms of Relational Grammar, such as *un peccato* 'a sin' in *fare/commettere un peccato* 'commit a sin'). However, this does not entail an increase in the number of arguments with respect to the synthetic verb (e.g. *peccare* 'sin'), since the further argument is nothing but the categorially nominal realization of the initiator-P. All the arguments licensed by the initiator-P are considered as arguments of the whole proposition, rather than of the noun phrase.

2 Light Verb Constructions as complex predicates: Features, typology and function

This volume is aimed at reinforcing the idea that LVCs can be considered as a subtype of complex predicates. As shown in the state of art, the inclusion of LVCs in the set of complex predicates mainly concerns argument structure. In addition to this issue, which is placed at the syntax-semantics interface, this volume also reflects on the meaning of LVCs as complex verbs from the event structure perspective, as well as on the lexical features of the LVC components. Indeed, if i) LVs are not only used to actualize the predicative noun by conveying agreement and TAM features (as functional elements licensing predication, i.e. auxiliaries, do), and hence if ii) LVs are not really semantically empty items, we can wonder whether the LV contribution to the predication might be richer and might go beyond the argument structure. Firstly, this means that if the argument structure is considered, the event structure also has to be taken into account. Actually, aspectual traits only rarely have been considered in relation to LVCs (Hook 1991, 1993) and more infrequently in lexical terms, i.e. actionality (Butt and Geuder 2013). Secondly, this perspective might entail a reconsideration of the relationship between the LV and the predicative noun, i.e. the relevance of lexical compatibility between them. Moreover, the relationship between the LV and its lexically full verb counterpart has to be re-examined in order to determine to what extent the LV is semantically full or empty.

The current volume is divided into four sections. The first two sections are devoted to the issues of LVC argument structure and event structure, respectively. The last two sections focus on the 'semi-lexical' status of the LV, exploring the degree of lexical fullness/emptiness of the LV with respect to the full equivalent. The different investigations contained in these sections are based on a variety of theoretical approaches (e.g. Neo-Constructionalist framework, Head-driven Phrase Structure framework, Generative Lexicon, Meaning-Text theory, Construction Grammar, Functional Generative Description theoretical perspective) and a large number of languages are investigated: from different Indo-European groups – both modern (Germanic, Slavic, Romance and Iranian languages) and ancient (Latin and Ancient Greek) – to Mandarin Chinese and different polysynthetic languages, such as Ket, Nivkh, Murrinhpatha, Kiowa, Bininj Gun-wok, Ainu and so forth. Such richness allows us to go deeper into LVC typology in terms of cross-linguistic comparison, thus highlighting to what extent languages exploit the strategy of LVCs to predicate: from Persian, which has only 150 lexically full verbs and employs LVCs as a primary strategy, to Ancient Greek, which strongly prefers full verbs, but provides interesting examples of LVCs in the field of motion, to polysynthetic languages, which shed light on peculiar LVCs. Furthermore, the chapters show evidence of the different features of LVCs, in terms of a variety of configurations that can be assumed by LVCs (not only Verb+Noun, but also Verb+Adjective, Verb+Adverb, Verb+Preposition+Noun, Verb+Verb) and assess the degree of cohesion between the components, from the referentiality of the second element to its incorporation. Finally, the different contributions allow for a reflection on the function of LVCs in the modulation of the situational content in terms of event structure and argument distribution; that is to say, they allow us to evaluate the effective correspondence of LVs to their synthetic counterparts. The whole set of findings allows the researcher to draw a complex picture of LV uses, challenging the original idea of the LV as an 'insignificant verb'.

2.1 Argument and event structure sharing

The volume opens with the analysis of LVCs in terms of argument structure. The first contribution by Václava Kettnerová fits within multilayer approaches to the issue. In particular, the author follows a Functional Generative Description theoretical perspective, which is a dependency-oriented theory providing an elaborated valency description that has been extensively applied in the Prague Dependency Treebank corpora and valency lexicons. The paper by Kettnerová concerns Czech

LVCs and stresses the idea that the semantic roles of LVCs are drawn from the noun within its lexical entry. The author proceeds from the semantic layer, i.e. from the noun as lexical entry, to the deep syntactic layer, where valency complementations take place, until the surface layer, where the LV provides the LVC's surface syntactic characteristics. Through the analysis of the behavior of LVCs in active and passive sentences, it is ultimately shown that the theoretical framework is able to represent the surface realizations of both kinds of sentences deriving the syntactic surface structures in the appropriate way.

The other paper in the first section is a contribution by Lars Hellan. The chapter is devoted to the analysis of Norwegian, in which a very large number of LVs is available. The author provides the formal representation of Verb+(Preposition)+ Noun LVCs according to the Head-driven Phrase Structure model, a multi-dimensional grammar. Given the large number of LVCs in Norwegian, the author chooses to show 39 verbs occurring with the series of nouns starting with *f-*. Interestingly this determines 250 constructions with Agents as subjects and 110 constructions with Theme/Patient/Undergoer subjects; constraints in the selection of nouns by verbs and *vice versa* are considered, and a number of parameters are included to differentiate among the combinations. Beyond the proposal of a possible annotation of LVCs in corpora, Hellan explores the integration of LVCs in the Norwegian valence catalogue *NorVal* and in the computational grammar *NorSource*; in the latter resource, in particular, the modelling of merging between features of the verb and the noun is developed in terms of 'unification', which allows for the representation of situational meaning and semantic composition. The formalism proposed by the author highlights that the function of the LV in LVCs is that of a semantic role bearer, which links the subject to the situational content expressed by the noun and, more interestingly, may add aspectual and viewpoint content to the situation.

With respect to previous studies, the contributions by Kettnerová and Hellan explore the application of the computational dimension to the formal analysis and representation of LVCs. Hellan's proposal also supports applications for language learning and teaching. Furthermore, it is not restricted to the consideration of the argument structure, but also takes into account the aspectual and viewpoint content of the situation.

The event structure of LVCs is further explored in the second section of the volume. The first article by Mahdie Eshaghi and Gholamhossein Karimi-Doostan deals with LVCs in Persian, one of the languages in which the use of LVs is more relevant than lexically full verbs for the encoding of predication. In this language, LVCs are constituted by the co-occurrence of Noun/Adjective/Prepositional Phrase (called 'preverbs') with an LV. Taking advantage of the Neo-Constructionalist approach, the authors take into account the features of [± INITIATIOR], [± PROCESS], [± DURATIVITY] and [± RESULT] and apply them to the six classes into which the 21 Persian LVs were previously divided. Each class can express a set of possible subevents; the subevent that is effectively expressed by the LVC depends on the preverb with which the LVs co-occur. In other words, the LV constrains the range of expressible subevents, one of which is selected by the preverb. Therefore, they conclude that the relevance of the LV in conveying eventuality is higher than that of the preverb.

The actional contribution of both LVC components is maintained in the paper of Anna Pompei and Valentina Piunno. The contribution proposes a comparative analysis of a number of Romance language (Portuguese, Spanish, French, Italian and Romanian) LVCs with the structure Verb+(Article)+Noun, where the LVs are 'have', 'do/make', 'give', 'take'. In this paper not only is verb *Aktionsart* considered, but also that of nouns, which are distinguished between stative and eventive; the latter include three groups based on the presence/absence of boundedness and durativity traits. The analysis highlights a prototypical use of LVs in co-occurrence with nouns having the same actionality. Beside these basic uses, all the LVs present some marked co-occurrences when the noun is non-coherent from the actional point of view. From these marked combinations some aspectual values originate, i.e. inchoative/incremental effects. More interestingly, the marked combination of the noun's and LV's *Aktionsart* also produces lexical diathetic effects, namely 'viewpoint' effects, as, for instance, when the LV 'do/make' combines with a stative noun (as also happens in Wichita, a polysynthetic language; cf. Mattissen, this volume). This means that the LV takes part in the LVC's semantics to a greater or lesser extent, depending on its basic or less prototypical function. The authors also suggest that an intermediate area should be supposed between LVs and LV extensions of the languages considered, in which LVs are less empty – developing their actional and diathetic effects starting from the meaning of their lexically full counterparts –, and LVCs are used to modulate different aspectual nuances and even configurations of the information structure. This is an important function of LVCs and a relevant reason for the choice of an LVC with respect to its synthetic counterpart in languages in which both kinds of predication strategies are present.

The third article of the event structure section, by Anna Pompei, is instead devoted to the use of the only LV *dare* 'give' in Latin, in co-occurrence with physical implication and motion nouns. This case study shows that the selection of this LV is strictly linked to the feature of boundedness. This constraint is explained as an inheritance of the semantic value of the lexically full verb, which is considered from a cognitive perspective, as basically denoting a possession transfer of a Theme from an Agent to a Recipient, which implies at least the existence of a trajectory and an energy source. Particular emphasis is placed on the two-places constructions of the LV co-occurring with nouns expressing motion Manner.

The last paper in the section is that of Roberta Mastrofini, concerning LVCs with LV extensions, namely made up by the combination of a fully lexical verb and an eventive or deverbal noun. The author proposes a corpus-based analysis of 444 LV extension patterns in English, a language in which the study of the phenomenon is still neglected. The fully lexical verb undergoes a semantic bleaching under certain syntagmatic conditions, namely by means of interaction with the semantic configuration of the nominal element it combines with. According to the author, the function of LV extensions is properly the expression of actional values, which are contextually licensed. The device through which these values emerge is the co-composition, in Generative Lexicon's terms.

2.2 The fullness and emptiness of LVs

The second section of the volume opens with Elisabetta Ježek's paper, dealing with semantic co-composition in LVCs. Interestingly, in this article the Generative Lexicon mechanism of co-composition is exploited to deny verb emptiness: in this perspective, both the LV and the noun influence each other's meanings in verb-argument combinations. The author proposes a corpus-based analysis of Italian LVCs with *prendere* 'take' and *fare* 'do' and demonstrates that noun and verb contribute to the unified predication. In particular, Ježek adopts a rich lexical semantic representation of noun meaning, including some predicative components at the sub-lexical level (i.e. the '*qualia* roles'), which allow the noun to act as a functor, concurring with the determination of LV meaning in the context of use.

In addition, the contribution by Marcos García Salido and Marcos Garcia questions the emptiness of LVs, dealing with the debated issue of the semantic predictability/arbitrariness of the LV choice in LVCs, with specific reference to the highly productive Spanish LV *tomar* 'take'. Through the use of a 'vector space' model and the investigation of different conversational Spanish corpora, the authors examine the distributional properties of *tomar* and its fuller counterparts (e.g. *coger* 'take', *adopter* 'adopt'), suggesting a distributional specialization of LVs. Starting from a Meaning-Text Theory perspective, the authors explain how the syntagmatic possibilities of *tomar* are in fact predictable on the basis of its core meaning. On the other hand, adopting a usage-based methodology, they highlight the relevance of frequency, and argue that a repertoire of LVCs and co-occurrence possibilities of their components are somehow specified in the speaker's lexicon.

The last contribution in the section by Noemi De Pasquale concerns LVCs expressing motion in Ancient Greek, where a clear preference for synthetic predication emerges; hence, special attention to a comparison with synthetic counterparts of LCVs is paid. If this issue sheds light on the function of LVCs, the article also reflects on the features of the predicative noun, the LV, and their combination. In particular, two LVC patterns prevail, i.e. Verb+Noun and Verb+Adjective. As for nouns, two types are employed, namely non-deverbal motion nouns, which can denote both entities and events, and deverbal motion nouns. Both kinds can be prefixed by a particle expressing the motion Path, as happens for motion verbs. Even though this means that all the components of motion are conveyed by the noun, interestingly the most productive LV in the Greek period at issue (*poiéo:* 'do, make') is inflected in the middle form when co-occurring with nouns denoting events – namely when forming LVCs – while it is in the active voice in combination with the same nouns denoting concrete entities – viz. when acting as a lexically full verb, expressing the creation of something (i.e. its entering into the state of existence). In other words, in Ancient Greek an important function of LVCs is a sort of 'anticausative' effect with regards to the non-light use of the same verb, and in this highly inflected language this diathetic function is carried out by the verb morphology. In addition to usages where LVCs seem to answer only stylistic needs of variation when used in the same text as the synthetic counterpart, two other functions of the analytical constructions have to be highlighted with regard to the equivalent synthetic verb, i.e. 1) an actional nuance stressing the single instantiation of an event (i.e. boundedness), and 2) the possibility of determining and modifying the noun, with some consequences on its referentiality.

The last section in the volume is devoted to what remains of the emptiness of LVs, once their 'not complete' lightness has been reaffirmed from the point of view i) of argument structure sharing – the notion from which LVs' consideration as complex predicates has developed –, as well as ii) of the eventive structure sharing, and iii) the (partial) sharing of the lexically full counterpart's core meaning.

The first contribution in the last section by Johanna Mattissen specifically takes stock of this point. The article deals with polysynthetic languages, in which LVs may be the dominant strategy and, interestingly, are an intermediate stage in a path of lexicalization or grammaticalization. In polysynthetic languages, LVs occur exclusively in the compositional type, which is characterized by complex verb forms allowing more than one lexical root. LVCs in polysynthetic languages show different kinds of template (Verb+Verb, Verb+Adjective, Verb+Noun, Verb+Particle/Adverb, Verb+ideophone/borrowing), in which the LV generally occurs synthetized with the other component of the construction, i.e. by means of incorporation. Although the author argues that LVs in polysynthetic languages are parallel in form and function to LVs in non-polysynthetic ones, which also partly exhibit synthetic LVCs, it is worth noting that the pattern Verb+PP only occurs in analytic LVCs of non-polysynthetic languages. Moreover, it is noteworthy that what is meant by LVs for polysynthetic languages is not limited to 'basic' LVs, but also includes, at least, LV extensions. After delimiting LVs with respect to other multiverb constructions, the author highlights that, diachronically, a transition from mono-clausal structures with shared participants and scope of negation to LVCs is possible, if one of the verbs reduces its lexical contribution, while the other loses its inflectability. Similarly, two further developments are possible, either 1) the lexicalization of LVCs having the patterns Verb+Verb and Verb+Noun on the path of opacity, or 2) the grammaticalization path, according to the cline drawn in Hopper and Traugott (2003: 11), towards the status of verbal classifiers, aspectoid markers, and valency and modal morphemes. In particular, aspectoid markers and valency are considered as the largest domains of grammaticalization of LVs, not only in polysynthetic languages. This paper is relevant both for the typology and function of LVs cross-linguistically. Moreover, it also takes into account light nouns in polysynthetic languages, which are similar to LVs in keeping their form and inflection while exhibiting a not (full) lexical semantics, as well as in taking over functions in the domains of valence-changing operations and classification.

The domain of LV grammaticalization is investigated by the second paper in the fourth section by Lu Lu and Chu-Ren Huang, who carry out a corpus-based diachronic analysis of the LVs of the GIVE group in Mandarin Chinese (i.e. *jiyu*, *yuyi*, and *jiayi* 'give') and explores the idea that the diachronic development of LVCs yields evidence of their synchronic properties. The paper questions the idea of verb lightness and shows that LVCs with *jiyu*, *yuyi*, and *jiayi* are not completely light. Within the framework of Construction Grammar and through a usage-based methodology, the authors show that the three LVs i) retain some of the uses of their corresponding independent verb (i.e. their lexically full counterpart) in classical and contemporary Chinese, and ii) are at different stages on the grammaticalization cline (with *jiyu* being at the earliest stage, *yuyi* following it, and *jiayi* as the most grammaticalized one). The hypothesis of intermediate stages coincides with the model of extension proposed by Heine and Kuteva (2007) for the transition from a less to more grammatical meaning. In particular, the grammaticalization stages can explain the differences among the three verbs in terms of aspectuality. The earlier the stage of grammaticalization, the more the compatibility with the realization of the perfective aspectual marker *-le*: while the perfective aspectual meaning needs the realization of the aspectual markers *-le* and *-guo* with the less grammaticalized LV *jiyu*, this rarely happens with *yuyi*; no marker is allowed with *jiayi*, which internally conveys the perfective value, and hence is incompatible with any perfective aspectual markers. In this perspective, LVs can be considered as 'light' in the sense that they retain little meaning of their lexically full counterpart, but they may be still considered as 'heavy' in the sense that they encode aspectual information.

The volume closes with Francesca Di Salvo's chapter, which analyzes two LVCs in Latin having the template PP+Verb, namely *in memoria habeo* ('remember', lit. 'in memory have') and *in animo habeo* ('have in mind/be thinking of/plan', lit. 'in soul have'); they are also attested in the variant $Noun_{abl}$+Verb (*memoria habeo* and *animo habeo*), where the noun is likewise an ablative but not governed by preposition. These two constructions realize experiential metaphors, in which the cognitive entity is conceived as a container; therefore, it may co-occur with the stative verb *habeo* 'have' and can establish a meronymic relationship with its locative subject. Although the pattern PP+Verb is only present in analytical LVCs of non-polysynthetic languages (cf. also Persian *be ya:d da:shtan* 'to have in mind'), the two Latin constructions undergo the same lexicalization process as noun incorporation and verb root serialization in polysynthetic languages. Moreover, starting from a compositional meaning, they exhibit different degrees of abstractness and opacity, depending on the different degree of noun referentiality, which in turn correlates with the noun syntactic autonomy, namely with different degrees of LCV cohesion (Heid 1994, Simone 2007).

Acknowledgements: We thank all the scholars who were so kind to review the chapters. A special thank goes to Elina Filippone.

References

Abeillé, Anne, Danièle Godard & Ivan A. Sag. 1998. Two kinds of composition in French complex predicates. In Erhard Hinrichs, Andreas Kathol & Tsuneko Nakazawa (eds.), *Complex Predicates in Nonderivational Syntax*. Syntax and Semantics. Vol. 30, 1–41. New York: Academic Press.
Adger, David. 2003. *Core Syntax: A Minimalist Approach*. Oxford: Oxford University Press.
Aissen, Judith & David Perlmutter. 1983. Clause reduction in Spanish. In David Perlmutter (ed.), *Studies in Relational Grammar*. Vol. 1, 360–403. Chicago: University of Chicago Press.
Alsina, Alex. 1996. *The Role of Argument Structure in Grammar*. Stanford: CSLI Publications.
Alsina, Alex, Joan Bresnan & Peter Sells (eds.), 1997. *Complex Predicates*. Stanford: CSLI Publications.
Alonso Ramos, Margarita. 1998. *Étude sémantico-syntaxique des constructions à verbe support*. PhD dissertation. Montréal: Université de Montréal.
Alonso Ramos, Margarita. 2001a. Constructions à verbe support dans des langues SOV. *Bulletin de la société de linguistique de Paris* 96(1). 79–106.
Alonso Ramos, Margarita. 2001b. Détermination, incorporation et phraséologie dans les constructions à verbe support. *Lingvisticae Investigationes* 23. 51–66.
Alonso Ramos, Margarita. 2004. *Las construcciones con verbo de apoyo*. Madrid: Visor.
Amberber Mengistu, Brett Baker & Mark Harvey (eds.), 2010. *Complex Predicates: Cross-linguistic Perspectives on Event Structure*. Cambridge: Cambridge University Press.
Bally, Charles. 1950. *Linguistique générale et linguistique française*. Bern: Francke Verlag.
Bresnan, Joan (ed.). 1982. *The Mental Representation of Grammatical Relations*. Cambridge, MA: The MIT Press.
Bresnan, Joan. 2001. *Lexical-Functional syntax*. Oxford: Blackwell.
Bustos Plaza, Alberto. 2005. *Combinaciones verbonominales institucionalizadas y lexicalizadas*. Frankfurt: Peter Lang.
Butt, Miriam. 1995. *The Structure of Complex Predicates in Urdu*. Stanford: CSLI Publications.

Butt, Miriam. 1998. Constraining argument merger through aspect. In Erhard Hinrichs, Andreas Kathol & Tsuneko Nakazawa (eds.), *Complex Predicates in Nonderivational Syntax*. Syntax and Semantics. Vol. 30, 73–113. New York: Academic Press.

Butt, Miriam. 2003. The Light Verb Jungle. *Harvard Working Papers in Linguistics* 9. 1–49.

Butt, Miriam. 2010. The Light Verb jungle: still hacking away. In Mengistu Amberber, Brett Baker & Mark Harvey (eds.), *Complex Predicates: Cross-linguistic Perspectives on Event Structure*, 48–78. Cambridge: Cambridge University Press.

Butt, Miriam. 2019. Complex Predicates and Multidimensionality in Grammar. *Linguistic Issues in Language Technology* 17(4). 1–14.

Butt, Miriam & Wilhelm Geuder. 2013. On the (semi)lexical status of light verbs. In Norbert Corver & Henk van Riemsdijk (eds.), *Semi-lexical Categories: The Function of Content Words and the Content of Function Words*, 323–370. Berlin/New York: Mouton De Gruyter.

Butt, Miriam & Aditi Lahiri. 2013. Diachronic pertinacity of light verbs. *Lingua* 135. 7–29.

Butt, Miriam & Gillian Ramchand. 2005. Complex aspectual structure in Hindi/Urdu. In Nomi Ertishik-Shir & Tova Rapoport (eds.), *The Syntax of Aspect*, 117–153. Oxford: Oxford University Press.

Cattell, Ray. 1984. *Composite Predicates in English*. Syntax and Semantics. Vol. 17. New York: Academic Press.

Choi, Soojung. 2005. *Multiple Verb Constructions in Korean*. PhD dissertation. Falmer: University of Sussex.

Davies, William. 1989. A union analysis of a Telugu complex predicate construction. In Manindra K. Verma (ed.), *Complex predicates in South Asian languages*, 47–61. New Delhi: Manohar.

Davies, William & Carol Rosen. 1988. Union as Multi-Predicate Clauses. *Language* 64. 52–88.

De Miguel, Elena. 2006. Tensión y equilibrio semántico entre nombres y verbos: el reparto de la tarea de predicar. In Milka Villayandre (ed.), *Actas del XXXV Simposio de la Sociedad Española de Lingüística*, 1289–1313. León: Ediciones del Dpto. de Filología Hispánica y Clásica – Universidad de León.

De Miguel, Elena. 2008. Construcciones con verbos de apoyo en español. De cómo entran los nombres en la órbita de los verbos. In Inés Olza Moreno, Manuel Casado Velarde & Ramón Gonzáles Ruiz (eds.), *Actas del XXXVII Simposio Internacional de la Sociedad Española de Lingüística*, 567–578. Pamplona: Servicios de Publicaciones de la Universidad de Navarra.

De Miguel, Elena & Olga Batiukova. 2017. Compositional mechanisms in a generative model of the lexicón. In Sergi Torner Castells & Elisenda Bernal (eds.), *Collocations and other lexical combinations in Spanish: Theoretical, Lexicographical and Applied perspectives*, 92–113. London: Routledge.

Dubinsky, Stanley. 1989. Compound 'suru' Verbs and Evidence for Unaccusativity in Japanese. in Caroline Wiltshire, Randolph Graczyk, Bradley Music (eds.), *Papers from the 25th Annual Regional Meeting of the Chicago Linguistic Society*, 157–189. Chicago: Chicago Linguistic Society.

Engelen, Bernhard. 1968. Zum System der Funktionsverbgefüge. *Wirkendes Wort* 18(5). 289–303.

Giry-Schneider, Jacqueline. 1987. *Les prédicats nominaux en français: les phrases à verbe support*. Genève/Paris: Droz.

Grimshaw, Jane & Armin Mester. 1988. Light verbs and θ-Marking. *Linguistic Inquiry* 19(2). 205–232.

Gross, Gaston. 1989. *Les constructions converses du français*. Genève/Paris: Droz.

Gross, Gaston. 2004a. Introduction. In Gaston Gross & Sophie De Pontonx (eds.), *Verbes supports. Nouvel état des lieux* 27(2). 167–169. [=Special issue of *Lingvisticae Investigationes*].

Gross, Gaston. 2004b. Pour un Bescherelle des prédicats nominaux. In Gaston Gross & Sophie De Pontonx (eds.), *Verbes supports. Nouvel état des lieux* 27(2). 343–358. [=Special issue of *Lingvisticae Investigationes*].

Gross, Maurice. 1981. Les bases empiriques de la notion de prédicat sémantique. *Langages* 63. 7–52.
Heringer, Hans J. 1968. *The opposition of 'come' and 'bring' as functional verbs*. Düsseldorf: Schwann.
Helbig, Gerhard. 1984. Probleme der Beschreibung von Funktionsverbgefügen im Deutschen.
 In Gerhard Helbig (ed.), *Studien zur deutschen Syntax*. Vol. 2, 163–188. Leipzig: Enzyklopädie.
Heid, Ulrich. 1994. On ways words work together. Topics in lexical combinatorics. In Willy Martin (ed.),
 Proceedings of the VI Euralex International Congress, 226–257. Amsterdam: Vrije Universiteit.
Heine, Bernd & Tania Kuteva. 2007. *The Genesis of Grammar: A Reconstruction*. Oxford: Oxford University
 Press.
Hook, Peter E. 1991. The emergence of perfective aspect in Indo-Aryan Languages. In Elizabeth
 Traugott & Bernd Heine (eds.), *Approaches to Grammaticalization*. Vol. 2, 59–89. Amsterdam:
 Benjamins.
Hook, Peter E. 1993. Aspectogenesis and the compound verb in Indo-Aryan. In Manindra K. Verma
 (ed.), *Complex Predicates in South Asian Languages*, 97–113. Delhi: Manohar.
Hopper, Paul J. & Elizabeth Traugott. 2003. *Grammaticalization*. 2nd ed. Cambridge: Cambridge
 University Press.
Huang, C.-T. James. 1992. Complex predicates in control. In Richard K. Larson, Sabine Iatridou & Utpal
 Lahiri (eds.), *Control and Grammar*, 109–147. Dordrecht: Kluwer.
Ibrahim, Amr Helmy. 1996. Les supports: le terme, la notion et les approches. *Langages* 121. 3–7.
Jespersen, Otto. 1942. *A Modern English Grammar on Historical Principles*. Vol. 6: *Morphology*. London:
 George Allen and Unwin Ltd.
Ježek, Elisabetta. 2011. Verbes supports et composition sémantique. *Cahiers de Lexicologie* 1. 29–43.
Kim, Sun-Hee. 2003. Light verbs, unaccusativity, and relational grammar. *Language Research* 39(2).
 305–336.
La Fauci, Nunzio. 2000. *Forme romanze della funzione predicative. Teorie, testi, tassonomie*. Pisa: Edizioni
 ETS.
La Fauci, Nunzio & Ignazio Mirto. 2003. *Fare. Elementi di sintassi*. Pisa: Edizioni ETS.
Leclère, Christian. 1971. Remarques sur les substantifs opérateurs. *Langue française* 11. 61–76.
Mastrofini, Roberta. 2004. Classi di costruzioni a verbo supporto in italiano: implicazioni semantico-
 sintattiche nel paradigma V + N. *Studi Italiani di Linguistica Teorica e Applicata* 33(3). 371–398.
Mattissen, Johanna. This volume, Light Verbs and 'light nouns' in polysynthetic languages. 275–303.
Mel'čuk, Igor. 1973. Towards a linguistic "meaning ⇔ text" model. In Ferenc Kiefer (ed.), *Trends in
 Soviet Theoretical Linguistics*, 33–57. Dordrecht: Reidel.
Mel'čuk, Igor. 1981. Meaning-text models: A recent trend in Soviet linguistics. *Annual Review of
 Anthropology* 10. 27–62.
Mel'čuk, Igor. 1988. Semantic description of lexical units in an explanatory combinatorial dictionary:
 Basic principles and heuristic criteria. *International Journal of Lexicography* 1(3). 165–188.
Mel'čuk, Igor. 1996. Lexical functions: A tool for the description of lexical relations in the lexicon.
 In Leo Wanner (ed.), *Lexical Functions in Lexicography and Natural Language Processing*, 37–102.
 Amsterdam: Benjamins.
Mel'čuk, Igor. 2003. Collocations dans le dictionnaire. In Thomas Szende (ed.), *Les écarts culturels dans
 les dictionnaires bilingues*, 19–64. Paris: Honoré Champion.
Mel'čuk, Igor. 2004. Verbes supports sans peine. In Gaston Gross & Sophie De Pontonx (eds.), *Verbes
 supports. Nouvel état des lieux* 27(2). 203–217. [=Special issue of *Lingvisticae Investigationes*].
Mel'čuk, Igor, Nadia Arbatchewsky-Jumarie, Lidija Lordanskaja, Suzanne Mantha & Alain Polguère.
 1999. *Dictionnaire explicatif et combinatoire du français contemporain: Recherches lexico-
 sémantiques*. Montréal: Presses de l'Université de Montréal.

Mel'čuk, Igor, André Clas & Alain Polguère. 1995. *Introduction à la lexicologie explicative et combinatoire*. Bruxelles: Duculot.
Mel'čuk, Igor & Alain Polguère. 2007. *Lexique actif du français*. Bruxelles: De Boeck.
Mohanan, Tara. 1990. *Arguments in Hindi*. PhD dissertation. Stanford: University of Stanford.
Mohanan, Tara. 1994. *Argument Structure in Hindi*. Stanford: CSLI Publications.
Mohanan, Tara. 1997. Multidimensionality of representation: NV complex predicates in Hindi. In Alex Alsina, Joan Bresnan & Peter Sells (eds.), *Complex Predicates*, 431–471. Stanford: CSLI Publications.
Perlmutter, David M. & Paul M. Postal. 1974. *Lectures on Relational Grammar*. Unpublished lectures presented at the Linguistic Institute, Amherst, MA: University of Massachusetts.
Polenz von, Peter. 1963. *Funktionsverben im heutigen Deutsch. Sprache in einer rationalisierten Welt*. Düsseldorf: Schwann.
Pompei, Anna. This volume. How light is 'give' as a Light Verb? A case study on the actionality of Latin light verb constructions (with some references to Romance languages). 149–200.
Pompei, Anna & Valentina Piunno. This volume. Light Verb Constructions in Romance languages. An attempt to explain systematic irregularity. 99–147.
Pustejovsky, James. 1995. *The Generative Lexicon*. Cambridge, MA: The MIT Press.
Rosen, Sara. 1989. *Argument Structure and Complex Predicates*. PhD dissertation. Waltham: Brandeis University.
Simone, Raffaele. 2007. Categories and constructions in verbal and signed languages. In Elena Pizzuto, Paola Pietrandrea & Raffaele Simone (eds.), *Verbal and Signed Languages. Comparing Structures, Constructs and Methodologies*, 197–252. Berlin/New York: Mouton de Gruyter.
Vivès, Robert. 1988. Verbes supports et nominalisations. *Lexique* 6. 139–159.
Wurmbrand, Susanne. 2001. *Infinitives: Restructuring and Clause Structure*. Berlin/New York: Mouton de Gruyter.
Žolkovskij, Aleksandr & Igor Mel'čuk. 1965. O vozmožnom metode i instrumentax semantičeskogo sinteza. [On the possible methods and instruments of semantic synthesis] *Naučno-texničeskaja informacija* 5. 23–28.
Žolkovskij, Aleksandr & Igor Mel'čuk. 1967. O semantičeskom sinteze [On semantic synthesis]. *Problemy kibernetiki* 19. 177–238.

Section 1: **Argument structure sharing**

Václava Kettnerová
1 Valency structure of complex predicates with Light Verbs
The case of Czech

Abstract: Concentrating on the example of Czech complex predicates consisting of a Light Verb and a predicative noun, this paper provides an in-depth analysis of the syntactic structure of Light Verb Constructions from a valency perspective. It argues that both the Light Verb and the predicative noun in the complex predicate have their own valency structures, i.e., a set of valency complementations, preserved in different complex predicates. What differentiates individual complex predicates from each other is the interaction between valency complementations of the Light Verb and those of the predicative noun through sharing semantic roles, which is manifested as their coreference. It is shown that the coreference, affecting the deep syntactic structure of the complex predicate, has consequences for both the semantic and the surface syntactic layer. From the semantic point of view, the coreference provides semantically unsaturated valency complementations of the Light Verb with their semantic specification. In the surface structure, it leads to the systemic ellipsis of the valency complementations of the predicative noun involved in the coreference. Czech, encoding syntactic relations through morphological cases, makes it possible to pinpoint the surface distribution of valency complementations in Light Verb Constructions and thus establish rules governing the surface expression of semantic participants in these constructions.

Keywords: valency structure, deep/surface syntactic structure, Czech, Functional Generative Description

1 Introduction

Light Verb Constructions (LVCs) have attracted considerable attention in current linguistics. They have been analyzed from various theoretical perspectives (for a brief overview, see Butt 2010). A crucial characteristic of LVCs, recognized across

---

Acknowledgements: The research reported in this paper has been using data provided by the Research Infrastructure LINDAT/CLARIAH-CZ (https://lindat.cz) supported by the Ministry of Education, Youth and Sports of the Czech republic (project No. LM2018101). I would like to thank the reviewers and Markéta Lopatková, Veronika Kolářová, Anna Vernerová, and Jakub Sláma for their valuable comments.

https://doi.org/10.1515/9783110747997-002

different theoretical approaches, is that LVCs are formed by a complex predicate consisting of a Light Verb and another predicative unit. Some formal mechanisms accounting for the formation of the complex predicate have been devised within generative frameworks: argument transfer in Government and Binding Theory (Grimshaw and Mester 1988), and argument fusion in Lexical-Functional Grammar (Butt 1998).[1] Despite variations rooted in their main tenets, the theories all posit argument structure as being where the complex predicate formation takes place.

Argument structure represents a central concept in dependency-oriented theories, although they use the term 'valency' instead (see Ágel et al. 2003). Valency refers to the set of obligatory and optional dependents of a predicate, typically a verb in a given sense, forming the nucleus of the sentence. In this paper, we demonstrate that a dependency analysis with an elaborated valency theory provides a good starting point for the description of LVCs. Namely, we make use of Functional Generative Description (FGD) with its multilayer design, dividing language description into separate layers, the units of which are connected by the relation of form and function (see esp. Sgall et al. 1986).[2] The principal focus of FGD lies in the deep syntactic layer, which is structured primarily by valency. The valency theory of FGD has been elaborated esp. by Panevová (1994) and basic postulates of this theory have been extensively applied in the Prague Dependency Treebank corpora (PDT) (Hajič et al. 2020) and in several valency lexicons (Lopatková et al. 2016; Urešová et al. 2021; Kolářová et al. 2020).

We summarize and further deepen the theoretical findings on Czech LVCs (Radimský 2010; Macháčková 1994; Kettnerová et al. 2018). We proceed from the semantic layer to the deep syntactic and the surface syntactic layer, aiming to establish all the linguistic information needed for the generation of LVCs and to formulate the rules governing this process. We suggest that LVCs can be adequately understood in a multilayer language description following the correspondence between semantic participants (as units of the semantic layer), valency complementations[3] (as units of the deep syntactic layer), and clause elements or surface positions (as units of the surface syntactic layer).

This study is limited to a central type of Czech LVCs that are formed by complex predicates consisting of a Light Verb and a predicative noun expressed as the direct

---

[1] Argument composition in Head-Phrase Structure Grammar (Hinrichs et al. 1998) and in Lexical-Functional Grammar (Alsina 1996, 1997), and argument merger in Government and Binding Theory (Rosen 1989) are also relevant here.
[2] The Meaning↔Text Theory (Mel'čuk 1988) represents another influential dependency theory. Here, LVCs are described by means of the so-called lexical functions (see esp. Mel'čuk 1996).
[3] The term complementation is often used for the situation where a predication functions as an argument of a predicate (see, e.g., Dixon and Aikhenvald 2006).

object of the Light Verb (e.g., *vést jednání* 'to hold talks', *mít potíže* 'to have difficulties', *udělat chybu* 'to make a mistake', *dostat příkaz* 'to get an order').[4] The language data are drawn esp. from the VALLEX lexicon, providing the syntactic annotation of more than 1,500 Czech complex predicates with Light Verbs,[5] with illustrative examples selected from the Czech National Corpus (CNC).[6]

The paper is structured as follows. First, the main tenets of the valency theory of FGD, the theoretical background of this study, are introduced in Section 2. Second, the defining characteristics of complex predicates with Light Verbs are provided in Section 3. The core of the paper is addressed in Sections 4–6, where the correspondence between semantic participants (Section 4), valency complementations (Section 5), and surface positions in LVCs (Section 6) is examined in detail. Based on this analysis, the principles governing the syntactic structure of complex predicates are formulated, making it possible to generate well-formed LVCs.

2 Valency theory of Functional Generative Description

2.1 Actants and free modifications

Valency complementations represent dependents of a predicate in the deep syntactic layer. Two distinctions concerning valency complementations are drawn in FGD. First, they are divided into actants and free modifications (this division roughly corresponds to the argument and adjunct dichotomy) (see esp. Panevová 1974–1975; 1994; Panevová et al. 2014). Two criteria are taken into account in determining whether a complementation is an actant or a free modification: (i) Can the complementation modify (a) any word or (b) a closed group of words that can be listed? (ii) Can the complementation modify a word (a) more than once or (b) only once (regardless of coordination and apposition)?

If a valency complementation can modify a word only once and satisfies the condition (ib), it is classified as an actant. Actants are structured on the surface as

---

[4] The predicative noun can also be expressed as an indirect object (e.g., *zahrnout někoho polibky* 'to shower somebody with kisses', *podléhat restrikcím* 'to be subject to restrictions', *vejít v platnost* 'to come into force'). The subject is available for the surface realization of the predicative noun as well (e.g., *Popadl ho strach* 'Fear gripped him'). It can be supposed that the results of the analysis provided here can be adopted for these LVCs as well.
[5] https://ufal.mff.cuni.cz/vallex/4.5/
[6] https://www.korpus.cz/

the subject, the direct object, or indirect objects of verbs, and as adnominal attributes. With verbs, five actants are distinguished: ACTor, ADDRessee, PATient, ORIGin, and EFFect, labeled by so-called functors, which mark the type of the dependency relation of actants to their governing verb. With nouns, MATerial is an additional actant.[7] If a verb has a single actant, it is always the ACTor. If it has two actants, they are the ACTor and the PATient.[8] For distinguishing the other three actants – ADDRessee, ORIGin, and EFFect – both syntactic and semantic criteria are taken into account.

Free modifications comply with criteria (ia) and (iia): they can modify any words more than once. They are typically structured on the surface as adverbials. In contrast to actants, free modifications are identified on the basis of their semantics: e.g., LOCative (the free modification 'where') or TWHEN (the free modification 'when').

2.2 Obligatoriness

The second distinction between valency complementations concerns their obligatoriness in the deep syntactic layer. It can be verified by the so-called dialogue test (Panevová 1974–1975). See the illustrative dialogue: a. 'John just came.' b. 'Where?' a. '*I do not know.' The unacceptability of the answer shows that the complementation of the direction 'where' (despite not being expressed on the surface) is obligatory in the deep syntactic layer for the verb 'to come' in contrast to, e.g., the free modification of the direction 'from where', which is only optional (cf. a. 'John just came.' b. 'From where?' a. 'I do not know.'). Both actants and free modifications can be either obligatory or optional.

2.3 Semantic participants

Each valency complementation, regardless of its type, has lexical semantic properties determined by the lexical meaning of its governing predicate. The lexical meaning of a predicate can be characterized in terms of a situation denoted by the predicate (cf. Mel'čuk 2004). Each situation denoted by a predicate consists of a set of semantic participants bearing some characteristic properties and enter-

---

[7] Valency of nouns within FGD has been described esp. by Kolářová (2014) and Kolářová et al. (2020).
[8] This approach is motivated by the fact that the first and the second actant are realized on the surface as ACTor and PATient, respectively, regardless of their semantics.

ing into some relations. These participants can described by means of semantic roles.[9] Each valency complementation of the predicate then typically corresponds to one of its semantic participants, which semantically saturates the valency complementation.[10]

FGD, following European structural linguistics in distinguishing between the so-called cognitive content and the meaning of linguistic structures, primarily focuses on the deep syntactic layer, perceived as the layer of linguistically structured meaning. As a result, a metalanguage for the description of lexical semantic properties of predicates, extending beyond the linguistically structured meaning, has not been sufficiently elaborated in FGD yet. For this purpose, we draw semantic roles from the semantically oriented lexicons in the CzEngClass project (Urešová et al. 2020), taking a first step in the lexical semantic annotation of predicates within FGD.

2.4 Valency complementations filled with predicative nouns

Predicative nouns together with Light Verbs form multiword predicates. The valency complementation of Light Verbs that is filled with predicative nouns then stands outside the distinction between actants and free modifications (see Section 2.1). It modifies only a closed set of verbs (Light Verbs in this case), and it modifies them only once. Thus it behaves similarly to actants. Unlike actants, however, it does not correspond to a semantic participant. This type of complementations is labeled here with the functor CPHR (the nominal part of complex predicates), as introduced in PDT.

2.5 Valency frames

In FGD, the valency structure of a single word predicate (typically a verb, a noun or an adjective) is captured by the *valency frame* stored in a lexicon. The valency frame consists of a set of valency slots, each filled with one valency complementation. Only actants (be they obligatory or optional) and free modifications that are obligatory are part of the valency frame (optional free modifications stand outside the valency frame). Each valency complementation is assigned with a functor and with information on obligatoriness. In addition, possible forms of the valency comple-

---

9 Despite the criticism of the concept of semantic roles (for an overview see, e.g., Levin and Rappaport Hovav 2005), semantic roles have been employed as an important tool in the analysis of various phenomena concerning valency. They are necessary for our further explanation too.
10 For exceptions see Section 2.4 and 4.2.

mentation, indicating its surface realization, can be provided. Forms are listed for actants as these forms are determined by the governing predicate; their list includes prepositionless and prepositional cases of nominals (typically nouns, sporadically adjectives), the infinitive, and dependent content clauses. Forms of free modifications are not explicitly declared in valency frames as these forms are implied by functors of free modifications, not by their governing predicates. However, valency of multiword predicates requires special treatment as discussed in Section 5.

3 Introductory characteristics

Before discussing the syntactic structure of LVCs, the defining characteristics of complex predicates with Light Verbs forming these constructions are provided. These predicates are composed of two elements: a Light Verb and a predicative noun. While the position of predicative nouns in the linguistic description appears to be more or less unproblematic, linguistic features of Light Verbs, esp. the semantic ones, still remain an open question. Butt (2010: 48) notes that these verbs "appear to be semantically *light* in some manner that is difficult to identify".

Currently, some scholars call for an extension of the inventory of Light Verbs; see the so-called Light Verb extensions introduced by Gross (1981) and recently elaborated, e.g., by Ježek (2011) and Mastrofini (under review).[11] The motivation behind this extension is that semantic and syntactic criteria formulated for Light Verbs with very general meaning (see esp. Gross 1981) are often satisfied also by verbs that are semantically more distinctive. First, these verbs can express various lexical aspectual properties (compare, e.g., *dostat strach* 'to get fear', *mít strach* 'to have fear' and *ztratit strach* 'to lose fear'). Further, they can change the perspective from which a situation is viewed (compare, e.g., *dát rozkaz* 'to give an order' with *dostat rozkaz* 'to get an order'). Moreover, semantic co-occurrence restrictions between Light Verbs and predicative nouns can be observed (compare, e.g., *dát pokutu* 'to give a fine' and *uložit pokutu* 'to impose a fine' with *dát pusu* 'to give a kiss' and **uložit pusu* '*to impose a kiss'). All these features testify against the complete semantic emptiness of Light Verbs (cf. Butt and Geuder 2001; Brugman 2001) and open the question of the semantic relation between Light Verbs and predicative nouns in complex predicates (cf. Apresjan 2009; Sanromán Vilas 2017).

We argue that Light Verbs are better identified on the basis of their function in complex predicates than by means of 'semantic lightness' (tested by deletion of a verb without resultant semantic loss) or by means of syntactic criteria operating

---

[11] See also Bosque (2001).

on the surface syntactic layer, such as the impossibility of their nominalization, the possibility of their passivization and clefting (see esp. Gross 1981). By the Light Verb, we mean a verb whose function is to provide some of its valency complementations for the surface expression of semantic participants of the noun with which the verb forms a complex predicate. This function will be thoroughly explained in the subsequent Sections 4–6. In Czech, this function is fulfilled by verbs that seem to be almost semantically empty (e.g., *provést analýzu* 'to carry out an analysis') but also by verbs that are semantically more distinctive (e.g., *vzdát poctu* 'to pay tribute').

As a point of departure, we introduce a definition of *complex predicates with the Light Verb*, although individual points of this definition will be elucidated further in Sections 4–6. As a complex predicate with a Light Verb, we understand a collocation of a noun and a verb that satisfies the following conditions:
- The noun is a valency complementation of the verb (and it is thus expressed in a surface position provided by the verb) (Section 5.2).
- The verb has no semantic participants of its own (Section 4.2).[12]
- Other valency complementations of the verb are semantically saturated by semantic participants of the noun (Section 5.3 and 5.4).
- Those semantic participants of the noun that saturate valency complementations of the verb are expressed in surface positions provided by the verb (Section 6.2).

4 Semantic structure

A key question concerning complex predicates with Light Verbs is which of their components – the Light Verb, the predicative noun, or even both of them – has semantic participants, semantically saturating their valency complementations. Here it is shown that the semantic participants in the complex predicate are provided by the noun (Section 4.1), except for the semantic participant Instigator, which is the only semantic participant that may be provided by the verb (Section 4.2).

---

[12] Only causative Light Verbs are an exception. See Section 4.2.

4.1 Predicative nouns

Nouns forming complex predicates with Light Verbs typically denote situations such as events (e.g., *pokus* 'experiment', *rozkaz* 'order', *výprava* 'expedition'), states (*nenávist* 'hatred', *radost* 'delight') or properties (*trpělivost* 'patience', *zvědavost* 'curiosity'). The situation denoted by the noun is typically characterized by a certain number and type of semantic participants. These semantic participants are the same regardless of whether the noun is used in a nominal structure or in an LVC as part of a complex predicate. For example, the predicative noun *radost* 'delight' denotes the state that is characterized by two semantic participants: the one who experiences the state (Experiencer) and the one who causes it (Stimulus). These participants are expressed in both nominal constructions and LVCs, as examples (1a-b) illustrate. The only difference between these constructions is the surface expression of the participant Experiencer (*Petr* 'Peter'): in the nominal construction in (1a), it is expressed as an adnominal possessive modifier, whereas in the LVC in (1b), it is realized as the subject of the Light Verb *mít* 'to have' (the surface expression of the Stimulus participant (*výlet* 'trip') remains the same in both cases). Let us repeat that the expression of nominal semantic participants in verbal surface positions is one of the defining characteristics of complex predicates with Light Verbs; see Section 3.

(1) a. *Petr-ov-a   radost-Ø   z výlet-u*
       Peter-POSS-NOM delight-NOM from trip-GEN
       'Peter's delight in the trip'
    b. *Petr-Ø   má   z výlet-u   radost-Ø.*
       Peter-NOM has   from trip-GEN delight-ACC
       'Peter takes delight in the trip.'

4.2 Light Verbs

Butt (2010) argues that one of the main characteristics of Light Verbs is that they are formally identical to full verbs. Czech Light Verbs support this claim and the same verb occurs as both the full verb and the Light Verb.[13] In this case, it can be observed that a Light Verb and its respective full verb counterpart denote similar situations.

---

[13] In limited cases, a verb is mostly used as the Light Verb and only peripherally as the full one. For example, the verb *provést* 'to carry out' is mostly used as the Light Verb (e.g., *provést analýzu, kontrolu, pokus* 'to carry out an analysis, an inspection, an experiment'), and only peripherally as the full verb (e.g., *provést plán* 'to execute a plan'). Radimský (2010) refers to such Light Verbs as 'generic'.

For example, both the full verb *dávat* 'to give' in (2a) and the Light Verb *dávat* 'to give' in (2b) can be interpreted as instances of the situation of giving. In the case of the full verb *dávat* 'to give', this situation is characterized by three semantic participants – Donor, Recipient, and Theme. The Donor and the Recipient are typically sentient beings, institutions or organizations (*rodiče* 'parents' and *děti* 'children' in example (2a)), and the Theme is a physical object (*jídlo* 'food' in example (2a)).

In the case of the Light Verb *dávat* 'to give' in (2b), the situation of giving is further semantically specified by the predicative noun *útěcha* 'comfort' and the number and nature of semantic participants are determined by the noun rather than by the verb. As example (2b) shows, the situation of giving comfort evokes two semantic participants instead of three, and their semantic characteristics are the same as with the verb *utěšovat* 'to comfort', representing the base verb of the noun *útěcha* 'comfort'; see example (2c). These participants can be thus characterized by the semantic roles of Stimulus and Experiencer. The Stimulus is sentient beings, events, ideas, beliefs etc. (*víra a filozofie* 'faith and philosophy' in examples (2b-c)), and the Experiencer is limited to sentient beings (*my* 'we' in examples (2b-c)).

(2) a. Předškolním dět-em dávají jídl-o rodič-e... (CNC)
    preschool child-DAT give food-ACC parent-NOM
    'Preschool children are given food by parents...'
 b. Vír-a a filosofi-e nám dávají
    faith-NOM and philosophy-NOM us.DAT give
    útěch-u. (CNC)
    comfort-ACC
    'Faith and philosophy give us comfort.'
 c. Vír-a a filozofi-e nás utěšuje.
    faith-NOM and philosophy-NOM us.ACC comfort
    'Faith and philosophy comfort us.'

The comparison of semantic participants in complex predicates and their single verb counterparts shows that semantic participants are contributed to complex predicates by predicative nouns rather than by Light Verbs.[14] There is only one exception: Light Verbs combined with some predicative nouns can gain causative features. In such a case, Light Verbs are endowed with the semantic participant that brings about the situation expressed by the predicative noun. To this participant,

---

14 Compare with the assumption that the Light Verb does not assign theta roles (Grimshaw and Mester 1988) and the idea of the Meaning↔Text Theory that it has no semantic actants (Alonso Ramos 2007).

we assign the role of Instigator. For example, the semantic participant expressed in the subject position in example (3a) (*standardy* 'standards') is not contributed to the complex predicate *dávat převahu* 'to give superiority' by the predicative noun *převaha* 'superiority'. As the nominal construction in example (3b) illustrates, this noun has only two semantic participants (*jeho* 'his' and *nad nepřítelem* 'over enemy'). Thus, the participant filled with *standardy* 'standards' in the LVC in (3a) necessarily belongs to the Light Verb.

(3) a. *Právní   standard-y   mu   dávají   převah-u*
       legal   standard-NOM   him.DAT   give   superiority-ACC
       nad nepřítel-em.   (according to CNC)
       over enemy-INSTR
       'Legal standards give him superiority over the enemy.'
   b. *jeho   převah-a   nad nepřítel-em*
      his.POSS.NOM   superiority-NOM   over enemy-INSTR
      'his superiority over the enemy'

5 Deep syntactic structure

This section examines the deep syntactic structure of LVCs determined by the valency of complex predicates. As the starting point, the following question should be addressed: (i) Do complex predicates as a whole have a valency structure that can be described by a single valency frame, or (ii) do the predicative noun and the Light Verb have their own valency structure and each should be assigned with its own valency frame? As shown below, option (ii) is better justified as individual predicative nouns and Light Verbs exhibit the same valency properties in different complex predicates. The valency structure of complex predicates is thus inferred from the valency of their components.[15]

---

[15] Option (ii) makes it possible to arrive at a more economical description of complex predicates as well. For example, instead of assigning separate valency frames to individual complex predicates with the same predicative noun, e.g., *mít strach* 'to have fear', *dostat strach* 'to get fear', *vyvolat strach* 'to evoke fear' etc., the valency of the noun *strach* 'fear' is captured by a single valency frame. Similarly, the Light Verb *mít* 'to have' is assigned with a single valency frame, regardless of its combination with different predicative nouns (e.g., *mít strach* 'to have fear', *mít radost* 'to have delight', *mít tendenci* 'to have a tendency').

5.1 Valency frames of predicative nouns

A predicative noun is characterized by a set of valency complementations, each of which corresponds to a semantic participant evoked by the situation denoted by the noun. Besides nominal constructions, the predicative noun can be used in LVCs as part of a complex predicate. As introduced in Section 4.1, the noun contributes the same set of semantic participants to both nominal constructions and LVCs. Thus, we can expect that the noun contributes its valency complementations corresponding to the respective participants to LVCs as well.

For example, the noun *hovor* 'conversation' is characterized by three semantic participants, namely Interlocutor_1, Interlocutor_2, and Topic, corresponding to the valency complementations ACTor, ADDRessee, and PATient, respectively; see the valency frame of the noun in (4). The forms indicated in the valency frame determine the surface expression of the valency complementations in nominal constructions; see example (5). The same set of semantic participants of the noun, and thus the valency complementations that these participants semantically saturate, is contained in LVCs as well. In this case, however, we can observe that the surface realization of the Interlocutor_1 differs. In the LVC, this participant is expressed as the ACTor of the verb as indicated by its nominative form while the ACTor of the noun corresponding to this participant is elided from the surface; see example (6). This issue is further elaborated in Section 6.

(4) *hovor* 'conversation': $ACT_{gen,poss}\ ADDR_{s\ 'with'+instr}\ PAT_{o\ 'about'+locat,dcc}$[16]

(5) *hovor-Ø   Polák-a*$_{ACT}$ *s Chalup-ou*$_{ADDR}$
    talk-NOM   Polak-GEN   with Chalupa-INSTR
    o drog-ách$_{PAT}$ (CNC)
    about drug-LOCAT
    'Polak's conversation with Chalupa about drugs'

(6) *Polák-Ø   vedl   hovor-Ø   s Chalup-ou*
    Polak-NOM   held   conversation-ACC with Chalupa-INSTR
    o drog-ách.
    about drug-LOCAT
    'Polak held a conversation with Chalupa about drugs.'

---

[16] In the case of prepositional groups, a preposition precedes the abbreviation indicating the respective case. Further, the information on obligatoriness is omitted from valency frames of nouns as it is not relevant for our further explanation.

5.2 Valency frames of Light Verbs

The valency frames of Light Verbs are typically identical to the valency frames of their full verb counterparts. They differ only in the functor of one of their complementations, typically PATient, which changes to CPHR, identifying the valency position reserved for a predicative noun. Compare the valency frame of the full verb *poskytovat* 'to provide' in (7) with the frame of the Light Verb *poskytovat* 'to provide' in (9). Unlike valency complementations of full verbs, valency complementations of Light Verbs do not, however, correspond to any semantic participants (see Section 4.2).[17] For example, the ACTor, ADDRessee, and PATient of the full verb *poskytovat* 'to provide' correspond to Donor (*pojišťovny* 'insurance companies'), Recipient (*pacienti* 'patients'), and Theme (*seznam* 'list'), respectively; see example (8). In contrast, the ACTor and ADDRessee of the Light Verb – the valency complementations present in its valency frame besides the CPHR complementation – do not by themselves correspond to any semantic participant (see Section 4.2) but remain semantically unsaturated until the Light Verb becomes part of a complex predicate with a particular predicative noun.

(7) *poskytovat$_{full}$* 'to provide': ACT$_{nom}^{obl}$ ADDR$_{dat}^{obl}$ PAT$_{acc}^{obl}$

(8) *Jiné   pojišťovn-y*$_{ACT}$ *poskytují   pacient-ům*$_{ADDR}$
    other   insurance company-NOM   provide   patient-DAT
    seznam-Ø$_{PAT}$ *nemocnic.*   (CNC)
    list-ACC   of hospitals.
    'Other insurance companies provide a list of hospitals for patients.'

(9) *poskytovat$_{light}$* 'to provide': ACT$_{nom}^{obl}$ ADDR$_{dat}^{obl}$ CPHR$_{acc}^{obl}$

5.3 Coreference of valency complementations

In accordance with the general principles of the deep syntactic representation, both valency complementations of the predicative noun and of the Light Verb are present in the deep structure of the complex predicate regardless of whether or not they are expressed on the surface. We can then observe that the deep structure of the complex predicate contains a pair(s) of nominal and verbal valency com-

---

[17] The only exception is the semantic participant Instigator with causative Light Verbs. See Section 5.4.

plementations filled with coreferential expressions where one of them cannot be expressed on the surface.[18] The valency complementations filled with coreferential expressions refer to the same semantic participants and thus have identical semantic roles. For simplification, we talk about *coreference* of valency complementations in complex predicates henceforth.

The pairs of coreferring valency complementations involve those complementations of the Light Verb that are semantically unsaturated (see above Section 5.2). The sharing of semantic roles with valency complementations of the predicative noun enables semantically unsaturated valency complementations of the Light Verb to obtain the semantic saturation from semantic participants of the noun. Whether the verbal complementation or the nominal one is then expressed on the surface can be unambiguously determined on the basis of their forms.

For example, in the deep structure of the complex predicate *poskytovat informace* 'to give information', both valency complementations from the valency frame of the Light Verb (9) and complementations from the frame of the noun (10) are contained. The noun *informace* 'information' is characterized by three semantic participants: Speaker (who gives a message to a recipient), Recipient (who receives the message from the speaker), and Message (the content of what the speaker communicates). These three participants are mapped onto the valency complementations ACTor, ADDRessee, and PATient of the noun, respectively; see the valency frame of the noun in (10) and the nominal construction in (11). When combined with the Light Verb *poskytovat* 'to provide', which has two semantically unsaturated valency complementations, ACTor and ADDRessee, in its valency frame (9), these unsaturated valency complementations enter into coreference with the ACTor and ADDRessee of the predicative noun, respectively, being thus semantically saturated by the Speaker and the Recipient. The fact that the involved valency complementations refer to these two semantic participants, and thus share semantic roles, is evident when the LVC with the complex predicate *poskytovat informace* 'to give information' in (12) is compared with the corresponding nominal construction in (11). In the LVC, the Speaker and the Recipient are not realized on the surface as the ACTor and the ADDRessee of the noun (these two valency complementations are elided) but as the ACTor and the ADDRessee of the Light Verb as their forms show. This fact can be best illustrated by the deep dependency trees of the LVC in (12) and the nominal construction in (11) displayed in Figure 1, where the sharing of semantic roles is captured by coreferential links.

---

[18] In this respect, complex predicates with Light Verbs stand close to, e.g., control verbs and they can be subsumed under so-called grammatical coreference (see Hajičová et al. 1985).

(10) *informace* 'information': ACT$_{\text{gen,poss,od 'from'+gen}}$ ADDR$_{\text{gen,dat,poss}}$ PAT$_{\text{o 'about'+locat,dcc}}$

(11) *informac-e   odborník-ů*$_{\text{ACTn}}$ *kolemjdouc-ím*$_{\text{ADDRn}}$[19]
    information-NOM   expert-GEN   passer-by-DAT
    o očkovacích centr-ech$_{\text{PATn}}$
    about vaccination center-LOCAT
    'information from experts to passers-by on vaccination centers'[20]

(12) *Odborníc-i*$_{\text{ACTv}}$ ... *poskytují   kolemjdouc-ím*$_{\text{ADDRv}}$ *informac-e*$_{\text{CPHRv}}$
    expert-NOM   ...   provide   passer-by-DAT   information-ACC
    o očkovacích centr-ech$_{\text{PATn}}$ ...
    about vaccination center-LOCAT (according to CNC)
    'Experts ... give passers-by information about vaccination centers ...'

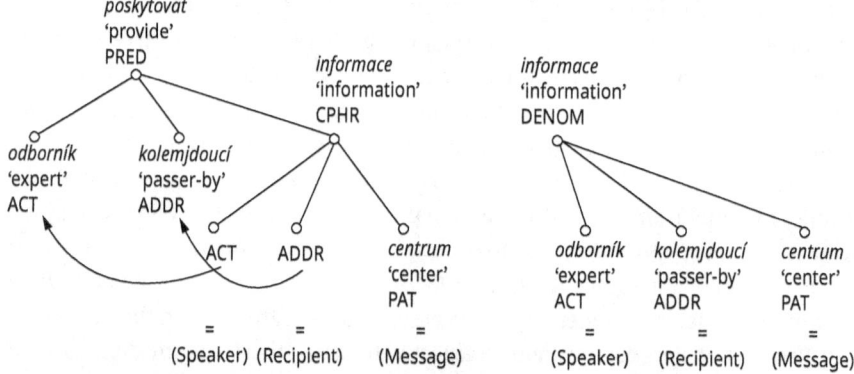

Figure 1: The simplified deep dependency trees of the LVC in (12) (on the left) and the corresponding nominal construction in (11) (on the right). Arrows indicate coreference; they point from the valency complementations unexpressed on the surface (the nominal ones in this case) to the expressed ones.[21]

---

19 The symbols n and v in the lower index with valency complementations distinguish whether they are nominal or verbal.
20 When a noun has more than two valency complementations in its valency frame, the expression of all of them on the surface is often limited by stylistic aspects as it may result in overloading nominal structures (Piťha 1984). Some of the valency complementations, still present in the deep syntactic structure, are then elided from the surface.
21 The semantic roles are not part of the deep syntactic representation. We introduce them only for the sake of clarity.

5.4 Variations in coreference

A Light Verb can form complex predicates with different predicative nouns. Semantically unsaturated valency complementations of the same Light Verb can then share semantic roles with different valency complementations of the predicative noun. The sharing of semantic roles, manifested in the deep syntactic structure by coreference of verbal and nominal valency complementations, is thus specific to individual complex predicates, as illustrated in this section through the example of complex predicates with the Light Verb *poskytovat* 'to provide'.

As mentioned above, the Light Verb *poskytovat* 'to provide' has two semantically unsaturated valency complementations – ACTor and ADDRessee – in its valency frame; see the valency frame in (9), repeated here for convenience as (13). In addition to the nominal ACTor and ADDRessee (see Section 5.3), the ACTor and ADDRessee of this Light Verb can share semantic roles, thus corefer, with the nominal ACTor and PATient as well, as manifested, e.g., by the complex predicate *poskytovat péči* 'to provide care'. The predicative noun *péče* 'care' has two semantic participants, Helper and Benefited_party, which are mapped onto its ACTor and PATient, respectively; see the valency frame of the noun *péče* 'care' in (14) and the nominal construction in (15). In the complex predicate *poskytovat péči* 'to provide care', the participants Helper and Benefited_party provided by the noun semantically saturate the semantically unspecified ACTor and ADDRessee of the Light Verb. See the LVC in (16), where the Helper and Benefited_party are expressed as the verbal ACTor and ADDRessee, respectively, as their forms indicate while the respective valency complementations of the noun, the ACTor and the PATient, remain unexpressed on the surface. The dependency trees of this LVC and of the corresponding nominal construction in (15) are displayed in Figure 2.

(13) *poskytovat*$_{light}$ 'to provide':   ACT$_{nom}$^{obl} ADDR$_{dat}$^{obl} CPHR$_{acc}$^{obl}

(14) *péče* 'care':   ACT$_{gen,poss}$ PAT$_{o\ \text{'for'+acc}}$

(15) *péč-e   tým-u*$_{ACTn}$ *o lid-i*$_{PATn}$ *s nízkými příjmy*
    care-NOM   team-GEN   for people-ACC   with low income
    'the team's care for people with low income'

(16) *Tým-Ø*$_{ACTv}$ *poskytuje péč-i*$_{CPHRv}$ *lid-em*$_{ADDRv}$ *s nízkými příjmy.* (CNC)
    team-NOM   provides   care-ACC   people-DAT   with low income
    'The team provides care to people with low income.'

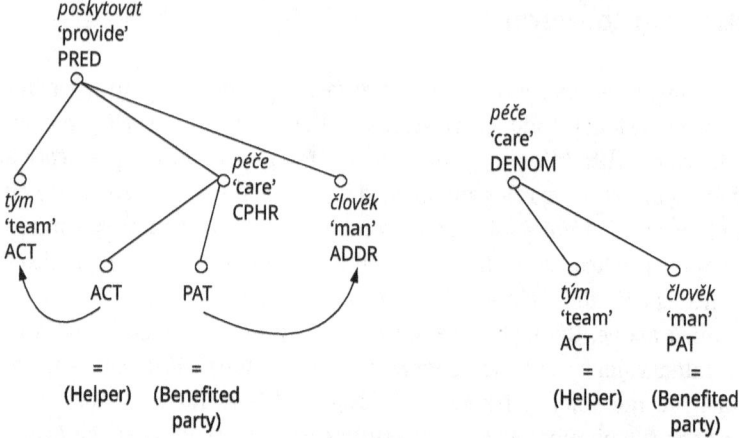

Figure 2: The simplified deep dependency trees of the LVC in (16) (on the left) and the corresponding nominal construction in (15) (on the right).

Further, a Light Verb, when combined with some predicative nouns, acquires causative features. In this case, the situation described by the complex predicate involves the semantic participant Instigator (Section 4.2), which is mapped onto a valency complementation of the verb. For example, when the Light Verb *poskytovat* 'to provide' combines with the predicative noun *uspokojení* 'satisfaction', the noun provides two semantic participants, Experiencer and Stimulus, for the complex predicate while the verb contributes an Instigator to it. The participants of the noun, Experiencer and Stimulus, are mapped onto the ACTor and the PATient of the noun; see the valency frame of the noun in (17) and the nominal structure in (18). As the comparison of this nominal construction and the LVC in (19) indicates, the LVC contains an extra participant (*postup* 'approach'). This participant with the role of Instigator is thus provided by the verb. It corresponds to the verbal ACTor; see the valency frame of the verb in (13). The ADDRessee of the verb then remains the only semantically unsaturated valency complementation in its valency frame. In the complex predicate *poskytovat uspokojení* 'to provide satisfaction', this ADDRessee is semantically saturated by the semantic participant Experiencer as the dative form of this participant shows while the nominal ACTor corresponding to this participant is elided. See the dependency trees of the LVC in (19) and of the nominal construction in (18) displayed in Figure 3.

(17) *uspokojení* 'satisfaction': $ACT_{gen,poss}$ $PAT_{nad\ 'over'+instr, s\ 'with'+instr, z\ 'from'+gen, dcc}$

(18) *mé*$_{ACTn}$ *uspokojen-í*   *z prác-e*$_{PATn}$
      my.POSS.NOM   satisfaction-NOM   from work-GEN
      'my job satisfaction'

(19) Tenhle terapeutický postup-∅_ACTv   mi_ADDRv vždycky poskytoval
     this   therapeutic approach-NOM   me.DAT   always   provided
     uspokojen-í_CPHRv   z prác-e_PATn. (according to CNC)
     satisfaction-ACC from job-GEN
     'This therapeutic approach has always brought me job satisfaction.'

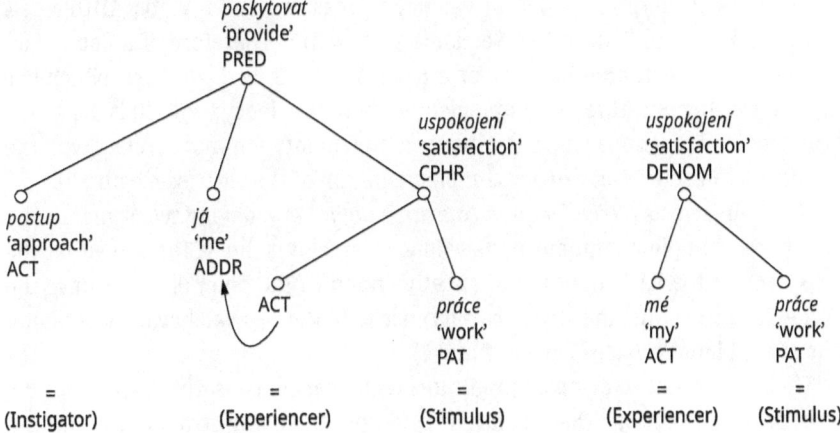

Figure 3: The simplified deep dependency trees of the LVC in (19) (on the left) and the corresponding nominal construction in (18) (on the right).

5.5 Restrictions on coreference

Which verbal and nominal valency complementations in complex predicates share semantic roles, and thus corefer, is restricted by two factors: the number of semantically unsaturated valency complementations of the Light Verb, and the systemic ordering of valency complementations of the predicative noun.

As for the first factor, only bivalent and trivalent Light Verbs with a predicative noun in the direct object position are attested in the data. It follows that if a Light Verb is *bivalent and non-causative*, then one valency complementation of the verb is reserved for the predicative noun and the other, being semantically unsaturated, shares a semantic role, and thus corefers, with a nominal valency complementation. When a *trivalent Light Verb* is *non-causative*, two semantically unsaturated complementations of the verb are available for coreference with nominal complementations. Causative Light Verbs, endowed with the semantic participant Instigator, have one less semantically unsaturated valency complementation in their valency frames. As a result, *bivalent causative Light Verbs* have no semantically unsaturated valency complementation in their valency frames at all since one of their valency complementations is filled with a predicative noun and the other with an Instigator. Finally, *trivalent causative Light Verbs* provide only one semantically unsaturated valency complementation for coreference.

Second, from the viewpoint of predicative nouns, we can observe that the coreference of their valency complementations in complex predicates typically respects their systemic ordering, applied in valency frames, which is ACTor, ADDRessee, PATient, EFFect, and ORIGin (see Section 2.1 as well).[22] Therefore, if a noun combines with a *bivalent non-causative* or a *trivalent causative Light Verb*, which has one semantically unsaturated complementation in its valency frame, it is the ACTor of the predicative noun as its first valency complementation that corefers with the semantically unsaturated valency complementation of the verb (see Figure 3).

If a noun selects a *trivalent non-causative Light Verb*, having two semantically unsaturated complementations in its valency frame, it is the ACTor and either the ADDRessee or the PATient of the predicative noun (if the noun does not have the ADDResse in its frame) that are in coreference with the two valency complementations of the Light Verb (see Figures 1 and 2).

The coreference in complex predicates with *bivalent causative Light Verbs* deserves special attention. These Light Verbs do not have any semantically unsaturated valency complementation in their valency frames. Nevertheless, the ACTor of the predicative noun combined with these Light Verbs still tends to corefer. In this case, the nominal ACTor typically makes use of an optional free modification of the Light Verb, standing outside its valency frame. See Section 2.5.

For example, the bivalent Light Verb *budit* 'to awaken', when combined with the predicative noun *touha* 'desire', behaves like a causative Light Verb. No semantically unsaturated valency complementation is contained in its valency frame: the ACTor corresponds to Instigator and the CPHR is occupied by the predicative noun; see the valency frame of the verb in (22). The noun *touha* 'desire' has two semantic participants, Experiencer and Focal_participant, mapped onto its ACTor and PATient, respectively, see its valency frame (20) and the nominal construction in (21). When combined with the Light Verb *budit* 'to awaken', the ACTor of the noun *touha* 'desire' can share its semantic role of Experiencer, thus corefer, with the LOCative, an optional free modification of the Light Verb as the LVC in (23a) illustrates. The Experiencer is then realized as the verbal LOCative complementation as its form indicates[23] while

---

[22] The systemic ordering complies with the unmarked word order (Sgall et al. 1986). The coreference violating the systemic ordering is very rare.

[23] The LOCative as an optional free modification is not part of the valency frame of the verb (see Section 2.5). The possible forms of the LOCative complementation (e.g., the prepositional group *v* 'in' + locat in (23a)) follow from the semantic type of this complementation.

the nominal ACTor corresponding to this participant is elided from the surface. When the ACTor of the noun does not corefer, the Experiencer is expressed as the nominal ACTor as is in the nominal construction (21); see the LVC in (23b). Compare the dependency trees of these LVCs provided in Figure 4.

(20) *touha* 'desire':   ACT$_{\text{gen,poss}}$ PAT$_{\text{po 'for' +locat,inf,dcc}}$

(21) *touh-a   lid-í*$_{\text{ACTn}}$ *po jistot-ách*$_{\text{PATn}}$
     desire-NOM people-GEN for security-LOCAT
     'people's desire for security'

(22) *budit*$_{\text{light}}$ 'to awaken': ACT$_{\text{nom,inf,dcc}}^{\text{obl}}$ CPHR$_{\text{acc}}^{\text{obl}}$

(23) a. *Nejistá   dob-a*$_{\text{ACTv}}$ *budí   v lid-ech*$_{\text{LOCv}}$ *touh-u*$_{\text{CPHRv}}$
        uncertain time-NOM awakens in people-LOCAT desire-ACC
        po jistot-ách$_{\text{PATn}}$ (CNC)
        for security-LOCAT
     b. *Nejistá   dob-a*$_{\text{ACTv}}$ *budí   touh-u*$_{\text{CPHRv}}$ *lid-í*$_{\text{ACTn}}$
        uncertain time-NOM awakens desire-ACC people-GEN
        po jistot-ách$_{\text{PATn}}$
        for security-LOCAT
        'Uncertain times awaken a desire for security in people.'

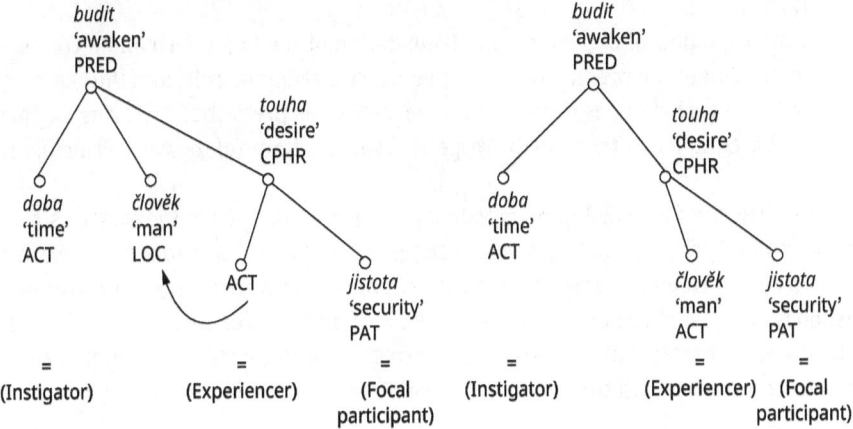

Figure 4: The simplified deep dependency trees of the LVC in (23a) (on the left) and the LVC in (23b) (on the right).

6 Surface syntactic structure

6.1 Distribution of valency complementations in the surface structure

Czech, an inflectional language, encoding syntactic relations by morphemic forms, provides a good starting point for studying the *distribution of valency complementations in the surface structure of LVCs* since forms of individual valency complementations expressed on the surface determine whether they are governed by the Light Verb or by the predicative noun. For example, in the LVC in example (23b), the nominative identifies the ACTor of the Light Verb *budit* 'to awaken'; see the valency frame of the verb in (22). The prepositionless genitive in the same example then encodes the ACTor of the predicative noun *touha* 'desire'; see the frame of the noun in (20).

Based on an analysis of forms of valency complementations expressed in LVCs, the following principles of their surface distribution can be formulated; these principles operate on valency frames of Light Verbs and of predicative nouns, making use of the information on the sharing of semantic roles between verbal and nominal valency complementations, or simply on their coreference:

- each valency complementation of the Light Verb and of the predicative noun that does not corefer with another complementation is expressed in the surface structure as prescribed by forms for this complementation in the respective valency frame of the verb (Principle 1)[24] or in the respective frame of the noun (Principle 2)
- from each pair of a valency complementation of the Light Verb and a complementation of the predicative noun that share a semantic role, and thus corefer, only the verbal one is expressed on the surface as prescribed by forms for this verbal complementation in the respective valency frame of the verb (Principle 3)

Let us illustrate the distribution of valency complementations in the surface structure of LVCs with the example of the complex predicate *budit touhu* 'to awaken a desire'. The valency frame of the Light Verb *budit* 'to awaken' (22) comprises two valency complementations: ACTor with the semantic role of Instigator and CPHR filled with the predicative noun *touha* 'desire'. Both these valency complementations are expressed on the surface as prescribed for them in the valency frame of

---

[24] Principle 1 applies also to the surface realization of the CPHR complementation, filled with the predicative noun. Unlike other valency complementations, this valency position is in principle excluded from coreference.

the verb as none of them share a semantic role, and thus corefer, with a nominal complementation (Principle 1). See the ACTor (*doba* 'time') and the CPHR (*touha* 'desire') in examples (23a-b) and Figure 4.

Further, the valency frame of the noun *touha* 'desire' contains ACTor and PATient; see its valency frame in (20). In the complex predicate *budit touhu* 'to awaken a desire', the ACTor can share its semantic role, thus corefer, with the optional LOCative complementation of the Light Verb. If it corefers, the verbal LOCative is expressed on the surface (Principle 3); see the LOCative complementation (*v lidech* 'in people') in example (23a) and Figure 4 on the left. If it does not corefer, the nominal ACTor is realized on the surface as determined in the valency frame of the noun (Principle 2); see the ACTor (*lidí* 'of people') in example (23b) and Figure 4 on the right. The surface expression of the PATient, the other valency complementation in the frame of the noun, is governed by Principle 2 as well since this PATient does not corefer with any valency complementation of the verb; see the PATient (*po jistotách* 'for security') in examples (23a-b) and Figure 4.[25]

Principle 3 reflects one of the most characteristic syntactic features of LVCs, namely that valency complementations of the predicative noun are often elided from the surface. This situation occurs when valency complementations of the predicative noun share their semantic roles (therefore corefer in the deep syntactic structure) with valency complementations of the Light Verb. In this case, nominal complementations are subject to systemic surface ellipsis.[26] For example, as shown in Section 5.3 and 5.4, the semantically unsaturated ACTor and ADDRessee of the Light Verb *poskytovat* 'to provide' (see the valency frame of the verb in (13)) can corefer in complex predicates with various nominal valency complementations. These ACTor and ADDRessee are then regularly expressed on the surface while the respective nominal complementations with which they corefer are deleted. See example (12) and Figure 1 on the left and example (16) and Figure 2 on the left.

---

[25] Valency complementations distributed according to these principles can be subsequently subject to various types of textual ellipsis.
[26] In a small number of cases, both the verbal ACTor and the nominal ACTor can be expressed in the surface structure of Czech LVCs although they corefer (e.g., *Jan*$_{ACTv}$ *činil svá*$_{ACTn}$ *rozhodnutí s nejlepší vůlí* 'John$_{ACTv}$ made his$_{ACTn}$ decisions with the best of intentions'). However, their stylistic appropriateness is often questionable. The conditions under which both ACTors can be expressed in LVCs require further research.

6.2 Surface expression of semantic participants

The analysis of the distribution of verbal and nominal valency complementations in the surface structure of LVCs, presented in Section 6.1, allows us to pinpoint how semantic participants are employed in LVCs:
- The semantic participants of the predicative noun that semantically saturate a valency complementation of the noun and at the same time a valency complementation of the Light Verb are expressed in the surface structure of LVCs as prescribed by forms for the verbal valency complementation in the valency frame of the Light Verb;
- The other semantic participants that semantically saturate only a single valency complementation, be they participants of the predicative noun or Instigator of the Light Verb, are realized in the surface structure of LVCs as prescribed by forms for the respective valency complementation in the valency frame of the noun or in the frame of the Light Verb.

7 Conclusion

This paper has addressed the syntactic structure of Czech Light Verb Constructions from the perspective of valency. We have argued that the Light Verb and the predicative noun have their own valency structures, which they retain in individual complex predicates. The valency structure of the Light Verb and that of the predicative noun should be thus captured by separate valency frames.

Further, we have shown that what differentiates individual complex predicates from each other is an interaction between valency complementations of the Light Verb and those of the predicative noun through the sharing of semantic roles, which enables semantically unsaturated valency complementations of the Light Verb to obtain their semantic specification. The sharing of semantic roles is manifested in the deep syntactic structure of the complex predicate as the coreference of the involved valency complementations. The coreference is specific for individual complex predicates and cannot be inferred from the valency structure of the Light Verb and that of the predicative noun. However, its variations are limited: on the side of Light Verbs by the number of their semantically unsaturated valency complementations and on the side of predicative nouns by the systemic ordering of valency complementations in their frames.

In specific cases where the Light Verb does not provide any semantically unsaturated valency complementation for coreference, the predicative noun is still inclined to employ its first valency complementation in coreference, making use of an optional free modification of the Light Verb. From this point of view, the sharing of semantic roles between verbal and nominal complementations, manifested as their coreference, appears to be a defining characteristic of complex predicates.

Finally, the coreference has implications for the surface realization of valency complementations as well since it typically leads to the surface ellipsis of the involved valency complementations of the predicative noun. Czech – as an inflectional language – makes it possible to survey the distribution of valency complementations in the surface structure of Light Verb Constructions and to accurately identify on the basis of their forms which of them are expressed on the surface. Based on this distribution, the principles governing the surface realization of semantic participants in Light Verb Constructions can then be established, corroborating that one of the main functions of the Light Verb is to open some of its valency positions for the surface expression of the nominal semantic participants.

Abbreviations

ACC	accusative
ACT	Actor
ADDR	Addressee
CNC	Czech National Corpus
CPHR	nominal part of complex predicates
DAT	dative
DCC	dependent content clause
DENOM	root of nominal clause
FGD	Functional Generative Description
GEN	genitive
INF	infinitive
INSTR	instrumental
LOC	locative complementation
LOCAT	locative
LVC	Light Verb Construction
n	nominal complementation
NOM	nominative
OBL	obligatory complementation
OPT	optional complementation
PAT	Patient
PDT	Prague Dependency Treebank
POSS	possessive pronouns or adjectives
PRED	root of verbal clause
v	verbal complementation

References

Ágel, Vilmos, Ludwig M. Eichinger, Hans-Werner Eroms, Peter Hellwig, Hans Jürgen Heringer & Henning Lobin. 2003. *Dependency and Valency. An International Handbook of Contemporary Research*. Berlin/New York: Walter de Gruyter.

Alonso Ramos, Margarita. 2007. Towards the synthesis of support verbs constructions: Distribution of syntactic actants between the verb and the noun. In Leo Wanner (ed.), *Selected Lexical and Grammatical Issues in the Meaning-Text Theory: In honour of Igor Mel'čuk*, 97–137. Amsterdam: Benjamins.

Alsina, Alex. 1996. *The Role of Argument Structure in Grammar. Evidence from Romance*. Stanford: CSLI Publications.

Alsina, Alex. 1997. A theory of complex predicates: Evidence from causatives in Bantu and Romance. In Alex Alsina, Joan Bresnan & Peter Sells (eds.), *Complex Predicates*, 203–246. Stanford: CSLI Publications.

Apresjan, Juri. 2009. The Theory of Lexical Functions: An Update. In David Beck, Kim Gerdes, Jasmina Milićević & Alain Polguère (eds.), *Proceedings of the Fourth International Conference on Meaning-Text Theory*, 1–14. Montréal: Observatoire de linguistique Sens-Texte (OLST).

Bosque, Ignacio. 2001. On the Weight of Light Predicates. In Julia Herschensohn, Enrique Mallén & Karen Zagona (eds.), *Features and Interfaces in Romance: Essays in honor of Heles Contreras*, 23–38. Amsterdam: Benjamins.

Brugman, Claudia. 2001. Light verbs and polysemy. *Language Sciences* 23. 551–578.

Butt, Miriam. 1998. Constraining Argument Merger through Aspect. In Erhard Hinrichs, Andreas Kathol & Tsuneko Nakazawa (eds.), *Complex Predicates in Nonderivational Syntax*. Syntax and Semantics. Vol. 30, 73–113. New York: Academic Press.

Butt, Miriam. 2010. The light verb jungle: still hacking away. In Mengistu Amberber, Brett Baker & Mark Harvey (eds.), *Complex Predicates: Cross-linguistic Perspectives on Event Structure*, 48–78. Cambridge: Cambridge University Press.

Butt, Miriam & Wilhelm Geuder. 2001. On the (semi)lexical status of light verbs. In Norbert Corver & Henk van Riemsdijk (eds.), *Semi-lexical Categories: The Function of Content Words and the Content of Function Words*, 323–370. Berlin/New York: Mouton de Gruyter.

Dixon, R. M. W. & Alexandra Y. Aikhenvald. 2006. *Complementation. A Cross-Linguistic Typology*. Oxford: Oxford University Press.

Grimshaw, Jane & Armin Mester. 1988. Light verbs and θ-marking. *Linguistic Inquiry* 19(2). 205–232.

Gross, Maurice. 1981. Les bases empiriques de la notion de prédicat sémantique. *Langages* 63. 7–52.

Hajič, Jan, Eduard Bejček, Jaroslava Hlavacova, Marie Mikulová, Milan Straka, Jan Štěpánek & Barbora Štěpánková. 2020. *Prague Dependency Treebank – Consolidated 1.0 (PDT-C 1.0)*. LINDAT/CLARIAH-CZ digital library at the Institute of Formal and Applied Linguistics (ÚFAL), Faculty of Mathematics and Physics, Charles University. http://hdl.handle.net/11234/1-3185.

Hajičová, Eva, Jarmila Panevová & Petr Sgall. 1985. Coreference in the Grammar and in the Text. Part I. *The Prague Bulletin of Mathematical Linguistics* 44. 3–22.

Hinrichs, Erhard, Andreas Kathol & Tsuneko Nakazawa (eds.), 1998. *Complex Predicates in Nonderivational Syntax*. Syntax and Semantics. Vol. 30. New York: Academic Press.

Ježek, Elisabetta. 2011. Verbes supports et composition sémantique. *Cahiers de lexicologie* 98(1). 29–43.

Kettnerová, Václava, Markéta Lopatková, Eduard Bejček & Petra Barančíková. 2018. Enriching VALLEX with light verbs: From theory to data and back again. *The Prague Bulletin of Mathematical Linguistics* 111. 29–56.

Kolářová, Veronika. 2014. Special valency behavior of Czech deverbal nouns. In Olga Spevak (ed.), *Noun Valency*, 19–60. Amsterdam: Benjamins.

Kolářová, Veronika, Anna Vernerová & Jana Klímová. 2020. *NomVallex I*. LINDAT/CLARIAH-CZ digital library at the Institute of Formal and Applied Linguistics (ÚFAL), Faculty of Mathematics and Physics, Charles University. http://hdl.handle.net/11234/1-3420.

Levin, Beth & Malka Rappaport Hovav. 2005. *Argument Realization*. Cambridge: Cambridge University Press.

Lopatková, Markéta, Václava Kettnerová, Eduard Bejček, Anna Vernerová & Zdeněk Žabokrtský. 2016. *Valenční slovník českých sloves VALLEX*. Praha: Karolinum.

Macháčková, Eva. 1994. Constructions with verbs and abstract nouns in Czech (analytical predicates). In Světla Čmejrková & František Štícha (eds.), *Syntax of Sentence and Text. A Festschrift for František Daneš*, 365–374. (*Linguistic and Literary Studies in Eastern Europe 42*). Amsterdam: Benjamins.

Mastrofini, Roberta. 2019. Aspectual classes and type coercion in English light verb extensions. Paper presented at at the 12th Annual International Conference on Languages & Linguistics (8–11 July 2019), organized by the Athens Institute for Education and Research (ATINER). https://www.athensjournals.gr/reviews/2019-2864-AJP-LNG.pdf

Mel'čuk, Igor. 1988. *Dependency Syntax: Theory and Practice*. Albany, NY: State University of New York Press.

Mel'čuk, Igor. 1996. Lexical functions: A tool for the description of lexical relations in a lexicon. In Leo Wanner (eds.), *Lexical Functions in Lexicography and Natural Language Processing*, 37–102. Amsterdam: Benjamins.

Mel'čuk, Igor. 2004. Actants in semantics and syntax I: Actants in semantics. *Linguistics* 42(1). 1–66.

Panevová, Jarmila. 1974–75. On Verbal Frames in Functional Generative Description I-II. The *Prague Bulletin of Mathematical Linguistics* 22 & 23. 3–40, 17–52.

Panevová, Jarmila. 1994. Valency Frames and the Meaning of the Sentence. In Philip A. Lueslsdorff (eds.), *The Prague School of Structural and Functional Linguistics: A Short Introduction*, 223–243. Amsterdam: Benjamins.

Panevová, Jarmila, Eva Hajičová, Václava Kettnerová, Markéta Lopatková, Marie Mikulová & Magda Ševčíková. 2014. *Mluvnice současné češtiny 2. Syntax češtiny na základě anotovaného korpusu*. Praha: Karolinum.

Piťha, Petr. 1984. Case frames of nouns. In Petr Sgall (ed.), *Contributions to functional syntax, semantics, and language comprehension*, 225–238. Amsterdam: Benjamins.

Radimský, Jan. 2010. *Verbo-nominální predikát s kategoriálním slovesem*. České Budějovice: Editio Universitatis Bohemiae Meridionalis.

Rosen, Sara T. 1989. *Argument Structure and Complex Predicates*. PhD dissertation. Waltham: Brandeis University.

Sanromán Vilas, Begoña. 2017. From the heavy to the light verb. An analysis of tomar 'to take'. *Lingvisticæ Investigationes* 40(2). 228–273.

Sgall, Petr, Eva Hajičová & Jarmila Panevová. 1986. *The Meaning of the Sentence in its Semantic and Pragmatic Aspects*. Dordrecht: Reidel.

Urešová, Zdeňka, Eva Fučíková, Eva Hajičová & Jan Hajič. 2020. SynSemClass Linked Lexicon: Mapping synonymy between languages. In Ilan Kernerman, Simon Krek, John P. McCrae, Jorge Gracia, Sina Ahmadi & Besim Kabashi (eds.), *Proceedings of the 2020 Globalex Workshop on Linked Lexicography (LREC 2020)*, 10–19. Marseille: European Language Resources Association.

Urešová, Zdeňka, Alevtina Bémová, Eva Fučíková, Jan Hajič, Veronika Kolářová, Marie Mikulová, Petr Pajas, Jarmila Panevová & Jan Štěpánek. 2021. *PDT-Vallex: Czech valency lexicon linked to treebanks 4.0 (PDT-Vallex 4.0)*. LINDAT/CLARIAH-CZ digital library at the Institute of Formal and Applied Linguistics (ÚFAL), Faculty of Mathematics and Physics, Charles University. http://hdl.handle.net/11234/1-3499.

Lars Hellan
2 Unification and selection in Light Verb Constructions
A study of Norwegian

Abstract: One characteristic of so-called *Light Verb Constructions* (*LVCs*) is that they unfold, mostly over a sequence '*Subject* **V** (**P**) **N**', a content that could in principle be carried by some verb **V** alone, where the **N** of the sequence expresses a situational content close to that of **V** (**N** thus being some kind of 'deverbal' variant of **V**). A typical role of (the 'light' verb) **V** in the LVC is to connect the *Subject* to this situational content as some kind of *role* bearer, and add *aspectual* content to the situational content expressed by **N**.

In languages where LVCs are seen as constituting a major category, the number of verbs serving as 'Light Verb' is low, and LVCs constitute formally recurrent patterns. In Norwegian the picture is different, with many verbs serving as possible Light Verbs, where these verbs select different nouns, and the nouns in turn select different verbs. In illustrating this, we outline a format for representation of LVCs in corpora. We in addition outline a format for representing LVCs in a valence lexicon, and for representing them in a sentence parsing formalism. The unification between the meaning of the Light Verb and the meaning of the noun is formally represented.

While a sizable number of LVC selection relations between verbs and nouns have been identified, and a large valence lexicon and parser constitute the frames for the formalizations mentioned, the formalizations have only to very small extents been implemented, being presented here only for formal consideration.

Keywords: situational meaning, semantic composition, Head-driven Phrase Structure, Norwegian, corpus annotation

1 Introduction

One characteristic of so-called *Light Verb Constructions* (*LVCs*)[1] is that they express, mostly over a sequence '*Subject* **V** (**P**) **N**', a content that could in principle be carried

---

[1] Many phenomena have been characterized in terms of the notion 'Light Verb'; Butt (2010) may be seen for a summary of many of them. The usage of the term here employed goes back at least to Jespersen (1942), more recently Grimshaw and Mester (1988), and is a topic of much current atten-

by some verb **V** alone, and where the **N** of the sequence carries the main part of the content, hence the term 'light' for the role of the verb. The **N** thus expresses a situational content, often being 'de-verbal', and a typical role of (the Light Verb) **V** in the LVC is to connect its *subject* to this situational content as a *role* bearer, and possibly add *aspectual* and *viewpoint* content to the situational content expressed by **N**.[2] (1a) to (1c) are examples from Norwegian; (1d) to (1f) are corresponding sentences where a related verb alone carries the relational content:

(1) a. *Han fant behag i innspilling-en*
    He find.PST pleasure in recording-MASC.DEF.SG
    'He found pleasure in the recording'
  b. *Han gjorde bruk av grammofon-en*
    He make.PST use of gramophone-MASC.DEF.SG
    'He made use of the gramophone'
  c. *Hun stil-te sak-en i bero*
    She pose-PST case-MASC.DEF.SG in rest
    'She suspended the case'
  d. *Innspilling-en behage-t ham*
    Recording-MASC.DEF.SG please-PST him
    'The recording pleased him'
  e. *Han bruk-te grammofon-en*
    He use-PST gramophone-MASC.DEF.SG
    'He used the gramophone'
  f. *Sak-en bero-r*
    Case-MASC.DEF.SG rest-PRES
    'The case rests'

In (1b), for instance, the noun *bruk* 'use' by itself represents at least an agent and a theme/patient, and the verb *gjorde* 'made' (infinitive *gjøre* 'make, do') effects a linking of the subject *han* 'he' to the agent role. In a contrasting construction like *Den hadde vært gjenstand for uforsiktig bruk* 'It had been subject to careless use', the subject *den* is linked to the patient/theme role of *bruk*. The interplay between *bruk* and the alternating Light Verb expression is thus one where the Light Verb is

---

tion, see, e.g., Pompei and Piunno (2015), Nagy et al. (2013). Other uses of the term, for instance in the Scandinavian oriented literature, pertain to auxiliary-like items (cf. Lødrup 2002).
2 There is rarely full semantic equivalence between a given LVC and the putative related *V*; a better perspective may lie in Tesnière's (1959) notion of *metataxis*, whereby the formation of LVCs can be seen as an extension of the *valency* properties of *V*, the N embodying the 'first step'.

defined for linking between a certain role and the grammatical function of subject, whereas the noun has no syntactic linking, but a richer content, including the role mediated by the verb.

Without making it a teleological issue, one may say that a situational content, in seeking linguistic expression, has more than one channel – most prominently the category of *verb*, bound to the patterns of valence offered by the grammar, but the category of *noun* is another, allowing situational content to be combined with expression of quantification, definiteness and such, and the LVC represents a manner in which the noun avails itself of the Light Verb to have its predicative content expressed in a sentential pattern.

It is well recognized that LVCs as here understood constitute a major category in, e.g., Persian (cf. Karimi-Doostan 2010, 2011, Eshaghi and Karimi-Doostan, this volume) and in Indic languages, Romance languages, and likewise in West African languages. In languages where LVCs are seen as constituting a major category, the number of verbs serving as 'Light Verb' (LV) is low, and LVCs constitute formally recurrent patterns. In Norwegian the picture is different, with many verbs serving as possible LVs. We will illustrate this in section 2.

In a lexicon accommodating LVCs, it will be reasonable to include in the entry of a verb lemma whether the verb can function as an LV, and if so, in combination with what kinds or nouns or individual nouns. A verb lexicon in addition should provide an account of the derivation potential of each verb lemma as to which adjectives and nouns it can be related to, be it as a source of derivation or as itself derived from such a source. In such a setting, the nouns of LVCs can be related to their verbal or adjectival networks, and patterns can be investigated relative to the senses and valences of the verbs compared with the sense or valence correspondents realized in the LVCs. Section 3 will outline a design for such an extension of a lexicon.

From a formal viewpoint, one can model the 'merger' or 'melting together' between features of the verb and the noun in terms of *unification*, which will be a theme developed in section 4. This perspective can be applied also in a formal account of *selection* within the LVC – the verb selecting the noun, and the noun selecting the verb (and with selection relating to possible intermediary nouns or prepositions). The unification perspective allows one to probe into the more detailed structures of senses and their interaction with structural factors. In order to abstract away from those aspects of the semantic specification of ***V*** which are tied to its status as a verb, we introduce a distinction between a word's *bound semantics*, which closely follows the word's syntactic properties, and its *free semantics*, which is grammatically independent (following the gist of many proposals, for instance Melchuk 2004, Levin and Rappaport Hovav 2005). What N retains from its 'verbal' core is its free semantics, and it is up to the LVC to integrate this into whatever syntactic frame it represents. On this basis we develop a design of semantic representation doing justice on the one hand to the 'unified' semantics of the LVC, and on the other to its word-by-word structure. Our approach will use *Typed Feature Structures* (Copestake 2002), as employed in HPSG (Pollard and Sag 1994), where the semantic distinctions mentioned can be consistently represented, and where at the same time the lexical/constructional representation of LVCs can be integrated in an explicit formal grammar of the language. This will also be a topic of section 4.

The lexicon serving as background for section 3 is the valence catalogue *NorVal* described in Hellan (2021a, 2021b). This catalogue does not represent LVCs, and the discussion in section 3 concerns how LVCs can be added and integrated into it. The background for the discussion in section 4 is the Norwegian computational grammar *NorSource*, which includes a large verb lexicon, in many respects corresponding to NorVal, and again not representing LVCs. It is written in a formalism aimed at grammatical combination, and in outlining how LVCs can be added and integrated in this system, we introduce a more detailed formal analysis of LVCs. In both respects, while NorVal and NorSource are large, complete systems, the discussion around LVCs is exploratory, serving as 'reconnaissance' for how to build LVCs into the systems, and by the same token, aimed at gaining understanding of aspects of LVCs as these formats of analysis allow for findings that will presumably be relevant also for other languages.

2 LVCs in Norwegian

Table 1 shows an array of LVCs in Norwegian. In line with what has been said, in each case, the perceived role, indicated to the right, is among the roles one can associate with the noun, and the LVC as a whole is interpreted as ascribing this role to the item marked X.

Table 1: Schematic examples of LVCs in Norwegian.

Schematic example	Translation	Role of 'X'
X gjør en feil	'X makes a mistake'	AGENT
X tar et oppgjør med Y	'X takes an issue with Y'	AGENT
X gir inntrykk av Y	'X gives impression of Y'	STIMULUS/ REPRESENT
X får inntrykk av Y	'X gets impression of Y'	EXPERIENCER
X har en fornemmelse av Y	'X has a feeling of Y'	EXPERIENCER
X får en fornemmelse av Y	'X gets a feeling of Y'	EXPERIENCER
X gir en fornemmelse av Y	'X gives a feeling of Y'	STIMULUS/ REPRESENT
X foretar et utvalg	'X makes a selection'	AGENT

Table 1 (continued)

Schematic example	Translation	Role of 'X'
X begår et mord	'X commits a murder'	AGENT
X undergår et forhør	'X is subjected to an interrogation'	MALEFACTIVE
X gir et tilbud	'X makes an offer'	AGENT
X får et tilbud	'X gets an offer'	RECIPIENT
X mottar en innbydelse	'X receives an invitation'	RECIPIENT
X hengir seg til drikk	'X engulfs in drinking'	AGENT
Det går et rykk igjennom X	'there goes a tremor through X'	PATIENT or LOCUS
X gjennomgår en forandring	'X undergoes a change'	THEME
X gjennomløper en utvikling	'X runs through a development'	THEME
X utfører en operasjon	'X executes an operation'	AGENT
X gjennomfører en undersøkelse	'X conducts an investigation'	AGENT
X tar en jafs av kaken	'X takes a bite of the cake'	AGENT

The role ascribed to 'X' is close to the role that the verb would give to its subject also in other contexts. The noun by itself has exactly as free a distribution as any other type of noun (except for not referring to 'things'), and is thus not tied to occurring in the kind of 'role providing' (or 'predicative') function as obtaining in LVCs. However, inside LVCs, it appears that verbs with 'L'-capacity – that is, being able in principle to serve as verb in an LVC – cannot freely choose among all nouns with 'N'-capacity: in many cases a verb can constitute an LVC only together with a few nouns. Moreover, a noun with N-capacity may be restricted in its LVC occurrences to combine with only very few verbs. An interesting question is how far such instances of restrictedness follow from the meaning of the items involved – i.e., to what extent in such cases the meaning compatibility requirement restricts the number of possible partners. For possible cases where such factors are not decisive, we will refer to the restrictedness as *selection* – whether as the verb selecting the noun, or as the noun selecting the verb.

The Norwegian lexicon may be estimated to include about 3500 de-verbal nouns, which may in principle serve as complements in LVCs. Table 2 shows relative to some verbs how many LVCs they head, relative to nouns starting with *f*. The rightmost column shows the nouns most frequently occurring in each such frame, and the mid column indicates the role typically profiled in the frame. The table is a summary from a concordance of 39 verbs with altogether 258 nouns starting with *f*, constituting 250 agent-profiled LVCs and 110 Theme/patient/undergoer-profiled LVCs; verbs heading 3 or less LVCs with nouns starting with *f* are not included.

The construction of this table, being based on native speaker knowledge, should be correlated with a corpus. For Norwegian, the largest corpus resource is

NB-digital, the National Library's assembly of digital texts. Table 3 shows numbers of occurrences for a small set of putative LVC strings from the set of combinations in Table 2:[3]

Table 2: LVCs with nouns starting with f, ordered according to number of occurrences with the verb (in the leftmost column) as head.

Head verb	English trans.	Profiled role(s)[4]	Number of LVCs	Examples of nouns occurring
foreta	conduct, do	Ag	72	*fengsling* 'imprisonment', *forbytting* 'mix-up', *fordrivelse* 'expulsion', *fordeling* 'distribution', *forenkling* 'simplification', *forfremmelse* 'promotion', *forhør* 'interrogation', *forskuttering* 'advance', *forsøk* 'attempt', *fortolling* 'customs clearance', *frakobling* 'detachment', *frigjøring* 'liberation', *forsøpling* 'pollution', *fortetning* 'densification'
være/bli gjenstand for	be subject to	Pat, Th, Ben, Mal	67	*forulempelse* 'insult', *forurettelse* 'abuse', *forutbestemmelse* 'predetermination', *fortielse* 'secrecy', *forslumming* 'slumping', *forsøk* 'attempt', *forsøpling* 'pollution', *fortetning* 'densification', *forundring* 'wonder'
drive	conduct	Ag	52	*forskning* 'research', *forvaltning* 'management', *filosofering* 'philosophising', *fotografering* 'fotographing', *fragmentering* 'fragmenting', *falsifikasjon* 'falsifying', *fordummelse* 'stupidity', *forherligelse* 'glorification', *forskjønnelse*, 'embellishment'
undergå	undergo	Pat, Th	44	*fortielse* 'secrecy', *forslumming* 'slumping', *forsøk* 'attempt', *forsøpling* 'pollution', *fortetning* 'densification', *forvandling* 'change', *forvitring* 'weathering'

---

3 Roles considered: Ag – agent, Ben – benefactive, C – content, Cg – cognizer, Cs – cause, E – experiencer, Initiator (Ag, Cs, E, M, St). M – mover, Mal - malefactive, Pat – patient, Rec – recipient, St – stimulus, Th - theme

4 The results are from 2016, and the NB-digital corpus was then 15 billion words. The strings of words were defined by the author, and submitted to the database for concordance search. I am grateful to Lars Johnsen at the National Library for conducting this search. Since the NB-digital corpus is not annotated, such search must be defined relative to the word strings; since the relevant items occur mainly adjacently, this can still be an efficient procedure.

Table 2 (continued)

Head verb	English trans.	Profiled role(s)	Number of LVCs	Examples of nouns occurring
begå	commit	Ag	28	*feilvurdering* 'misjudgment', *forbrytelse* 'crime', *fortielse* 'secrecy', *fornærmelse* 'offense', *forstyrrelse* 'disturbance', *fusk* 'cheating'
gi	give	Initiator	17	*forlatelse* 'redemption', *fritak* 'exemption', *forklaring* 'explanation', *forelesning* 'lecture', *forestilling* 'performance', *forordning* 'regulation', *fortolkning* 'interpretation', *fremføring* 'performance', *fornemmelse* 'sensation'
gjøre	do	Ag	16	*fangst* 'catch', *fortjeneste* 'gain', *fritak* 'exemption', *feilvurdering* 'misjudgment', *foranstaltning* 'measure', *forbedring* 'improvement', *forfalskning* 'fraud', *forsøk* 'attempt', *forberedelse* 'preparation'
ha	have		11	*forbruk* 'use', *forståelse* 'understanding', *formening* 'opinion', *fornemmelse* 'sensation', *følelse* 'feeling', *forankring* 'anchoring', *forløp* 'course'
utløse	release, cause	Stim	9	*forargelse* 'indignation', *forbarmelse* 'mercy', *forbauselse* 'surprise', *forbitrelse* 'resentment', *forbløffelse* 'astonishment', *forferdelse* 'horror', *forskrekkelse* 'fright'
få	get	Rec, Ben, Mal	7	*flyt* 'fluency', *forløsning* 'release', *forståelse* 'understanding', *fornemmelse* 'sensation', *følelse* 'feeling', *forankring* 'anchoring'
hengi seg til			4	*forlystelse* 'amusement', *fornøyelse* 'amusement'

Table 3: Number of occurrences for some LVC strings in *NB-digital*.

'gi forklaring'	'give explanation'	4140
'gi forlatelse'	'give redemption'	50
'foreta fordeling'	'make a distribution'	240
'ilegge forelegg'	'give a fine'	45
'inngå forlik'	'enter a reconciliation'	1500
'drive forskning'	'do research'	330
'vise forakt'	'show contempt'	660
'få forståelse'	'receive understanding'	4800
'holde foredrag'	'give a talk'	5000+
'være gjenstand for'	'be subject to'	5000+
'inngå forlovelse'	'enter an engagement'	80
'forhold opptrer'	'conditions obtain'	100
'fant behag i'	'found pleasure in'	352

In general terms, such a search can instantiate a procedure where, from speaker's knowledge, one defines strings which constitute LVCs and can be part of sentences in any corpus. The concordances can be used to establish actual sentence corpora, where each sentence contains an LVC. These corpora can then be annotated in various ways.[5]

Information which one might want to represent in such a sorted corpus is for instance in what *domain of discourse* the LVC is used, and at what kind of *style/register* level. For the nouns, a possible set of annotation parameters are suggested in Table 4:[6]

Table 4: Parameters for annotation of nominalizations.

Parameter	Abbreviation	Description	Value marks
Ontological status	Ontstat	Situation vs. Thing	s, t
Resultativity	Res	Result of event vs. not	1, 0
Agentivity	Ag	Agentive vs. Non-agentive	1, 0
Aspect	Asp	Aspectual types	Type name(s)
Institutionalization	Instit	Institutionalized vs. not	1, 0
Domain	Dom	Physical vs. Cognitive vs. Emotional vs. Apriori vs. Social vs. *FinanJurAdminManag* (=fjam)	phys, cog, emot, aprio, soc, fjam (connected with '&' when many)
Valence preservation	Val	Valence preserving vs. not	1, 0
Theta-role, for things	Th	The role that the entity has relative to the situation type expressed by the root	Role name(s) (connected with '&' when many)

Table 5 lists examples of how some of the annotations may be assigned in a word inventory (given by word form list rather than full noun entries). Here '–' stands for 'does not apply' (as with aspect specification of a 'thing'), and 'inh' stands for 'inherent object'. '&&' standing in a column by itself means 'can be all/either of the options defined for the column', a situation often obtaining when a word is char-

---

5 This procedure is notably different from one where, in a large corpus, one tries to automatically detect LVCs – see, for instance, Nagy et al. (2013), Grefenstette and Teufel (1995). Neither procedure is by itself more 'empirical' than the other, as long as metadata-confirmed data in the end is what supports the analyses. But given the lack of formal distinguishing features of LVCs in Norwegian, designing an automatic detection procedure would be quite a challenge.
6 Relative to categories under 'Domain', a full-fledged ontological system is Dornseiff (2020), on which a development from the present sketch could be based.

acterized in isolation (and has many uses in principle), less so when annotated as a corpus occurrence.

Table 5: Annotation parameters of Table 4 applied to a partial inventory of bare nominalizations.

		Ont-stat	Res	Ag	Asp	Instit	Domain	Val	Role
bønn_s	'prayer'	s	0	1	dur	1	cog	0	
bønn_t	'prayer'	t	0	1	–	1	cog	0	inh
begjær	'desire'	s	0	0	dur	0	emot	0	
begrep	'concept'	t	0	0	–	1	cog	0	inh
behag	'pleasure'	s	0	0	dur	0	emot	0	
behov	'need'	s	0	0	dur	0	&&	1	
besøk	'visit'	s	0	1	dur	&&	soc&fjam 0		
bifall	'approval'	s	0	1	dur	&&	soc&fjam	0	
bistand	'support'	s	0	1	&&	&	fjam 0		
bitt	'bite'	t	1	1	–	0	phys	0	inh
brak	'crash'	s	&&	0	inst	0	phys	0	
brann	'fire'	s	&&	0	dur	0	phys	0	

For annotation of nominalization occurrences in a corpus, one can in turn pull sequences of expressions as exemplified in Table 5 together as short-hand expressions, as indicated in Table 6 below in an annotation snippet for a construction including the Light Verb expression *finne behag i* 'find pleasure in'. The shorthand expression for *behag*, viz. 's00dur0emot0-', reflects the sequence:

'situational' + 'non-resultative' + 'non-agentive' + 'durative' + 'non-institutionalized' + 'emotive' + 'non-valence-preserving'

Table 6: Snippet of annotation of *finne behag i* using categories from Table 4.

finne	behag	i
find	pleasure	in
V	N=s00dur0emot0-	P

The categories used here will be concise enough to be telling of content, but also general enough that a human annotator can assign them with reasonable speed, be it for an inventory like in Table 5 or a lexicon, or in a running corpus.[7]

---

[7] Formulaic expressions like N= s00dur0emot0 can be processed by finite-state-like procedures, be it for building up other types of structure, or for being expanded into readable prose.

3 Representing LVCs in a dictionary

The Norwegian valence catalogue *NorVal* uses two categories of classification. A *lexval* is an entry consisting of a lemma together with *one* of the valence frames in which it can occur. A *valpod* ('pod' in the sense 'assembly') is a lemma together with the *full set* of valence frames in which it can occur. (2a,b) below represent two *lexvals* for the verb *foreta* 'perform, conduct', each lexval accompanied by a short example, and (2c) represents the *valpod* constituted by (2a,b). The valence representation code is explained in Hellan 2021a; in the representations in question, `ditr-iobRefl` in (2a) means 'ditransitive frame where the indirect object is the 'light reflexive' pronoun, and `tr` in (2b) means 'transitive with a nominal subject and nominal object, both with full argument status'.

(2) Lexvals (a and b, exemplified) and valpod (c) for *foreta*:[8]
    a. `foreta__ditr-iobRefl`; Ex: *hun foretar seg noe* (Engl_transl: 'she does something')
    b. `foreta__tr`; Ex: *de foretar handlingen* (Engl_transl: 'they conduct the act')
    c. `foreta: {V__ditr-iobRefl & V__tr}`

An example of an LVC with *foreta* as head is *foreta et forhør* 'make an interrogation'. This LVC instantiates the transitivity pattern of (2b), and will now be used as example of how an LVC specification can be added to a lexval: In (3) below, the lexval format is expanded with a feature `LVC-COMPLEMENTS`, which can be either defined in terms of general properties, or listed as a set of lemmas. Exemplifying here with the latter option, and, since the relevant set of nouns is rather large, using only the nouns in the upper line in Table 2 (thus, only nouns starting with *f*) as LVC complements, the expanded version of the lexval (2b) will be (3):

---

[8] In the NorVal specifications, the `courir` format is used for formal terms in entries, including the heads of lexvals and valpods, while *standard italics* is for mention of linguistic entities. **Boldface italics** is for the head of a **lemma**.

(3) Lexval (2b) extended with possible nominal complements constituting LVCs with the verb:

    foreta__tr; {
        Ex: *de foretar handlingen* (Engl_transl: 'they conduct the act');
        LVC-COMPLEMENTS:
            BY DEFINITION: ...
            BY STRINGS:
                NOUN LEMMAS *{fengsling, forbyttelse, fordrivelse, fordeling, forenkling, forfremmelse, forhør, forskuttering, forsøk, fortolling, frakobling, frigjøring, forsøpling, fortetning}*
    }

In the LVC *foreta et forhør*, it is *forhør* 'interrogation' which carries the main content, and we represent this noun relative to its sense and valence potential. In the noun lexicon, part of its specification is as follows:

(4) Lexical entry for the noun *forhør* 'interrogation':

    forhør
    {
    GENDER: neuter;
    INFLECTION_PARADIGM: sg.indef. -Ø, sg.def. -*et*, pl.indef. -Ø,
        pl.def. -*ene*;
    N-TYPE: sO1durO&&soc&fjamO;[9]
    SELECTED_PREP.: *av* (participant), *om* (matter);
    SENSE: *interrogation*;
    ENGLISH_GLOSS: 'interrogation'
    }

The noun has an obvious relation to the verb *forhøre*. In the verb valence lexicon, this verb has the following *lexval* entries (the selected preposition *om* is indicated as hyphenated to the lemma):

---

[9] Using the notation introduced in Table 4 and 5; the value is much like that of *besøk* in Table 5.

(5) Lexvals for *forhøre*:
   a. forhøre-om__trObl-oblN; Ex: *de forhører dem om det* (Engl_transl: 'they interrogate them about it')
   b. forhøre-om__trObl-obRefl-oblN; Ex: *hun forhører seg om dem* (Engl_transl: 'she makes queries about them')
   c. forhøre__tr-obRefl; Ex: *hun forhører seg* (Engl_transl: 'she makes queries')
   d. forhøre__tr; Ex: *de forhører dem* (Engl_transl: 'they interrogate them')
   e. forhøre-om__trObl-obRefl-oblINTERR; Ex: *hun forhører seg om hvorvidt det går an* (Engl_transl: 'she makes queries as to whether it is possible')
   f. forhøre-om__trObl-oblINTERR; Ex: *vi forhører dem om hvorvidt det går an* (Engl_transl: 'we interrogate them as to whether it is possible')

The versions with the reflexive pronoun have the meaning of 'querying' or 'finding out', while those without the reflexive pronoun will imply a more 'face off' type of interrogation. The latter is the sense one finds with the noun *forhør* 'interrogation' represented in (4). The selected preposition *om* used with *forhør* has the same range of meanings and combinations as it has with the verb, whereas the preposition *av* used with *forhør* is one of the productively used prepositions connecting a noun with a constituent which could have been a direct object if used with a verb. It may thus be inviting to say that the noun *forhør* 'inherits' one of the verb's senses together with the lexically specific selected preposition *om* of the verb.

While the word 'inherit' here could be used in a loose sense of 'carry over', a recognized issue in connection with so-called de-verbal nouns is that while some noun forms may be said to be *derived* from the verb, such as nouns ending with –*ing* or –*else*, with a stem identical to a verbal stem and gender determined by the suffix, other forms must be defined as basic, non-derived lexical items. These are forms whose connection to a verbal stem is less regular, and which have a gender inherent to the noun, not ascribable to a suffix like those just mentioned. These forms are in Hellan (2017) defined as *bare nominalizations*, and *forhør* belongs to this group. Suggested in that work is a 'super'-lexeme specified in the respects shared between the words but otherwise not fully specified as a lexical item. The 'super'-form connecting *forhøre* and *forhør* will have a phonological specification shared between the words, a sense we may dub '*quer-interr*' subsuming 'interrogate' and 'query', and the selected preposition *om*, but no part-of-speech, no inflectional information and no valence specification. The latter come as standard specifications of lexical items proper, that is, when the 'super'-item gives rise to the standard lemmas *forhøre* and *forhør*, each receiving a full lemma specification but still inheriting the relevant aspects of information from the 'super'-item. In this inheritance configuration, the information associated with the higher node is thus present in both of the lower nodes, possibly expanded:

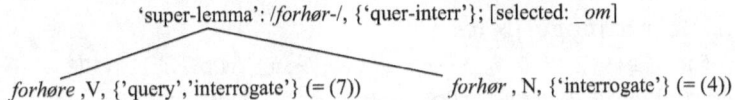

Figure 1: Schematic view of V and N separately inheriting from a 'super'-lemma.

We may say that the words in this case are *co-inheritors*. In a lexicon we can use the term *v-n-correlatedness* when wishing to leave open whether lemmas are in a co-inheritance relationship or a derivational relationship.

The noun in an LVC can be either derived from or co-inherited with a given verb,[10] which means that in both a noun lexicon and a verb lexicon we want to specify *v-n-correlatedness* jointly between the noun of the LVC and the verb to which it is related. A format for this is now outlined.

As a first step, *senses* must be represented. As illustrated in (5), a lemma may be associated with more than one sense, and although senses may distribute differently over the lexvals, it is convenient to also list them as a set associated with the lemma as such, just as the set of lexvals of a lemma is represented as a set in its *valpod*; the set of senses we may call the *sensepod* of the lemma. For *forhøre* the sensepod will be '{'interrogate', 'query'} (cf. Figure 1). We leave open at this point how senses are to be formally represented, as placeholders we use just English translations.

To illustrate the use of these notions, we first state the valpod of *forhøre* (reflecting the valence frames in (5)):

(6) Valpod for *forhøre*:

   forhøre:{V__tr & V__tr-obRefl & V-om__trObl-oblINTERR & V-om__trObl-oblN & V-om__trObl-obRefl-oblINTERR & V-om__trObl-obRefl-oblN}

A representation of the distribution of senses across the lexvals in (6) will have the form in (7), where the attribute *VAL-SENSES* represents all the combinations of lexvals and senses. To this structure we add the feature *V-N-CORRELATES*; for *forhøre* there is only one such correlate, namely *forhør*. For this item we in turn specify its *VAL-SENSES*, and also the verbs by which *forhør* can be headed in an LVC, these being *foreta* and *gjennomgå* ('be subject to').

---

10 They may also have no verbal counterpart, but still situational content.

(7) Partial lexical entry for the verb *forhøre* 'interrogate, query':

forhøre
{
SENSEPOD: {[a]'*interrogate*', [b]'*query*'}
VALPOD: forhøre:{V__tr & V__tr-obRefl & V-om__trObl-oblINTERR
& V-om__trObl-oblN & V-om__trObl-obRefl-oblINTERR & V-om__trObl-obRefl-oblN}
VAL-SENSES:[11]{< [a], V__tr> & <[b], V__tr-obRefl> & <[a],
V-om__trObl-oblINTERR> & <[a], V-om__trObl-oblN> & <[b],
V-om__trObl-obRefl-oblINTERR> & <[b], V-om__trObl-obRefl-oblN>}
V-N-CORR: *forhør* {
    VAL-SENSES:{<[a],N__>,<[a],N-om__intrObl-oblN>, <[a],
    N-om__intrObl-oblINTERR>;
    LVC-GOVERNORS: {*foreta, gjennomgå*}
    }
}

The lemma-reference *forhør* in (7) points to the same structure as the one entered in (4), so that the specifications shown in (4) and in (7) are to be understood as merged to one structure, i.e., (8); here the semantic specification indicated by '[a]' is still co-referring with the marker '[a]' in the structure for *forhøre*:

(8) Lexical entry for the noun *forhør* 'interrogation', fully unified relative to the specifications in (4) and (7):

forhør
{
GENDER: neuter;
INFLECTION_PARADIGM: sg.indef. -Ø, sg.def. -*et*, pl.indef. -Ø,
    pl.def. -*ene*;
N-TYPE: sO1durO&&soc&fjamO;[12]
SELECTED_PREP.: *av* (participant), *om* (matter);
SENSE: *interrogation*;
ENGLISH_GLOSS: 'interrogation';

---

[11] In this case, the senses divide the lexvals neatly between them, each lexval being associated with only one sense. It is however not excluded that a lexval can be associated with many senses, there being then one ordered pair for each association.
[12] Using the notation introduced in Table 4 and 5; the value is much like that of *besøk* in Table 5,

```
VAL-SENSES: {<[a],N__>,<[a],N-om__intrObl-oblN>,<[a],N-m__intrObl-
    oblINTERR>;
LVC-GOVERNORS: {foreta, gjennomgå}
}
```

Thus, we assume a powerful design of identities and unifications across lexical entries and parts of lexical entries, across verbs and nouns (and in due course adjectives).

When the sense of the verb *forhøre* as 'interrogate' and the sense of the noun *forhør* 'interrogation' are here set as identical, through the common marker '[a]' in (7) in the specifications of the verb and the noun, we are highlighting the co-relatedness of the lexical items across lexical entries. A further issue is whether 'identity' is necessarily the notion to use for semantic relatedness across co-related items: in the case in question, 'unifiability' ('compatibility') may be a safer term in view of possible differences reflecting differences in parts-of-speech of the lexical items, and when also derivational relations of co-relatedness are taken into account, for instance inducing causality, the semantic relations involve more than just compatibility. At the present stage, though, all we want to capture are these types of semantic relationships across lexical entries, as they enter into considerations of integrating the representation of LVCs into a larger valence lexicon setting. We suggest in the next section a semantic analysis framework where more detailed questions of semantic relatedness can be pursued. For a format of representation suited for a large verb and noun inventory (as here, 6000 verbs and 3-4000 nouns with 'verbal' or situational content), it is essential to have a system of 'pointers' to semantic relatedness rather than detailed representations thereof.

That being said, we have shown, for the triple of words *foreta*, *forhør* and *forhøre*, how they can be lexically represented relative to their potential of forming LVCs, as in *foreta et forhør*, and to their co-relatedness as lexical items (*forhøre* vs. *forhør*). For every LVC in a language, one can envisage such a triple of lexical items to be involved, and amenable to specification along the lines shown.

4 Unification and selection within LVCs

The notion of *sense* is represented in many different ways across fields and analytic traditions, from definitions in plain prose, or enumerations of synonyms or near-synonyms, in lexicography, to various formats of formalization in formal and computational linguistics. We here explore one such type of formalism, suited both for representing senses per se and for representing the key function of meaning compatibility and syntactic combination in LVCs.

4.1 Grammar formalism of features and unification

As a representation of (1b), repeated,

(1b)   Han gjorde bruk av grammofonen
       'He made use of the gramophone'

we can model the combination of verb and noun as in (9) as one where the semantic contents of verb and noun 'melt together'. This is indicated schematically by the contents of the brackets introduced by the attribute 'SIT' (for 'Situation Structure', see 4.2 below), where the combination resides in merging, or unifying, these situational contents into one.

(9)   VP
                    [SIT *UNIFICATION-of-[1]-and [2]*
                    SUBJ [INDEX [3]]

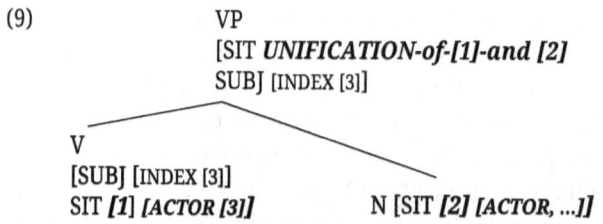

V
[SUBJ [INDEX [3]]
SIT *[1] [ACTOR [3]]*   N [SIT *[2] [ACTOR, ...]]*

The verb has ACTOR as role, as does the noun, and the situational contents can unify, with the role 'ACTOR' carried by the VP as a unified role. The referential linking of the role to *subject* of the VP remains as encoded with the verb, since the verb's subject specification is carried up to the VP.

We now develop a formal analysis of LVCs partly highlighting the merger of verb and noun contents now indicated, using the framework of analysis *Head-Driven Phrase Structure Grammar* (HPSG).[13] We first indicate how the constellation in (9) above comes out in a formal HPSG analysis. To outline this, we first give a brief exposition of the essential combinatorial mechanism of HPSG for the verb-object constellation, namely its treatment of *valence satisfaction*.

Relating to a sentence like *The cat bites the dog*, we may say that *bite* has a 'program' of valence satisfaction; such 'programs' of valence satisfaction are for-

---

[13] Pollard and Sag (1994), Sag et al. (2003).

malized in HPSG as *lists* of constituents for the verb to be combined with, one list for complements, named *COMPS*, and one for the subject, called *SPR*. For *bite*, in its use in question, these lists thus have one member each, as illustrated in (10):

(10) $\begin{bmatrix} \text{SPR} \langle NP \rangle \\ \text{COMPS} \langle NP \rangle \end{bmatrix}$

Following a general strategy originally stemming from *Categorial Grammar*, valence satisfaction is registered through *deletion* of items in these lists, referred to as *cancellation*. Thus, the rule, or statement, effecting satisfaction of the valence requirements of an *object* will have schematically the form (11), where the identity symbols '[1]' enforce compatibility between the NP actually occurring as object, and the NP item specified in the valence list:[14]

(11)   VP [COMPS < >]
        ╱   ╲
  V [COMPS < [1] >]   [1] NP

A similar cancellation constellation applies for subject, so that in the representation of the top S node, both lists will be empty, this counting technically as a well-formedness requirement on the S node.[15]

Applying this formalism to the case of an LVC, the shared SIT specification between V, NP and VP can be represented as in (12), the identical SIT values representing the circumstance that these specifications are unifiable:

---

14 For instance, if a COMPS specification were to ask for a genitive NP and the NP in question were accusative (in a grammar where case is relevant), the unification enforced by the identity symbols would not work, and the combination would fail.

15 A representation where both the SUBJ list and the COMPS list are empty, is not very informative about what is contained in the sentence. However, information about the sentence's 'logical form' will be available, and the framework also offers constructs for keeping track of the syntactic constituents, one such being 'ARG-ST', which is a list displaying the constituents in an order corresponding to their grammatical function (GF) status, without naming GFs explicitly (cf. Sag and Wasow 1999, Sag et al. 2003). Alternative formats of display more like the f-structure format in LFG (cf. Bresnan 2001) have also been developed (cf., for instance, Hellan 2019, and Hellan and Bruland 2015).

(12)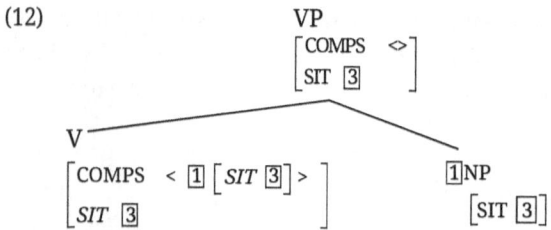

The SIT content of the verb unifies with the SIT content of the NP, encoded as a as requirement in the italicized part of the V specification, and in turn satisfied by the sister NP. This SIT content in turn is projected to the VP.

4.2 Sense specification within a formalism of features and unification

We now illustrate how one can construe *unifiability*, or *compatibility*, between the SIT specification of the verb and the SIT specification of the NP.

One way in which the notions of unifiability or compatibility can be formally modeled is through *typed feature structures*, a format used in HPSG. These representations typically involve attribute-value matrices (AVMs), where features, or attributes, are listed with their values. Values may in turn introduce attributes, so that information of any complexity can be modeled in an AVM. *Types* can be used to define which combinations of attributes are possible in an AVM, and given the recursion possibility mentioned, they also serve as values of attributes. The AVM format is suitable for representing many aspects of linguistic information, among them what we may call *situational meaning*.[16]

An example of a representation of situational meaning is given below, representing a semantic type labeled *run*, where the outermost attributes indicate situational parameters and the innermost attributes list properties specific to one who runs:[17]

---

[16] The notion covers the type of semantic space explored in traditions like Lexical Semantics and Situation Semantics (Barwise and Perry 1983); a division between such a space on the one hand and a more grammatically defined argument structure has been proposed in Melchuk (2004), and in another form in Grimshaw (2005), Levin and Rappaport Hovav (2005) and Rappaport Hovav and Levin (1998). Relative to semantic designs in HPSG, our proposal for situational specification has most in common with Davis (2000). See Hellan (2019) for an exploration of situation structure along the same lines as here, explicitly drawing on typed feature structures as defined in Copestake (2002).
[17] In (13), 'zip-lock' refers to the interlocking interplay between legs in walking/running.

(13)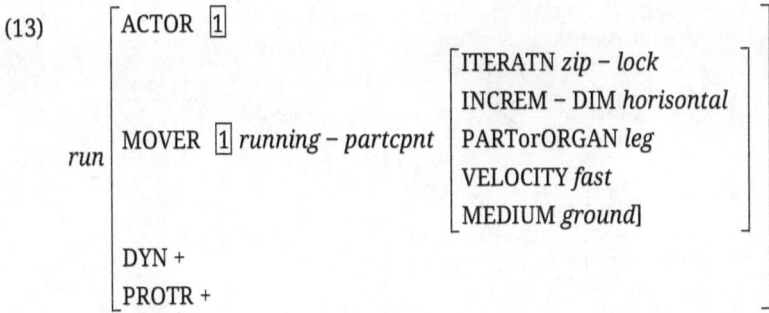

The use of *run* here envisaged is the standard one, where directionality and dynamicity are combined, as opposed to the 'running' of a motor, and to the lack of dynamicity of a line 'running'.

The general governing regulations for the interplay between types and attributes can be summarized as in (14):[18]

(14) *[A]* A given type introduces the same attribute(s) no matter in which environment it is used.
[B] A given attribute is declared by one type only (but occurs with all of its subtypes).

The type *run* is introduced as one of the leaf types in the partial situation type hierarchy in Figure 2. Under a type node we indicate which attributes (if any) are introduced by the type, obeying the general regulations (14). The hierarchy combines Aktionsart (cf. Vendler 1967, Smith 1997) with standard situational notions. Note that the English verb name 'run' under the leaf node is just a mnemonically convenient name of a *type* as defined in terms of the inheritances shown, not of the English *verb* so named.[19]

With such a system in the background, in the analysis of an LVC like *make a run*, the SIT representation of *make* would have a role ACTOR, and this SIT representation and the one in (13) for *run* would unify. In these terms, the combination of the article *a* with *run* would induce the specification 'COMPL+' added to the specifications in (13), representing 'a run' as a completed event, but otherwise with the same content of 'run' as it has a as verb (and not as the running of a motor or the directionality of a line); this is a typical effect of the nominalization option provided in LVCs.

---

18 See Copestake (2002).
19 While this type hierarchy accounts for the shared carrier of the roles ACTOR and MOVER, the information entered inside of ACTOR in (13) is provided by another type hierarchy serving as values of attributes like ACTOR, viz. *participant*; for details, see Hellan (2019).

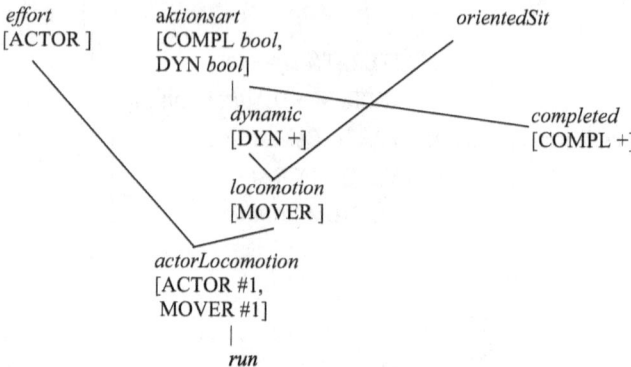

Figure 2: Partial type system integrating situation types and *Aktionsarten*.

4.3 Syntactic combination using sense specification

Given a general format of SIT specification as outlined, and a syntactic combination formalism as sketched in 4.1, the lexical specification of *foreta* can be given as follows in the AVM format – what corresponds to the label tr in (2b) is the content of the COMPS list in (15), and the DOMAIN requirement on the object is among the types in Table 4. The feature 'KEY' takes as value a label specific to the use of *foreta* as a LV:

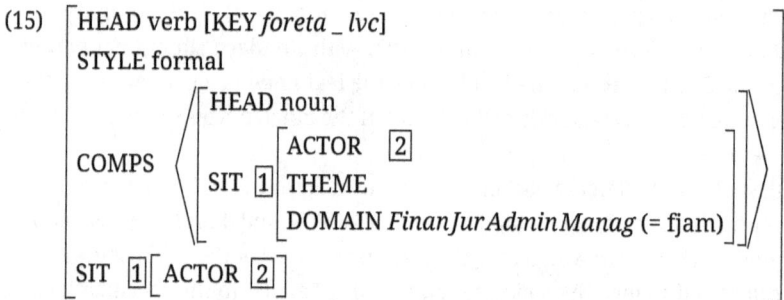

The relevant AVM for *forhør* for the combination *foreta et forhør* is in turn (16) (notice that co-indexing is valid only inside of a given AVM, so that '[1]' in (15) has no bearing on the content of '[1]' in (16)):

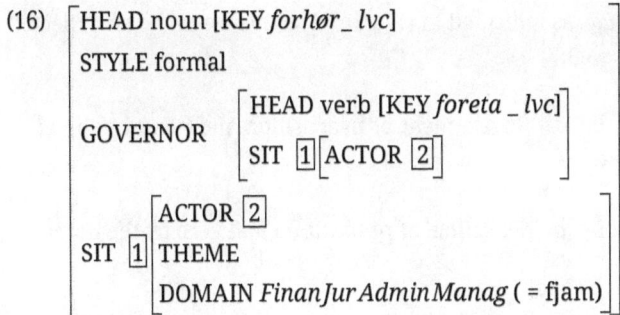

Given that the SIT specification in (12) matches the specification on the path 'COMPS| SIT' in (15), the combination *foreta et forhør* is licensed. This demonstrates how the semantic unification requirement in LVCs can be implemented in a grammar combination formalism based on typed feature structures.

Mechanisms of item-specific *selection* are also shown: in (16), the attribute GOVERNOR has information about the verb by which *forhør* can be governed in an LVC, viz. *foreta* (corresponding to the first item in the list GOVERNORS in the line 'LVC-GOVERNORS: {*foreta, gjennomgå*}' in (7); *forhør* thus also has a corresponding entry with *gjennomgå* as value of GOVERNOR). For *foreta*, the array of nouns that it selects is, for nouns starting with *f*, the list under 'LEMMAS' in (3), which may ultimately mean 2-300 item-specific entries, unless a concise common denominator is found ((15) in this respect is too wide as a concise denominator, and serves more as a schema of the entries to be deployed).

Further constellations of selection in LVCs include prepositions, exemplified by (1c) above, repeated with parts of speech indicated:

(1c) Hun   stil-te   sak-en   i   bero
     She   pose-PST   case-MASC.DEF.SG   in   rest
     Pron   V   N   P   N
     'She suspended the case'

The verb *bero* ('rest', as for a court case being rested) has the corresponding noun *bero*, and the typical LVC for this noun is *stille i bero* ('suspend'), as in (1c). The verb *stille* 'put, position' can take many environments, being a verb of general positioning, whereas the noun *bero* has hardly any other environments than the one in (1c). This means that, in intuitive terms of 'selection', the noun *bero* may be seen as selecting the preposition *i* as well as the verb *stille*, as schematically indicated in (17b) below. This constellation contrasts with the general view of selection as going via the line of *government*: the preposition *i* syntactically governs *bero*, and is itself governed by the verb *stille*, as indicated in (17a), and so this would be an expected direction of selection as well:

(17) a. *stille   i   bero*   Government of preposition and noun by the verb
    |───▶|───▶|

   b. *stille   i   bero*   'Selection' of preposition and verb by the noun
    |◀───|◀───|

From the perspective of the *verb*, the specification corresponding to (17a) can be indicated as in (18). Here the COMPS list has two items, the object (*saken*) and the PP; in the PP, the preposition is marked as taking *bero* as governed item, which is thus represented in a COMPS list in turn.[20] The selection by *stille* of 'NP *i bero*' thus is expressed with a COMPS list of two items, one containing a COMPS list in turn. The semantics of the construction is here also represented: The noun *bero* has a situational meaning with THEME as only role. This role has index '4', which is also the index of the object, *saken*, meaning that 'saken' is represented as the theme of 'bero'. *Stille*, as the verb, has a causative meaning, represented in the outermost SIT specification, with the arguments ACTOR, co-indexed with the subject, and CAUSED, coindexed with the SIT expressed by the noun *bero*.

(18) $\begin{bmatrix} \text{HEAD}[verb[\text{KEY } stille\_lvc]] \\ \text{SUBJ } \langle [\text{INDEX } \boxed{3}] \rangle \\ \text{COMPS } \left\langle \begin{bmatrix} \text{HEAD } noun \\ \text{INDEX } \boxed{4} \end{bmatrix}, \begin{bmatrix} \text{HEAD } prep \text{ [KEY } i] \\ \text{COMPS } \left\langle \begin{bmatrix} \text{HEAD } noun[\text{KEY } bero\_lvc] \\ \text{SIT } \boxed{2}[\text{THEME } \boxed{4}] \end{bmatrix} \right\rangle \end{bmatrix} \right\rangle \\ \text{SIT } \boxed{1} \begin{bmatrix} \text{PRED } cause \\ \text{ACTOR } \boxed{3} \\ \text{CAUSED } \boxed{2} \end{bmatrix} \end{bmatrix}$

---

[20] In implementations of HPSG grammars like the LKB platform (Copestake 2002), the specification of a list within a list, as in the specification of a COMPS list within COMPS, is not licit. However, using attributes more corresponding to those used in LFG in parallel to the valency lists allows one to make specifications with the same effect as in (18). This formalism is used extensively in the Norwegian LKB grammar Norsource (cf. Hellan and Bruland 2015), but for the purposes of the present exposition we do not show this extension.

From the viewpoint of the selected noun, *bero*, the situation of selection is still a bit more complicated since, as pictured in (17b), there is a chaining of selections, *bero* selecting *i*, and *i* selecting *stille*. As far as the relation between *bero* and *i* is concerned, it can be represented with the attribute GOVERNOR, as in (19), while to cover the next selection relation up, with *stille*, it must be represented by another GOVERNOR attribute inside the first one; cf. (20) (we omit the semantic specifications, which will reflect the one given in (18)):[21]

(19)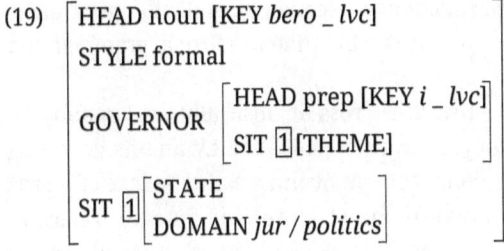

(20)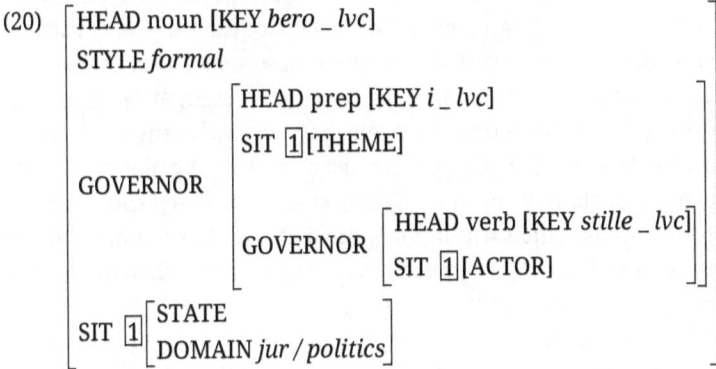

These examples illustrate how both semantic specification and syntactic combination of LVCs, including selection, can be represented in the typed feature structure formalism considered. While it addresses a more granular level of analysis, connections to the dictionary format outlined in the previous section can in principle be defined, although not to be shown here.[22]

---

[21] The same point about specification of lists within lists holds as relative to (18).
[22] Thus, one can envisage procedures by which, from entries using the format in section 3, one can automatically generate lexical entries in the typed feature formalism.

5 Concluding remarks

We have outlined strategies and formalisms for analyzing Light Verb Constructions (LVCs) in Norwegian, based on structures and complexities revealed in a sizeable set of sample constructions. Underlying resources reside in a large valence catalogue and a large computational grammar for Norwegian. One of the strategies outlined for analyzing LVCs concerns annotation of corpora (section 2), another strategy addresses the overall organization of senses and valence frames relative to each other in a large scale valence dictionary (section 3), and still one strategy reflects principles of syntactic and semantic combination in a formal grammar and parser (section 4).

The latter two strategies address what is cross-linguistically presumably the main defining aspect of LVCs, namely the way in which the LV and its governed noun interact in articulating a situational content over a small sequence of words rather than in just one word. The organization of senses and valence frames in a dictionary can in principle be addressed independently of what formalism by itself is optimal for representing meaning. In dealing with the former in section 3, we thus employ a simple string-based notation for valence frames, sets of valence frames, and sense-identifiers distributed over these. In section 4, as a key formalism for representing situational meaning and semantic composition, we use typed feature structures. It is possible that these systems can be built together in a larger architecture, but for research they support distinct strategies, one aiming at large coverage relative to a dictionary, the other aiming at understanding and articulating the principles of combination within the individual LVC. We assume that the formats of these approaches can be applied cross-linguistically, although the constructions discussed here are restricted to Norwegian.

Aside from its analytical interest, the integration of the representation of LVCs in a valence dictionary can sustain general dictionaries of the language, and support applications for language learning and teaching. LVCs constitute a powerful stylistic tool, allowing for nuanced and concise expression, but their mastery requires knowledge of exactly which verbs and nouns (and prepositions) can combine with each other, and with what meaning. An L2 environment for Norwegian accommodating these circumstances is a practical goal associated with the enlarged valence dictionary envisaged.

References

Barwise, John & John Perry. 1983. *Situations and Attitudes*. Cambridge, MA: The MIT Press.
Bresnan, Joan. 2001. *Lexical Functional Syntax*. Oxford: Blackwell.
Butt, Miriam. 2010. The light verb jungle: still hacking away. In Mengistu Amberber, Mark Harvey & Brett Baker (eds.), *Complex Predicates: Cross-linguistic Perspectives on Event Structure*, 48–78. Cambridge: Cambridge University Press.
Copestake, Ann. 2002. *Implementing Typed Feature- Structure Grammars*. Stanford: CSLI Publications.
Davis, Anthony. 2000. *The Hierarchical Lexicon*. Stanford: CSLI Publications.
Dornseiff, Franz. 2020. *Der deutsche Wortschatz nach Sachgruppen*. Berlin/New York: Mouton De Gruyter.
Eshaghi, Mahdiyeh & Karimi-Doostan Gholamhossein. This volume. Persian light verbs as event determiners. 73-97.
Grefenstette, Gregory & Simone Teufel. 1995. Corpus-based method for automatic identification of support verbs for nominalization. In *Proceedings of the 7th Meeting of the European Chapter of the Association for Computational Linguistics* (EACL'95). March 1995, 98–103.
Grimshaw, Jane & Armin Mester. 1988. Light verbs and Θ-marking. *Linguistic Inquiry* 19(2). 205–232.
Grimshaw, Jane. 2005[1993]. Semantic structure and semantic content in lexical representation. In Jane Grimshaw, *Words and Structure*, 75–89. Stanford: CSLI Publications.
Hellan, Lars. 2017. A design for the analysis of bare nominalizations in Norwegian. In Maria Bloch-Trojnar & Anna Malicka-Kleparska (eds.), *Aspect and Valency in nominals*, 181–199. Berlin/Boston: Mouton De Gruyter.
Hellan, Lars. 2019. Construction-Based Compositional Grammar. *Journal of Logic Language and Information* 28. 101–130.
Hellan, Lars. 2021a. A valence catalogue for Norwegian. In Roussanka Loukanova (eds.), *Natural Language Processing in Artificial Intelligence – NLPinAI 2021*, 49–104. Cham: Springer.
Hellan, Lars. 2021b. Norwegian Valence Dictionary (NorVal). Talk presented at SLE 2021.
Hellan, Lars & Tore Bruland. 2015. A cluster of applications around a Deep Grammar. In Zygmnut Vetulani & Joseph Mariani (eds.), *Human Language Technology. Challenges for Computer Science and Linguistics*, 503–508. Cham: Springer.
Jespersen, Otto. 1942. *A Modern English Grammar on Historical Principles*. Vol. 6: *Morphology*. London: George Allen and Unwin Ltd.
Karimi-Doostan, Gholamhossein. 2010. Lexical categories in Persian. *Lingua* 1719. 1–14,
Karimi-Doostan, Gholamhossein. 2011. Separability of light verb constructions in Persian. *Studia Linguistica*. 1–26.
Levin, Beth & Malka Rappaport Hovav. 2005. *Argument Realization*. Cambridge: Cambridge University Press.
Lødrup, Helge. 2002. The syntactic structures of Norwegian pseudocoordinations. *Studia Linguistica* 56(2). 121–143.
Mel'čuk, Igor. 2004. Actants in semantics and syntax I: actants in semantics. *Linguistics* 42(1). 1–66.
Nagy, István T., Veronika Vincze & Richárd Farkas. 2013. Full-coverage Identification of English Light Verb Constructions. In Ruslan Mitkov & Jong C. Park (eds.), *Proceedings of the Sixth International Joint Conference on Natural Language Processing*. Nagoya, Japan, 14–18 October 2013, 329–337. https://aclanthology.org/I13-1000.pdf.
Pollard, Carl & Ivan Sag. 1994. *Head-driven Phrase Structure Grammar*. Chicago: Chicago University Press.

Pompei, Anna & Valentina Piunno. 2015. Light Verb Constructions. An interlinguistic analysis to explain systemic irregularities. Talk presented at SLE 2015, Leiden.

Rappaport Hovav, Malka & Beth Levin. 1998. Building verb meaning. In Miriam Butt & Wilhem Geuder (eds.), *The Projection of Arguments*, 97–134. Stanford: CSLI Publications.

Sag, Ivan, Tom Wasow & Emily Bender. 2003. *Syntactic Theory. A formal introduction*. Stanford: CSLI Publications.

Samardzíc, Tanja & Paola Merlo. 2010. Cross-lingual variation of light verb constructions: Using parallel corpora and automatic alignment for linguistic research. In Fei Xia, William Lewis & Lori Levin (eds.), *Proceedings of the 2010 Workshop on NLP and Linguistics: Finding the Common Ground, Uppsala, Sweden, July 2010*, 52–60. https://aclanthology.org/W10-21.pdf.

Smith, Carlota. 1997. *The Parameter of Aspect*. Dordrecht: Kluwer.

Tesnière, Lucien. 1959. *Éleménts de syntaxe structurale*. Paris: Klincksieck.

Vendler, Zeno. 1967. *Linguistics in Philosophy*. Ithaca, NY: Cornell U. Press.

Section 2: **Event structure sharing**

Mahdie Eshaghi and Gholamhossein Karimi-Doostan
3 Persian Light Verbs as event determiners

Abstract: Light Verbs, first introduced by Jespersen (1942), are a group of verbs that are supposed to be semantically bleached. To function as a predicate in a sentence, they must be combined with other predicative elements to form Light Verb Constructions. Understanding Light Verb Constructions is thus one of the challenges of modern linguistics. Since the verbal system of Persian consists largely of Light Verb Constructions, the present study aims to investigate the role of Persian Light Verbs (Karimi-Doostan and Eshaghi, 2019) in determining the event structure of sentences in which Light Verb Constructions function as predicates. We adopt a Constructivist view (Marantz, 2013) and develop a detailed aspectual classification of Persian Light Verbs, using the findings of Harley (2009) and Ramchand (2008), to show that Light Verbs directly influence the event type of sentences with Light Verb Constructions.

Keywords: Event Structure, Light Verb Constructions, Subevents, Constructivist

1 Introduction

The notion of Light Verb (hereafter LV), first introduced by Jespersen (1942), became one of the challenging topics in modern linguistics after it was dealt with in Grimshaw and Mester (1988), focusing on Japanese *suru* 'to do' constructions. LVs are generally known as a group of verbs that carry some grammatical properties of a verb, but are semantically bleached or partially devoid of meaning. They are combined with nouns, prepositional phrases, or adjectives[1] to form Light Verb Constructions (hereafter LVCs) to function as predicates. LVCs have been studied by many researchers from different points of view.

The verb system of Persian consists mainly of LVCs rather than heavy (lexical) verbs.[2] For this reason, a large and growing body of literature has investigated LVs in this language. Mohammad and Karimi (1992), Dabir-Moghadam (1995), Vahedi-Langrudi (1996), Karimi (1997), Karimi-Doostan (1997, 2005, 2011), Megerdoomian (2001), and Folli et al. (2004) are among the researchers who have studied

---
[1] The position of these elements is preverbal, so we call them preverbs (hereafter PVs).
[2] Mohammad and Karimi (1992) write that the number of Persian heavy verbs are 115, whereas Karimi-Doostan (1997) claims that their number is about 150.

Persian LVCs from different angles. In light of these studies, many issues related to LVCs have been accounted for, but less attention has been paid to other important issues. This paper attempts to deal with these questions: 1) what role do LVs play in realizing the event structure of sentences containing LVCs as predicate, and 2) do LVs determine the event structure of the sentences independently of PVs, or is this the result of their inseparable cooperation?

In answering these questions, three hypotheses are possible:

Hypothesis A: The event structure of LVCs originates from the aspectual properties of LVs without the involvement of PVs.
Hypothesis B: The event structure of LVCs originates both from the LVs and the PVs.
Hypothesis C: The event structure of LVCs originates predominantly from the aspectual properties of LVs, and PVs affect it within the bounds set by the LVs.

A quick look at the LCP corpus[3] shows that in this language, an LV can appear in sentences with different kinds of event structures. For example, the most productive Persian LV *kardan* 'to do' appears in sentences either with [+initP$_{cause}$] (1a), [+initP$_{do}$] (1b), or without an initiator (1c), and with a result (1a) and (1c) or without a result (1b; see Section 2).

(1) a. ?a:nha: ?in bakhsh ra: **sa:ma:ndehi kard-and.** (+initP$_{cause}$)
   they this department OM organization do.PST.3PL.
   'They organized this department.'
 b. ?ali ta: ?omq 180 metri **shena: kard.** (+initP$_{do}$)
   Ali to depth 180 meter swim do.PST.3SG.
   'Ali swam to a depth of 180 meters.'
 c. ?u diru:z **fout kard.** (-initP)
   she yesterday death do.PST.3SG.
   'She died yesterday.'

These observations allow us to refute hypothesis A. Therefore, to find an answer to the research question, we should focus on the other two hypotheses.

---

[3] This corpus has been developed out of a post doctorate project done by the authors under the support of the Iran National Science Foundation. It is named The linguistic corpus of Light Verb Constructions of Persian (LCP) and is available at https://literature.ut.ac.ir/compound-verb.

In LVCs, two or more elements act as a single predicate. Based on the principles of the constructivist view, we deal with PVs as acategorial roots and LVs as categorizers. Focusing on the aspectual properties of LVs in determining the event type of the LVCs they appear in, we aim to find out to find out whether the role of these predicative elements in encoding the event structure can be identified, and if so, which element is more dominant.

Some scholars such as Mohammad and Karimi (1992), Karimi-Doostan (1997, 2005), Megerdoomian (2001), and Folli et al. (2004) have already addressed this issue in their studies, but in a different framework than the one used in this paper. Folli et al. (2004) argue that PVs are responsible for the variation in the event types of LVs, but only with some LVs; for instance, they consider the LV *shodan* 'to become' an exception, it being responsible for event type variation, and relate this to the semantic properties of this verb. Moreover, they fail to provide a coherent account of the behavior of LVs in realizing the event structure of sentences with LVCs.

The paper is organized as follows. Section 2 introduces the model of grammar used in this work. Section 3 discusses the role of LVs in determining the eventuality. Section 4 outlines a detailed aspectual classification for the six Persian LV classes and discusses the role of Persian LVs in determining the event structure of sentences containing LVCs. In section 5 some conclusions are drawn.

2 Constructivist view and LVs' event structure

Events were first introduced by Davidson (1967) as an additional participant in the argument structure of sentences with transitive verbs. After that, Parsons (1990) introduced the Neo-Davidsonian view; they believed in the existence of an event variable in every predicate, which specifies the event type of the sentence. James Pustejovsky (1991), following Grimshaw (1990) and Williams (1981), who introduced the argument structure level, on the one hand, and Jackendoff (1983) and Rappaport and Levin (1998), who introduced lexical conceptual structure, on the other hand, used the term 'event structure' to refer to the internal structure of events as a separate level in natural language lexical representations. There are different views in the study of event structure, such as the Lexical view (Levin and Rappaport Hovav, 1995, 1999), the Constructional view (Goldberg 1995, 2006 or Croft 2001) and the Constructivist view (Hale and Keyser, 1993, 2002; Marantz, 2013). Although there are differences between these views, according to Lyutikova and Tatevosov (2013), they all share the idea that event structure determines the grammatical behavior of verbal predicates.

The Constructivist view applies some notions from Chomsky's Minimalism (1995) and some notions from Halle and Marantz's Distributed Morphology (1994). Marantz (2013) defines constructivism[4] as the theoretical marriage of the Minimalist Program and Distributed Morphology, which shares with the Minimalist Program the assumption that syntax is the sole generative engine of the grammar, and in which, like in Distributed Morphology, "late insertion" is assumed. According to late insertion, the phonological identity of morphemes is determined after the syntax via the process of vocabulary insertion. This approach enables us to deal with a limited number of syntactic structures, into which different LVCs try their hand at entering the structure through late insertion, encoding events of different types. Moreover, within the principles of this framework, we divide LVCs into acategorial roots (PVs) and eventuality determiners and categorizers (LVs) in the same sense as Marantz (2013). This helps us to reduce the redundant burden of the categories of roots in our analysis.

Among the possible approaches to the Constructivist view, we choose the decomposition model of Ramchand (2008, 2017).[5] As illustrated in Figure 1, she assumes three subevents in the study of event structure: the initiatory subevent, the process subevent and the result subevent. Each of these subevents has its own projection, ordered in a hierarchical embedding relation.

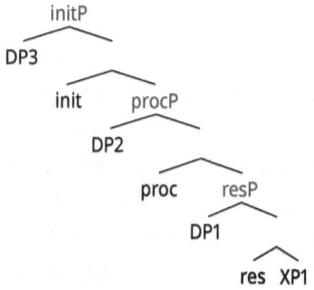

Figure 1: Hierarchical embedding relation of Ramchand's subevents (2008: 46).

According to Ramchand (2008: 47),[6] these three subevents represent the maximal possible decomposition of an event, and a verbal projection may exist without

---

[4] Ramchand (2008: 11) refers to the same view as generative constructivist.
[5] Cf. also Van Hout (1996), Borer (2003), Åfarli (2007), Ramchand (2008), Lohndal (2012), Marantz (2013), and Åfarli and Jin (2014) for an overview.
[6] The hierarchy of Ramchand's event structure provides a basis for investigating the role of LVs in realizing the subevents of an event. We consider two values for the initiatory phrase, [±initP]: LVCs with a positive value for [initP] can encode one of the possible initiatory phrases of the types [+initP$_{cause}$], [+initP$_{do}$], or [+initP$_{state}$], while those with a negative value are sentences with no ex-

either the *init, proc* or *res* subevents. The initiatory phrase (initP) denotes an initial state, and the initiator is an argument which causes an event and is placed in the specifier of initP (§ 3.2.1). As a matter of fact, it appears to license the external argument. The Process Phrase (procP) exists in dynamic events. It is considered the heart of the dynamic predicate. The argument affected by the process is called the Undergoer and is located in the specifier of procP (§ 3.2.2). The Result Phrase (resP), or result subevent, expresses a result state. It denotes the result of the dynamic change in the meaning of the verb (§ 3.2.3). The resultee, something that attains a final state, is placed in its specifier.[7]

Ramchand (2008:31) clarifies the notion of initiator and concept of causation relevant to it in this way:

> I will assume (with Rappaport-Hovav and Levin 2000 and many others) that the relevant abstract category to causation is that of 'initiator'. An initiator is an entity whose properties/behaviors are responsible for the eventuality coming into existence. Thus, 'stinking' has an external argument which is the initiator by virtue of inherent properties of dirtiness or smelliness; the water is the initiator of a spewing event by virtue of the fact that it has the requisite properties of kinetic energy; volitional agents have intentions and desires that lead them to initiate dynamic events; instrumental subjects are entities whose facilitating properties are presented as initiating the event because they allow it to happen. There is a sense in which all of these 'thematic roles' are just real world instantiations of the more abstract concept of causation. Among transitive verbs as well, external arguments can be volitional agents, instrumentals, abstract causes/sources showing the generality and abstractness of the external argument relation.

Ramchand's definition of initiator reminds us of Harley's (2009) little v flavors of little v.[8] These theoretical views, as well as the empirical observations of the behavior of LVCs in encoding the subevents of an event, lead us to assume an aspectual classification (§ 3.2) for the six Persian LV classes proposed by Karimi-Doostan and Eshaghi (2019) (§ 3.1).

---

ternal argument. In the case of [+initP$_{cause}$], there is an external argument which causes something to be done or the appearance of a state; this means that we deal with different subevents. Two values are considered for the process phrase too, [±procP], which has a positive value for eventive LVs and a negative one for stative ones. [resP] expresses the result of a dynamic change which is present in eventive LVs; so, result subevent can only occur in sentences with eventive LVCs and not in sentences with stative LVCs. More detailed information is presented in § 3.2.

7 An argument can occupy more than one specifier and hence bear more than one role.

8 Harley (2009) in discussing English verbalizing morphemes referring to Harley (1999), Harley (2005) and Folli and Harley (2006), Folli and Harley (2007) suggests that there must be different varieties, or 'flavours,' of v°, all serving the verbalizing function, but expressing distinct meanings to do with the initiation or lack thereof of the verbal event. Assuming the distinctions caused by v° in event types, she applied feature clusters such as as [±dynamic], [±change of state], [±cause] to introduce different flavours for v°, i.e. v_{cause}, v_{become}, v_{do}, v_{be}.

3 Light Verbs and the determination of events

To gain a deeper insight into the role of LVs in expressing the event structure of sentences with LVCs, in this section we present some real language examples and examine first their role in determining eventuality (§ 3.1) and then in encoding the subevents of an event (§ 3.2).

3.1 Light Verbs and eventuality

Eventuality means the stativity or eventivity of a proposition, and this section specifically examines the role of LVs in determining the eventuality of the sentences. States do not happen and are not associated with change. In contrast, events happen and take place. As mentioned in section 2, Karimi-Doostan and Eshaghi (2019) proposed a new classification for the 21 productive Persian LVs (Figure 2), in which they first divided Persian LVs into two primary classes, i.e. stative Light Verbs (SLVs) and dynamic/ eventive Light Verbs (ELVs).

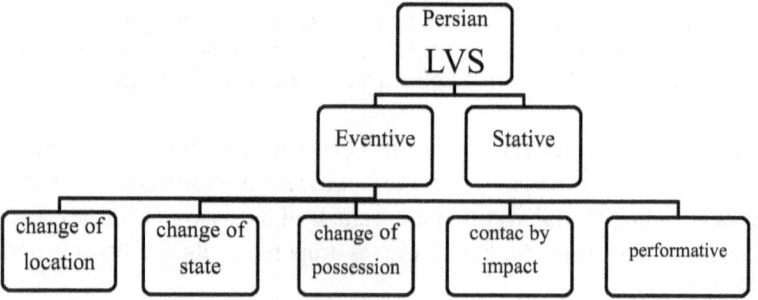

Figure 2: The new classification for Persian LV proposed by Karimi-Doostan and Eshaghi (2019).

The SLV class (V_S) has only one member *da:shtan* 'to have', while the remaining 20 verbs lie in the 5 subclasses of the ELV class; change of location (V_{CL}) (*goza:shtan* 'to put', *keshidan* 'to pull', *ʔa:madan* 'to come', *ʔa:vardan* 'to bring', *residan* 'to arrive', *raftan* 'to go', *ʔofta:dan* 'to fall', *ʔanda:khtan* 'to throw', *bordan* 'to take'), change of state (V_{CS}) (*shodan* 'to become', *gashtan* 'to turn', *didan* 'to see', *ya:ftan* 'to gain'), change of possession (V_{CP}) (*da:dan* 'to give', *bakhshidan* 'to give', to grant', *gereftan* 'to get'), contact by impact (V_{CI}) (*khordan* 'to collide', *zadan* 'to hit', *bastan* 'to tie'), and performative (V_{PRF}) (*kardan* 'to do').

Karimi-Doostan (1997, 2008) used tests such as the progressive test and cooccurrence with the aspectual/temporal adverb *na:gaha:n* 'suddenly' to assess the role of LVs in determining eventuality. In this way, he convincingly demonstrates that the LVs here labelled as SLVs express stativity, whereas all the others (ELVs) express eventivity. We provide some examples to further support his idea.

(2) SLVCs
    a. mu-y-e   sepid-ash dar miya:n-e mardom   **hormat da:sht.**
        hair-HIA-EZ white-POSS.3SG in among-EZ people respect have.PST.3SG.
        'Her white hair was respectable among people.'
    b. ?u be mehma:ni **da?vat   da:sht.**
        she to party   invitation have.PST.3SG.
        'She was invited to the party.'
    c. ?u tama:m da:sta:n ra: **be ya:d da:sht.**
        she whole story   OM to mind have.PST.3SG.
        'She had the whole story in her mind.'

Examples (2a) to (2c) contain SLVCs as their verbal predicates. To identify the type of eventuality realized in these sentences, we use the Persian progressive auxiliary *da:shtan* 'to have' with these LVs as a test to distinguish stativity from eventivity (3a) to (3c).[9]

(3) a. *mu-y-e   sepid-ash   *da:sht*   dar miya:n-e   mardom
        hair-HIA-EZ white-POSS.3SG PROG-AUX in   among-EZ people
        hormat *mi*-da:sht.
        respect PROG-have.PST.3SG.
        'Her white hair was having respect among people.'
    b. *?u *da:sht*   be mehma:ni **da?vat   *mi*-da:sht.**
        she PROG-AUX   to party   invitation PROG-have.PST.3SG.
        'She was having an invitation to the party.'
    c. *?u *da:sht*   tama:m da:sta:n ra: **be ya:d *mi*-da:sht.**
        she PROG-AUX whole   story   OM to mind PROG-have.PST.3SG.
        'She was having the whole story in her mind.'

The incompatibility of these sentences with progressive aspect shows that the Persian SLV *da:shtan* 'to have' only encodes stative sentences, not eventive ones.

---

[9] The basis of the "progressive test" is the use of progressive aspect, which is compatible with eventive LVs, but not with stative ones.

Another interesting point is that *da:shtan* still expresses a state in these examples despite being accompanied by different types of PVs.[10] This confirms the idea of Karimi-Doostan (1997, 2008) about the role of LVs in determining eventuality. The replacement of SLVs by ELVs (4a) to (4c), which causes a change in their eventuality from stativity to eventivity, can be seen as another piece of evidence to show that determining eventuality is the job of LVs independently of PVs.

(4) a. mu-y-e   sepid-ash   dar miya:n-e mardom **hormat ya:ft.**
       hair-HIA-EZ white-POSS.3SG in   among-EZ people   respect gain.PST.3SG.
       'Her white hair became respectable among people.'
   b. ?a:nha: ?u ra: be mehma:ni **da?vat   kard-and.**
       they   him OM   to party   invitation do.PST.3PL.
       'They invited him to the party.'
   c. ?u tama:m da:sta:n ra: **be ya:d ?a:vard.**
       she whole story   OM to mind bring.PST.3SG.
       'She remembered the whole story.'

The progressive test has already shown that the sentences with SLVCs (3a) to (3c) become ill-formed in the progressive form, which means they can only encode stativity. Conversely, their counterparts with ELVCs remain grammatical in the progressive in (5a) to (5c). The compatibility of these sentences with progressive aspect clearly shows the fact that ELVs encode eventivity.

(5) a. mu-y-e   sepid-ash   *da:sht*   dar miya:n-e   mardom
       hair-HIA-EZ white-POSS.3SG PROG-AUX in   among-EZ people
       hormat   *mi*-ya:ft.
       respect   PROG-gain.PST.3SG.
       'Her white hair was gaining respect among people.'
   b. ?a:nha: *da:sht-and* ?u ra: be mehma:ni **da?vat   *mi*-kard-and.**
       they   PROG-AUX him OM to party   invitation PROG-do.PST.3PL.
       'They were inviting him to the party.'
   c. ?u   *da:sht*   tama:m da:sta:n ra: **be ya:d *mi*-a:vard.**
       she PROG-AUX whole   story   OM to mind PROG-bring.PST.3SG.
       'she was bringing the whole story to her mind.'

---

10 Eshaghi (2020:109) has proposed a classification for Persian PVs (acategorial roots) in which they are divided into state-denoting and event-denoting PVs. The state-denoting class does not contain subclasses, but there are 3 subclasses in the event-denoting class, namely action-naming, entity-naming, and directional naming.

Aspectual/temporal adverbs such as 'suddenly' can be used in sentences referring to events, but they are odd with statives, since states do not refer to change or dynamic actions. Indeed, the use of this adverb in sentences with SLVCs is ungrammatical in (6a) to (6c), whereas its use in sentences with ELVCs yields grammatical sentences in (7a) to (7c), supporting the role of LVs in determining eventuality.

(6) a. *mu-y-e   sepid-ash   na:gaha:ni   dar miya:n-e
       hair-HIA-EZ white-POSS.3SG   suddenly   in   among-EZ
       mardom **hormat da:sht.**
       people respect have.PST.3SG.
       'Her white hair suddenly had respect among people.'
   b. *?u   na:gaha:ni be mehma:ni **da?vat   da:sht.**
       she suddenly   to party   invitation   have.PST.3SG.
       'She suddenly had an invitation to the party.'
   c. *?u   na:gaha:ni tama:m da:sta:n ra: **be ya:d da:sht.**
       she suddenly   whole   story   OM   to mind have.PST.3SG.
       'She suddenly had the whole story in her mind.'

(7) a. mu-y-e   sepid-ash   na:gaha:ni dar miya:n-e   mardom
       hair-HIA-EZ white-POSS.3SG   suddenly   in   among-EZ   people
       hormat ya:ft.
       respect gain.PST.3SG.
       'Her white hair suddenly gained respect among people.'
   b. ?a:nha: na:gaha:ni ?u   ra: be mehma:ni **da?vat   kard-and.**
       they   suddenly   him OM   to party   invitation   do.PST.3PL.
       'They suddenly invited him to the party.'
   c. ?u   na:gaha:ni tama:m da:sta:n ra: **be ya:d ?a:vard.**
       she suddenly   whole   story   OM   to mind bring.PST.3SG.
       ' She suddenly remembered the whole story.'

The most obvious insight from this evidence is that LVs in Persian are able to determine the eventuality of sentences as states with SLVs and as events with ELVs.

3.2 LVs and the subevents of an event

Having identified the role of Persian LVs in determining the eventuality of LVCs, we will now elaborate on the role of LVs in encoding the initiatory subevent, the process subevent and the result subevent of an event. In the following, we provide a schematic overview of the application of Ramchand's (2008) subevents model to the six Persian LV classes proposed by Karimi-Doostan and Eshaghi (2019).

(8) Persian Light Verb Aspectual Classes[11]
    a. V_S: +init, – proc, -res
    b. V_{PRF}: +init, +proc, +dur, -res
    c. V_{CS}: -init, +proc, -dur, +res
    d. V_{CL}: ± init,[12] +proc, ±dur, ±res
    e. V_{CP}: ±init, +proc, -dur, +res
    f. V_{CI}: ±init, +proc, ±dur, +res

We introduce different possibilities for LVs in encoding the three subevents of an event through features with binary values. Considering the notion of causation in the sense of Ramchand (2008) and the flavors of little v of Harley (2009), we outline the ability of LVs to encode the initiatory subevent with the feature [±init]. The value of initP is positive in sentences where we find initiators of the type "holder of a property" [+initP$_{state}$],[13] "volitional/nonvolitional cause" [+initP$_{cause}$], "doer of the action" [+initP$_{do}$]; in contrast, the value of initP is negative in sentences where there is no initiator and the first argument is an Undergoer [-initP]. The ability of an LV to encode a process subevent is expressed by [±proc]: this feature is positive in all members of dynamic classes and negative in stative ones; the feature [±dur] as a sub-feature of [procP] is used to express the duration of the process subevent, i.e. whether it contains a single minimal transition [-dur] or continued transitions

---

[11] It is noteworthy that these aspectual features have been derived from the behavior of verbs in isolation, i.e. before being accompanied by PVs; we see how PVs affect them in §§ 3.2.1–3.2.3, so the mismatches you may find in what is stated here and what is represented there are due to this fact.
[12] It should be noted that ± is used in cases where a subevent is present in the event structure of some members of a class and not in others. For example, in the change of location class, ?ofta:dan 'to fall' does not realize the initiator subevent in its event structure, but ?anda:khtan 'to throw' does. The same is true with [±dur] and [±res].
[13] Ramchand (2008:41) defines stative verbs as follows: "In stative verbs, there is no dynamicity/process/change involved in the predication, but it is merely the description of a state of affairs". Then, to discuss the subevents in the event structure of stative verbs, she explains that "a stative verb cannot have a proc element in its first phase syntax or any UNDERGOER argument, but only RHEMATIC or non-aspectual internal arguments. I will assume that stative verbs therefore simply consist of an init projection, with rhematic material projected as a complement of init, rather than a full processual procP. The subject of initP is then straightforwardly interpreted simply as the holder of the state" (Ramchand 2008: 63). In the same spirit, and on the basis of her notion of cause discussed in § 2, we assume the value of the initiatory subevent of stative verbs as [+initP$_{state}$].

[+dur]. Since a result subevent expresses the result of a process, it is only applicable to dynamic verbs.

Illustrating whether LVs exhibit consistent, predictable behavior in expressing the three subevents discussed above is best done under three separate headings, as we do in what follows.

3.2.1 Persian LVs and the initiatory subevent

The initiatory subevent, which appears in the hierarchy of Ramchand's event structure as 'initP', licenses the external argument. Following the aspectual classification in (8), which provides a basis for investigating the role of LVs in realizing the subevents of the Ramchand model, we consider two values for the initiatory phrase, [±initP]. LVCs with a positive value for [initP] can encode one of the possible initiatory phrases of the types [+intP$_{cause}$], [+intP$_{do}$], or [+intP$_{state}$], while those with a negative value are sentences with no external argument. In this type of sentences, the first participant is an Undergoer.

In order to find out the role of LVs in the realization of the initiatory subevent, examples have been taken from the LCP corpus (see footnote 3). In the following, we describe the types of initiatory subevents realized by each member of the six Persian LV classes.

We begin our investigation with the performative class, which contains one member, *kardan* "to do". It can occur in sentences containing [±initP] (9a) to (9c).

(9) a. ?a:nha: ?in bakhsh ra: **sa:ma:ndehi kard-and.** (+initP$_{cause}$)
    they this department OM organization do.PST.3PL.
    'They organized this department.'
   b. ?ali ta: ?omq 180 metri **shena: kard.** (+initP$_{do}$)
    Ali to depth 180 meter swim do.PST.3SG.
    'Ali swam to a depth of 180 meters.'
   c. har boshke naft 50 dollar **tanazol kard.** (-initP)
    each barrel oil 50 dollar decrease do.PST.3SG.
    'The price of oil decreased by 50 dollars a barrel.'

The second class of LVs under consideration is the class of change of location LVs, in which there are 9 members: *?a:madan* 'to come', *?a:vardan* 'to bring', *residan* 'to arrive', *raftan* 'to go', *?ofta:dan* 'to fall', *?anda:khtan* 'to throw', *bordan* 'to take', *keshidan* 'to pull', *goza:shtan* 'to put'. Three of them; *?a:madan* 'to come', *raftan* 'to go', *?ofta:dan* 'to fall', can encode [+initP$_{Do}$] (10a) to (10c) or [-initP] (11a) to (11c).

(10) a. ʔu   ba: tala:sh-e farava:n bar moshkela:t **fa:ʔeq**   **ʔa:mad**. (+initP_do)
       she   with effort-EZ great   on difficulties overcoming come.PST.3SG
       'she overcame the difficulties with great effort.'
   b. niru:-ha: dar   sava:hel-e   Makra:n **rezhe** xa:h-and
      army.force-PL   in   coast-PL-EZ Makran   march   FUT.AUX.3PL
      raft. (+initP_do)
      go.PST.
      'The army forces will march on Makran coasts.'
   c. police **be   donba:l**-e khodro **ʔofta:d.** (+initP_do)
      police to   rear-EZ   car   fall.PST.3SG.
      'The police chased the car.'

(11) a. taqira:t-i   dar   ʔin   hoze   **padid ʔa:mad.** (-initP)
       changes-INDEF   in   this field visible come.PST.3SG.
       'Some changes emerged in this field.'
   b. ʔaz   khastegi   **ʔaz   hush   raft.** (-initP)
      from   overwork   from   consciousness go.PST.3SG.
      'He fainted from overwork.'
   c. roshd-e   ʔeghtesa:di-y-e   ʔira:n   **ʔaz   nafas ʔofta:d.** (-initP)
      growth-EZ   economic-HIA-EZ   Iran   from   breath fall.PST.3SG.
      'The economic growth of Iran stagnated.'

Five of these verbs i.e. *goza:shtan* 'to put', *ʔa:vardan* 'to bring', *ʔanda:khtan* 'to throw', *keshidan* 'to pull', *bordan* 'to take' are capable of encoding [±initP]. The examples (12a) to (12e) show the realization of [+initP_cause] in the sentences containing these LVs.

(12) a. sherkat-e   mosha:ver   ka:r   ra: marhale be   marhale
       company-EZ   advisor   work   OM   step   to   step
       be ʔejra: goza:sht. (+initP_cause)
       to performance put.PST.3SG.
       'The advisor company performed the work step by step.'
   b. vazir-e   jadid   yek   neza:m-e   ʔeqtesa:di-y-e   no
      minister-EZ   new   one   system-EZ   economic-HIA-EZ   new
      padid ʔa:vard. (+initP_cause)
      visible bring.PST.3SG.
      'The new minister creates a new economic system.'
   c. masʔul-an   ba:zgosha:ʔi-y-e   esta:dium   ra: ta: nova:mber
      authority-PL   reopening-HIA-EZ   stadium   OM   till November

      be ta?viq   **?anda:kht-and.** (+initP$_{cause}$)
      to postponement throw.PST.3PL.
      'The authorities postponed the reopening of the stadium to November.'
  d. shureshgar-a:n hame ja: ra: **be vira:ni**   **keshid-and.** (+initP$_{cause}$)
     revolutionist-PL every where OM to destruction pull.PST.3PL.
     'The revolutionists destroyed everywhere.'
  e. moha:jem-a:n ?amva:l-e   mardom-e bi-defa:?   ra:
     invader-PL   possession-EZ people-EZ helpless   OM
     be yaqma: **bord-and.** (+initP$_{cause}$)
     to despoilment take.PST.3PL.
     'The invaders despoiled the helpless people's possessions.'

The last member of the V$_{CL}$ class is *residan* "to arrive" which occurs only in sentences without an external argument and consequently without an initiatory subevent, i.e. [-initP] (13a) and (13b).

(13) a. tarh-e   ?akhir **be tasvib**   **resid.** (-initP)
     plan-EZ recent to approval arrive.PST.3SG.
     'The recent plan was accepted.'
  b. ?ahda:f-ash   **be tahaqoq**   **resid.** (-initP)
     aims-POSS.3SG to   accomplishment arrive.PST.3SG.
     'His aims were accomplished.'

The third group of LVs studied is the change of state class, having four members: *shodan* 'to become', *gashtan* 'to turn', *ya:ftan* 'to gain', *didan* 'to see'. Of these *ya:ftan* 'to gain' encodes only sentences without an initiatory subevent [-initP] (14a).

(14) a. divist-o-chehel   milya:rd riya:l be proje-y-e   sad
     two.hundred-and-forty billion   rial   to project-HIA-EZ dam
     takhsis   **ya:ft.** (-initP)
     allocation gain.PST.3SG.
     'Two hundred forty billion rials was allocated to the dam project.'

While the other members of this class are capable of encoding initiatory phrases of the types [+initP$_{cause}$] (15a) and (15b), [+initP$_{do}$] (16a) and (16b), as well as non-initiatory phrases[-initP] (17a) and (17b).

(15) a. kha:mushi- y-e ?ede?i ?az mardom **sabab**-e dava:m-e za:lema:n
silence-HIA-EZ some of people cause-EZ stability-EZ oppressors
gasht. (+initP_cause)
become.PST.3SG.
'The silence of some people caused oppressors to last.'
b. ?ekhtela:fa:t-e ?akhir **ba?es**-e qat?-e rava:bet-e siya:si
disputes-EZ recent cause cutting-EZ ties-EZ political
miya:n-e do keshvar **shod.** (+initP_cause)
between-EZ two countries become.PST.3SG.
'The recent disputes caused the political ties between the two countries to break.'

(16) a. ra?isjomhu:r vaza:yef-e veza:ratkha:ne-ha: ra:
president duties-EZ ministry-PL OM
motezaker shod. (+initP_do)
remind become.PST.3SG.
'The president reminds the duties of the ministries.'
b. ?u khata:-y-e bozorg-i **mortakeb shod.** (+initP_do)
she mistake-HIA-EZ big-INDEF blunder become.PST.3SG.
'She made a big mistake.'

(17) a. ?ahda:f-e doval-e ?este?ma:ri **padida:r gasht.** (-initP)
aims-EZ governments-EZ colonial apparent become.PST.3SG.
'The aims of the colonial countries become apparent.'
b. khodro-y-e Takfiri-ha: **monhadem shod.** (-initP)
car-HIA-EZ Takfiri-PL destroyed become.PST.3SG.
'Takfiris' car was destroyed.'

The last member of V_CS class is *didan* 'to see' which can encode [+initP_do] (18a) and [-initP] (18b).

(18) a. ?a:n-ha: ?eqda:ma:ti ra: bara:ye residan be hadaf
they measures OM for gaining to goal
tadarok did-and. (+initP_do)
preparation see.PST.3PL.
'They prepared measures to gain the goal.'
b. va:hed-ha:-y-e masku:ni-y-e ?in shahr **khesa:rat did-and.** (-initP)
unit-PL-HIA-EZ residential-HIA-EZ this city damage see.PST-3PL.
'The residential units of this city were damaged.'

The fourth group of LVs is the change of possession class, with three members: *da:dan* 'to give', *bakhshidan* 'to give, to grant', *gereftan* 'to get'. The latter verb can encode sentences with [+initP$_{Do}$] (19a) and without an initiatory subevent [-initP] (19b).

(19) a. darva:zeba:n tu:p ra: dar **?a:qush gereft.** (+initP$_{do}$)
goalkeeper ball OM in hug get.PST.3SG.
'The goalkeeper hugged the ball.'
b. ?enteqa:da:t be mava:ze-?-e dolat **shedat gereft.** (-initP)
criticisms to stances-HIA-EZ government increase get.PST.3SG.
'The criticisms to the governments' stances increased.'

The second member of this class, *da:dan* 'to give', can encode [+initP$_{cause}$] (20a), [+initP$_{do}$] (20b) and [-initP] (20c).

(20) a. a?za:-y-e shora:-y-e shahr mozu?-e ?entekha:b-e
members-HIA-EZ council-HIA-EZ city issue-EZ election-EZ
shahrda:r ra: **feysale da:d-and.** (+initP$_{cause}$)
mayor OM termination give.PST.3PL.
'City council members terminated the mayor election issue.'
b. man mashin-ash ra: be da:khel-e darre **hol**
I car-POSS.3SG OM to inside-EZ valley push
da:da-am. (+initP$_{do}$)
give.PRES.PF-1SG.
'I pushed his car to the valley.'
c. diva:r **nam da:de.** (-initP)
wall moist give.PRES.PF-3SG.
'The wall has moistened.'

The last member of this class, *bakhshidan* 'to give, to grant', encodes [+initP$_{cause}$] in all its corpus samples (21a) (21b).

(21) a. khoda: be ?u **shafa: bakhshid.** (+initP$_{cause}$)
God to her heal grant.PST.3SG.
'God healed her.'
b. Veza:rat-e ?a:muzesh va parvaresh sava:da:muzi ra:
Ministry-EZ education literacy OM
?omumiyat bakhshid. (+initP$_{cause}$)
publicity grant.PST.3SG.
'The ministry of education publicized literacy.'

The next class of LVs is that of contact by impact, which includes three members: *khordan* 'to collide', *zadan* 'to hit', *bastan* 'to tie'. Among them, *zadan* 'to hit' is capable of encoding initiatory subevents of the types [+initP$_{cause}$] (22a) and [+initP$_{Do}$] (22b), and in some cases [-initP] (22c).

(22) a. ka:rgar-a:n dar marhale-y-e ?a:khar bar ?in mahsula:t
worker-PL in step-HIA-EZ last on these products
barchasb mi-zan-and. (+initP$_{cause}$)
label PROG-hit.PRES.3PL.
'The workers are labelling these products ultimately.'
b. ?u sa:?at-ha: be ?aks-e ma:dar-ash **zol zad.** (+initP$_{do}$)
she hour-PL at picture-EZ mother-POSS.3SG stare hit.PST.3SG.
'She stared at her mother's picture for hours.'
c. bakhsh-i ?az ta:la:b **yakh zad.** (-initP)
part.INDEF of lagoon ice hit.PST.3SG.
'A part of the lagoon froze.'

The other two members of this class, *bastan* 'to tie' and *khordan* 'to collide', are seen in sentences with initiatory subevent of the types [+initP$_{Do}$] (23a) and (23b), as well as without initiatory subevent [-initP] (24a) and (24b).

(23) a. ba: khoda:-y-e khod **?ahd bast-am.** (+initP$_{do}$)
with God-HIA-EZ self promise tie-PST.1SG.
'I made a promise to my God.'
b. man **teka:n na-khord-am.** (+initP$_{do}$)
I movement negative-collide-PST.1SG.
'I didn't move.'

(24) a. labkhand-I bar ru-y-e lab-ha:-y-ash **naghsh bast.** (-initP)
smile-INDEF on-HIA-EZ lip-PL-HIA-POSS.3SG appearance tie-PST.3SG.
'A smile appeared on her lips'.
b. hasan ?az bara:dar-ash **kotak khord.** (-initP)
Hasan from brother-POSS.3SG beating collide-PST.3SG.
'Hasan was beaten by his brother.'

Finally, *da:shtan* 'to have' is the only member of Persian stative verbs that can encode an initiatory subevent of the type [+initP$_{state}$] (25a) and (25b).

(25) a. ʔu   bar   harif-e   khod   **bartari   da:sht.**
       he   to   opponent-EZ   self   superiority   have.PST.3SG.
       'He was superior to his opponent.'
   b. barna:me   be   maba:hes-e   varzeshi   **ʔekhtesa:s da:sht.**
       program   to   topics-EZ   sport   dedication have.PST.3SG.
       'The program was dedicated to sport topics.'

So far, we have listed the possible initiatory types that can be realized by each of the LVs under study. However, a question remains: are LVs the only elements of LVCs having a role in the realization of the initiatory phrases in the event structure of sentences containing LVCs? Or can PVs also have a role in affecting the event structure of sentences?

What stands out in our findings is the existence of different types of initiatory subevents in the event structure of sentences containing LVCs with the same LV. This makes the contribution of both LVC components in determining event type inevitable. We offer compelling evidence to support the dominance of the role of LVs in this regard. The first piece of evidence is the impact of the semantic properties of LVs on the type of [initP] they express. According to the data, it appears that a group of LVs can encode three types of initiatory subevents. Strictly speaking, these are LVs in whose lexically full equivalent a causal meaning can be observed. For example, *kardan* 'to do' – in its general meaning expresses senses such as creation and performing – which are processes depending on a cause; *goza:shtan* 'to put', *ʔa:vardan* 'to bring', *ʔanda:khtan* 'to throw', *keshidan* 'to pull', *bordan* 'to take' can express the cause of a change of location; *zadan* 'to hit' can act as the cause of contact; *da:dan* 'to give', *bakhshidan* 'to give' convey a change of possession and express the causer of the events. In addition to encoding [+initP$_{cause}$], these LVs may express the initiatory subevent of the type [+initPdo] or they may occur in sentences without an initiatory subevent [-initP]. This behavior is fully consistent with decompositional theories of event structure, which envisage a sequence of subevents in causative event structures: a CAUSE subevent may imply a DO or BECOME subevent as its consequence. When referring to LVCs in which the predication function is divided between two elements, we can think of the headedness of a subevent of the causative event structure other than the CAUSE subevent (in the sense of Pustejovsky 1991), i.e. DO or BECOME subevents, due to the PVs with which the LVs co-occur. Another piece of evidence that can support our claim is represented by verbs that do not have a CAUSE participant in their lexically full equivalent, such as *ʔa:madan* 'to come', *raftan* 'to go', *ʔofta:dan* 'to fall', *gereftan* 'to get', *didan* 'to see', *bastan* 'to tie', *xordan* 'to collide', which can encode initiatory phrases of the type [+initP$_{do}$] or [-initP]. Semantically, they are a group of DO verbs, whose first participant is the "doer of an action". Accordingly, they can occur in sentences with

[+initPdo]. Since we are talking about a group of verbs that have lost part of their semantic content in the process of light verbalization and share their predication role with a PV, their occurrence in sentences with [-initP] is not far from expectation. We can imagine a situation in which these bleached verbs no longer need the "doer" as one of their participants. Consequently, they do not need the initiatory phrase and the Undergoer becomes the first participant in their semantic realization. The last piece of evidence to be mentioned here refers to the LV *da:shtan* 'to have', which encodes an initiatory phrase [+initP$_{state}$]. As the only member of the class of stative LVs, *da:shtan* 'to have' is a verb that denotes the presence of a property in someone or something (the holder of a property in the sense of Ramchand, 2008), so the initiatory phrase appears as [+initP$_{state}$] in its event structure. From this evidence, we can conclude that LVs impose some constraints on the realization of their initiatory subevents. PVs comply with or may partially affect one of these potentially existing initiators. They never go beyond the boundaries constrained by the LVs.[14] Therefore, LVs play a dominant role in encoding the initiatory subevent.

3.2.2 Persian LVs and process subevent

The process subevent is represented as ProcP in Ramchand's hierarchy of event structure. Ramchand (2008) considers ProcP to be at the heart of dynamic predicates, expressing a changing process. Thus, it has to be present in any dynamic verb. ProcP licenses the entity undergoing a change or process.

As mentioned earlier, we have divided Persian LVs into SLVs and ELVs in their first classification. In our aspectual classification of LVs (8), procP has a positive value for ELVs, which means that it is present in the event structure of all the sentences containing ELVs, while it is negative for SLVs, which means that procP is not present in the event structure of sentences containing SLVs. We even claim that LVs are the elements that enable the realization of procP in the event structure of the sentences that contain them.

To support this claim, we propose a test to verify the presence of ProcP in the event structure of a sentence. The test is based on the fact that ProcP licenses the

---

14 One exception is noteworthy in the results, concerning *gashtan* 'to turn', and *shodan* 'to become'. Although in their lexically full equivalent they have no CAUSE participants, they show two cases of realization of the initiatory phrase [+intP$_{cause}$], namely, in their combination with two PVs, i.e. *sabab* and *ba?es*, which both mean 'cause' in Persian. This behavior is justified for two reasons: 1. the degree of their lightness (*shodan* is one of the lightest LVs in Persian and *gashtan* is its formal counterpart); 2. the power of the meaning of these two PVs.

entity undergoing a change or process. Therefore, the presence of a participant undergoing the change or process confirms the presence of its licenser, ProcP.

To illustrate the point let's look at some examples.

(26) a. hey?at-e   dolat   moza:kera:t   ra: **be jarya:n ?anda:xt-and.**
         cabinet-EZ government negotiations   OM   afoot   throw.PST.3PL.
         'The government's cabinet set afoot the negotiations.'
     b. mardom ba: va?de-ha-y-e   dolat   **?omidvar šod-and.**
         people   with promise-PL-HIA-EZ government hopeful become.PST.3PL.
         'The people become hopeful with the government's promises.'
     c. man be yek   khane-y-e   shakhsi   **nia:z da:shtam.**
         I   to   one   home-HIA-EZ private   need have.PRES.1SG.
         'I need a private home.'

In (26a), a process is predicated by the ELVC *be jaryan ?andaxtan* 'to set afoot'; as expected, there exists an Undergoer, i.e. *mozakera:t* 'negotiations', in this sentence. In (26b), the change is predicated by the ELVC *?omidvar šodan* 'to become hopeful', and an Undergoer is present in this sentence too, i.e. *mardom* 'people'. Conversely, in (26c) the predicate is an SLVC and, in accordance with our claim, there is no Undergoer and consequently no ProcP in the sentence.[15]

We considered [±dur] as a sub-feature of procP in our aspectual classification. This feature determines whether the change or process realized by procP contains a single minimal transition [-dur] or a repeated/continued transition [+dur]. Indeed, this distinction is necessary to distinguish two types of events, i.e. accomplishments and achievements. The difference between these two event types is related to the punctuality[16] of the process in Ramchand's (2008) terms, and [±dur] in our term. Achievements encode a procP$_{[-dur]}$, whereas accomplishments encode a procP$_{[+dur]}$.

However, it should be noted that although Ramchand (2008) originally tried to introduce duration as a redundant feature, she has applied it in her (2017) classifi-

---

[15] It is worth mentioning that based on the definition LVs are supposed to be semantically bleached, so "have" as a part of an LVC is no longer a transitive possession verb, which needs an object undergoer.

[16] Ramchand (2008: 86) distinguishes between achievements and accomplishments through the feature of punctuality. It seems that achievements are considered by her to be punctual verbs, while accomplishments are considered to be verbs which identify non-punctual processes. She argues that verbs expressing a non-punctual process do not simultaneously identify both process and result, i.e. two different verbs head the process and result subevents, unlike what happens with punctual verbs, where a lexical verb identifies both the process and the result.

cation. We apply her punctuality test to identify [±dur]. According to this punctuality test, example (26a) has the feature [+duration] while (26b) has the feature [-duration]. To explore the role of LVs in determining the duration of the Proc subevent, we compared the behavior of LVs and their fully lexical equivalents in encoding the feature of duration. The result of our observation indicated that, independent of the presence or the absence of the duration feature in fully lexical verbs, all ELVs possibly encode [±dur] procP in their event structure. Therefore, ELVs can express ProcP, but PVs may have an effect on the type of ProcP, i.e in determining whether it contains a single minimal [-dur] transition or repeated or continued transitions [+dur].

3.2.3 Persian LVs and result subevent

Having discussed the role of LVs in encoding initiatory and process subevents in the last two subsections, a look at the role of LVs in encoding the result subevent is in order here. The result subevent appears as [resP] in Ramchand's (2008) hierarchy of event structure. It expresses a result state and exists only to express a property that is the result of a dynamic change in the meaning of a verb: [resP] licenses the entity that comes to hold the result state (resultee). Many works (*inter alia* Tenny 1987, Kiparsky 1998, Ritter and Rosen 1998 and Borer 1998) describe this subevent as a semantic component of verbs. Due to the fact that the result subevent [resP] expresses the result of a dynamic change, the existence of a [procP] is a definite prerequisite of the existence of [resP]. For this reason, it can be concluded that a result subevent can only occur in sentences with ELVCs and not in sentences with SLVCs; in other words, it is the type of LV which permits the entrance of a result subevent into the event structure.[17]

Let's look at some examples.

(27) a. ʔejra:-y-e   tarh-ha:-y-e   jadid   sarma:ye-y-e   šerkat-ha:
       performing-HIA-EZ plan-PL-HIA-EZ   new   capital-HIA-EZ firm-PL
       ra: **ʔafza:yeš da:d.**
       OM   increase   give.PST.3SG.
       'Performing new plans increased the capital of the firms.'
    b. moškela:t-e ziyadi   bara:ye   ka:rgar-a:n   **be vojud   ʔa:mad.**
       troubles-EZ a.lot.of for   worker-PL   to existence come.PST.3SG.
       'Lots of troubles arose for the workers.'

---

[17] Note that we do not mean that [resP] exists in the event structure of all sentences with ELVCs. It may exist depending on the type of LV and PV in the sentence.

c. ba:yad tama:m-e java:neb ra: **dar nazar da:sht.**
   must all-EZ aspects OM into consideration have.PST.
   'All aspects must be considered.'

As expected, in (27a) and (27b) the resultee and consequently the result subevent are present, due to the presence of ELVCs: in (27a) the resultee is *sarmaye-y-e šerkat-ha* 'firm's funds', while in (27b) is *ka:rgara:n* 'workers'. On the other hand, there is no resultee and no result subevent in (27c), due to the occurrence of an SLVC.[18]

4 Conclusion

Light Verb Constructions, as a subgroup of complex predicates, are multi-word predicates. Therefore, it is a challenging and difficult task to illustrate the role of each component of an LVC in determining its event structure and its subevents. We have argued and attempted to show the role of LVs in determining the eventuality of sentences and their role in realizing the subevents of an event in accordance with Ramchand's (2008, 2017) model of event structure. To achieve this goal, we have developed a detailed aspectual classification for Persian Light Verbs. Firstly, using the findings of Harley (2009) and Ramchand (2008), we have investigated the role of LVs in determining event structure. Applying some tests on the sentences containing LVCs, we have shown that, in the spirit of Karimi-Doostan (1997), LVs determine the eventuality of the sentences containing them. We then investigated the role of LVs in realizing the subevents of Ramchand's (2008) model of event structure, and we have also shown that LVs play a dominant role in this respect. The results of our analysis are represented in Table 1.

---

[18] Once again, it should be noted that examining only one of the three subevents in the examples presented in each section does not mean that the other subevents do not occur in them. Each section focuses on one of the subevents, in order to present the behavior of LVs in encoding each one of the subevents separately.

Table 1: The possibilities of Persian LVs in encoding subevents of an event.

LVs			+initP$_{cause}$	+initP$_{do}$	+initP$_{state}$	-initP	+dur	-dur	+res	-res
ELVs	V$_{PRF}$	kardan "to do"	√	√		√	√	√	√	√
	V$_{CL}$	goza:shtan "to put"	√	√		√	√	√	√	√
		?a:madan "to come"		√		√	√	√	√	√
		?a:vardan "to bring"	√	√		√	√	√	√	√
		residan "to arrive"				√	√	√	√	
		raftan "to go"		√		√	√	√	√	√
		?ofta:dan "to fall"		√		√	√	√	√	
		?anda:khtan "to throw"	√	√		√	√	√	√	√
		keshidan "to pull"	√	√		√	√	√	√	√
		bordan "to take"	√	√		√	√	√	√	
	V$_{CS}$	ya:ftan "to gain"				√	√	√	√	√
		gashtan "to turn"	√	√		√	√	√	√	√
		didan "to see"		√		√	√	√	√	√
		shodan "to become"		√		√	√	√	√	√
	V$_{CP}$	gereftan "to get"		√		√	√	√	√	√
		da:dan "to give"	√	√			√	√	√	√
		bakhshidan "to give"	√					√	√	√
	V$_{CI}$	zadan "to hit"	√	√		√	√	√		
		bastan "to tie"				√	√	√	√	√
		khordan "to collide"		√		√	√	√	√	√
SLVs		da:shtan "to have"			√					

Abbreviations

DUR	duration
EZ	ezafe (which is used as a particle between two nouns or a noun and its modifier)
FUT	future
HIA	hiatus (which is used for the separation of two consecutive vowels that occur in adjacent syllables)
INDEF	indefinite
initP	initiatory phrase
LV	Light Verb
LVC	Light Verb Constructions
OM	object marker
PL	plural

POSS	possessive
procP	process phrase
PROG-AUX	progressive auxiliary
PRES	present tense
PRES.PF	present perfect
PST	past tense
PV	preverbal element
resP	result phrase
SG	singular
V_{CS}	change of state
V_{CI}	contact by impact
V_{CL}	change of location
V_{CP}	change of possesion
V_{PRF}	performatives
V_S	statives

References

Åfarli, Tor A. 2007. Do verbs have argument structure? In Eric J. Reuland, Tanmoy Bhattacharya & Giorgos Spathas (eds.), *Argument Structure*, 1–16. Amsterdam: Benjamins.

Åfarli, Tor A. & Fufen Jin. 2014. Syntactic frames and single-word code-switching: A case study of Mandarin Chinese – Norwegian bilingualism. In Tor A. Åfarli & Brit Maehlum (eds.), *The Sociolinguistics of Grammar*, 153–170. Amsterdam: Benjamins.

Borer, Hagit. 1998. Deriving passives without theta-grids. In Steven G. Lapointe, Diane K. Brentari & Patrick M. Farrell (eds.), *Morphology and its Relations to Phonology and Syntax*, 60–99. Stanford: CSLI Publications.

Borer, Hagit. 2003. Exo-skeletal vs. endo-skeletal explanations: syntactic projections and the lexicon. In John C. Moore & Maria Polinsky (eds.), *The nature of explanations in linguistic theory*, 37–67. Chicago: Chicago University Press.

Chomsky, Noam. 1995. *The minimalist program*. Cambridge, MA: The MIT Press.

Croft, William. 2001. *Radical Construction Grammar*. Oxford: Oxford University Press.

Dabir-Moghaddam, Mohammad. 1995. Compound verbs in Persian. *Journal of Iranian Linguistics* 12(1). 2–46.

Davison, Donald. 1967. The logical form of action sentences. In Nicholas Rescher (ed.), *The Logic of Decision and Action*, 81–95. Pittsburgh: University of Pittsburgh Press.

Eshaghi, Mahdie. 2020. *The emergence and productivity of Light verb and its role in event structure*. PhD dissertation. Tehran: Tehran University.

Folli, Raffaella, Heidi Harley, & Simin Karimi. 2004. Determinants of event type in Persian complex predicates. *Lingua* 115. 1365–1401.

Folli, Raffaella & Heidi Harley. 2006. Waltzing Matilda. *Studia Linguistica* 60(2). 1–35.

Folli, Raffaella & Heidi Harley. 2007. Causation, obligation and argument structure: On the nature of little v. *Linguistic Inquiry* 38(2). 197–238.

Goldberg, Adele. 1995. *Constructions. A Construction Grammar Approach to Argument Structure*. Chicago: University of Chicago Press.

Goldberg, Adele. 2006. *Constructions at Work. The Nature of Generalization in Language*. Oxford: Oxford University Press.
Grimshaw, Jane. 1990. *Argument Structure*. Cambridge, MA: The MIT Press.
Grimshaw, Jane & Armin Mester. 1988. Light verbs and θ-theory. *Linguistic Inquiry* 19(2). 205–232.
Hale, Kenneth & Samuel J. Keyser. 1993. On argument structure and the lexical expression of syntactic relations. In Kenneth Hale & Samuel J. Keyser (eds.), *The View from Building 20: A Festschrift for Sylvain Bromberger*, 53–109. Cambridge, MA: The MIT Press.
Hale, Kenneth & Samuel J. Keyser. 2002. *Prolegomenon to a Theory of Argument Structure*. Cambridge, MA: The MIT Press.
Halle, Morris & Alec Marantz. 1994. Some key features of Distributed Morphology. In Andrew Carnie & Heidi Harley (with Tony Bures) (eds.), *Papers in Phonology and Morphology*. MIT Working Papers in Linguistics. Vol. 21, 275–288. Cambridge, MA: MIT Working Papers in Linguistics.
Harley, Heidi. 1999. Denominal verbs and *Aktionsart*. In Liina Pylkkänen, Angeliek van Hout and Heidi Harley (eds.), *Papers from the UPenn/MIT Roundtable on the Lexicon*. MIT Working Papers in Linguistics. Vol. 35, 73–86. Cambridge, MA: MIT Working Papers in Linguistics.
Harley, Heidi. 2005. How do verbs get their names? The *Aktionsart* of denominal verbs and the ontology of verb roots in English. In N. Erteschik-Shir, T, Rappaport (eds), *The Syntax of Aspect*, 42–64. Oxford: Oxford university Press.
Harley, Heidi. 2009. The morphology of nominalizations and the syntax of vP. In Monika Rathert & Anastasia Giannankidou (eds.), *Quantification, Definiteness and Nominalization*, 320–342. Oxford: Oxford University Press.
Jackendoff, Ray. 1983. *Semantics and Cognition*. Cambridge, MA: The MIT Press.
Jespersen, Otto. 1942. *A Modern English Grammar on Historical Principles*. Vol. 6: *Morphology*. London: George Allen and Unwin Ltd.
Karimi, Simin. 1997. Persian Complex Verbs: Idiomatic or Compositional. *Lexicology* 3. 273–318.
Karimi-Doostan, Gholamhossein. 1997. *Light Verb Constructions in Persian*. PhD dissertation. Colchester: Essex University.
Karimi- Doostan, Gholamhossein. 2005. Light verb and structural case. *Lingua* 115(12). 1737–1756.
Karimi-Doostan, Gholamhossein. 2008. Event Structure of verbal nouns and light verbs. In Simin Karimi, Vida Samiian & Donald Stilo (eds.), *Aspects of Iranian linguistics*, 206–226. Newcastle: Cambridge Scholars Publishing.
Karimi-Doostan, Gholamhossein. 2011. Separability of Light Verb Constructions in Persian. *Studia Linguistica* 65. 1–26.
Karimi-Doostan, Gholamhossein & Mahdie Eshaghi. 2019. Systematic light verbalization in Persian. *Journal of Researches in Linguistics* 11(2). 157–186.
Kiparsky, Paul. 1998. Partitive case and aspect. In Miriam Butt & Wilhelm Geuder (eds.), *Projecting from the Lexicon*, 265–307. Stanford: CSLI Publications.
Levin, Beth & Malka Rappaport Hovav. 1995. *Unaccusativity. At the Syntax-Lexical Semantics Interface*. Cambridge, MA: The MIT Press.
Levin, Beth & Malka Rappaport Hovav. 1999. Two structures for compositionally derived events. *Semantics and Linguistic Theory* 9. 199–223.
Lohndal, Terje. 2012. *Without Specifiers: Phrase Structure and Events*. PhD dissertation. College Park: University of Maryland.
Lyutikova, Ekaterina & Sergei Tatevosov. 2013. Complex predicates, eventivity, and causative-inchoative alternation. *Lingua* 135. 81–111.
Marantz, Alec. 2013. Verbal argument structure: Events and participants. *Lingua* 130. 152–168.

Megerdoomian, Karine. 2001. Event structure and complex predicates in Persian. *Canadian Journal of Linguistics* 46(1/2). 97–125.
Mohammad, Jan & Simin Karimi. 1992. Light verbs are taking over: complex verbs in Persian. In Joel A. Nevis & Vida Samiian (eds.), *Proceedings of WECOL* 5, 195–212. Fresno: Fresno State University.
Parsons, Terence. 1990. *Events in the Semantics of English. A Study in Subatomic Semantics*. Cambridge, MA: The MIT Press.
Pustejovsky, James. 1991. The syntax of event structure. *Cognition* 41. 47–81.
Ramchand, Gillian. 2008. *Verb Meaning and the Lexicon. A First Phase Syntax*. Cambridge: Cambridge University Press.
Ramchand, Gillian. 2017. The event domain. In Roberta D'Alessandro, Irene Franco & Ángel J. Gallego (eds.), *The Verbal Domain*, 233–254. Oxford: Oxford University Press.
Rappaport Hovav, Malka & Beth Levin. 1998. Building verb meanings. In Miriam Butt & Wilhelm Geuder (eds.), *The Projection of Arguments: Lexical and Compositional Factors*, 97–134. Standford: CSLI Publications.
Rappaport Hovav, Malka & Beth Levin. 2000. Classifying single argument verbs. In Peter Coopmans, Martin B.H. Everaert & Jane Grimshaw (eds.), *Lexical Specification and Insertion*, 269–304. Amsterdam: Benjamins.
Ritter, Elizabeth & Sara Thomas Rosen. 1998. Delimiting events in syntax. In Miriam Butt & Wilhelm Geuder (eds.), *The Projection of Arguments: Lexical and Syntactic Constraints*, 135–164. Standford: CSLI Publications.
Tenny, Carol Lee. 1987. *Grammaticalizing Aspect and Affectedness*. PhD dissertation. Cambridge, MA: Massachusetts Institute of Technology.
Vahedi-Langrudi & Mohammad-Mehdi. 1996. *The Syntax, Semantics and Argument Structure of Complex Predicates in Modern Farsi*. PhD dissertation. Ottawa: University of Ottawa.
Van Hout, Angeliek. 1996. *Event Semantics and Verb Frame Alternations*. PhD dissertation. Tilburg: Tilburg University.
Williams, Edwin. 1981. Argument structure and morphology. *The Linguistic Review* 1. 1–34.

Anna Pompei and Valentina Piunno

4 Light Verb Constructions in Romance languages

An attempt to explain systematic irregularity

Abstract: The chapter provides a comparative analysis of a set of Light Verb Constructions of some Romance languages (Portuguese, Spanish, French, Italian and Romanian) employng the Light Verbs 'have', 'do/make', 'give', 'take'. Light Verb Constructions are classified according to the *Aktionsart* of nouns. From the cross-linguistic data analysis, prototypical and marked uses of Light Verbs in co-occurrence with nouns regularly emerge: the former concern nouns and Light Verbs having the same actionality, while the latter refer to Light Verb Constructions including Light Verbs and nouns which are not coherent from the actional point of view. Marked combinations may produce inchoative/incremental and lexical diathetic effects. The investigation demonstrates that Light Verbs participate in the Light Verb Construction's semantics based on their basic or less prototypical function. According to this perspective, Light Verbs are not considered truly empty, and Light Verb Constructions are used to modulate different aspectual nuances and even configurations of the information structure. Finally, the cross-linguistic investigation also provides explanations for irregularities among the languages considered, according to some diachronic and areal considerations.

Keywords: Romance languages, noun actionality, prototypical Light Verbs uses, marked Light Verbs uses

1 Introduction

Light Verb Constructions (henceforth LVCs) are word combinations composed of a semantically bleached verb, the so-called Light Verb (henceforth LV), and a second element, commonly a predicative noun. The verb of an LVC is usually polysemic and its semantic value is highly generic; it generally covers a grammatical function, expressing tense, mood or aspectual information. The nominal element, which is generally scarcely referential, is the nucleus of the predication, since it is lexically full and bears the semantics of the construction.

LVCs are particularly productive in some languages, where they represent the typical verbal construction (e.g. Persian, Kalam and some Northern Australian languages; cf. Mattissen, this volume), but are also very common in other languages, which may show both LVCs and their synthetic verbal counterparts (e.g. Romance languages). This investigation deals only with LVCs showing the syntactic configuration [Verb + (Article) + Noun]. In particular, our proposal is aimed at carrying out a comparative analysis of Portuguese, Spanish, French, Italian and Romanian LVCs. Indeed, the comparative perspective proves to be helpful in showing and explaining idiosyncrasies and irregularities.

The analysis is also aimed at evaluating whether irregularities are due to lexical constraints, or if synchronic and diachronic explanations are also possible. The paper[1] is divided into seven sections. We firstly identify the irregularities in the selection of LVs in the Romance languages considered (Section 2). Subsequently, we explore the notion of lightness and predicativeness (Section 3) of nouns (Section 3.1) and verbs (Section 3.2) in LVCs, according to the literature. Section 4 shows the criteria used to select and classify data, which are discussed in Sections 5 and 6. In Section 7 some areal, diachronic and typological considerations are presented. Finally, some conclusive remarks are drawn in Section 8.

2 Idiosyncrasies in Romance languages

The association between an LV and a predicative noun seems to be arbitrary. Nevertheless, some scholars have pointed out that LVCs may exhibit some regular features (*inter alia*, Gross 1981, Wierzbicka 1982). Indeed, a comparison between LVCs of Romance languages may reveal some regularities in the selection of the LV by a specific, and interlinguistically equivalent, noun, as in the following examples:[2]

(1) 'give a slap'
    PT: dar *uma bofetada*
    SP: dar *una bofetada / dar un bofetón*
    FR: donner *une gifle*

---

[1] The article has been planned and elaborated jointly by the authors. However, for academic purposes, sections 1-5.1 are attributed to Valentina Piunno, and sections 5.2-8 to Anna Pompei. This investigation could not have been completed without native speakers' judgements about the acceptability of our data. We are especially grateful to Ana Paula Loureiro and Silvia Brambilla for Portuguese, to José Miguel Baños Baños and María Dolores Jiménez López for Spanish, to Gilles Authier and Dominique Longrée for French, and to Mira Mocan and Nicoleta Neşu for Romanian. We would also like to thank Jaume Mateu for the contrastive data from Catalan.
[2] As far as the English translations are concerned, we render the LVC meanings through an equivalent LVC in American English, when available. When the source construction differs from the target one, we include a literal translation.

    IT: dare *uno schiaffo*
    RO: a da *palmă*

(2) 'make a choice'
    PT: fazer *uma escolha*
    SP: hacer *una elección*
    FR: faire *un choix*
    IT: fare *una scelta*
    RO: a face *o alegere*

(3) 'take a decision'
    PT: tomar *uma decisão*
    SP: tomar *una decisión*
    FR: prendre *une décision*
    IT: prendere *una decisione*
    RO: a lua *o decizie*

Nevertheless, the comparison may also show a certain degree of variability in the selection of the LV by an equivalent noun. This may be exemplified, for instance, by the interlinguistic irregularities in the following LVCs:

(4) 'take a shower'
    PT: tomar *duche/banho*
    SP: darse *una ducha*
    FR: prendre *une douche*
    IT: fare(-si) *una doccia*
    RO: a face *un duş*

(5) 'have courage'
    PT: ter *coragem*
    SP: tener *valor*
    FR: avoir *du courage*
    IT: avere *coraggio*
    RO: a avea *curaj*

(6) 'evoke envy'
    PT: fazer *inveja*
    SP: dar *envidia*
    FR: faire *envie*

IT: fare *invidia*
RO: a provoca *invidie*

(7) 'take a walk'
PT: dar *um passeio*
SP: dar *un paseo*
FR: faire *une promenade*
IT: fare *una passeggiata*
RO: a face *o plimbare*

In the case of LVCs with eventive nouns such as 'shower' (4), the Western Romance languages select the verb 'take' (PT, FR) or 'give (oneself)' (SP), while Italian and Romanian prefer the verb 'do/make'. In the case of LVCs including nouns expressing psychological states, the verb changes whether the state is felt (5) or caused (6). In the former (5), languages of the Iberian area use the continuance of the Latin verb *tenere* 'hold', while the continuance of Latin *habere* 'have' is preferred by French, Italian and Romanian; as far as the latter is concerned (6), only Spanish continues the Latin verb *dare* 'give' instead of Latin *facere* 'do/make', like Portuguese, French, and Italian do. On the other hand, the selection of *dar* 'give' in combination with the eventive noun 'walk' (7) is common to both the Iberian languages, whereas all the other languages prefer 'do/make'. Next to the interlinguistic dimension, variation may also result at the intralinguistic level. In the same language, nouns which are apparently similar – as 'choice' and 'decision' (2)–(3) – may select different verbs. On the other hand, different verbs can be selected by the same noun, with different diathetic and aspectual nuances (see ex. (8) in Section 3.2).The explanations of the intralinguistic data may be similar to those of the interlinguistic ones. However, our main goal is to better understand whether cross-linguistic variations in the LVs selection by nouns are completely arbitrary, or if some constraints can be identified; and, in this case, how they can be explained. Indeed, the cross-linguistic dimension of Romance LVCs is scarcely explored in literature.

3 Lightness and predicativeness in Light Verb Constructions

The first studies devoted to LVCs mainly concentrated on the lightness of the verb (Jespersen 1942, Gross 1981, Giry-Schneider 1987), and on the sole predicativeness of the noun (among others, Gross 1996). In this perspective, the verb was generally considered as a light element only codifying TAM traits and the agreement with the subject, in order to 'actualize' the predicative noun (*prédicat nominal*, Gross 1999: 74–75), thus playing the same role as verbal predicate endings. For this reason, in the French tradition the notion of 'verbe support' is adopted.

Verbs having richer semantic features have been considered as LV 'extensions'. For instance, Maurice Gross (1981: 33; cf. also Vivès 1984) compares in French *avoir de l'influence* 'have influence' with *prendre de l'influence* 'take influence', *conserver de l'influence* 'keep influence', *perdre de l'influence* 'lose influence', which realize the inchoative, progressive and terminating values respectively, as opposed to the basic form *avoir* 'have'. On the other hand, Gaston Gross (1994; 2004b: 347) identifies all the verbs that frequently occur with a specific lexical class of predicative nouns (i.e. *classe d'objects*), distinguishing i) the generic verb, i.e. the verb which is typical to different aspectual classes, ii) the basic verb, i.e. the verb which is neutral for a specific class of objects, and iii) many others that he classifies in different categories, all considerable as LV extensions. For example, as far as the class of objects of ‹battles› (e.g. FR *guerre* 'war', *combat* 'fight', *bataille* 'battle') is concerned, French requires *faire* 'do/make' – both as a generic LV, which is shared by all other classes of objects with the same *Aktionsart*, and as a basic LV, which is specific for such a class – but it can also co-occur with many other LV extensions, conveying different nuances of meaning.³

On the other hand, the non-complete semantic neutrality of the LV has been questioned. In the Generative Lexicon perspective (Pustejovsky 1995), LVCs are considered as built from the co-composition of semantic features of both the noun and the verb, which share the predicativeness of an LVC, and cooperatively select each other (cf. De Miguel 2006, 2008; Ježek 2004, 2011, this volume). In this framework, the selection of an LV depends at the same time on the semantic features of the noun and on the lexical meaning of the verb. Thus, the noun and the LV have been considered as semantically homogenous (*concordancia de los rasgos léxicos del N y del V*, De Miguel 2008; *semantic compatibility*, Sanromán Vilas 2011; *semantic coherence*, Bosque 2011). In the following we will go through the main investi-

---

3 The class of objects of ‹battles› can co-occur with several 'appropriate' support verbs, i.e. specific to that class such as 'conduct', 'fight' (FR *mener, livrer*), with support verbs that realize the lexical passive (FR *subir*) or the reciprocal meaning (FR *se faire, se livrer*), as well as with a series of support verbs that encode particular aspectual values – 'inchoative' (FR *engager*), 'iterative' (FR *renouveler*), 'progressive' (FR *continuer*), 'terminative' (FR *cesser*) – and, finally, with 'eventive' or 'existential' verbs having the predicative noun as their subject and meaning 'take place/occur' (FR *avoir lieu*); cf. Gross (2004b: 357). It is worth noting that the notion of 'eventive verbs' of this classification is narrower than the notion of events at the basis of Ježek's (2016) classification of noun classes, which we use in this article (Section 4); cf. also Ježek (2004) for a classification of Italian LV extensions as codifying other values besides the aspectual one (e.g. modality, intensification, quantity, connotation, register).

gations and classifications of Romance LVCs, which aim to identify the semantic contribution of the noun (Section 3.1) and of the verb (Section 3.2).

3.1 The predicative noun

For Romance languages, scholars have tried to demonstrate that the selection of LVs in LVCs, far from being arbitrary, is often sensitive to the semantics of the predicative noun they combine with. In particular, some recent investigations have highlighted that the selection of an LV is linked to lexically coherent groups of nouns (Bosque 2011; cf. also Samvelian et al. 2011; Koike 2001; Gross 1994, 2004b), having the role of 'base' in combination with an LV (cf., among others, Apresjan 2009, Bosque 2011).

The type of semantic classification of the predicative noun may depend on the theoretical framework, on the goal and on the type of analysis.[4] From a contrastive perspective, nouns have been collected into different lexical classes in order to identify interlinguistic differences (usually between two languages) in the selection of LVs. As far as Romance languages are concerned, differences have been highlighted in the selection of the LV by nouns describing psychological states, events, blows, sounds or communication (cf. Sidoti 2014, Moncó Taracena 2011, Sanromán Vilas 2014 on Spanish, French and Italian). In particular, within the semantic field of emotion (Section 5.1.1), nouns have been distinguished among *internal cause emotion nouns* (where "the emotion is born in the experiencer", i.e. SP. *admiración* 'admiration') and *external cause emotion nouns* (where an external fact "triggers the emotion", i.e. SP *disgusto* 'upset') (Sanromán Vilas 2011: 260): when the subject is the Experiencer, in Spanish internal cause emotion nouns combine with *tener* 'to have' and *sentir* 'to feel', while external cause emotion nouns co-occur with *llevarse* 'to take away'. Nouns denoting blows always select the verb 'give' (Section 5.2.3; cf. Gross 2004b for French). Being punctual, these nouns describe a single instance of

---

4 Many investigations are devoted to translating problems; some studies analyze LVCs taking care of L2 learning problems (Sidoti 2014), others have been elaborated for lexicographical goals (such as Bosque 2011, devoted to the building of the REDES dictionary). In addition to the studies quoted in this section, at least the following references can be considered: on French, M. Gross (1981), Vivès (1983; 1984; 1988), Giry-Schneider (1987), G. Gross (1993, 1999, 2004a, b), G. Gross and Pontonx (2004); on Italian, Elia et al. (1985), La Fauci (1997), La Fauci and Mirto (2003), Mastrofini (2004; 2013), Vietri (2004), Ježek (2004, 2011, this volume), and Cantarini (2004), who proposes a contrastive analysis between Italian and German; as for Spanish, Alonso Ramos (1991, 2004), Corpas Pastor (1996), Mendívil Giró (1999), Blanco Escoda (2000), Bustos Plaza (2005), De Miguel (2006, 2008), Moncó Taracena (2011), Sanromán Vilas (2011; 2014), Sidoti (2014); on Portuguese, Neves (2002), Duarte et al. (2010); on Romanian, Ciocanea (2011).

the event, whereas their pluralizability implies iterativity: in Italian *dare un colpo* 'give a blow' means to give a single blow; the pluralized construction *dare colpi* 'give blows' means to repeat the action for a number of times. The demarcation of either the unicity or the plurality of the number of blows cannot be expressed by the equivalent synthetic form *colpire* 'hit'.

The selection of a specific LV by lexical classes of nouns has also been explained on the basis of the aspectual values of the noun. For instance, for Portuguese, Duarte et al. (2010) note that punctual nouns select the LV *dar* (e.g. PT *dar um chute* 'kick'), as well as nouns denoting processes (e.g. PT *dar um passeio* 'take a walk'), and resultative events (*dar uma limpeza* 'clean'). Nevertheless, nouns denoting processes can also co-occur with the verb *fazer* (i.e. *fazer uma caminhada* 'take a walk') or with the verb *ter* (i.e. *ter uma viagem agradável* 'have a nice trip'; cf. Section 5.2.2). On the relevance of aspectual agreement of the combinatorial profile of a predicate, cf. also Apresjan (2009: 3).

According to Bosque (2011), the semantic value of LVCs is not only deducible through sets of semantically related nouns, but is also interlinguistically comparable.

3.2 The Light Verb

If the noun bears most of an LVC's predicativeness, the verb does not really play a neutral role. As Butt (2010: 73) points out, LVs "do not instantiate a full event predication of their own and given that they often predicate about the causation or result (boundedness) of an event, one intuitive avenue of analysis is that Light Verbs correspond to, or predicate parts of an event, i.e., subevents".

The non-complete semantic bleaching of the verb is particularly clear when the verb is the only part of an LVC which is subject to variation, the noun being the same, as De Miguel (2008: 570–571) notes for Spanish. The following examples show that this is also true for other Romance languages:

(8) 'be cold' (lit. 'have cold') 'be cold' (lit. 'do/make cold') 'get cold' (lit. 'take cold')
    PT: a. *ter frio*   b. *fazer frio*   c. *apanhar frio*
    SP: a. *tener frío*   b. *hacer frío*   c. *coger frío*
    FR: a. *avoir froid*   b. *faire froid*   c. *prendre froid*
    IT: a. *avere freddo*   b. *fare freddo*   c. *prendere freddo*
    RO: a. *a îi fi frig*   b. *a fi frig*   c. –

In the examples in (8), the equivalents of *cold* are preceded by different LVs: constructions with 'have' (8a) and 'do/make' (8b) denote a state, while those with 'take' (8c) have an incremental value. As it is clear, the combinatorial properties of the three types of construction are different: in a. and c. the subject is usually [+ HUMAN] or [+ ANIMATE] (i.e. IT *Giovanni ha freddo* 'John is cold', *Giovanni prende freddo* 'John gets cold'), while in b. the construction is impersonal (i.e. IT *fuori fa freddo* 'it's cold outside'). This means that LVs can also impose semantic constraints for the selection of the type of subject.

The semantic contribution of the LV can be also highlighted in cases like (9)-(11):

(9) a. SP: *tener sueño* 'be sleepy' b. SP: *dar sueño* 'make someone be sleepy'

(10) a. IT: *avere la febbre* 'have a fever' b. IT: *dare la febbre* 'make someone have a fever'

(11) a. FR: *avoir froid* 'be cold' b. FR: *donner froid* 'make someone be cold'

While the Romance counterparts of 'have' (9a)–(11a) describe a state, those of 'give' (9b)–(11b) express a causative value (see also ex. (6), with 'do/make'). This means that the LV can convey semantic diathetic values (Sections 5.1.1–5.1.2). Actually, Gross (2004b) also takes into account the realization of 'passive', 'reciprocal', 'eventive' or 'existential' values by LVs which are different from the basic ones (i.e. respectively *subir* 'undergo'/*se faire* 'make (oneself)'/*avoir lieu* 'take place' *un combat* 'a fight', as opposed to the basic support verb *faire* 'do/make' in *faire un combat* 'have a fight').

Moreover, if the LV is considered as completely empty from the semantic point of view, this should imply that the argument structure totally depends on the noun (Gross 2004a: 167). However, both LVs and predicative nouns may contribute to the selection of the arguments of LVCs, as largely demonstrated in the literature (among others, Grimshaw and Mester 1988; Baker 1989; Mohanan 1994; Butt 1995, 1998, 2010; Collins 1997; Culicover and Jackendoff 2005).[5] Therefore, next to the concordance of lexical properties, other features also have to be considered, such as the aspectual compatibility between the predicative noun and the LV, as well as the distribution of the arguments.

---

5 This is shown, for instance, by the LVCs including 'give', for which the third argument does not depend on the noun. For instance, in Italian, in a sentence such as *Luigi ha dato un colpo a Mario* 'Luigi gave a blow to Mario', the PP *a Mario* can be replaced by a clitic (*Luigi gli ha dato un colpo* 'Luigi gave him a blow'), which means that it is governed by the verb (cf. Levin and Rappaport Hovav 2005).

4 Data selection and classification

For the purpose of this investigation, a set of 120 LVCs from different Romance languages (i.e. the standard varieties of Italian, Portuguese, Spanish, French and Romanian)[6] has been collected through monolingual and bilingual standard and combinatory dictionaries. Firstly, for Italian, the GRADIT dictionary (De Mauro 1999), the *Dizionario Combinatorio Italiano* (Lo Cascio 2013) and *CombiNet* lexicographic tool (Simone and Piunno 2017, Lenci et al. 2017) were used. Subsequently, Italian data were contrasted with the other Romance languages. Spanish data were gathered through the *Diccionario de la lengua española* (www.rae.es), as well as the monolingual combinatory dictionaries *REDES* (Bosque 2004) and *Práctico* (Bosque 2006). French data refer to the *Trésor de la Langue Française informatisé* (www.atilf.fr/tlfi), and to the *Combinaisons de mots* dictionary (Le Fur 2007). Portuguese data refer to the *Infopédia* (www.infopedia.pt) dictionary, and to the *Dicionário Priberam da Língua Portuguesa* (https://dicionario.priberam.org). Finally, Romanian data were collected through the *Dictionar explicativ al limbii romane* (https://dexonline.ro). Each translational equivalence was then tested according to native speakers' judgement of acceptability.

For the purpose of this analysis, we have considered only LVCs including a limited set of LVs, namely the signifiers for 'have', 'do/make', 'give', 'take', as described in Table 1:[7]

Table 1: The set of Light Verbs considered.

	'have'	'do/make'	'give'	'take'
Portuguese	ter	fazer	dar	tomar
Spanish	tener	hacer	dar	tomar
French	avoir	faire	donner	prendre
Italian	avere	fare	dare	prendere
Romanian	a avea	a face	a da	a lua

---

[6] In particular, as for Spanish, French and Portuguese, we have considered the standard national variety of Spain, France and Portugal respectively. Although we firstly considered Catalan as well, we subsequently excluded it from the analysis because, from a sociolinguistic perspective, not being the standard national variety, it is not homogeneous, and it shows a great amount of contact phenomena. However, we will refer to Catalan when significant phenomena emerge.
[7] The verb 'be' also has been taken into account, in relation to states (Sections 5.1.1–5.1.2). Beyond these verbs, the collection of the data has shown that different signifiers for the same meaning are possible, both from cross- and intralinguistic points of view; the variants are often LV extensions. It is worth pointing out that, among the set of LVs, the signifiers for 'put' have not been considered.

The set of LVCs we have considered (i.e. Verb + (Article) + Noun) was firstly distinguished into different groups, mainly on the basis of the aspectual features of the predicative noun. The presence of an event structure in nominalizations dates back to at least Grimshaw (1990), who refers to Pustejovsky (1988). A seminal work related to the event structure in LVCs' predicative nouns is by Gross and Kiefer (1995). Indeed, a number of studies on French have been devoted to the analysis of *Aktionsart* in nouns, in terms of aspectual features (cf., among others, Haas et al. 2008, Huyghe 2011). An important work about this topic is Simone (2003), who distinguishes three groups of nouns, i.e. *indefinite process nouns* [+ PROC] [- TEL], *definite process nouns* [+ PROC] [+ TEL], and *'nouns of once'* [- PROC] [+ TEL], on the basis of the Arabic grammar model. By 'processuality' (± PROC), he means dynamism and duration, while telicity (± TEL) is described as the possibility that the process may or may not be bounded, conceiving the *télos* as a temporal boundary, without any explicit entailment of culmination. Starting from this classification, Ježek (2016: 147) identifies four noun classes, namely state-denoting nouns [- DYNAMIC] [+ DURATIVE] [- TELIC], such as *fear, richness*, and event-denoting nouns which are distinguished in three classes: i) nouns of indefinite process [+ DYNAMIC] [+ DURATIVE] [- TELIC], such as *swimming*; ii) nouns of definite process [+ DYNAMIC] [+ DURATIVE] [+/- TELIC], such as *walk* and *construction*; iii) punctual nouns [+ DYNAMIC] [- DURATIVE] [+ TELIC], such as *start* and *hit*. Definite process nouns can be both telic and atelic: nouns such as *construction* are telic, because they entail an intended terminal point, that is a culmination; on the other hand, definite process nouns such as *walk* are atelic, since they do not have any culmination, but only a temporal boundary. In fact, both telic and atelic nominalizations can be derived from activity verbs, such as *construct* and *walk*. However, both formations are bounded, being the feature of boundedness "irrespective of whether the situation has an intended or inherent endpoint or not" (Depraetere 1995: 2–3; cf. also Talmy 2000). Actually, a major difference with respect to verb actionality is the fact that boundedness seems to be more relevant than telicity for nouns' *Aktionsart*, since the latter implies the former, as well as atelicity implies unboundedness. For this reason, beyond the traits of durativity, dynamicity and telicity, boundedness also has been considered here. As far as punctual nouns are concerned, in this class Ježek (2016: 148) merges both achievements and Simone's (2003) 'nouns of once', which are semelfactive, such as *hit* or *flash*, i.e. they express a single instance of a potential larger event. Conversely, if the event expressed by achievements (such as *start* or *arrival*) is repeated, the repetition does not form any larger event, but several instances of different events.

According to the semantic dimensions discussed above, two main groups of nouns can be identified, i.e. states and events. These can be in turn distributed among four classes, as Table 2 shows:

Table 2: Classification of nouns.

	Type of noun	Durativity	Dynamicity	Telicity	Boundedness
States	States nouns	+	–	–	–
Event	Indefinite process nouns	+	+	–	–
	Definite process nouns	+	+	+/–	+
	Punctual nouns	–	+	+	+

The different classes have been identified through co-occurrence and substitution tests.

As is well known, the relevant feature to distinguish states from events is dynamicity. This trait was evaluated through the following tests:
- co-occurrence with 'eventive' verbs, such as *take place, occur, happen* (not allowed in the case of states)

(12) *the anxiety *took place/occurred/happened yesterday*

vs

(13) the run *took place/occurred/happened yesterday*

- substitution of the entire LVC with 'do' (not admitted in the case of states, since the verb 'do' can typically substitute (dynamic) events)

(14) *I am cold* --> *You do the same*

vs

(15) *I took a walk* --> *You did the same*

Within the class of eventive nouns, indefinite and definite processes are characterized by durativity, which, on the other hand, is absent in punctual nouns. The following tests were considered to evaluate this feature:
- co-occurrence with durative expressions (e.g. *last*)

(16) his shower *lasted one hour*

vs

(17) *the blow *lasted one hour*

- co-occurrence with phasal verbs (e.g. *start, continue, end*)

(18) a. the talk *ended/started at 10.00 pm*
   b. the talk *continued for an hour*

vs
(19) a. *the scream *ended/started at 10.00 pm*
     b. *the scream *continued for an hour*

– co-occurrence with the preposition *during*

(20) during the *stroll*, he stopped frequently
vs
(21) *during the *jump*, he stopped frequently

On the other hand, when the durativity is equal, definite processes are distinguished from indefinite ones according to the presence of temporal boundaries. Boundedness was evaluated through the following test:
– co-occurrence with the adverbial construction '*of* X time' (typical of bounded nouns)

(22) *I took a* nap *of two hours*
vs
(23) **I did* gardening *of two hours*

Finally, when durativity and boundedness are equal, definite processes can be classified in turn into telic and atelic nouns. As a matter of fact, beyond the temporal boundary, telicity also entails culmination. The latter was evaluated through the following traditional test:
– co-occurrence with the adverbial time-constructions '*in* X time'

(24) *The* construction *of the building in nine months*
vs
(25) **My morning* walk *in half an hour*

5 Data discussion: the noun

In our hypothesis, the cross-linguistic (and intralinguistic) variation in the selection of LVs can be explained, at least to a certain extent, from the semantic (and syntactic) viewpoint, as this is not just a matter of idiosyncrasy. In this section, LVCs are described starting from the relationship between the *Aktionsart* of the noun and the verb, also making some considerations about the argument distribution, if relevant. This section is organized from the perspective of different noun classes.

First, Italian LVCs are taken into account and, secondly, a comparison to the other Romance languages is provided.

5.1 Stative nouns

Among the stative nouns occurring in the LVCs, for the purpose of this analysis, psychological and physiological states have been considered. They are analyzed separately, since their combinatorial behavior may slightly differ in the selected languages.

5.1.1 Psychological states

As far as psychological states are concerned, the class includes nouns of emotional states or feelings (e.g. IT *allegria* 'cheerfulness', *ansia* 'anxiety', *paura* 'fear'), sensations (e.g. IT *fastidio* 'annoyance'), mental states and aptitudes (e.g. IT *rispetto* 'respect', *costanza* 'perseverance', *competenza* 'competence'), as exemplified in Table 3, which contains a significant sample of the collected data:

Table 3: LVCs including psychological state nouns.

	Italian	French	Spanish	Portuguese	Romanian
'be scared'	avere paura	avoir peur	tener miedo	ter medo / estar com medo	a îi fi frică
'have anxiety'	avere ansia	éprouver de l'anxiété	tener ansiedad	ter ansiedade / estar com ansiedade	a fi îngrijorat
'have courage'	avere coraggio	avoir du courage	tener valor	ter coragem	a avea curaj
'have competence'	avere competenza	avoir de la compétence	tener competencia	ter competência	a avea competență
'have perseverance'	avere costanza	avoir de la constance	tener constancia	ter constância	a avea constanță / tenacitate
'have respect'	avere rispetto	avoir du respect	tener respeto	ter respeito	a avea respect
'cause joy'	dare allegria	donner de la joie	dar alegría	dar alegria	a înveseli
'give anxiety'	dare ansia	donner de l'anxiété	dar ansiedad	dar ansiedade	a provoca anxietate
'cause annoyance'	dare fastidio	déranger	fastidiar	chatear / irritar	a deranja
'give trust'	dare fiducia	donner confiance	dar confianza	dar confiança	a da încredere

Table 3 (continued)

	Italian	French	Spanish	Portuguese	Romanian
'give strength'	dare forza	donner de la force	dar fuerza	dar força	a da forță
'give courage'	fare / dare coraggio	donner du courage	dar ánimo	dar coragem	a da curaj
'evoke envy'	fare invidia	faire envie	dar envidia	fazer inveja	a provoca invidie
'move to pity'	fare compassione	faire pitié	dar lástima	–	a stârni compasiune
'scare'	fare paura	faire peur	dar miedo	fazer medo	a provoca frică

In all these cases, the basic LV in Italian is the verb *avere* 'have'.[8] The same LV selection occurs in all the Western Romance languages which have been considered. As a matter of fact, in the Iberic languages the signifiers conveying the central meaning of 'have' – namely, the notion of possession – are represented by the Portuguese *ter* and the Spanish *tener*, because of a homogenous change in the meaning of the Latin *tenere* 'hold'. As far as the event structure is concerned, in such cases there is a full semantic coherence between the nouns and the verb. As a matter of fact, the lexically full counterpart of the LV 'have' also denotes a state (i.e. possession). This means that the same *Aktionsart* is present in both the predicative noun and the verb constituting the LVC.[9] When the same aspectual values are shown by both the verb and the noun, the prototypical LVC is realized. This semantic compatibility also implies coreference between the first argument of the predicative noun and the subject of the verb; this coreference is considered one of the most important

---

8 By 'basic LV' we mean the LV prototypically selected by a certain aspectual class of nouns. Actually, in the French tradition the verbs *avoir* 'have', *faire* 'do/make' and *avoir lieu* 'take place' – which prototypically occur with 'states', 'actions' and 'eventive' or 'existential' nouns respectively –, are called *verbes génériques*, whereas by *verbe basique* the neutral verb for a specifc class of objects is meant (Section 3). Although our use of basic LV is more similar to the French use of *verbe générique*, we adopt it because i) the adjective *generic* might evoke the lexically full counterpart of the LV, and ii) our classification of predicative nouns according to their *Aktionsart* is different from the one of the French tradition.

9 Of course, with emotional states or feelings such as 'joy', 'anxiety', 'fear', the verb 'have' is used as an LV only to denote a non-permanent state developing in a specific situation. Otherwise, with more permanent states, the verb 'be' is selected. This implies the different selection of the copula in the languages that distinguish between permanent/non-permanent states (e.g. SP *ser ansioso/estar ansioso* ≈ *tener ansiedad*, PT *ser ansioso/estar ansioso/com ansiedade* ≈ *ter ansiedade*). Therefore, for these languages the construction *estar* + adjective is the effective equivalent of LVCs with 'have'. As for French, it avoids the selection of 'have' with *anxiété*, only allowing LV's extensions, such as *éprouver* or *ressentir* 'feel'.

tests for the identification of LVCs (cf. Giry-Schneider 1987: 27–28, and Gross 1989: 38). As for the argument structure, in this case the predicative psychological noun maps the semantic role of its first argument (the Experiencer) onto the argument playing the syntactic function of subject of 'have':

(26) IT *Giovanni*$_{\text{xsubject}}$ ha   *paura*$_{\text{xExperiencer}}$
         John   has fear
         'John is scared'

The semantic role of the subject is the Possessor when 'have' is lexically full. As a matter of fact, the Experiencer and the Possessor are put together in the same place of the macroroles hierarchy elaborated by Van Valin and LaPolla (1997: 127, 146; verbs denoting a state, such as 'have', usually refer to the place where something is located, according to De Miguel 2008: 575). Differently from Western Romance languages, Romanian mainly codifies possession through the verb 'be' and a locative structure (e.g. *a îi fi frică* 'be scared', lit. 'be at someone fear', *a îi fi milă* 'have compassion', lit. 'be at someone compassion'), which is a close reminder of the so-called dative of possession in Latin. This is particularly true for emotional states or feelings. Another strategy employing the verb 'be' is also frequent in Romanian, namely the copulative + adjective (e.g. *a fi îngrijorat* 'be anxious'). According to our data, the former strategy is used in the case of non-permanent states, whereas the latter describes (more) permanent states. Conversely, if the category of possession alienability fits psychological states, the former mechanism seems to be employed in the case of 'alienable possession', while the latter in the case of 'inalienable possession'. When the possession is 'inalienable', also the verb *a avea* 'have' might be used, as happens in particular with mental states and aptitudes (e.g. *a avea competență* 'have competence', *a avea curaj* 'have courage', *a avea respect* 'have respect').[10]

When the aspectual features of the noun and of the verb are not coherent, some marked lexical diathetic effects can arise, i.e. the causativity expressed by 'give' or 'do/make' in combination with a stative noun (on the concept of diathesis as the lexical counterpart of the syntactic voice, see, among others, García-Hernández 1989, 1998, 2003). In this case the LV clearly participates in the building of the semantics of the construction, as a causative marker, denoting a state caused by an event or an individual; the argument structure does not show any coreference between the subject of the LV and the first argument of the psychological noun, i.e. the coreference principle is not respected (Ježek 2004: 188):

---

[10] As to this point, it is noteworthy that French also mantains the structure with the locative + 'be' to denote the alienable possession (e.g. *Ce livre est à moi* 'this book is mine').

(27) IT Giovanni$_{\text{ysubject}}$ fa   paura$_{\text{xExperiencer yStimulus}}$ a tutti$_x$
         John   makes   fear   to everybody
         'John scares everybody'

As far as Italian is concerned, it is worth noting a split selection of *fare* 'do/make' and *dare* 'give' in the realization of the causative LVCs involving psychological nouns. In particular, *fare* 'do/make' is selected when the subject of the LV is the Stimulus, regardless of his/her will, and the indirect object is the Experiencer who enters in an emotional state strictly connected to the subject of the LV (e.g. IT *fare paura* 'scare', *fare pena* 'evoke pity', *fare invidia* 'evoke envy', *fare compassione* 'move to pity'). In this use, *fare* 'do/make' marks the 'production' of the state in which the Experiencer enters, i.e. the state codified by the basic LV *avere* 'have':

(28) IT X fa *paura* a Y   = X fa avere *paura* a Y   = Y ha *paura* di X
         X makes fear to Y   = X makes Y have fear   = Y has fear of X
         'X scares Y'   = 'X makes Y be scared'   = 'Y is scared by X'

It should be noted that in the basic LVC, i.e. the stative one (*Y ha paura di X*), the Stimulus (X) is governed by the psychological noun,[11] denoting an emotion whose emergence is directly caused. The choice between the causative LVC and its stative counterpart is often due to pragmatic reasons, i.e. the foregrounding of the Stimulus.

Also in the case of LVCs with *dare* 'give', the indirect object is the Experiencer and the subject encodes the Stimulus (e.g. IT *dare ansia* 'cause anxiety', *dare allegria* 'cause joy', *dare fastidio* 'cause annoyance'); hence, there is no coreference between the subject of the LV and the first argument of the psychological noun, namely the coreference principle is not respected:

(29) IT L'esame$_{\text{ysubject}}$ mi$_x$ dà   ansia$_{\text{xExperiencer yStimulus}}$
         The exam   me   gives   anxiety
         'The exam makes me anxious'

However, when 'give' is selected, the psychological nouns denote emotional states which may exist regardless of the presence of a Stimulus, like a latent state. There-

---

11 Indeed, the synthetic verb equivalent to the LVC is usually transitive (*avere paura* 'be scared' = *temere* 'fear', *avere invidia* 'have envy' = *invidiare* 'envy', *avere compassione* 'have compassion' = *compatire* 'pity'). This is the reason why the existence of a Stimulus – realised as the object in case of a synthetic verb – is also compulsory for the stative noun, be it realised or retrievable from the context.

fore, the Stimulus is a mere trigger indirectly causing the emergence of the state which is codified by the LVC with *avere* 'have', i.e. the raising of the emotion in the Experiencer:

(30) *X dà ansia a Y*   = *X fa avere ansia a Y*   = *Y ha ansia a causa di X*
      X gives anxiety to Y   = X gives Y anxiety   = Y has anxiety because of X
      'X makes Y anxious'   = 'X makes Y feel anxiety'   = 'Y feels anxiety because of X'

In this case, the noun encoding the psychological state does not syntactically govern the Stimulus. Moreover, while the stative counterparts of LVCs with *fare* 'do/make' are completely grammatical, those with *dare* 'give' are more marked in Italian. This is probably because of the non-obligatoriness of the Stimulus, as the causative construction is used when the Stimulus is foregrounded.[12]

The selection of the LV in the causative LVC is present also in other Romance languages. French behaves similarly to Italian. In Portuguese, the causative with the noun *compaixão* 'compassion' is impossible, whereas the stative structure is admitted (e.g. *eu tenho compaixão de alguém* 'I feel compassion of someone'); on the other hand, *dar* is selected by *pena* 'pity', which however denotes the state of suffering provoked by something (e.g. *algo dá-me pena* 'something makes me feeling compassion'), and not by somebody. Conversely, in Spanish, *dar* 'give' is chosen in all cases:

(31) a. SP *dar ansiedad* 'cause anxiety', *dar alegría* 'cause joy', *dar fuerza* 'cause force'
      b. SP *dar miedo* 'scare', *dar pena* 'evoke pity', *dar envidia* 'evoke envy', *dar lástima* 'move to pity'

The hyperextension of 'give' in this language also occurs with other nouns (Section 5.2). As far as Romanian is concerned, it choices *a da* 'give' in the same way as the other languages, while it does not employ *a face* 'do/make' as a causative marker,

---

[12] Other aspects related to these LVCs may be highlighted. As for the stative construction, in Italian the LV extension *provare* 'feel/experience' or the LV *essere in* 'be in' are generally preferred to the verb *avere* 'have' (e.g. *provare ansia* 'feel anxiety', *essere in ansia* 'be in anxiety/anxious' vs *avere ansia* 'have anxiety'). Furthermore, as for the causative LVC with *dare* 'give', the Stimulus can be [+/- HUMAN], while a preference for a [+ HUMAN] Stimulus occurs with *fare* 'do/make'. This difference is also one of the reasons for the selection of *fare/dare* by the noun *coraggio* 'courage'. While *fare coraggio* 'make courage' means 'express words of encouragement or exhortation', *dare coraggio* 'give courage' means 'make the courage emerge in someone else'. As for IT *dare fastidio* 'cause annoyance', it is noteworthy that in all other Romance languages a synthetic verb is used to express the equivalent meaning.

preferring either LV extensions (*a provoca frică* 'scare', *a stârni milă* 'evoke pity') or synthetic verbs (e.g. *a înveseli* 'give joy').

5.1.2 Physiological states

Among the set of states, it is also important to distinguish stative nouns conveying experiential meanings such as physical states or sensations (e.g. *freddo* 'cold', *caldo* 'hot'), as well as physiological states such as illnesses (e.g. *febbre* 'fever') or basic physiological needs (e.g. *fame* 'hunger', *sete* 'thirst', *sonno* 'sleep'), as exemplified in Table 4:

Table 4: LVCs including physiological state nouns.

	Italian	French	Spanish	Portuguese	Romanian
'be hot'	avere caldo	avoir chaud	tener calor	ter calor / estar com calor	a îi fi cald
'be cold'	avere freddo	avoir froid	tener frío	ter frio / estar com frio	a îi fi frig
'be hungry'	avere fame	avoir faim	tener hambre	ter fome / estar com fome	a îi fi foame
'be thirsty'	avere sete	avoir soif	tener sed	ter sede / estar com sede	a îi fi sete
'be sleepy'	avere sonno	avoir sommeil	tener sueño	ter sono / estar com sono	a îi fi somn
'have a cold'	avere il raffreddore	avoir un rhume	tener un resfriado	estar constipado	a fi răcit
'have a fever'	avere la febbre	avoir de la fièvre	tener fiebre	ter febre	a avea febră
'make someone (be) sleepy'	dare sonno	donner sommeil	dar sueño	dar sono	a provoca somn
'give heat'	dare caldo	donner chaud	dar calor	dar calor	–
'give cold'	dare freddo	donner froid	dar frío	dar frio	–
'be hot'	fare caldo	faire chaud	hacer calor	estar / fazer calor	a fi cald
'be cold'	fare freddo	faire froid	hacer frío	estar / fazer frio	a fi frig
'get cold'	prendere freddo	prendre froid	coger frío	apanhar frio	–
'take fire'	prendere fuoco	prendre feu	prender fuego	pegar fogo	a lua foc

Table 4 (continued)

	Italian	French	Spanish	Portuguese	Romanian
'get a fever'	prendere la febbre	attraper la fièvre (e.g. jaune)	coger fiebre (e.g. amarilla)	ficar com febre	a face febră
'get the flu'	prendere l'influenza	attraper la grippe	coger la gripe	apanhar / ficar com gripe	a lua gripă
'take a cold'	prendere il raffreddore	attraper un rhume	coger(se) un resfriado	apanhar um resfriado	a lua răceală

In Italian all the physiological states can combine with the stative verb 'have', which is semantically coherent (e.g. IT *avere la febbre* 'have a fever', *avere fame* 'be hungry', *avere sonno* 'be sleepy', *avere caldo* 'be hot'). The same happens in French: *avoir de la fièvre* 'have a fever', *avoir faim* 'be hungry', *avoir sommeil* 'be sleepy', *avoir chaud* 'be hot'. As happens for psychological states, the Iberic languages select as signifier the verb developed from the Latin *tenere* 'hold', instead of that developed from the Latin *habere* 'have'. On the other hand, Romanian typically employs the locative structure with *a fi* 'be' (i.e. RO *a îi fi*) in all the cases of nouns denoting short non-permanent physiological states (e.g. *a îi fi sete* 'be thirsty', *a îi fi somn* 'be sleepy', *a îi fi frig* 'be cold'), while *a avea* 'have' (e.g. *a avea febră* 'have a fever') – or the copulative *a fi* 'be' plus an adjective (e.g. *a fi răcit* 'have a cold') – with nouns describing more long-lasting physiological states.

As happens with psychological nouns, a causative semantics can be retrieved also in LVCs with physiological and physical ones. However, differently from the previous group, in Italian only *dare* 'give' in this case can be selected (e.g. IT *dare la febbre* 'give a fever', *dare fame* 'give hunger', *dare sonno* 'make someone sleepy', *dare caldo* 'give heat'). Actually, physiological states may also exist regardless of the presence of a Stimulus, which is a simple trigger indirectly causing the raising of the state:

(32) X dà *la febbre a Y*   = X fa avere *la febbre a Y*   = Y ha *la febbre a causa di X*
  X gives the fever to Y   = X makes have the fever to Y   = Y has the fever because of X
  'X makes Y have a fever'   = 'X makes Y have a fever'   = 'Y has a fever because of X'

Also in this case, the Stimulus is realized as the subject of the LV, and the Experiencer is the indirect object. There is no coreference between the first argument of the noun and the LV's subject, which is often a non-human entity:

(33) IT *L'aria condizionata*$_{ysubject}$ *mi*$_x$ dà *la febbre*$_{xExperiencer\ yStimulus}$
The air conditioning me gives the fever
'The air conditioning gives me a fever'

As far as the other Romance languages are concerned, the causative form with physiological nouns is always conveyed by 'give', with the exception of Romanian, which prefers LV extensions (*a provoca somn* 'make someone be sleepy'), and does not employ the causative expression with physical nouns (in fact, the expression *a da căldură* 'give heat' existed in Romanian, but with a very specific meaning, and it is not used anymore).

As a matter of fact, in Italian *fare* 'do/make' is selected by a very restricted set of nouns of physical state (e.g. IT *fare caldo* 'be hot', *fare freddo* 'be cold'). In such cases, it is used as an impersonal verb, as happens when the verb *essere* 'be' is selected (e.g. IT *essere caldo* 'be hot', *essere freddo* 'be cold'). The subject being a null expletive, in both cases the Stimulus is not expressed. Although being basically equivalent, the two alternatives show some slight differences in semantic terms: the selection of *fare* 'do/make' evokes the physiological perception of the physical state, namely the fact that somebody can experience the state of hot or cold. On the other hand, the selection of *essere* 'be' only refers to the meteorological state (without the implication of the perception by somebody). Hence, in the case of the selection of *fare* 'do/make' by physical state nouns, a (weak) causative feature can be identified. The non-expressed Stimulus is represented by the physical state itself. The same happens in all the Western Romance languages considered, even though, according to the native speakers, in Portuguese *estar* is also more natural than *fazer* with meteorological nouns. On the other hand, Romanian only allows the selection of *a fi* 'be' (*a fi cald* 'be hot', *a fi frig* 'be cold').

In Italian, both physiological and physical nouns can also select *prendere* 'take'. As happens with *dare* 'give' and *fare* 'do/make', also in the case of LVCs with *prendere* 'take' the aspectual features of the noun and of the verb are not coherent. In particular, with *prendere* 'take' an inchoative or incremental value arise, since the verb acquires the meaning of 'X (gradually) enters in a state', regardless of the fact that the coreference between the first argument of the predicative noun and the subject of the LVCs is kept, exactly as happens in stative LVCs (e.g. IT *avere la febbre* 'have a fever'):[13]

---

[13] For the difference between inchoative and incremental, see Haspelmath (1987). The inchoative aspectual value emerges in the case of illnesses (e.g. IT *prendere il Covid* 'catch Covid'), while it is incremental in the case of perception of physical states (e.g. IT *prendere freddo* 'take cold'). In the case of illnesses, Italian also selects *prendersi* 'take oneself', where the clitic *-si* highlights the male-factive nature of the Experiencer. Also in the case of a physical state usually not physiologically per-

(34) IT   Gianni$_{\text{xsubject}}$ ha preso la febbre$_{\text{xExperienceyStimulus}}$
          John   has taken the fever
          (a causa dell'aria condizionata/da Luigi$_y$)
          (due to the air conditioning/from Luis)
          'John has taken fever (due to the air conditioning/from Luis)'

Furthermore, some diathetic effects can arise when *prendere* 'take' is selected, namely a sort of 'anticausative effect' (Haspelmath 1993: 91–92) in alternance to the construction with *dare* 'give'. This alternative is chosen when the entry in the physiological state is considered from the perspective of the Experiencer, without a Stimulus, or when the Stimulus is backgrounded, opposite to what happens in causative LVCs. If the Stimulus cannot be expressed or understood, only the aspectual – inchoative (or incremental) – meaning is relevant (i.e. IT *prendere sonno* 'fall asleep').

It is worth noting some differences concerning the anticausative/inchoative structure, where the extended use of the Italian *prendere* 'take' has no perfect correspondence in the other Romance languages, with the exception of French *prendre* with nouns of physical state, such as *froid* 'cold' and *chaud* 'hot', but not as *sommeil* 'sleep' (with which the synthetic verb *s'endormir* is preferred). As for *prendere sonno* 'fall asleep' also Spanish, Portuguese and Romanian prefer a synthetic verb, e.g. *dormirse* and *adormecer, a adormi* respectively. Physical states, instead, select *coger* 'take' in Spanish and *apanhar* 'take' in Portuguese, both differing from the basic LV *tomar* 'take'. It is worth noting that Spanish also selects *coger* for illnesses (e.g. SP *coger la gripe* 'get the flu', *coger una nuemonía* 'get pneumonia', *coger el Covid* 'catch Covid'), while Portuguese and French prefer the LV extensions *apanhar* and *attraper* 'catch' respectively (in Brazilian Portuguese *pegar* is preferred to *apanhar* both for physical and physiological states).[14] As far as Romanian is concerned,

---

ceived, the inchoative/incremental value can be expressed by *prendere* 'take' (e.g. IT *prendere fuoco* 'take fire', the anticausative counterpart of *dare fuoco* 'give fire'). On the other hand, in Italian the initial phase of the physiological state of 'being thirsty' or 'hungry' cannot be expressed by *prendere* 'take' LVCs (e.g. IT **prendere fame* 'take hunger', **prendere sete* 'take thirst'). It is important to note that the use of *prendere* 'take' is even less regular with psychological states (e.g. *prendere coraggio* 'take courage', *prendersi uno spavento* 'take fright' vs **prendere ansia* 'take anxiety'), where the entry in a state from the perspective of the Experiencer may not always be focused. In the case of *prendere coraggio* 'take courage', the same meaning can be expressed by *farsi coraggio* 'make oneself courage'. A more in-depth investigation is needed on this point.

14 As for Iberic languages, we thank María Dolores Jiménez López for her insightful comments on the use of LVs with 'fever': in the case of SP *fiebre*, the LV *coger* is not used as in other cases (e.g. *coger el Covid, coger la gripe*), since the fever is only an epiphenomenon of an illness. As a matter of fact, *coger la fiebre* 'take a fever' can only occur if it is modified by a specification of the 'type' of fever, actually denoting a disease (e.g. *coger la fiebre amarilla* 'take yellow fever'). The same

virally diffused illnesses, namely taken from outside, require *a lua* 'take' (e.g. *a lua gripă* 'get the flu', lit. 'take flue', *a lua Covid* 'catch Covid', lit. 'take Covid'), while those internally developed (e.g. *febră* 'fever', *pneumonie* 'pneumonia' and *indigestie* 'indigestion') employ *a face* 'do/make', which seems to have the 'effective' meaning of 'production' of the illness.

5.2 Eventive nouns

Eventive nouns have been distinguished into three classes, i.e. indefinite process nouns (Section 5.2.1), definite process nouns (Section 5.2.2) and punctual nouns (Section 5.2.3), in order to evaluate whether their combinatorial features differ in the selected languages. Differently from stative nouns, this group more frequently selects dynamic verbs, such as 'do/make', 'give', 'take'.

5.2.1 Indefinite process nouns

As far as indefinite process nouns are concerned, the occurrences in an LVC are rather restricted, as the small set of examples included in Table 5 shows:

Table 5: LVCs including indefinite process nouns.

	Italian	French	Spanish	Portuguese	Romanian
'go swimming'	fare nuoto	faire du natage	hacer natación	fazer natação	a face înot
'do aerobics'	fare aerobica	faire de l'aérobic	hacer aeróbic	fazer aeróbica	a face aerobică
'make chaos'	fare caos	faire du desordre	provocar el caos	fazer estragos	a face dezordine
'make confusion'	fare confusione	faire du desordre	provocar confusión	fazer confusão	a face zgomot
'make noise'	fare rumore	faire du bruit	hacer ruido	fazer barulho	a face zgomot

---

happens in French, and the issue probably also emerges in Portuguese as well, where *febre* 'fever' selects *ficar com*, whereas *resfriado* 'cold' selects *apanhar*. In Italian *prendere la febbre da qualcuno* 'take a fever from someone else' has the meaning of 'get the flu'; if the fever develops because of an external cause (e.g. the air conditioning), the construction with the *-si* clitic (*prendersi*) seems more natural.

Table 5 (continued)

	Italian	French	Spanish	Portuguese	Romanian
'give assistance'	dare / fare assistenza	porter / prêter assistance	dar asistencia	dar assistência	a oferi asistență
'give help'	dare aiuto	donner de l'aide	dar ayuda	dar ajuda	a da o mână de ajutor

The scarce presence of these nouns in LVCs may be due to their specific aspectual properties: being unbounded eventive nouns, they are necessarily atelic, like their synthetic verb equivalents (e.g. IT *fare nuoto* 'go swimming' vs *nuotare* 'swim'). Thus, the analytic and synthetic verbs seem to overlap semantically. In fact, in Italian *fare nuoto* 'go swimming' differs from *nuotare* 'swim' since the former denotes a regular sport activity, while the latter describes swimming in general, without any implications of practicing a physical activity. Indeed, these LVCs typically include also sports nouns (e.g. *aerobics, fitness, judo, athletics, gymnastics*), which do not necessarily have a (synthetic) verbal counterpart. In all these cases, the basic LV is *fare* 'do/make' in Italian, as well as in the other languages considered. Other indefinite process nouns which only select *fare* 'do/make' are those denoting a situation of disorder or tumult (e.g. IT *confusione* 'confusion', *rumore* 'noise', *caos* 'chaos'). In this case, *fare* 'do/make' seems to keep the meaning of 'production' of its semantically full equivalent, however what is produced is not a concrete object, but rather an effect. Also in this case, the synthetic verbal counterpart does not exist, so that such LVCs fill a gap in the language lexicon. For all these occurrences, 'do/make' is employed in all the Romance languages, although in Spanish the use of the LV extension *provocar* (or of the synthetic verb *liar*) is preferred.

This group of LVCs also seems to include other kinds of indefinite process nouns, such as, in Italian, *aiuto* 'help' and *assistenza* 'assistance', requiring either *fare* 'do/make' or *dare* 'give'. The ones selecting *fare* 'do/make' (IT **fare aiuto* is, in fact, impossible) typically give birth to LVCs denoting professions or the tasks such professions entail (e.g. IT *fare assistenza a un esame* 'assist with an exam'),[15] while the ones selecting *dare* usually denote economical and charitable aid; even though they express indefinite processes, they probably have to be conceived as the pluralization of singular episodes of instantiation of the state of affairs. Furthermore, the selection of *dare* 'give' seems to imply the involvement of a Recipient (e.g. IT

---

15 This is different from *assistere a un esame* 'to attend to an exam'. The LV *fare* 'do/make' is also used with *nomina agentis* (e.g. IT *fare l'assistente* 'do the assistant'). On this, cf. La Fauci and Mirto (2003).

dare assistenza a qualcuno 'give assistance to someone'), which is not compulsorily required by *fare* 'do/make' (e.g. IT *fare assistenza online* 'assist in online'). These types of LVCs probably deserve an in-depth analysis, since in such cases the selection of an LV extension (e.g. FR *fournir de l'aide, porter/prêter assistance*; SP *prestar ayuda/asistencia*, PT *prestar ajuda/auxílio/assistência*, RO *a oferi asistență*) seems more natural to all the speakers contributing as informants of the other Romance languages.[16]

5.2.2 Definite process nouns

The group of LVCs including nouns of definite process is very large and heterogenous. Among others, nouns describing motion and other physical activities (e.g. IT *nuotata* 'swim', *camminata* 'walk', *bagno* 'bath'), as well as communication (e.g. IT *spiegazione* 'explanation', *risposta* 'answer') and cognitive process nouns (e.g. IT *scelta* 'choice', *decisione* 'decision') occur in this set of LVCs (see Table 6):

Table 6: LVCs including definite process nouns.

	Italian	French	Spanish	Portuguese	Romanian
'go for a stroll'	fare un giro	faire un tour	dar una vuelta	dar uma volta	a da o tură
'take a walk'	fare una passeggiata	faire une promenade	dar un paseo	dar um passeio	a face o plimbare
'take a swim'	fare una nuotata	nager	nadar	dar um mergulho	a înota
'take a run'	fare una corsa	faire une course	dar(se) una carrera	dar uma corrida	a alerga
'take a walk'	fare una camminata	faire une balade	dar(se) / hacer(se) una caminata	fazer uma caminhada	a face o plimbare
'do a trip'	fare una gita	faire une excursion	hacer una excursión	fazer uma excursão	a face o excursie
'do a journey'	fare un viaggio	faire un voyage	hacer un viaje	fazer uma viagem	a face o călătorie
'take a nap'	fare una dormita	faire un somme	echar(se) una siesta	tirar uma soneca	a trage un pui de somn

---

16 According to the native speakers that we have consulted, the usual expression for Romanian is *a da o mână de ajutor*, to which *a da ajutor* is equivalent. Actually, also in Italian *aiuto* 'help' can be used both as an indefinite process noun (*dare aiuto* 'give help') and a definite process one (*dare un aiuto* 'give a help'; see Section 5.2.2).

Table 6 (continued)

	Italian	French	Spanish	Portuguese	Romanian
'take a bath'	fare il bagno	prendre un bain	darse un baño / bañarse	tomar banho	a face baie
'take a shower'	fare una doccia	prendre une douche	darse una ducha / ducharse	tomar duche	a face duș
'make a choice'	fare una scelta	faire un choix	hacer una elección	fazer uma escolha	a face o alegere
'take a decision'	prendere una decisione	prendre une decision	tomar una decisión	tomar uma decisão	a lua o decizie
'ask a question'	fare una domanda	poser une question	hacer una pregunta	fazer uma pergunta	a pune o întrebare
'make a comment'	fare un commento	faire un commentaire	hacer un comentario	fazer um comentário	a face un comentariu
'make a compliment'	fare un complimento	faire des compliments	hacer un halago / cumplido	fazer / dar um elogio	a face un compliment
'give a speech'	fare un discorso	faire un discours	hacer / dar un discurso	fazer um discurso	a ține un discurs
'do / give a conference'	fare / dare una conferenza	faire / donner une conférence	dar una conferencia	dar uma conferência	a ține o conferință
'have a chat'	fare una chiacchierata	faire la causette	tener una charla	ter uma conversa	a povesti
'make a list'	fare un elenco	faire une liste	hacer una lista	fazer uma lista	a face o listă
'make criticism'	fare una critica	critiquer / faire la critique (de)	hacer una crítica	fazer uma crítica	a face o critică
'make a promise'	fare una promessa	faire une promesse	hacer una promesa	fazer uma promessa	a face o promisiune
'make a proposal'	fare una proposta	faire une proposition	hacer una proposición / propuesta	fazer uma proposta	a face o propunere
'give a suggestion'	dare un consiglio	donner un conseil	dar un consejo	dar um conselho	a da un sfat
'give an answer'	dare una risposta	donner une réponse	dar una respuesta	dar uma resposta	a da un răspuns
'give an explanation'	dare una spiegazione	donner une explication	dar una explicación	dar uma explicação	a da o explicație

As far as physical activities are concerned, the group of motion nouns corresponding to inergative (thus, atelic) motion verbs emerges (e.g. IT *fare una nuotata* 'take a swim', *fare una camminata* 'take a walk'). Such nouns denote the excerpting of a portion of an atelic activity, to which some external boundaries are added

(Talmy 2000: 51). Thus, the Italian noun *nuotata* 'swim' denotes a single occurrence of the event described by *nuotare* 'swim'. In the case of *nuotata* (but also *camminata* 'walk', *passeggiata* 'stroll'), the notion of 'a single instantiation' is given by the Italian suffix *-ata* (Gaeta 2002) – which is also realized in some other Romance languages (*-ada/-ata/-ato* suffix of Spanish, *-ada* of Portuguese, as well as French *-ade*). In such cases, the single instantiation implies countability, and this allows co-occurrence with the indefinite article (e.g. IT **fare un nuoto* 'do a swimming' vs *fare una nuotata* 'take a swim'). As a matter of fact, the indefinite article implies *per se* the portion excerption; therefore, in these cases, part of the semantics lies on the construction itself. It is worth noting that the indefinite article also precedes motion nouns not employing the suffix (e.g. IT *fare un giro* 'go for a stroll'). French behaves like Italian. Conversely, in the 'lateral' Romance languages (cf. for instance Bartoli 1925), the situation seems to be more complex. In Spanish and Portuguese motion nouns mainly select *dar* 'give', with the exception of long-lasting motion activities (e.g. SP *hacer una excursión* 'do an excursion', PT *fazer uma viagem* 'do a trip').[17] Romanian shows a broader extension of *a face* 'do/make' (e.g. *a face o plimbare* 'take a walk'), but in the case of short-lasting motion nouns it can select *a da* 'give' (e.g. *a da o tură* 'go for a stroll'); sometimes in Romanian the portion excerption is not expressed (cf. *a înota* 'swim', which has no bounded counterparts, as also happens in French and Spanish with the equivalent synthetic verbs).

Italian coherently selects *fare* 'do/make' also to express other physical activities, such as *fare una dormita* 'take a nap', *fare un bagno* 'take a bath' or *fare una doccia* 'take a shower'. In these cases, the definite article is also admitted in Italian (e.g. *fare il bagno* 'take a bath' lit. 'do the bath', *fare la doccia* 'take a shower' lit. 'do the shower'). Even though the latter are not deverbal nouns, they correspond to an activity which can be either transitive or reflexive, as it is expressed by the synthetic counterparts *lavare* 'wash, shower' (transitive) or *lavarsi* 'wash oneself, shower oneself' (reflexive). In the reflexive variant the clitic *-si* can be added to the LV (e.g. IT *fare una doccia* 'take a shower' vs. *farsi una doccia* 'take (oneself) a shower'), to highlight the coreference between the Agent and the beneficiary. This coreference implies middle semantics, whose distinctive trait is the affectedness of the subject (Kemmer 1993). This semantics is conveyed in French and Portuguese by the verb 'take' (i.e. FR *prendre une douche*, PT *tomar duche* 'take a shower'), which highlights the perspective of the subject, whereas in Spanish its converse *dar* 'give' together with the clitic *-se* is preferred (i.e. *darse una ducha* 'take a shower'

---

[17] It is worth noting the twofold possibility of *dar/hacer* in Spanish also in co-occurrence with *caminata* 'walk'. In Portuguese the duration of the motion event can also be highlighted by the verb *ter* (Duarte et al. 2010: 28; fn. 6).

lit. 'give oneself a shower', *darse un baño* 'take a bath' lit. 'give oneselfe a bath'; cf. also the synthetic verb *ducharse*, which is much more frequent than the LVC. As regards the equivalent of Italian *fare una dormita* 'take a nap', French behaves likewise, whereas in Spanish the reflexive *echarse* 'throw' is selected; Portuguese and Romanian make a similar lexical choice through the selection of *tirar* and *a trage* 'pull' respectively. That is to say, while the choice of *fare* 'do/make' marks the development of the process, the selection of the signifiers for 'take' and 'give' plus a reflexive clitic (or of less basic LVs such as 'throw' or 'pull') can be conceived as bringing to the foreground the coincidence of the Agent with the beneficiary of the action. As a matter of fact, according to Kemmer (1993: 55), physical actions – not only body care, but also motion – are prototypical instances of the middle category, since either a unique affected participant (e.g. SP *dar un paseo* 'take a walk', *darse una carrera* 'take a run')[18] or two potential coreferential participants (e.g. SP *darse una ducha*) are involved.

The distinctive trait of middle semantics – i.e. the involvement of the subject by undertaking the responsibility of the decision as the endpoint of an evaluation process – can also be invoked to explain the selection of 'take' not only in Italian *prendere una decisione* 'take a decision', but also, coherently, in the other languages considered.[19] On the other hand, the verb *fare* 'do/make' is selected by the noun *scelta* 'choice', because the construction highlights the internal development of the process of choice; also in this case, this is true not only for Italian, but for the other Romance languages as well (FR *faire un choix*, SP *hacer (una) elección*, PT *fazer uma escolha*, RO *a face o alegere*).

In Italian, the LV *fare* 'do/make' is usually required by definite process nouns derived by performative verbs such as *fare una domanda* 'ask a question', *fare una proposta* 'make a proposal', *fare un complimento* 'make a compliment'. Some occurrences, on the other hand, require the LV *dare* 'give' (e.g. IT *dare una spiegazione* 'give an explanation', *dare un consiglio* 'give a (piece of) advice'). In the latter, the

---

18 Cf. also IT *farsi una passeggiata* 'take a walk'.
19 The decision is undertaken by somebody in his/her own interest (and, potentially, another's). This coincides with the traditionally called 'middle of interest'. On the other hand, the aspect of the noun 'decision' is not completely clear. Indeed, the noun does not answer uniformly to the different tests detecting durativity (e.g. IT *la decisione è durata un'ora* 'the decision lasted one hour', *durante la decisione* 'during the decision', but ?*una decisione di un'ora* 'a decision of one hour' and **iniziare una decisione* 'start a decision'). This means that the duration probably pertains to the discussion phase preceding the moment in which the decision is effectively taken. In this perspective, the choice of 'take' is not only due to diathetic reasons, but also to aspectual reasons, focalizing the final and real moment of decision, as the equivalence with *prendere una risoluzione* 'take a resolution' confirms.

selection of *dare* 'give' is related to the fact that the noun represents an act of verbal communication usually stimulated by the Recipient (e.g. IT *dare una risposta* 'give an answer'), whereas, when *fare* 'do/make' is selected, the potential Recipient is not salient. On the other hand, the presence of an audience may allow both the selection of *fare* 'do/make' – when the focus is on the action – and of *dare* 'give' – if the Recipient is foregrounded (e.g. IT *fare/dare una conferenza* 'do/give a conference'). These uses generally correspond in the other Romance languages, with the exception of a preference for *dar* 'give' in Iberic languages, in cases such as 'conference' (e.g. SP *dar una conferencia*, PT *dar uma conferência*), where Romanian prefers *a ține* 'hold', instead.[20]

5.2.3 Punctual nouns

The class of punctual nouns includes nouns of blow (e.g. IT *frustata* 'lash', *calcio* 'kick', *pugno* 'punch'), gestures of love (e.g. IT *abbraccio* 'hug', *bacio* 'kiss'), motion nouns (e.g. IT *balzo* 'leap', *salto* 'jump', *passo* 'step'), nouns of verbal or non-verbal communication (e.g. IT *ordine* 'order', *permesso* 'permission', *consenso* 'consensus'), as well as nouns of vocal sounds (e.g. IT *grido* 'shout', *urlo* 'scream', *sospiro* 'sigh'); see Table 7:

---

[20] In the case of *conferenza* 'conference', as well as with other nouns of definite processes that imply a large participation of people (e.g. *riunione* 'meeting', *cerimonia* 'cerimony', *spettacolo* 'show'), the event is bounded, but it has a duration which is usually not brief. In Italian such items might also co-occur with the LV *avere* 'have', which highlights the long duration of the event denoted by the noun (e.g. *avere una conferenza* 'have a conference', *avere una riunione* 'have a meeting': for instance, I can answer "Scusa, ho una riunione" 'sorry, I have a meeting' if my husband calls me when I am having a meeting). Likewise, in Italian the LV *tenere* 'hold' can be selected (e.g. *tenere un discorso* 'hold a speech', *tenere una conferenza* 'hold a conference') – as in Romanian – when the event is viewed in the perspective of the person who manages it. This is the only possibility for Romanian (e.g. *a ține un discurs, a ține o conferință*). In the Iberic languages, definite process nouns expressing acts of bidirectional verbal communication, inherently long-lasting, such as 'chat', always select 'have' (SP *tener una charla*, PT *ter uma conversa*), whereas those requiring an audience sometimes allow both 'do/make' and 'give' (e.g. SP *hacer un discurso* vs *dar un discurso*; PT *fazer um discurso* vs *dar um discurso*) – as in Italian. In other cases, the selection of 'do/make' is extremely rare and is not accepted by informants (cf. SP **hacer una conferencia*), whereas LV extensions are preferred (e.g. SP *pronunciar* 'pronounce', and, more refined, *dictar* 'dictate'). In French with *questionne* 'question' the extension *poser* 'put' is used, because *faire une questionne* means 'bring something up for discussion'.

Table 7: LVCs including punctual nouns.

	Italian	French	Spanish	Portuguese	Romanian
'give a whiplash'	dare una frustata	donner un coup de fouet	dar un latigazo	dar um açoite	a biciui
'give a blow'	dare un colpo	donner un coup	dar un golpe	dar um golpe	a da o lovitură
'give a punch'	dare un pugno	donner un coup de poing	dar un puñetazo	dar um soco / um murro	a da un pumn
'give a kick'	dare un calcio	donner un coup de pied	dar una patada / un puntapié	dar um chuto / um pontapé	a da un şut
'give a slap'	dare uno schiaffo	donner une gifle	dar una bofetada	dar uma bofetada	a da o palmă
'give a hug'	dare un abbraccio	embracer	dar un abrazo	dar um abraço	a îmbrăţişa
'give a kiss'	dare un bacio	donner un baiser	dar un beso	dar um beijo	a săruta / a da un sărut
'give a caress'	dare / fare una carezza	donner / faire une caresse	dar / hacer una caricia	dar / fazer uma carícia	a mângâia
'make a leap'	fare un balzo	faire un bond	dar un brinco	dar um pulo / um salto	a face o săritură
'make a step'	fare un passo	faire un pas	dar un paso	dar um passo	a face un pas
'make a jump'	fare un salto	faire un bond	dar un salto	dar um salto	a face un salt
'give a shout'	fare / dare un grido	pousser un cri	dar un grito	dar um grito	a striga / a da a strigăt
'take a sigh'	fare / dare un sospiro	pousser un soupir	dar un suspiro	dar um suspiro	a ofta / a suspina
'sneeze'	fare uno starnuto	éternuer	dar un estornudo	dar um espirro	a strănuta
'give consent'	dare il consenso	donner son accord	dar el consentimiento	dar (o) consentimento	a da consimţământul
'give permission'	dare il permesso	donner la permission	dar permiso	dar permissão	a permite / a da voie
'give an order'	dare un ordine	donner un ordre	dar una orden	dar uma ordem	a da un ordin
'give a signal'	dare un segnale	donner un signal	dar la señal	dar um sinal	a da un semnal

In Italian, nouns denoting a blow select the LV *dare* 'give'. These LVCs imply a transfer of the blow from an Agent towards a Recipient, which is always present. In this case, the Agent is the origin of the movement of a body part coming into contact with the Recipient; the contact may sometimes be mediated by the instrument which is used to strike. This is a general use among the languages we have considered. It is worth noting that French never employs deverbal nouns for blows, but a so-called 'support noun' (cf. Simone 2013: 251) *coup* 'blow', which – being a prototypical instance of Simone's (2003) 'nouns of once' (Section 4) – highlights the punctuality of the event and co-occurs with the noun denoting the concrete instrument or body part employed to strike (e.g. FR *coup de fouet* 'whiplash', *coup de poing* 'punch'). While synthetic blow verbs are usually transitive, the LVCs with 'give' imply the expression of the hit entity as an indirect object, as in the following examples:

(35) a. IT *Maria* schiaffeggia *Luigi*
         'Mary slaps Luis'
     b. IT *Maria* dà uno schiaffo *a Luigi*
         'Mary gives a slap to Luis'

Even in the case of *bacio* 'kiss' and *abbraccio* 'hug', in Italian the selected LV is *dare*, whereas *carezza* 'caress' can select both *dare* 'give' and *fare* 'do/make'; when *dare* 'give' is selected, the transfer of the metaphorical object (caress) to the Recipient is foregrounded. It is important to note that the use of 'give' signals the fact that the transfer is unidirectional (36a), while the synthetic counterpart – in particular 'kiss'– usually denotes bidirectional transfer, being realized as a reflexive with the reciprocal function (37a). Clearly, this does not exclude the occurrence of the synthetic verb in the case of the unidirectional transfer (36b), as well as the LVC in the case of the bidirectional one (37b). Nevertheless, the uses in (36a-37a) are the unmarked ones:

(36) a. IT *Maria* dà un bacio *a Luigi*
         'Mary gives a kiss to Luis'
     b. IT *Maria* bacia *Luigi*
         'Mary kisses Luis'

(37) a. IT *Maria e Luigi* si baciano
         'Mary and Luis kiss each other'
     b. IT *Maria e Luigi* si danno un bacio
         'Mary and Luis give each other a kiss'

On the other hand, when in Italian *fare* 'do/make' is selected by *carezza* 'caress', it highlights the occurrence of the event itself. With gestures of love, the contact specifically concerns a body part (e.g. the lips, the arms), but also involves the movement of the whole body of the Agent. Both with blow nouns and gestures of love nouns, a discretization of an atelic activity occurs (e.g. the hitting, the punching, the kicking, and the kissing, the embracing, the caressing), which can imply a unique occurrence or its pluralization (e.g. IT *dare un colpo* 'give a blow' vs *dare colpi* 'give blows'). The same happens in all the Romance languages considered; nevertheless, Romanian does not always express this discretization, preferring the corresponding synthetic verb, mainly with nouns of gesture of love.

Conversely, a relevant and well-known difference concerns the selection of the verb by motion nouns such as 'step' and 'jump': in Portuguese and Spanish 'give' is selected, while in French, Italian and Romanian 'do/make' is chosen. Even in this case, the selection of 'do/make' highlights the production of the event itself, whereas the choice of 'give' is coherent with what happens with definite process nouns expressing motion (Section 5.2.2): in both cases the potential atelic event (e.g. SP *pasear*, PT *passear* 'walk') is bounded. In the case of definite process nouns, boundedness is conveyed by a portion excerption (e.g. SP *dar un paseo*, PT *dar um passeio* 'take a walk'); in the case of punctual nouns it is expressed by the excerption of a unit, which can be pluralized (e.g. SP *dar un paso*, PT *dar um passo* 'make a step').[21]

The use of *dare* 'give' may often be connected to the foregrounding of the Recipient. This is more evident with nouns of verbal or non-verbal communication that promote a reaction by the Recipient, i.e. a perlocutive act (e.g. *dare un ordine* a qualcuno 'give someone an order', *dare un permesso* a qualcuno 'give someone permission', *dare il consenso* a qualcuno 'give someone consent'). In these cases, a sort of causative value may be implied: it emerges thanks to the presence of a causer (the Agent) who orders, permits, consents, making the causee (the Recipient) doing something. Differently from instances such as *dare ansia* 'give anxiety', where a state is caused (cf. Section 5.1.1 and ex. (29)), in these cases there is coreference between the subject of the LV and the first argument of the noun (*Luigi$_x$* dà un ordine$_{xAgent\ yRecipient}$ *a Maria$_y$* 'Luis gives an order to Mary'). This means that *dare* is the basic LV in co-occurrence with these substantially deontic nouns.[22] Also

---

21 As for nouns of blow and gesture of love, Catalan is worth noting: for the former, this language, as French, can employ 'support nouns' (e.g. *cop* 'blow' in *donar un cop de puny* 'give a punch', *donar un cop de fuet* 'give a whiplash'), next to 'nouns of once' formed by the suffix *-ada* plus a noun of the concrete instrument which is used to hit (e.g. *puntada de peu* 'kick'); for the latter, Catalan always selects the verb *fer* 'do/make' (e.g. *fer una abraçada* 'give a hug', *fer un petó* 'give a kiss', *fer una carícia* 'caress'). The LV *fer* is also selected by motion nouns (e.g. *fer un salt* 'make a leap', *fer una passa* 'make a step').
22 On the other hand, when an order/permission/consent is 'given', the causee 'has' it. The selection of 'have' with this type of nouns might seem rather odd, given the durativity of this LV. However, in this case 'have' means to possess the order/permission/consent received as the result of ordering/permitting/consenting. Therefore, in 'have an order/permission/consent', 'have' seems to co-occur more with result nouns than with eventive nouns, since what they denote is more similar to 'things' than to 'events'. From this perspective, the pertinent feature of such nouns in these LVCs is perhaps

in the other Romance languages considered, the causative value of these LVCs is expressed through the counterparts of *dare* 'give'.

Finally, the presence of a Recipient may also be entailed in the case of LVCs with nouns of vocal sound (*dare un grido (a qualcuno)* 'give a shout to someone', *dare un urlo (a qualcuno)* 'give a scream to someone'). In these cases, either the nouns might have a communicative content, which is transferred to the Recipient, or the Recipient is the potential perceiver of the sound, even when it is missing. As a matter of fact, if the Recipient is absent, *dare* 'give' highlights the force of emission of the first and unique argument, which is the sound source, as shown by the Italian extensions *mandare* 'send', *gettare* 'throw', *emettere* 'emit' (i.e. IT *mandare un grido* lit. 'send a shout', *gettare un grido* lit. 'throw a shout', *emettere un urlo* lit. 'emit a scream'). It is worth noting that Italian also admits the verb *fare* 'do/make' with *grido* and *urlo*, differently from the other Romance languages, which typically employ 'give'. On the other hand, in the case of vocal sounds which do not possess any communicative content (e.g. IT *starnuto* 'sneeze', *sospiro* 'sigh'), in Italian the LV *fare* 'do/make' is selected, which underlines the event production. Conversely, all the other Romance languages analyzed univocally select 'give' (i.e. Spanish and Portuguese) or highlight the force of emission through an LV extension, such as *pousser* 'push' in French, which sometimes prefers the synthetic strategy (e.g. *éternuer* 'sneeze'); this strategy is the only possibility for Romanian (e.g. *a ofta / a suspina* 'suspire', *a strănuta* 'sneeze').

---

persistence, namely a trait of objects and not of actions (Croft 1991: 62-65), which is different from the effective aspectual trait of stativity; persistence is very similar to Givón's (1979: 320-324) the notion of 'time stability', characterizing the long-persisting entities, like trees, books, houses. This means that the order/permission/consent is 'had' as happens for concrete objects. Consequently, in these cases 'have' has the meaning of 'possession', which is similar to that of the semantically full counterpart of the LV. From this perspective, these nouns are very close to 'pure nouns' along the verb-noun continuum (cf. Simone 2003) and in this case the LV is less empty. In fact, 'have' can co-occur also with indefinite process nouns expressing the practice of physical activities (e.g. IT *nuoto*: *avere nuoto alle cinque* 'have swimming at five o'clock') and with definite process nouns (e.g. IT *viaggio*: *in luglio ho un viaggio in Cina* 'in July I have a trip to China'); also in these cases the nouns do not effectively denote events, but the result of a commitment, which persists until it is fulfilled. This is also a possible interpretation when 'have' co-occurs with communication nouns (e.g. IT *riunione* 'meeting'/*conferenza* 'conference'; Section 5.2.2, fn. 20), if the event is scheduled rather than ongoing. This issue would deserve more attention.

6 Data discussion: the Light Verb

This section is aimed at focusing on the compatibility between the two LVC components from the perspective of the LV. In particular, we provide a general overview of the uses of each LV considered – 'have' (Section 6.1), 'do/make' (Section 6.2), 'give' (Section 6.3), 'take' (Section 6.4) – with the different classes of nouns analyzed in Section 5. Table 8 summarizes the LVs selected in the Romance languages considered:

Table 8: Correspondence between LV and noun classes in the different languages considered.

Type of noun			Italian	French	Spanish	Portuguese	Romanian
States	Psychological nouns	'have' 'give' 'do/make'	avere dare fare	avoir donner faire	tener dar	ter dar fazer	a avea / a fi[23] a da
States	Physiological nouns	'have' 'give' 'do/make' 'take/get'	avere dare fare prendere	avoir donner faire prendre	tener dar hacer coger / prender	ter dar fazer apanhar / pegar	a avea / a fi a da a lua / a face
Event	Indefinite process nouns	'give' 'do/make'	dare fare	donner faire	dar hacer	dar fazer	a da a face
Event	Definite process nouns	'give' 'do/make' 'take/get'	dare fare prendere	donner faire prendre	dar hacer tomar	dar fazer tomar	a da a face a lua
Event	Punctual nouns	'give' 'do/make'	dare fare	donner faire	dar hacer	dar fazer	a da a face

In particular, Table 8 suggests some correlations between the nouns' aspectual properties and those of the LVs they combine with.[24] In the following, we systematize such correlations, in order to i) sketch a homogenous picture of each LV distribution within the LVCs having different aspectual classes, and ii) highlight the prototypical selection vs the aspectual/diathetic effects that emerge in the non-prototypical combinations.

---

23 As for Romanian, *a fi* 'be' has been included together with *a avea* 'have', since in this language the possession is also codified through 'be' + locative structure (Section 5.1.1–5.1.2).
24 This also confirms what has been highlighted in some analyses devoted to single languages: for example, the close compatibility between the Spanish *tener* and nouns denoting states, as well as the one between LVs like *dar, hacer, tomar* and nouns referring to actions, which have been demonstrated by Sanromán Vilas (2011). Cf. also Gross (2004b: 347) for French.

6.1 'Have'

The Romance signifiers for 'have' typically co-occur with nouns denoting non-dynamic situations, i.e. states (Section 5.1). As observed above, this is due to the aspectual compatibility between such nouns and the lexically full 'have', which is a stative verb. This implies that signifiers for 'have' are the basic LVs for states in Romance languages. When the LV is basic both (i) the coreferential and (ii) the reduction tests (see Gross 1981: 39, Giry-Schneider 1987: 28) can be applied: thus, i) if someone 'has', for instance, a psychological state such as fear, he/she is the subject of the LV and the Experiencer of the psychological noun at the same time (see ex. (26): *Giovanni*$_{\text{xsubject}}$ *ha paura*$_{\text{xExperiencer}}$); ii) if the LV 'have' is omitted, the whole predication stands on the stative noun, which governs the constituent being the subject of the LVC as its argument (e.g. *la paura di Giovanni*$_x$). In these conditions, the selection of the basic LV shows the perspective of the Experiencer, which is probably the most relevant participant in such a frame. In Romanian, the locative structure with *a fi* 'be' is largely preferred to *a avea* 'have', with emotional, physiological and physical states requiring an Experiencer. In these cases, the Experiencer is not realized in the subject position – which is occupied by the stative noun – but as a locative. Of course, for Romanian, the coreference and the reduction tests are inapplicable, unless one considers the coreference with the locative – rather than the subject – both of the Experiencer (test of coreference) and the constituent governed by the stative noun in the absence of the LV (reduction test).

When 'have' co-occurs with definite process nouns instead of 'do/make' or 'give' (e.g. SP *tener una charla*, PT *ter uma conversa* 'have a chat'), it highlights the long duration of the event (Section 5.2.2, fn. 20). On the other hand, when it co-occurs with punctual nouns expressing verbal/non-verbal communication (e.g. IT *avere il permesso* 'have permission'), 'have' highlights the persistence of the result of the commissive/exercitive acts expressed with 'give'. Likewise, it might highlight the persistence of a commitment until it is fulfilled (e.g. IT *avere nuoto alle cinque* 'have swimming at five o'clock'; Section 5.2.3, fn. 22).

6.2 'Do/make'

The signifiers for 'do/make' can be typically selected by dynamic nouns, codifying events (Section 5.2). Indeed, 'do/make' is a dynamic verb, and this entails the aspectual compatibility with this kind of noun. Nevertheless, some clarifications are needed.

As far as Italian is concerned, it is clear that mainly definite process nouns select *fare*. The selection by indefinite process nouns is lexically constrained

(Section 5.2.1). This LV mainly occurs with indefinite nouns denoting the regular practice of sports activities (e.g. IT *fare nuoto* 'go swimming'), because the general physical activity is expressed by the synthetic verb equivalent (e.g. IT *nuotare* 'to swim'). This lexical constraint is probably due to the fact that indefinite eventive nouns are unbounded, namely necessarily atelic, as their synthetic verb counterparts. Thus, the lexical specialization economically avoids the overlapping between the LVC and its synthetic counterpart. On the other hand, there is no synthetic verbal counterpart for LVCs with *fare* including nouns which denote a situation of disorder or tumult. The two semantic sets of nouns also select the signifiers for the LV 'do/make' in the other Romance languages considered.

In the case of definite process nouns (Section 5.2.2), the semantics of LVCs generally differs from that of their atelic synthetic counterparts; indeed, these predicative nouns are durative but bounded, differently from their verb bases (e.g. IT *fare una nuotata* 'take a swim' vs *nuotare* 'swim'). This probably explains the large number of LVCs formed with definite process nouns. As far as Italian is concerned, *fare* is the basic LV in co-occurrence with nouns denoting motion, other physical and communication activities (where the Recipient is not foregrounded). Among the other Romance languages considered, French behaves similarly to Italian, since it selects uniformly *faire* except for physical activities such as *douche* 'shower', *bain* 'bath', which select *prendre* 'take'. Likewise, Romanian mostly selects *a face* 'do/make', although it employs *a da* 'give' with short-lasting motion nouns, and generally prefers LV extensions or even the synthetic equivalent, thus not expressing portion excerptions. On the other hand, Iberic languages select *hacer/fazer* only in the case of long-lasting motion nouns and communication nouns without the foregrounding of the Recipient, like SP *propuesta* / PT *proposta* 'proposal'. In all the other cases *dar* 'give' is selected.

The LV 'do/make' is a minor choice with punctual nouns. In Italian, *fare* is selected only by vocal sound and motion nouns, and, rarely, by nouns expressing gestures of love such as *carezza* 'caress'. In all these cases, *fare* highlights the occurrence of the event itself. From the interlinguistic perspective, the equivalents of 'do/make' are uniformly selected in the case of love gestures such as 'caress', as an alternative of 'give'. Romanian is the only exception, since it prefers synthetic equivalents with this type of noun (e.g. *a mângâia* 'caress'), as well as with other punctual nouns, thus not always expressing the unit excerption; indeed, the Romanian LV *a face* 'do/make' only occurs with motion nouns. Similarly, French requires *faire* with motion nouns, while the LV extension *pousser* 'push' or a synthetic verb are preferred in the case of vocal sound nouns. In all the other instances, Romance punctual nouns co-occur with 'give', which is basically the unique possibility with the Iberic languages.

The LV 'do/make' can also occur with stative nouns. Since there is no aspectual compatibility with these nouns, the resulting LVCs acquire a causative value. In Italian this happens both with psychological and physical nouns. As far as the former are concerned, the LVCs with *fare* 'do/make' mark the 'production' of the state by the Stimulus, which is the LVC's subject (e.g. IT *Giovanni fa paura a tutti* 'John makes everybody scared', lit. 'John makes fear to everyone' vs *tutti hanno paura di Giovanni* 'everybody is afraid of John', lit. 'everybody has fear of John'). This means that in the absence of the Stimulus the state does not exist (e.g. IT ??*tutti hanno paura* 'everybody is scared', lit. 'everybody has fear'). The LV 'do/make' provides a causative interpretation of LVCs with psychological nouns also in French and Portuguese, whereas Spanish prefers the LV *dar* 'give'. As for physical states, *fare* is selected by a very restricted set of nouns in Italian (i.e. *caldo* 'hot' and *freddo* 'cold'), and its competition with *essere* 'be' may be connected to the perception of the state of hot or cold by somebody; hence, the potential causative value of *fare* is extremely weak in this case. Only 'do/make' is available to express meteorological states in Spanish and in French, where the alternative 'be' is not possible.[25] On the contrary, Portuguese prefers *estar* 'be' and Romanian exclusively selects *a fi* 'be'.

Generally speaking, it is possible to note a minor bleaching of the meaning of 'creation/production' of the lexically full 'do/make' in its causative function. In the case of psychological nouns, the subject of 'do/make' is the Stimulus (the causer) which creates the state felt by the Experiencer (the causee).[26] In the case of physical nouns, even if the Stimulus is represented by the physical state itself, which is understood (being the subject a null expletive), a perception by an Experiencer-causee can be always supposed. Likewise, when co-occurring with indefinite process nouns such as 'noise' or 'chaos', the subject of 'do/make' is still the causer, producing an effect which might be perceived by another potential participant; indeed, if in this case there is an agentive source rather than a proper Stimulus, there can still be an Experiencer. We can call this causative use 'effective', since a cause-effect situation is implied. All these cases are very different from the basic uses of this verb as an LV, which lacks every lexical meaning of production, as for example happens in Italian in *far(si) una passeggiata* 'take a walk', lit. 'do (oneself) a walk'.

As is well known, the reduction test – together with that of coreference – is relevant for the identification of the basic uses of an LV. Both tests work perfectly when 'do/make' co-occurs with process nouns, for instance in Italian with *passeg-*

---

[25] Since Spanish usually does not select *hacer* 'do/make' to realize the lexical causative construction, the selection of this LV with meteorological nouns probably does not convey any causative value even in this case.

[26] It is worth noting that this is the only case when in Romanian LV extensions such as *a provoca* 'provoke' are preferred to *a face*, which cannot be employed.

giata 'walk' (e.g. IT *Giovanni*$_{xsubject}$ (*si*) *fa una passeggiata*$_{xTheme}$ 'John takes a walk', lit. 'John does (oneself) a walk'; *la passeggiata*$_x$ *di Giovanni*$_x$ 'the walk of John'). On the other hand, when the reduction test is applied with psychological nouns (e.g. IT *la paura*$_{xy}$ *di Giovanni*$_x$ 'the fear of John'), it is interpreted as the omission of the stative LV 'have' (e.g. IT *Giovanni*$_x$ *ha paura*$_{xy}$ 'John has fear'), rather than of the causative verb 'do/make' (e.g. ex. (27): IT *Giovanni*$_y$ *fa paura*$_{xy}$ *a tutti*$_x$ 'John scares everibody', lit. 'John makes fear to everybody'; cf. Ježek 2004: 188). The same happens with the other causative uses.[27]

This means that, at least the lexical causative uses in the case of stative nouns – but maybe also the 'effective' ones – display a lesser degree of semantic bleaching with respect to the lexical meaning of the full verbal counterpart, while the occurrences in prototypical LVCs are 'lighter'.

6.3 'Give'

The signifiers for 'give' typically co-occur with eventive nouns, like those for 'do/make'. This is compatible with the full meaning of the verb, which entails dynamicity, as it expresses a transfer of a Theme from an Agent towards a Recipient. Since in the case of the full meaning of the verb the prototypical transfer concerns an object, namely a concrete and countable entity, the usual co-occurrence of 'give' is with bounded nouns, mainly punctual ones (Sections 5.2.2–5.2.3). In fact, the selection of the verb by indefinite process nouns such as 'help' and 'assistance' is not easily explainable (Section 5.2.1). Firstly, in this case the unboundedness can be considered as resulting from the repetition of a set of different instances; secondly, such occurrences are constrained from the lexical point of view; and last but not least, the selection of 'give' is connected to the involvement of the Recipient. This means

---

[27] Indeed, in the case of physical nouns, the reduction test (e.g. IT *il freddo*$_{xy}$ *di Giovanni*$_x$ 'John's feeling of cold', lit. 'the cold of John') similarly refers to the stative LVC with 'have' (e.g. IT *Giovanni*$_x$ *ha freddo* 'John is cold', lit. 'John has cold'). When co-occurring with indefinite process nouns such as 'noise', even if the argument of the noun is, in this case, the Agent, in our opinion, the result of the reduction test is not completely grammatical in this interpretation (IT ?*il rumore di Giovanni* 'the noise of John', ?*il caos di Giovanni* 'the chaos of John'). As a matter of fact, 'the chaos of John' seems to refer to the state of mental confusion, rather than to 'the production of the chaos by John'. For a different opinion on the grammaticality of the reduction test with the Italian indefinite process noun *rumore*, see Ježek (2004: 188). Maybe also the selection of *a face* 'do/make' by nouns of internally-developed illnesses in Romanian (e.g. RO *a face febră* 'get a fever'; Section 5.1.2) can be referred to the 'effective' function of the verb. Nevertheless, the comparison with the selection of *a avea* 'have' by the same nouns also suggests the presence of an inchoative nuance in *a face* in this case.

that in this case the LV 'give' keeps the argument structure of its full counterpart. Indeed, the scarce lightness of these uses is also shown by the high competition with the alternative selection of LV extensions.

The Recipient is usually salient also when the verb co-occurs with definite process nouns. This in particular happens with nouns denoting an act of communication either stimulated by the Recipient or allowing its focalization. Iberic languages show a peculiar preference for *dar* 'give' also in 'lighter' uses, having a reduced argument structure with respect to the full verbal counterpart, as happens with motion nouns denoting short-lasting events; the same selection appears sometimes in the other 'lateral' area, i.e. in Romanian (e.g. RO *a da o tură* 'go for a stroll'). However, Spanish is the Romance language presenting a broader extension of 'give'. This language also employs the reflexive variant of *dar* with the clitic *-se*, not only in co-occurrence with motion nouns, but also with body care nouns such as *ducha* 'shower', where the reflexive pronouns highlight the middle nature of such physical actions.

Iberic languages also select *dar* 'give' in co-occurrence with punctual motion nouns, which differ from definite ones only in the excerption operation (of a unit in the former, and of a portion in the latter). As a matter of fact, the semelfactivity of the event is the distinctive feature of punctual nouns. This characteristic is particularly coherent with the semantics of transfer of the lexically full 'give', usually concerning a unique object, which is potentially pluralizable. This is the reason why 'give' is the only choice with blow nouns, and generally the unique possibility with nouns of gestures of love, in all the Romance languages considered. With both kinds of nouns, the presence of a Recipient is involved. The discretization and the existence of a possible Recipient also explain the strong preference for 'give' in the case of vocal sound nouns, mainly those having a communicative content such as 'shout'; in the absence of the Recipient, 'give' highlights the force of emission of the sound source, as is revealed by the selection of the LV extension *pousser* 'push' in French. The foregrounding of the Recipient is also at the base of the choice of 'give' with verbal or non-verbal communication nouns which promote a perlocutive act; in these cases, a causative value may be implied, as there is a causer who makes the Recipient do something. However, this is a (weak) causative use of 'give', as the application of the coreference and the reduction tests suggest (cf. Section 5.2.3). We can call this causative use 'perlocutive', since an illocutive-perlocutive relation is implied.[28]

---

[28] In fact, a 'perlocutive' use of 'give' can also be identified in the case of vocal sound nouns having a communicative content (e.g. IT *dai un urlo al cane* lit. 'give a scream to the dog', for instance to make it come back). On the other hand, an 'effective' use of 'give' might be seen in the effects of blows on the potential Recipient.

The selection of the LV 'give' conveys a causative value also in co-occurrence with stative nouns (in Romanian only with psychological stative nouns). The notion of transfer typically conveyed by the lexically full counterpart of 'give' is probably at the basis of its causative value. In all these cases, the reduction test cannot be applied, since there is no coreference with the LVC's subject: for instance, in Italian *l'ansia$_{xy}$ di Giovanni$_x$* 'the anxiety of John' can be interpreted as the omission of the stative LV *avere* 'have' (e.g. IT *Giovanni$_x$ ha ansia$_{xy}$* 'John has anxiety'), rather than of the causative verb *dare* 'give' (e.g. IT *Giovanni$_y$ mi$_x$ dà ansia$_{xy}$* 'John gives me anxiety').

This means that also 'give', like 'do/make', can have weaker or stronger causative uses. Weaker causative uses are lighter, whereas stronger ones are rather close to the lexically full counterpart in terms of argument structure and distribution of semantic roles. On the other hand, the lightest uses of 'give' are those with motion nouns, which characterize Spanish.

6.4 'Take'

The signifiers for 'take' typically co-occur as converses of the causative 'give', and rarely of the causative 'do/make'. This means that the main use of the LV 'take' is as a marker of anticausativity. Indeed, the lexically full counterpart of the LV 'take' expresses the endpoint of a transfer starting from an Agent/Source and ending into a Recipient, namely the opposite directionality of 'give'. This properly entails punctuality or, at least, short-time boundedness.

Actually, we can suppose the converse occurrence of 'take' for almost all 'perlocutive' and 'effective' uses of 'give' with punctual nouns. This can often occur with nouns of verbal and non-verbal communication (e.g. IT *prendere un ordine*, FR *prendre ses ordres*, RO *a lua permisiunea* 'take an order') and nouns of blow (e.g. IT *prendere un pugno (in faccia)*, FR *se prendre un coup de poing (dans la figure)*, RO *a lua un pumn (în față)* 'take a punch (on the face)'). Although two participants can be entailed in the situation, the selection of 'take' foregrounds the Recipient, which is placed in the subject position; this is due to the fact that the state of affairs is only conceived from the point of view of one participant, namely by reducing the argument structure. The impossibility to apply the reduction test[29] reveals that the

---

[29] For instance, in Italian *l'ordine$_{xy}$ dell'ufficiale$_x$* 'the order of the official' can be considered as the reduced form of *l'ordine$_{xy}$ che l'ufficiale$_x$ ha dato (al soldato$_y$)* 'the order that the official has given (to the soldier)', rather than *l'ordine$_{xy}$ che ha preso l'ufficiale$_y$ (dal generale$_x$)* 'the order that the official has taken (from the general)'. It is worth noting that in the Iberic languages the verb 'take' cannot be employed in these uses (PT *receber uma ordem*, SP *recibir orden* 'receive an order').

anticausative choice made by using 'take' is secondary to that of the alternative causative one, where this test works.

On the other hand, the co-occurrence with definite process nouns shows some uses where the second participant cannot be realized; either it coincides with the first participant – when the Agent is coreferent to the beneficiary (e.g. FR *prendre une douche*, PT *tomar duche* 'take a shower') – or it is not conceivable, as happens with 'decision'. This means that, even if the comparison between the use of 'take' and causative LVs might lead one to suppose that the former always codifies the lexical 'passive' – i.e. the 'anticausative' –, here it effectively behaves as a lexical middle, simply highlighting the subject. Indeed, what is relevant in these occurrences is the involvement of the subject, as either it does something for itself or it undertakes the responsibility of its actions. The reduction test is applicable in all these uses. Indeed, these are the only uses where 'take' is the basic LV (e.g. FR *la douche$_x$ de Marie$_x$* 'the shower of Mary' ≈ *la douche$_x$ que Marie$_x$ a prise* 'the shower that Mary has taken').

In the co-occurrence with psychological, physical and physiological stative nouns the foregrounding of the subject is similarly very clear, as it is an Experiencer, thus an affected entity. However, in all these uses 'take' is a marked choice just as 'give' and 'do/make'. In these cases the entry into a new state is implied, but 'give' and 'do/make' realize a causative construction, whereas 'take' an anticausative one, although the link to a causative counterpart might be extremely weak (e.g. FR *faire peur* 'scare' ~ *prendre peur* 'take fright'; SP *hazer/dar frío* 'be/give cold' ~ *coger frío* 'take cold'; RO *a da foc* 'give fire' ~ *a lua foc* 'take fire'; IT *dare sonno* 'make someone (be) sleepy) ~ *prendere sonno* 'fall asleep'). The result of the reduction test always corresponds to the basic LVs for states, i.e. 'have' (with the exception of Romanian, when the construction with 'be' + locative is selected). Of course, the entry into a new state produces an aspectual effect, namely an inchoative or incremental value, in the case of anticausative LVs as well as in the one of causative LVs, due to the differences in the *Aktionsart* between the verb and the noun.

7 Areal and diachronic considerations

As the data discussion has shown, the verbs under analysis (i.e. 'have', 'do/make', 'give', 'take') may either be basic LVs or entail a causative/aspectual interpretation. They are basic LVs when they co-occur with aspectually coherent predicative nouns, whereas they acquire a causative/aspectual value in combination with nouns not sharing the same aspectual features. As far as causativity is concerned, the coreference test is sufficient to detect it when it implies the causee's entry into a new state. However, the test does not allow one to distinguish the so-called 'effective' and 'perlocutive' causativity from the basic uses of the LVs (Sections 6.2–6.3). On the other hand, middle inchoative and incremental effects are identified through the reduction test, whose application always refers to the basic LV (Section 6.4).

Among the basic LVs, 'have' and 'do/make' are the most relevant. On the one hand, the stative verb 'have' is the basic LV for stative nouns. When co-occurring with eventive nouns, it highlights durativity and persistence in time. On the other hand, the dynamic verb 'do/make' is the basic LV for nouns of event; its co-occurrence with stative nouns determines the emergence of a causative value. Both in the co-occurrence with eventive nouns and as a causative trigger, 'do/make' is in competition with the LV 'give'. Since the prototypical selection of 'give' requires the expression of the Recipient, the preference of 'give' rather than 'do/make' in LVCs is usually linked to the foreground of the participant having this role (or that of Experiencer). In the absence of the Recipient/Experiencer, the competition with 'do/make' seems to be ruled according to the more/less durativity of the event. Indeed, the choice of 'give' can be due to the short lastingness of the event, and the co-occurrence with punctual nouns seems to be the basic one. Finally, 'take' usually appears to be the converse of 'give', namely an anticausative; like causative LVs, it has inchoative/incremental effects in co-occurrence with stative nouns. The only occurrences of 'take' as a basic LV in Romance languages seem to be the ones including definite process nouns, where the causative counterpart is not pertinent; in such a case the coreference and the reduction tests are applicable. For these uses, we have employed the term 'middle', which highlights the involvement of the argument in subject position. Actually, this 'middle' orientation is always present when the LV 'take' is selected, in the anticausative uses as well.

This picture is in line with the very general system of oppositions which can be drawn for Latin (García-Hernández 1998, 2003), although this language, being more synthetic than Romance languages, often resorts to extensions, prefixed LVs and synthetic verbs, besides having LVs which have not been inherited (e.g. LT *agere* 'drive', *gerere* 'carry/bear', *ferre* 'carry'). In particular, García-Hernández (2003: 140) refers to an aspectual/diathetic trimember structure *dare* 'give' – *sumere* (*capere*) 'take' – *habere* 'have' in Latin, calling its first element 'causative', the second 'not causative and not resultative', and the third 'not causative but resultative'. He also observes that, already in Latin, there are two different constructions for *dare* 'give', one 'with dative' and the other 'without dative' (i.e. without Recipient/Experiencer: e.g. LT *saltum dare* 'make a jump', lit. 'jump give'), pointing out that the construction without dative might overlap with *facere* 'do/make'.[30] Furthermore, according to García-Hernández (2003: 148), within this general system of oppositions, the spread of the causative uses of *dare* 'give' in Latin is strictly linked to the diffusion of the expression of the possession by a verb (i.e. LT *habere* and then *tenere* 'have') rather than by the inherited locative structure with 'be' (the so-called dative of possession: e.g. LT *fames alicui esse* lit. 'hunger be to someone' > *famem habere* lit. 'have hunger', 'I am hungry'). Finally, the causative Latin verb *dare* 'give' shows a tendency to be substituted by the denominal verb *donare* 'give/offer', at least in the Gallo-Romance branch of the Romance languages, which implies a redistribution of the LV's uses of *dare* between *donner* 'give' and *faire* 'do/make' in French.

Considering this system, it is possible to make some areal and diachronic comments on the data that have been analyzed. Starting from 'lateral' areas, Romanian appears to be particularly conservative. For instance, it keeps the locative structure with *a fi* 'be' in co-occurrence with non-permanent psychological (emotions or feelings) and physiological states[31], reserving the selection of *a avea* 'have' to long-lasting psychological (mental states and aptitudes) and physiological states (e.g. illnesses). It is also worth noting that Romanian largely employs synthetic verbs and extensions, in particular with gestures of love and vocal sound nouns without communicative content; in all these cases the other Romance languages considered use 'do/make' or 'give'. Moreover, Romanian seems to be sensitive to the duration of the event in the selection of either *a da* 'give' or *a face* 'do/make' when co-occurring with motion definite process nouns, despite only selecting *a face* 'do/make' with motion punctual nouns.

As far as the Western 'lateral' area is concerned, two relevant and well-known traits can be noted with respect to Latin, namely the large expansion of *dar* 'give' and the substitution of the signifier of the verb expressing possession. The expansion of *dar* emerges in particular i) in the causative uses with psychological nouns expressing emotions directly caused by the foregrounded Stimulus, ii) with short-lasting definite motion nouns and punctual ones, and iii) with vocal sounds. This means that the spread of *dar* concerns the verb uses both with and without a Recipient. From the areal point of view, it is worth noting that the diffusion of *dar* is more restrained in Portuguese, where *fazer* is preferred with some psychological nouns (e.g. *inveja* 'envy', *medo* 'fear') and with some definite motion nouns (e.g. *caminhada* 'walk'). As

---

30 On the uses of Latin *dare* 'give' see also Martín Rodríguez (1996, 1999) and Pompei (2018, 2019, this volume). Cf. also Baños (2014) for the different values of the Latin noun *consilium* in the selection of *dare* 'give', *capere* 'take' or *habere* 'have' (i.e. 'advice', 'decision', 'meeting for deliberation' respectively).
31 This phenomenon has been linked to the hypothesis of the Romance origin of the genitive-dative syncretism in the Balkan *Sprachbund* (cf. Catasso 2011).

a result of the change in the meaning of the Latin *tenere* 'hold', the signifiers conveying 'have' are *tener* in Spanish and *ter* in Portuguese, both as lexically full verbs and as LVs, whereas the auxiliary is inherited from Latin *habere* 'have' in both languages.

In the 'middle' area, there is a resystematization in the distribution of 'give' and 'do/make' with respect to Latin. The most relevant phenomenon is the total regression in the selection of 'give' concerning bounded motion nouns, i.e. both definite process nouns and punctual ones. A small difference between Italian and French is the possible use of *dare* 'give' in particular cases in Italian, while French prefers a synthetic verb (e.g. FR *déranger* 'cause annoyance', *éternuer* 'sneeze', *embracer* 'embrace') or even an LV extension (FR *pousser un cri/un soupir* 'let out a cry/sigh', lit. 'push a cry/sigh'). On the other hand, Italian selects *fare* 'do/make' with nouns of body care activities, while French prefers to highlight the coreference between the beneficiary and the Agent employing the middle *prendre* (IT *fare una doccia* vs FR *prendre une douche* 'take a shower'). Differently from Latin, in Italian *fare* and in French *faire* are selected with meteorological nouns, as also happens in the Iberic languages, but not in Romanian, which keeps the use of 'be' with all non-permanent states. Finally, Italian is the only language which has chosen a unique signifier – i.e. *prendere* 'take' – to express the meaning of taking in all its functions, namely as a basic LV, as inchoative/incremental and/or anticausative LV. On the other hand, the other Romance languages considered select other signifiers, which are clearly, in many cases, LV extensions accompanying the basic LVs, namely *prendre* in French, *tomar* in Spanish and Portuguese, *a lua* in Romanian. This variegated situation is similar to that of Latin, where the idea of 'take' is conveyed by *sumere, capere, prehendere*, in addition to the same verbs with different prefixes (e.g. LT *adsumere* 'take as acquiring', *accipere* 'take as receiving', *apprehendere* 'take as seizing'), which realize different nuances of meaning.

In general, all the Romance languages considered show a wider presence of LVCs than (at least literary) Latin.

8 Conclusions

With respect to the main purposes of this paper, the analysis has shown that some regularities can be identified in the selection of LVs in the Romance languages considered. The apparently different behavior that may be detected can actually be systematized firstly taking into account the *Aktsionsart* of the verb and the noun.

We have dealt with the main basic LVs, i.e. the Romance equivalents for 'have', 'do/make', 'give' and 'take'. From the analysis, it clearly emerges that these LVs are really the basic ones when they co-occur with nouns which are compatible from the aspectual point of view: the stative verb 'have' is the basic LV for stative nouns; the dynamic verb 'do/make' is the basic LV for nouns of event. To these two LVs, 'give' and 'take' may be added: the former can be preferred to 'do/make' when the Recipient/Experiencer is foregrounded, and/or when the event is short-lasting; the latter has a very limited use as a basic LV, restricted to preferably short-lasting events having a unique participant. Beside these basic uses, all the verbs present some marked co-occurrences when the noun is non-coherent from the aspectual viewpoint. The effect of these combinations is the expression of non-basic values such as diathetic and aspectual ones. In particular, 'do/make' and 'give' can convey causative values in combination with stative nouns, even though a sort of 'effective' and 'perlocutive' causativity can also emerge in combination with eventive nouns. On the other hand, the equivalents of 'take' usually encode anticausative and inchoative/incremental values.

This means that between the basic LVs and the LV extensions that have been identified in the literature an intermediate area has to be assumed. Here the basic LVs considered show some non-prototypical uses, which could also be fulfilled by more proper and less generic LV extensions. This is an important issue, which has not yet received proper attention. For instance, Gross (1981: 33) considers *prendre* 'take' as an inchoative extension of the French LVC *avoir de l'influence* 'have influence', in the same way as the progressive extension *conserver* 'keep' and the terminative one *perdre* 'lose'. However, differently from *prendre*, extensions such as *conserver* and *perdre* cannot be used as basic LVs; hence, they are different in nature, and cannot be treated in the same way. Similarly, no adequate attention has been paid to the non-prototypical uses of verbs such as 'do/make', which have been dealt with only as basic LVs.

From these considerations, another important issue of this paper derives, namely the fact that the LV contributes to the semantics of the LVCs to a greater or a lesser extent, depending on its basic or less prototypical function. This also means that, in addition to the basic LVC of a predicative noun, other LVCs exist, whose function is to modulate the different aspectual nuances and the configurations of the information structure. It is worth noting that similar diathetic and aspectual configurations can be found not only within the same language, but also, to a certain extent, from the cross-linguistic point of view. This is a powerful resource for the organization of this area of the lexicon.

Further explanations for peculiar 'irregularities' (e.g. the use of *a fi* 'be' in Romanian, the extended use of *dar* 'give' in the Iberic area, as well as the use of *faire/fare* 'do/make' in French and in Italian) are provided by diachronic and areal considerations. For instance, the 'lateral' Eastern area represented by Romanian seems to be reluctant in its use of LVs, perhaps because this language is more synthetic than the others and closer to Latin. Furthermore, the inherited LVs have developed differently in each Romance language considered, according to its own system. For instance, in Spanish the expansion of the LV *dar* 'give' is probably connected to the lack of a proper lexical causative function for *hacer* 'do/make', as well as to the large use of LV extensions such as *echar* 'throw' and *provocar* 'provoke'.

Last but not least, another significant finding of this analysis concerns the fact that LVCs do not seem to be truly equivalent to their synthetic counterparts, as their scarce co-occurrence with indefinite process nouns with respect to the other aspectual groups of nouns shows. This means that their main function proves to be the encoding of single instantiations of the synthetic verb (more generic) meaning through the mechanism of the portion/unit excerption (e.g. IT *nuotare* 'swim' vs *fare una nuotata* 'take a swim'), as well as the filling of lexical gaps and the expression of particular senses (e.g. IT *nuotare* 'swim' vs *fare nuoto* 'go swimming').

In our opinion, this comparative approach could be adjusted to explain intra-linguistic irregularities as well.

References

Alonso Ramos, Margarita. 1991. Verbes supports et fonctions lexicales. *Lingvisticae Investigationes* 15. 203–223.
Alonso Ramos, Margarita. 2004. *Las construcciones con verbo de apoyo*. Madrid: Visor.
Apresjan, Jurij. 2009. The theory of lexical functions: An update. In David Beck, Kim Gerdes, Jasmina Milićević & Alain Polguère (eds.), *Proceedings of the Fourth International Conference on Meaning-Text Theory*, 1–14. Montréal: Observatoire de linguistique Sens-Texte (OLST).
Baker, Mark C. 1989. Object sharing and projection in serial verb constructions. *Linguistic Inquiry* 20(4). 513–553.
Baños, José Miguel. 2014. *Consilium (habere, capere, dare)*: un sustantivo hecho predicado. In José Miguel Baños, María Felisa del Barrio Vega, María Teresa Callejas Berdonés & Antonio López Fonseca (eds.), *Philologia, Universitas, Vita. Trabajos en honor de Tomás González Rolán*. 103–114. Madrid: Escolar y Mayo.
Bartoli, Matteo-Giulio. 1925. *Introduzione alla neolinguistica: principi, scopi, metodi*. Genève: Olschki.
Blanco Escoda, Xavier. 2000. Verbos soporte y clases de predicados en español. *Lingüística Española Actual* 22(1). 1–12.
Bosque, Ignacio. 2004. *REDES. Diccionario Combinatorio del español contemporáneo*. Madrid: Ediciones SM.
Bosque, Ignacio. 2006. *Práctico. Diccionario combinatorio práctico del español contemporáneo*. Madrid: Ediciones SM.
Bosque, Ignacio. 2011. Deducing collocations. In Igor Boguslavsky & Leo Wanner (eds.), *Proceedings of the 5th International Conference on Meaning-Text Theory*, 1006–1023. Barcelona. Observatoire de linguistique Sens-Texte (OLST).
Bustos Plaza, Alberto. 2005. *Combinaciones verbonominales institucionalizadas y lexicalizadas*. Frankfurt: Peter Lang.
Butt, Miriam. 1995. *The Structure of Complex Predicates in Urdu*. Stanford: CSLI Publications.

Butt, Miriam. 1998. Constraining argument merger through aspect. In Erhard Hinrichs, Andreas Kathol & Tsuneko Nakazawa (eds.), *Complex Predicates in Nonderivational Syntax*. Syntax and Semantics. Vol. 30, 73–113. New York: Academic Press.

Butt, Miriam. 2010. The light verb jungle: still hacking away. In Mengistu Amberber, Brett Baker & Mark Harvey (eds.), *Complex Predicates: Cross-linguistic Perspectives on Event Structure*, 48–78. Cambridge: Cambridge University Press.

Cantarini, Sibilla. 2004. *Costrutti con verbo supporto*. Bologna: Pàtron.

Catasso, Nicholas. 2011. Genitive-Dative Syncretism in the Balkan Sprachbund: An Invitation to Discussion. *Journal of Theoretical Linguistics* 8. 70–93.

Ciocanea, Cristiana. 2011. *Lexique-grammaire des constructions converses en a da / a primi en roumain*. PhD dissertation. Paris: Université Paris-Est.

Collins, Chris. 1997. Argument sharing in serial verb constructions. *Linguistic Inquiry* 28(3). 461–497.

Corpas Pastor, Gloria. 1996. *Manual de fraseología española*. Madrid: Gredos.

Croft, William. 1991. *Syntactic Categories and Grammatical Relations: The Cognitive Organization of Information*. Chicago: University of Chicago Press.

Culicover, Peter W. & Ray Jackendoff. 2005. *Simpler Syntax*. Oxford: Oxford University Press.

De Mauro, Tullio (ed.). 1999. *Grande Dizionario Italiano dell'Uso*. Torino: UTET.

De Miguel, Elena. 2006. Tensión y equilibrio semántico entre nombres y verbos: el reparto de la tarea de predicar. In Milka Villayandre (ed.), *Actas del XXXV Simposio de la Sociedad Española de Lingüística*, 1289–1313. León: Ediciones del Dpto. de Filología Hispánica y Clásica - Universidad de León.

De Miguel, Elena. 2008. Construcciones con verbos de apoyo en español. De cómo entran los nombres en la órbita de los verbos. In Inés Olza Moreno, Manuel Casado Velarde & Ramón Gonzáles Ruiz (eds.), *Actas del XXXVII Simposio Internacional de la Sociedad Española de Lingüística*, 567–578. Pamplona: Servicios de Publicaciones de la Universidad de Navarra,

Depraetere, Ilse. 1995. On the necessity of distinguishing between (un)boundedness and (a)telicity. *Linguistics and Philosophy* 18. 1–19.

Duarte, Inês, Anabela Gonçalves, Matilde Miguel, Amália Mendes, Iris Hendrickx, Fátima Oliveira, Luís Filipe Cunha, Fátima Silva & Purificação Silvano. 2010. Light verbs features in European Portuguese. In Pier Marco Bertinetto, Anna Korhonen, Alessandro Lenci, Alissa Melinger, Sabine Schulte im Walde & Aline Villavicencio (eds.), *Proceedings of Verb 2010 Interdisciplinary Workshop on Verbs: The Identification and Representation of Verb Features*, 27–31. Pisa: Università di Pisa.

Elia, Annibale, Emilio D'Agostino & Maurizio Martinelli. 1985. Tre componenti della sintassi italiana: frasi semplici, frasi a verbo supporto e frasi idiomatiche. In Annalisa Franchi De Bellis & Leonardo Maria Savoia (eds.), *Sintassi e morfologia della lingua italiana d'uso. Teorie e applicazioni descrittive. Atti del XVII congresso internazionale della Società di Linguistica Italiana*, 311–325. Roma: Bulzoni.

Gaeta, Livio. 2002. *Quando i verbi compaiono come nomi*. Milano: FrancoAngeli.

García-Hernández, Benjamín. 1989. Complémentarité lexicale et voix verbale. In Gualtiero Calboli (ed.), *Subordination and Other Topics in Latin. Proceedings of the Third Colloquium on Latin Linguistics*, 289–309. Amsterdam: Benjamins.

García-Hernández, Benjamín. 1998. Diathèse et aspect verbal dans les structures lexicales. *Bulletin de la Société de Linguistique de Paris* 93. 211–227.

García-Hernández, Benjamín. 2003. Fraseología latina y románica. Desarrollo del sistema clasemático 'dar'-'tener'. El testimonio de las Glosas de Reichenau. *Revista de Estudios Latinos* 3. 133–153.

Giry-Schneider, Jacqueline. 1987. *Les prédicats nominaux en français: les phrases à verbe support*. Genève/Paris: Droz.

Givón, Talmy. 1979. *On Understanding Grammar*. New York: Academic Press.

Grimshaw, Jane. 1990. *Argument Structure*. Cambridge, MA: The MIT Press.

Grimshaw, Jane & Armin Mester. 1988. Light verbs and θ-marking. *Linguistic Inquiry* 19(2). 205–232.
Gross, Gaston. 1989. *Les constructions converses du français*. Genève/Paris: Droz.
Gross, Gaston. 1993. Trois applications de la notion de verbe support. *L'Information grammatical* 59. 16–23.
Gross, Gaston. 1994. Classes d'objets et description des verbes. *Langages* 115. 15–30.
Gross, Gaston. 1996. Prédicats nominaux e compatibilité aspectuelle. *Langages* 121. 54–72.
Gross, Gaston. 1999. Verbes supports et conjugaison nominale. *Revue d'études francophones* 9. 70–92.
Gross, Gaston. 2004a. Introduction. In Gaston Gross & Sophie De Pontonx (eds.), *Verbes supports. Nouvel état des lieux*. 27(2). 167–169. [=Special issue of *Lingvisticae Investigationes*].
Gross, Gaston. 2004b. Pour un Bescherelle des prédicats nominaux. In Gaston Gross & Sophie De Pontonx (eds.), *Verbes supports. Nouvel état des lieux* 27(2). 343–358. [=Special issue of *Lingvisticae Investigationes*].
Gross, Gaston & Ferenc Kiefer. 1995. La structure événementielle des substantifs. *Folia Linguistica* 29(1–2). 43–66.
Gross, Gaston & Sophie De Pontonx (eds.), 2004. *Verbes supports. Nouvel état des lieux*. [=Special issue of *Lingvisticae Investigationes* 27(2)].
Gross, Maurice. 1981. Les bases empiriques de la notion de prédicat sémantique. *Langages* 63. 7–52.
Haas, Pauline, Richard Huyghe & Rafael Marín. 2008. Du verbe au nom: calques et décalages aspectuels. In Jacques Durand, Benoît Habert & Bernard Lacks (eds.), *Congrès mondial de linguistique française 2008* (CMLF 2008), 2051–2065. Paris: Institut de Linguistique Française.
Haspelmath, Martin. 1987. *Transitivity Alternations of the Anticausative Type*. Arbeitspapiere des Instituts für Sprachwissenschaft der Universität zu Köln. Vol. 5. Köln: Universität zu Köln.
Haspelmath, Martin. 1993. More on the typology of inchoative/causative verb alternations. In Bernard Comrie & Maria Polinsky (eds.), *Causatives and Transitivity*, 87–120. Amsterdam: Benjamins.
Huyghe, Richard. 2011. (A)telicity and the mass-count distinction: the case of French activity nominalizations. *Recherches linguistiques de Vincennes* 40. 101–126.
Jespersen, Otto. 1942. *A Modern English Grammar on Historical Principles*. Vol. 6. *Morphology*. London: George Allen and Unwin Ltd.
Ježek, Elisabetta. 2004. Types et degrés de verbes supports en italien. In Gaston Gross & Sophie De Pontonx (eds.), *Verbes supports. Nouvel état des lieux* 27(2). 185–201. [=Special issue of *Lingvisticae Investigationes*].
Ježek, Elisabetta. 2011. Verbes supports et composition sémantique. *Cahiers de Lexicologie* 1. 29–43.
Ježek, Elisabetta. 2016. *The Lexicon: An Introduction*. Oxford: Oxford University Press.
Ježek, Elisabetta. This volume. Semantic Co-composition in Light Verb Constructions. 221–238.
Kemmer, Suzanne E. 1993. *The Middle Voice*. Amsterdam: Benjamins.
Koike, Kazumi. 2001. *Colocaciones léxicas en el español actual: estudio formal y lexico-semántico*. Alcalá: Universidad de Alcalá.
La Fauci, Nunzio. 1997. Sulla struttura proposizionale delle costruzioni con nome predicativo e verbo supporto. In Riccardo Ambrosini, Maria Patrizia Bologna, Filippo Motta & Chatia Orlandi (eds.), *Scríbthair a ainm n-ogaim. Scritti in memoria di E. Campanile*, 467–490. Pisa: Pacini.
La Fauci, Nunzio & Ignazio Mirto. 2003. *Fare. Elementi di sintassi*. Pisa: Edizioni ETS.
Le Fur, Dominique. 2007. *Dictionnaire des combinaisons de mots: les synonymes en contexte*. Paris: Le Robert.
Lenci, Alessandro, Francesca Masini, Malvina Nissim, Sara Castagnoli, Gianluca E. Lebani, Lucia C. Passaro & Marco S. G. Senaldi. 2017. How to harvest Word Combinations from corpora. Methods, evaluation and perspectives. *Studi e Saggi Linguistici* 55(2). 45–68.

Levin, Beth & Malka Rappaport Hovav. 2005. *Argument Realization*. Cambridge: Cambridge University Press.
Lo Cascio, Vincenzo. 2013. *Dizionario Combinatorio Italiano*. Amsterdam: Benjamins.
Martín Rodríguez, Antonio María. 1996. *Dare*, auxiliaire lexical en latin. In Michèle Fruyt & Claude Moussy (eds.), *Structures lexicales en latin*, 49–64. Paris: Presses de l'Université de Paris-Sorbonne.
Martín Rodríguez, Antonio María. 1999. *Los verbos de 'dar' en latín arcaico y clásico. Análisis estructural de un campo semántico*. Las Palmas: Universidad de Las Palmas.
Mastrofini, Roberta. 2004. Classi di costruzioni a verbo supporto in italiano: implicazioni semantico-sintattiche nel paradigma V + N. *Studi Italiani di Linguistica Teorica e Applicata* 33(3). 371–398.
Mastrofini, Roberta. 2013. *Classi di verbi inglesi tra pesantezza e leggerezza*. Roma: Aracne.
Mattissen, Johanna. This volume. Light Verbs and 'light nouns' in polysynthetic languages. 275–303.
Mendívil Giró, José Luis. 1999. *Las palabras disgregadas. Sintaxis de las expresiones idiomàticas y los predicados complejos*. Zaragoza: Prensas Universitarias de Zaragoza.
Mohanan, Tara. 1994. *Argument Structure in Hindi*. Stanford: CSLI Publications.
Moncó Taracena, Sofía. 2011. Étude constrastive des verbs *dar* (espagnol) et *faire* (français). In *Méthodes et analyses comparatives en Sciences du langage. Actes de la 3eme édition des Journées d'Etudes Toulousaines*, 125–134. Toulouse: Université de Toulouse.
Neves, Maria H. 2002. Estudo das construções com verbo-suporte em português. In Ingedore Koch (ed.), *Gramática do Protuguês Falado*, 209–238. Vol. 6. Desenvolvimentos: Campinas: UNICAMP.
Pompei, Anna. 2018. *Facere saltum* ou *dare saltum*? Verbes supports et noms de mouvement. In Colette Bodelot & Olga Spevak (eds.), *Les constructions à verbs support en latin*. 169–186. Clermont-Ferrand: Presses Universitaires Blaise Pascal.
Pompei, Anna. 2019. *Dare, facere* e i nomi di implicazione fisica e di movimento in latino. In Anna Pompei & Lunella Mereu (eds.), *Verbi supporto. Fenomeni e teorie*, 111–153. München: LINCOM.
Pompei, Anna. This volume. *How light is 'give' as a light verb? A case study on the actionality of Latin Light Verb Constructions (with some references to Romance languages)*. 149–200.
Pustejovsky, James. 1988. Event Semantic Structure. Unpublished manuscript. Waltham: Brandeis University.
Pustejovsky, James. 1995. *The Generative Lexicon*. Cambridge, MA: The MIT Press.
Samvelian, Pollet, Laurence Danlos & Benoît Sagot. 2011. On the predictability of light verbs. In Fryni Kakoyianni-Doa (ed.), *Penser le Lexique-Grammaire, perspectives actuelles*, 209–22. Paris: Honoré Champion.
Sanromán Vilas, Begoña. 2011. The unbearable lightness of light verbs. Are they semantically empty verbs? In Igor Boguslavsky & Leo Wanner (eds.), *Proceedings of the 5th International Conference on Meaning-Text Theory*, 253–263. Barcelona: Observatoire de linguistique Sens-Texte (OLST).
Sanromán Vilas, Begoña. 2014. La alternancia *dar/hacer* en construcciones con verbo de apoyo y nombre de comunicación. *An International journal of Hispanic linguistics* 3(2). 185–222.
Sidoti, Rossana. 2014. Interferencias colocacionales en construcciones con verbo de apoyo + sustantivo entre lenguas fines. *Lingue e Linguaggi* 11. 215–224.
Simone, Raffaele. 2003. Maṣdar, 'ismu al-marrati et la frontière verbe/nom. In José Luis Girón Alconchel (ed.), *Estudios ofrecidos al profesor J. Bustos Tovar*, 901–918. Madrid: Universidad Complutense de Madrid.
Simone, Raffaele. 2013. *Nuovi fondamenti di linguistica*. Milano: McGraw-Hill.
Simone, Raffaele & Valentina Piunno. 2017. Combinazioni di parole che costituiscono entrata. Fenomeni, rappresentazione lessicografica e aspetti lessicologici. *Studi e Saggi Linguistici* 55(2). 13–44.

Talmy, Leonard. 2000. *Toward a Cognitive Semantics*. Cambridge, MA: The MIT Press.
Van Valin, Robert D. & Randy J. LaPolla. 1997. *Syntax: Structure, Meaning and Function*. Cambridge: Cambridge University Press.
Vietri, Simonetta. 2004. *Lessico-Grammatica dell'italiano. Metodi, descrizioni e applicazioni*. Torino: UTET.
Vivès, Robert. 1983. Avoir, prendre, perdre: *constructions à verbe support et extensions aspectuelles*. PhD dissertation. Paris: LADL Université Paris 8.
Vivès, Robert. 1984. L'Aspect dans les constructions nominales prédicatives: *avoir, prendre*, verbe support et extension aspectuelle. *Linguisticae Investigationes* 3(1). 161–185.
Vivès, Robert. 1988. Verbes supports et nominalisations. *Lexique* 6. 139–159.
Wierzbicka, Anna. 1982. Why can you *have a drink* when you can't **have an eat*? *Language* 58(4). 753–799.

Anna Pompei
5 How light is 'give' as a Light Verb?
A case study on the actionality of Latin Light Verb Constructions (with some references to Romance languages)

Abstract: This article deals with the actual emptiness of Light Verbs with particular reference to the Light Verb 'give' in constructions with the pattern [V+N]. The paper specifically focuses on the contribution given by both the verb and the noun to the *Aktionsart* of Light Verb Constructions, starting from the idea that these are complex predicates. The history of the notion of Light Verb Construction is first briefly outlined, with special emphasis on the linguistics of Romance languages. The usefulness of approaching the concept of the Light Verb Constructions as complex predicates from the perspective of cognitive linguistics is then shown. This is a valid approach 1) for understanding what the lexical meaning present in the so-called 'empty' verbs consists of, 2) for overcoming the theoretical difficulties related to the sharing of the argument structure by the components of the construction, and 3) for better understanding the event structure of Light Verb Constructions. A case study concerning Latin shows that the selection of the Light Verb *dare* 'give' is closely linked to the feature of boundedness, at least in co-occurrence with physical implication and motion nouns. This actional constraint is explained in terms of inheritance of the semantic value of the lexically full verb. These conditions of use are considered akin to those of *dar* 'give' in the Iberic languages.

Keywords: 'give' Light Verb, eventive nouns, boundedness, Latin, Romance languages

1 Introduction

This paper is aimed at providing a reflection on the effective emptiness of the verb in Light Verb Constructions (henceforth LVCs) having the pattern [V+N], with particular regard to 'give' co-occurring with physical implication nouns (henceforth PhINs) and motion nouns (henceforth MNs), especially in Latin.

In the first part of the article the notion of Light Verb (henceforth LV) is introduced, and both its development under the label of *support verb* (Section 2) and the subsequent reinterpretation of LVCs as instances of complex predicates are dealt with, with special emphasis on the Romance linguistics tradition (Section 2.1). In describing the evolution of the notion, special attention is paid to the consequences of re-evaluating the LV semantic contribution to the LVC in terms of (a) distance in meaning from the lexically full counterpart, (b) argument structure sharing, and (c) event structure sharing.

The second section is devoted to the interpretation of the meaning of 'give' as a heavy verb and to the reasons for its selection as an LV, both in Romance languages (Sections 3–3.1) and from a typological viewpoint (Section 3.1.1). The central hypothesis of the article is proposed here, namely that the inheritance of 'give' full lexical meaning implies a constraint on the *Aktionsart* of the LVCs, in terms of boundedness. This actional feature is then analyzed, dealing with lexical aspect in eventive nouns (Section 3.2).

In the last section of the article, the hypothesis of the boundedness constraint is tested on Latin, taking into account LVCs made up of *dare* 'give' plus PhINs (Section 4.1) and MNs (Section 4.2). As regards the former, the semantic classes of hitting (Section 4.1.1) and sound nouns (Section 4.1.2) are considered; the latter are further divided into punctual nouns (Section 4.2.1) and nouns of definite and indefinite processes (Section 4.2.2). Some conclusive remarks are drawn at the end (Section 5).

2 Light Verbs and Romance linguistics tradition

The structures studied in this article are usually considered as LVCs. The label of LV has its origins in the field of English linguistics:[1] according to Jespersen (1942: 117), LV means "an insignificant verb, to which the marks of person and tense are attached, before the really important idea" conveyed by a deverbal noun, which usually expresses "the action or an isolated instance of the action". This is the case, for instance, of [V+N] constructions such as *have a swim*, *take a walk*, and *give a sigh* in English. Such an idea of verb lightness highlights the semantic bleaching of the verb.

On the other hand, in Romance linguistics the French definition of *verbe support* is usually adopted, from which Italian *verbo supporto* and Spanish *verbo soporte* (in addition to *verbo de apoyo*) originate. From this perspective, the exclusively morpho-syntactic function of the verb is pointed out. Indeed, as a mere support, the verb only encodes grammatical categories, such as TAM and agreement features, but it does not predicate: it only 'actualizes' the predicative noun (*prédicat nominal*) – in which the whole predication stands – thus having the same

---

[1] This will be the only label used in this article, apart from in this section. For simplicity, in English and Latin examples the language abbreviations are not shown.

function as verb endings (Gross 2004a: 167). Therefore, both labels – i.e., LV and *verbe support* – assume a binary partition between a predicative noun, on the one hand, and an empty verb, on the other.

A battery of tests has been developed to recognize LVCs (*inter alia*, recently Langer 2004). Among them, (a) the possibility of the LVC replacement by a synthetic verb, usually morphologically related to the predicative noun (e.g., *give a slap* ≈ *slap*), and (b) the so-called reduction text (e.g., *John gave a slap to Mary → John's slap to Mary*) (Gross 1981: 39; Giry-Schneider 1987: 28) have been considered as particularly relevant to revealing the predicativeness of the noun, and hence the emptiness of the LV. The reduction text firstly shows that the meaning does not seem to be affected by the deletion of the verb; secondarily, it shows that the notion of noun predicativeness entails not only the encoding of the predicative lexical meaning, but also the argument structure. Indeed, starting from the first approach to these constructions in the French tradition, the coreference between the verb subject and the first argument of the predicative noun has been considered as a distinctive feature for identifying the use of a verb as a 'support' (Giry-Schneider 1986: 52): for instance, in *John gave a slap to Mary*, the subject *John* is also the Agent of the predicative noun *slap*. This implies that a clause where the subject of the support verb and the first argument of the predicative noun are distinct rather than coreferent is ungrammatical (e.g., **John gave Andrew's slap to Mary*, where *Andrew* realizes the Agent of the predicative noun *slap*, this role being already realized by the subject *John*) – unlike what happens in 'normal' clauses, where the verb is semantically full, and the noun is a full referential one (e.g., *John gave Andrew's book to Mary*, where the role of Agent is assigned to the subject *John* by *gave*, whereas *Andrew* realizes the Possessor of the non-predicative noun *book*). According to the French school, this ungrammaticality is due to the fact that there cannot be two predicates in a clause (Gross 1996: 55). In particular, in support verb constructions the predication is conceived as completely noun-dependent, which implies that arguments are selected by the noun (Gross 2004a: 167).

It is worth noting that in this framework, since the whole predication of support verb construction is ascribed to the noun, the lexical aspect of nouns has been studied as well. Indeed, actionality is a feature of all predicates, including nominal ones. A seminal work on the *Aktionsart* of nouns occurring with support verbs is Gross and Kiefer (1995). In addition to nominalizations, i.e., deverbal nouns, they identify two further types of predicative non-deverbal nouns: those having the eventive reading in their lexical representation (e.g., FR *orage* 'storm' and *coup* 'bump'), and those whose eventive interpretation is due to a conceptual shift to a dynamic reading (e.g., FR *film* when standing for 'film showing'). According to this study, deverbal predicative nouns inherit the *Aktionsart* of the verbs they are derived from, and thus they can be activities (e.g., FR *course* 'running'), accomplishments (e.g., FR *construction* (*d'une maison*) 'construction (of a house)'), achievements (e.g., FR *arrivée* 'arrival'), and semelfactives (e.g., FR *sursaut* 'start' and *frappe* 'strike'). Non-deverbal nouns are, instead, either processes (i.e., a series of quasi-identical events, according to Pustejovsky (1991a, b), such as FR *orage* 'storm' and *film* 'film showing') or semelfactives (FR *coup* 'blow'). As a matter of fact, Gross and Kiefer (1995: 45) strongly emphasize that duration is the only relevant feature in predicative nouns, generally speaking. As far as support verbs are concerned, within the model of object classes (*classes d'objets*) – in which the semantic classes of predicative nouns and of the typically co-occurring support verbs are classified – Gaston Gross (2004b: 347) considers *faire* 'do/make' and *avoir* 'have' as the French 'generic support verbs' for action nouns (e.g., FR *Paul a fait un voyage en Italie* lit. 'Paul did a trip to Italy') and state ones (e.g., FR *Paul a un bon caractère* 'Paul has a good character'), respectively. Furthermore, he points out that a specific class of objects might require a 'basic support verb' which is different from the generic one characterizing the entire aspectual class, as happens with the ‹*coups*› 'blows' class, selecting *donner* 'give' in French, although it is considered as an action class. Eventually, aspectual features are recognized for the so-called 'support verb extensions' (Gross 1981: 33; Vivès 1984), i.e., semantically full verbs in paradigmatic relation with basic support verbs, as variants adding nuances of meaning (e.g., FR *engager* 'begin', *poursuivre* 'continue', *cesser* 'stop' with the ‹*combats*› 'combats' class).

2.1 Light Verb Constructions as complex predicates and Romance linguistics tradition

From another perspective, LVCs have been included in the broader class of complex predicates, a notion which originated in syntactic approaches such as Lexical-Functional Grammar and Relational Grammar. Complex predicates are multi-headed predicates, i.e., they are "composed of more than one grammatical element (either morphemes or words), each of which contributes part of the information ordinarily associated with a head" (Alsina et al. 1997: 1). This is, for instance, the position of Butt (2010: 49), who argues that "the term complex predicate designates a construction that involves two or more predicational elements (e.g., nouns, verbs and adjectives) which predicate as a single unit, i.e., their arguments map onto a monoclausal syntactic structure". She specifically deals with Urdu [V+V] LVs, but considers also [V+N] constructions as LVCs. According to Butt (1995), the salient features of complex predicates are (a) the complexity of the argument structure, since two or more semantic heads contribute to it; (b) the grammatical functional structure of a simple predicate, as the subject is unique; and (c) the morphological or syntactic formation. As we have seen (Section 2), the fact that the subject is unique in LVCs has been claimed since the original development of the notion. On the other hand, the idea that two or more predicational elements constitute a single unit marks an important shift in viewpoint, dramatically questioning the actual lightness of the LV.

Within the literature on LVCs in Romance languages, an analysis that recognizes the lexical contribution of the verb to the LVC has been carried out within the Generative Lexicon framework (Pustejovsky 1995), for instance by De Miguel (2006, 2008, 2011) for Spanish (see also Ježek, 2011, this volume, for Italian). In this case, the focus is more on the meaning than on the syntactic mechanism of argument sharing between the two components of the LVC. According to De Miguel (2008: 571), a first hint of the fact that the verb in an LVC is not a mere support of the inflection is given by the existence of LVCs having the same noun but different LVs and a different meaning (see, e.g., SP *tener frío* 'be cold' ~ *coger frío* 'get cold' ~ *dar frío* 'give cold'; on this, cf. also Butt 2010: 1). Within the Generative Lexicon framework, the meaning of words is considered as underspecified: this lack of specification enables them to occur in different syntactic structures and in different operations of semantic composition, such as co-composition, which is a mechanism of concordance of lexical features (e.g., De Miguel 2006: 1302–1304; Pustejovsky 1995: *passim*; see Section 3.1). From this perspective, when the verb is combined with a noun that predicates an event compatible with its meaning, the concordance mechanism of lexical features occurs, resulting in lexical redundancy: this means that the LV in not empty or emptied, but that it predicates the same as the noun. According to De Miguel (2008: 575), this explains (a) the possibility of verb deletion, thanks to the redundancy, and (b) the LVC's semantic equivalence to a synthetic verb. Nevertheless, LVCs cannot always be considered as analytical predications equivalent to the synthetic counterparts, which is a further hint of the not-actual emptiness of the verb. This is true, for instance, in cases that seem to involve the *Aktionsart* – e.g., SP *dar un hervor* lit. 'give a boil' (*La leche dio un hervor* (**durante un rato*) lit. 'The milk gave a boil (*for a while)') ~ *hervir* 'boil' (*La leche hirvió durante un rato* 'the milk boiled for a while') – as well as further semantic features, such as [±HUMAN] – e.g., SP *dar un golpe* 'give a blow' ~ *golpear* 'hit' (*Juan golpeó el coche* 'Juan hit the car' ≈ *Juan dió un golpe al coche* 'Juan gave the car a blow' vs. *El fuerte viento golpeó el coche* 'The wind hit the car' ~ **El viento dió un golpe al coche* lit. 'The wind gave the car a blow'); nevertheless, the latter feature is not relevant in every usage, as *dar un hervor* clearly shows as for Spanish (De Miguel 2006: 1299). In addition, the fact that the meaning of the verb originates from the co-composition with the predicative noun can explain why the meaning of the LV can be specified by the noun it combines with (e.g., in IT *fare un sospiro* 'take a sigh', *fare* 'do/make' specifically means 'emit'; in SP *dar una explicación* 'give an explanation', *dar* 'give' stands for 'provide'; Ježek

2004: 186; De Miguel 2008: 569). Moreover, De Miguel (2008: 570) claims that LVCs may imply the lack of syntactic autonomy of the noun and the verb, i.e., syntactic cohesion. This is a logical consequence of the fact that the co-composition between the verb and the predicative noun generates a unique predication, in which the two elements share lexical features and denote the same event. For this reason, there can be noun arguments that become the arguments of the whole LVC (e.g., *John [[gave her an explanation] [of his reaction]]*), under strong cohesion conditions. This is shown by the possibility of moving these arguments out of the noun phrase (*The explanation that John gave her of his reaction*), while 'normal' verbal phrases (e.g., *John [gave her [a bouquet of flowers]]*) do not allow such an extraction (**The bouquet that John gave her of flowers*), and only allow the movement of the whole noun phrase (*The bouquet of flowers that John gave her*), as also LVCs under weak cohesion conditions do (*The explanation of his reaction that John gave her*) (Langer 2004: 182). The possibility of double syntactic analysis is another distinctive feature of LVCs, according to de Miguel (2008: 575).

On the other hand, an analysis focusing on the mechanism of argument sharing in LVCs as complex predicates has been proposed by Samek-Lodovici (2003), fitting into the syntactic thread. He deals with Italian LVCs with the LVs *dare* 'give' and *fare* 'do/make' in co-occurrence with *-ata* nominalizations (e.g., IT *Dare una lavata alle camicie* 'To wash the shirts' vs. *Gianni ha fatto una interminabile camminata* 'John walked endlessly'). Samek-Lodovici (2003) explains the lightness of both *dare* 'give' and *fare* 'do/make' in terms of decomposition of arguments into argument-variables – encoding argumenthood but isolated from the Lexical Conceptual Structure, hence void of interpretation – and thematic indices – linking argument-variables to the Lexical Conceptual Structure and thus making them interpretable. He argues that the formation of a complex predicate is due to two operations: (a) the erasure of the thematic indices in the verb argument structure, whereby the LVs *fare* 'do/make' and *dare* 'give' 'emerge' from their full semantics; (b) the transfer of the thematic indices associated with the nominalization argument-variables to the indexless verb argument-variables. In the end, both the LV and nominalization arguments are linked to the same Lexical Conceptual Structure variables. This mechanism determines the overall meaning of the LVC, preserving the original argument adicity – i.e., the number of arguments – of the full verb but not its interpretation. This means that *dare* 'give' as an LV remains a ditransitive verb and *fare* 'do/make' a monotransitive one. In both cases the external argument of the LV obligatorily coincides with the external argument of the nominalization; in this way, there is a single subject. In the case of *dare* 'give', the index transfer is extended to the indirect object, obligatorily coinciding with the second argument of the verbal base of the nominalization (e.g., IT *lavare le camicie* 'wash the shirts' ≈ *una lavata alle camicie* lit. 'a wash to the shirts'). From this perspective, the selection of either *dare* 'give' or *fare* 'do/make' as LVs directly follows from the adicity: the nominalizations derived from transitive verbs select *dare* 'give' (e.g., IT *lavata* 'wash'), whereas the nominalizations of intransitive select *fare* 'do/make' (e.g., IT *camminata* 'walk'). Indeed, from this perspective, if nominalizations of intransitive verbs selected *dare* 'give', either one of its three argument-variables would remain indexless, and thus uninterpretable, or there would be a violation of the Theta Criterion (Chomsky 1981: 36) by the assignment of the same thematic index to two argument-variables. On the other hand, the selection of *fare* 'do/make' by nominalizations of transitive verbs is considered as grammatical, albeit not very productive; in this case, only two thematic indices are transferred and the third is considered to be realized as a local argument of the nominalization, introduced by *di* 'of' (e.g., IT *Fare una lavata di camicie* 'To wash shirts'; Samek-Lodovici 2003: 857). Delving further into the issue of LVCs' argument structure would take us too far afield.[2] For the purposes of this article, two aspects are of interest: (a) the fact that this approach seems to exclude the possibility that *dare* 'give' might also occur in monotransitive structures, linking the selection of the LV to the adicity of the full counterpart, and (b) the fact that the presence of an argument structure in -*ata* nominalizations has, in fact, been questioned in the literature.

Indeed, Folli and Harley (2013) and Tovena and Donazzan (2017) argue that Italian -*ata* nominalizations have no argument structure. This means that, for example, in the Italian phrase *la caduta del muro* 'the fall of the wall', *muro* 'wall' can be considered as a participant in the event of falling, but it does not instantiate an argument of the noun (Tovena and Donazzan 2017: 87). In other words, while deverbal nouns, in Grimshaw's (1990) terms they are not complex event nominals, but simple event ones (like non-deverbal forms classified as predicative nouns by Gross and Kiefer 1995; Section 2). From the aspect point of view, Italian nominalizations in -*ata* denote in the domain of event occurrences, or acts: e.g., the count noun *sciata* does not refer to the activity of skiing – in Italian denoted by the nominal infinitive (*lo*) *sciare* – but to the single act of going on skis (on this cf., *inter alia*, Gaeta 2000, 2002). Since Grimshaw (1990: 55), nominals expressing a single instance of an event, i.e., having an individual reference, have been classified together with result nominals. For instance, they cannot co-occur with 'in/for-x-time' aspect modifiers (e.g., IT **La passeggiata di Maria in due ore / per due ore è stata stancante a causa della tremenda afa* lit. 'Mary's walk in two hours / for two hours was exhaust-

---

2 Among the other mechanisms that have been proposed to explain the presence of two semantic heads in complex predicates, see, at least, the notions of 'argument transfer' (Grimshaw and Mester 1988), 'argument raising' (Butt 1998), 'predicate composition' (Alsina 1996), and of 'clause union' in the multistratal approach of Relational Grammar (*inter alia*, La Fauci and Mirto 2003: 45–59).

ing because of the tremendous mugginess'), like simple event nominals and unlike complex event ones. Tovena and Donazzan (2017: 91–92) present a complex predicate composition rule of the LVC made up of -*ata* nominalizations and the LVs *fare* 'do/make' and *dare* 'give', the explanation of which is beyond the scope of this paper. For our purposes, it is sufficient to say that the composition of the nominalization with the LV allows the predication to have an external argument, and that the nominalization imposes some constraints on the participants in the event, although being devoid of argument structure. Moreover, it is worth noting that the authors point out that this rule preserves the semantically active role of both the nominalization and the LV involved in the LVC, avoiding the conception of LV selection as a mere matter of number of arguments that have been transferred or licensed. The most relevant constraint imposed by the nominalization on the participants in the event is the property of Initiator, which is considered as more general and abstract than animacy, viz., a cover term for semantic roles such as Agent and Cause, which can be instantiated, for instance, by animate entities, instruments and natural forces. The Initiator is conceived as a thematic trace of the external argument of the eventive base, and as a predicate that constrains the event, but does not introduce a semantic role nor does it license a syntactic argument. This property is considered as closely linked to the unacceptability of sentences such as Italian **Nel 1989, il muro di Berlino ha fatto una (brutta) caduta* 'In 1989, the Berlin Wall had a (great) fall', with respect to the acceptability of *Ieri Mario ha fatto una (brutta) caduta* 'Yesterday, Mario had a (great) fall', as the semantic properties of the subject are different: the ungrammaticality of the former sentence is due to the fact that the Berlin Wall is not the Initiator of its falling in 1989, as someone broke it down. From the aspectual point of view, -*ata* nominalizations characterize the event as dynamic, durative and bounded, since it is the expression of a single instance of an event: after all, Jespersen (1942: 117) already observed that deverbal nouns co-occurring with LVs can express "the action or an isolated instance of the action"; on the other hand, the insertion of a simple event nominal as predicative noun in LVC inevitably leads one to the conclusion that, even if the noun expresses the "important idea", it is not possible that the LV is really an "insignificant verb" (Section 2). In fact, Borer (2013: 56) notes that "'simple' events are fully compatible, syntactically, with 'complex' events, insofar as arguments and event modification are possible providing a light verb is present".

This implies a sort of rebalancing of the imbalance placed on the noun not only by the early studies concerning LVCs, but also within perspectives closer to the concept of complex verb. In this perspective, it is very likely that LVs give their own contribution to the actionality of LVCs.

3 The selection of the Light Verb 'give' in Romance languages

A cursory comparative glance at the selection of the signifiers for 'give' and 'do/make' in the major Romance languages clearly reveals that the adicity cannot be the (only) LV choice criterion, as the following examples show:

(1) 'give a slap': PT *dar uma bofetada*, SP *dar una bofetada*, FR *donner une gifle*, IT *dare uno schiaffo*; RM *a da o palmă*

(2) 'give a shout': PT *dar um grito*, SP *dar un grito*, FR *pousser un cri*, IT *fare / dare un grido*, RM *a striga / a da un strigăt*

(3) 'take a jump': PT *dar um salto*, SP *dar un salto*, FR *faire un bond*, IT *fare un salto*, RM *a face un salt*

(4) 'take a walk': PT *dar um passeio*, SP *dar un paseo*, FR *faire une promenade*, IT *fare una passeggiata*; RM *a face o plimbare*

Obviously, these examples do not only concern LVCs with -*ata* nominalizations or their equivalents (PT -*ada*, SP -*ada*, FR -*ade*, RM -*ăt*). As a matter of fact, the nouns in these LVCs are not completely comparable either from the word formation (e.g., PT *passeio* / SP *paseo*, IT *passeggiata*) or etymological viewpoint (e.g., PT *salto* / SP *salto* / IT *salto* / RM *salt* vs. FR *bond*). It is also noteworthy that sometimes the synthetic equivalent counterpart is preferred to the basic LV (e.g., RM *a striga* ≈ *a da un strigăt*), as well as LV extensions (FR *pousser un cri* 'push a shout'; cf. Pompei and Piunno, this volume). However, the interchangeability of 'give' and 'do/make' both cross-linguistically and even within the same language (e.g., IT *fare / dare un grido*) clearly emerges. Therefore, i) if hitting nouns for 'slap' (1) can readily refer to transitive predicate, so that their selection of the LV 'give' seems to be predictable starting from the adicity, and ii) if sound nouns such as 'shout' (2), although usually intransitive, can sometimes involve an addressee, so justifying the selection of 'give' (Section 4.1.2), yet, this explanation seems not to apply in the case of MNs such as 'jump' and 'walk' (3–4). They refer to intransitive predicates, so that they should select the LV 'do/make'; nevertheless, they co-occur with *dar* 'give' in the Iberic languages. These findings make the results of the fine-grained analyses proposed to explain the selection of the LV with Italian -*ata* nominalizations not completely extensible to the data considered here. In other words, the data aggregated on a morphological basis can be explained based upon the argument structure sharing in LVCs. Conversely, when dealing with lexically coherent groups of nouns, LV selection has been explained not only by taking into account the adicity, but especially the meaning of the lexically full verbal counterpart (Section 3.1). On the other hand, the aspectual feature of boundedness attributed to -*ata* formations among others by Tovena and Donazzan (2017) deserves further investigation as a constraint on the nouns co-occurring with the LV 'give', due to an inheritance of meaning of its lexically full counterpart (Sections 3.1.1, 4).

After presenting the adopted aspectual classification of nouns, which includes boundedness (Section 3.2), the last section of this article is aimed at testing the hypothesis of boundedness centrality in the event structure of LVCs having 'give' as an LV. To this purpose, a case study is carried out on Latin [V+N] LVCs in which the LV *dare* 'give' co-occurs with PhINs (Section 4.1) and MNs (Section 4.2).

3.1 'Give' as a full, a figurative, and a Light Verb in Romance languages

From a contrastive perspective, the reasons for the selection and the partial overlapping of the LVs 'do/make' and 'give' in Romance languages LVCs of the types in (1)-(4) have mainly been sought in the argument structure and in the basic semantic value of the lexically full counterpart of the two LVs. For instance, comparing Spanish and French, Moncó Taracena (2011: 126–127) reflects on the conditions of the overlapping between Spanish *dar* / French *donner* 'give' and Spanish *hazer* / French *faire* 'do/make' and makes reference to the basic meaning of the two lexically full verbs and their argument structure. As well known, 'give' has a concrete, core semantic value of transfer, and coherently is a three-slot transitive verb, since it requires an Agent as the first argument, transferring a Theme, which is the second argument, to a Recipient, namely the third one. On the other hand, 'do/make' has the core semantic value of creation, viz., realization, and consistently is a two-slot predicate, which requires an Agent as the first argument, creating the second argument, that is an (incremental) Theme. The possibility of the overlapping of the two verbs may be due either (a) to the addition of a third participant to the scene evoked by the verb 'do/make', with a semantic value of Beneficiary rather than of actual Recipient – as happens, for instance, in French, in *Louis a fait un gâteau pour sa soeur* 'John made a cake for his sister' – or (b) to the missing third argument of the verb 'give', perhaps when the Recipient is recoverable from the context or generic – as happens, for example, in Spanish *La viña da un vino excelente* lit. 'The vineyard gives an excellent wine'. According to Moncó Taracena (2011: 127), in the latter case, a mere transitive – rather than ditransitive – construction is envisaged for 'give'. In the former case, a verb not usually expressing a transfer can denote it because of its insertion in the so-called 'Dative Construction' (cf. Palancar 2003: 201; below) through pronominal encoding of the Beneficiary (e.g., FR *Louis lui a fait un gâteau* 'John made her a cake'). Starting from these two constructions that either full lexical verbs can have in common, the overlapping between the use of Spanish LV *dar* 'give' and French LV *faire* 'do/make' is explained. It is worth noting that such explanations fit constructionist approaches well. For example, Hilpert (2014: 32) considers occurrences where a usually transitive verb occurs in a ditransitive construction (e.g., *bake* in *Sally baked her sister a cake*) as an instance of *valency-increasing construction*; together with the opposite *valency-decreasing construction*, this can be included in the more general notion of *valency coercion* (see *inter alia* Michaelis 2004; Perek and Hilpert 2014; Perek 2015) (Section 3.1.1).

From another perspective – i.e., of internal-language overlapping, but equally referring to the lexically full verb – De Miguel (2011: 144) points out that in Spanish, when both the LVs *dar* 'give' and *hacer* 'do/make' are possible (as happens in SP *dar un masaje* 'give a massage' vs. *hacer un masaje* 'do a massage'), in the latter case a creation event is encoded, while in the former it is, rather, a transfer event. Indeed, according to De Miguel (2008: 575), 'give' has an underspecified meaning of 'to pass something from a source to a goal', either when the object is a concrete entity (e.g., a piece of candy) or the verb co-occurs, as an LV, with an abstract one (e.g., an explanation). Moreover, De Miguel (2008: 576–577) observes that in Spanish *dar* 'give' as an LV can combine with compatible eventive nouns such as *besos* 'kisses', *abrazos* 'hugs', *golpes* 'blows' (1) y *gritos* 'shouts' (2) because they involve a muscular effort that 'exits' from the body and reaches an external goal, namely they share with the LV the lexical feature 'trajectory'. Similarly, from a cognitive and constructionist perspective, for Spanish Palancar (2003: 202–203) establishes a connection between the so-called 'Dative Construction' – the three-slot construction of *dar* 'give' – and what he calls the 'Construction of Hitting Events' (e.g., SP *el borracho le dio un puñetazo a su amigo* 'the drunk gave a punch to his friend'); he refers to Goldberg (1995: 149) in considering intentional actions directed at other people as a metaphor for the transfer of a physical entity. Starting from this extension, Moncó Taracena (2011: 130–131), in turn, extends Palancar's (2003) 'Construction of Hitting Events' to the use of Spanish *dar* 'give' with sound nouns, in which the Experiencer is not truly physically 'affected' and may even be missing (e.g., SP *dar un silbido (al perro)* 'give a whistle (to the dog)'); she calls this more inclusive and complex structure 'Physical Implication Construction'. Moreover, Moncó Taracena (2011: 131) proposes that the semantic extension of Spanish *dar* 'give' from the meaning of concrete transfer to the metaphorical meaning in co-occurrence with PhINs goes all the way to MNs (3–4), according to the metaphorical chain "Transfer Construction > Physical Implication Construction > Motion Construction". It is worth noting that Moncó Taracena (2011) considers the abstract extensions of *dar* 'give' in Spanish as LV uses, whereas Palancar (2003) never refers to this notion and merely speaks of 'polysemous networks', in which the mechanism of semantic variation is related to the insertion of the verb into specific constructions, where meaning extensions occur. They are 'extensions' because from a cognitive perspective the starting point is the basic verb meaning, which is related to spatial context.

Actually, as Sanromán Vilas (2011: 255–256) clarifies, among the approaches which have considered LVs as not truly empty, two main groups can be identified, namely i) those which have focused on the relationship between LVs and their heavy counterparts, and ii) those which have centered on the connection between the LV and the predicative noun. The former thread mostly concerns scholars who adhere to cognitive frameworks, considering the verb uses that are different from the heavy one as extensions of a polysemous word, as well as assuming that the meaning is also determined by the construction in which the LV is placed. On the other hand, the latter group especially includes scholars with lexicological interests, who research the semantic reasons for the 'semantic agreement' (Apresjan 2009: 4) of a certain LV with a certain predicative noun (such as the mechanism of co-composition within the Generative Lexicon framework; Section 2.1). This is an excellent summary of the different theoretical approaches to the challenges that LVs continue to pose to linguistic theory, even when they are considered as complex predicates. Sometimes, the reasons for the semantic compatibility between the LV and the predicative noun have been pinpointed in actional features, also in a more complex way than the mere identification of the co-occurrence of stative verbs with stative nouns and of dynamic verbs with eventive nouns (Section 2). For instance, for Portuguese Duarte et al. (2010: 29) explain the compatibility of the LV and the MN in *dar um passeio* 'take a walk' considering (a) the LV *dar* 'give' as endowed with the features [+DYNAMIC], [±CHANGE], [±CAUSE], [±DURATIVE], where only one ([+DYNAMIC]) is specified, and (b) the eventive noun *passeio* 'walk' as endowed with the specified features [+DYNAMIC], [-CHANGE], [-CAUSE], [+DURATIVE], whose values are inherited by the whole Portuguese LVC *dar um passeio* 'take a walk' ([+DYNAMIC], [-CHANGE], [-CAUSE], [+DURATIVE]). On the other hand, in Spanish an instance such as *dar un hervor* lit. 'give a boil' cannot have the same atelic interpretation as the synthetic verb *hervir* 'boil' (Section 2.1) likely because of the feature of boundedness entailed by the LV *dar* 'give'.

The compatibility of LV and predicative noun from the event structure viewpoint has been scarcely studied. However, evidence exists of some boundedness constraints linked to the selection of 'give', not only in Romance languages (see Pompei and Piunno, this volume).

3.1.1 ... and beyond

Butt and Geuder (2001) deal with LVCs having the [V+V] pattern in Urdu, in which one of the verbs is the so-called 'main verb', whereas the other is the LV *de* 'give'. They exclude the possibility that LVs in Urdu mark perfectivity (Hook 1991) as a result of a grammaticalization process, as if they were auxiliaries. Rather, they consider LVs as semi-lexical heads, since they cannot make independent reference to events, but are not a totally empty element: "what is involved is some type of lexically specified content which interacts with the semantics of the main verb" (Butt and Geuder 2001: 336). To grasp what this content consists of, they compare Urdu [V+V] LVCs with the LV *de* 'give' and English [V+N] LVCs with the LV *give*, highlighting that in both languages LVs are formally identical with lexically full counterparts. However, English LV *give* usually occurs in the same ditransitive construction as its lexically full counterpart, while Urdu LVs can be distinguished from the heavy counterpart both from the semantic and the syntactic viewpoint. Starting from prototypical concrete ditransitive occurrences such as *give him the ball* – where a change in possession as well as in location is involved – other different uses are considered, including LV uses, such as *give someone a kiss / a punch* and *give the car a wash*. The conclusion of the in-depth discussion of the instances is that "[t]he array of different uses of *give* in English yields the impression that the semantic features present in light verb constructions can be understood as continual extensions from the prototypical concrete meaning of *give*, with the extension of the meaning being correlated to the increasing abstractness of the referents filling the Theme argument slot" (Butt and Geuder 2001: 343). The same seems to happen in monotransitive *give* occurrences, from concrete ones (*to give milk*) to abstract ones (*give a scream*), which have been much less studied and are not even dealt with in Butt and Geuder's (2001) study. Such an extension of abstractness implies the semantic weakening of the verb, namely, lightness. The authors, however, express perplexity about the real possibility that LVs are exclusively due to lexical sense extension, and attribute this impression to the occurrence of both lexical fully verbs and LVs "in the very same grammatical construction" (Butt and Geuder 2001: 343). In particular, they criticize the possibility of connecting *give* LV uses to the prototypical meaning of the heavy verb counterpart through the sharing of an abstract 'transfer schema', such as the one shown in Figure 1, which refers to Newman's (1996) typological study on 'give', within the cognitive framework. Here, the object of 'give' (Theme) can be both a noun denoting a concrete entity (e.g., *ball*), in the domain of spatial transfer, and one denoting an abstract entity (e.g., *regards* in *give someone one's regards*), in the domain of abstract transfer:

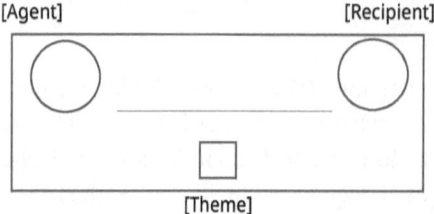

Figure 1: 'transfer schema' (from Butt and Geuder 2001: 353).

Butt and Geuder (2001: 354) encounter difficulties in extending this schema to LVCs such as *to give someone a kiss* or *to give the soup a stir*, as they identify a problem in the referential distinctiveness of what is denoted by the verb and the object, respectively. As long as the object denotes an entity, even an abstract one, this distinctiveness subsists, and the transfer represents a relationship between three individuals, which itself constitutes an event. Nevertheless, a kiss does not subsist independently of its 'transfer'; nor is it clear to the two authors how 'a stir' can be conceived independently of the event of 'stirring' that the schema is supposed to represent: indeed, in the latter case, "the mere application of an action to an entity is all that is left of the transaction meaning of *give*" (Butt and Geuder 2001: 342). However, they note that in the various figurative uses of *give*, including those with greater semantic weakening, i.e., the LV ones, some features of meaning always remain: (a) the agentivity of the subject (in ditransitive constructions), who is always a sentient being performing an intentional act; (b) an entailment of control over the resulting state affecting the Recipient, who is also a sentient being, at least until the result is reduced to the mere exercise of an effect (as happens, e.g., in *to give the soup a stir*); (c) a vague sense of emission (cf., e.g., *I gave it a good throw* ~*I gave the ball a good catch*); and, last but not least, (d) the constant boundedness of the events co-occurring with *give*, as an effect of the fact that the entity in object position is always forced into the reading of a specific quantity. Actually, the verb meaning involves a constraint on the amount of matter that can be transferred, even in the presence of a mass noun: for instance, if we say *I gave milk to the child*, this is not an unbounded event of giving that goes on as long as there is milk, but a single event of giving a specific quantity of milk, e.g., a cupful. Since the boundedness-unboundedness opposition is the counterpart for events of the count-mass distinction, it is highly likely that the actionality of event-denoting nouns occurring in LV uses of *give* equally implies boundedness (Section 3.2). This is a crucial point for our analysis.

LVs conveying a special type of meaning – which consists of features such as volitionality, benefaction, forcefulness, boundedness – is also true for Urdu [V+V] LVs. To explain this modulation, after dealing with the weakening of meaning of the verb *give* in terms of lexical decomposition,[3] Butt and Geuder (2001) consider LVs similar to modifiers, such as manner adverbs in neo-Davidsonian representation (Parsons 1990). In detail, they postulate an event predicate GIVE-TYPE(e) – e.g., *John gave the car a wash* = wash(e)(John, the car) & GIVE-TYPE(e) – where the contents of GIVE-TYPE(e) can be variously expanded: GIVE-TYPE(e) = (a) e has beneficial effects on THEME(e) or (b) e involves the force transmission pattern AGENT(e)-THEME(e), etc. (Butt and Geuder 2001: 356). In this way, the semantic interpretation is dependent on the adducing of contextual factors through a mechanism of non-monotonous inference capable of accounting for the enormous flexibility of meaning. This means that LVs do not denote classes of events on their own, but only add some semantic features to the event like modifiers, which is different from the usual denotation of verbs. This is a very interesting proposal, which clearly explains the Urdu [V+V] pattern as a complex predicate made up of a main verb and an LV. It is also noteworthy that, in addition to event modification, complex predicates also show other types of relationship between the two components, such as event summation – when the relation is a symmetric one – and event augmentation – when the relation is a functor-argument one, changing the sort of the event conveyed by the lexical verb, as happens when adding a predicate to another yields causative, inchoative, resultative effects (Butt and Geuder 2001: 358–361). On the other hand, according to Butt and Geuder (2001: 356), their proposal is problematic for the [V+N] LVC pattern, since the modifier is encoded as a verb, whereas the modified as its object. Moreover, constant reference to semantic roles certainly creates some difficulty in the case of constructions with MNs, where it is hardly tenable that the subject is always an agentive one.

For these reasons, a cognitive perspective is preferable for our purposes. Indeed, the main aim of this article is to gather what it means to consider the LV 'give' as a complex predicate from the actionality perspective. To this end, the representation in the vein of Newman's (1996) typological findings seems to be particularly appropriate for modeling the 'boundedness constraint' that this LV seems to entail. At the same time, this perspective easily allows us to understand which features of the full verb lexical meaning are present in 'give' usages as LV. Likewise, argument structure is closely related to these features, which turn out to be semantically shared with the noun.

As a matter of fact, Newman's (1996: 37–60) cognitive shaping takes into consideration four domains making up the frame evoked by 'give', i.e., the 'literal give'

---

3 The proposal is DO (x, [x CAUSE CHANGE <HAVE(x,z), HAVE(y,z)>]); DO encodes the agentive-intentional role of x and excludes the inadvertent causation, which is absent in the literal meaning of *give* (Butt and Geuder 2001: 340).

transfer schema (where a person who has something passes it over with his/her hands to another person receiving it with his/her hands): (a) the spatio-temporal domain, (b) the control domain, (c) the force-dynamics domain, and (d) the domain of 'human interest'. Through these four domains, all of the features of meaning seen above – from trajectory to agentivity/volitionality, control/benefaction, sense of emission/forcefulness, and boundedness – can be accounted for.

The spatio-temporal domain is the basic one, as the frame of 'give' necessarily involves a change in the position of the thing being passed, and this occurs in a temporal dimension. Moreover, 'give' includes a profile, namely a GIVER, a THING, a RECIPIENT, and the relations holding between these entities. Eventually, the hands of the GIVER and the RECIPIENT are also 'active zones' (Langacker 1987: 271–274), i.e., entities involved in the interaction, even if they are not overtly spelled out. The predicate profile involves one or more instances of trajector/landmark organization, viz., an asymmetry relation between profiled entities. This is a core notion that the cognitive perspective takes from the *Gestalt* psychology relationship figure/ground, where "the figure is a substructure perceived as 'standing out' from the remainder (the ground) and accorded special prominence as the pivotal entity around which the scene is organized" (Langacker 1987: 120). A type of asymmetry between the trajector and the landmark is, for instance, that between the subject and the object, at the syntactic level, but it is not the only one possible. Indeed, given a clause such as *The teacher gave the girl a book*, according to the subject/object asymmetry, there is an agentive GIVER, the teacher, who is the trajector, controlling the movement of the book, which is the landmark. On the other hand, the most literal interpretation of the trajector/landmark relation is that of a moving entity – i.e., the book, in this case – with respect to a stationary ground – i.e., the girl, in this case. Actually, in human cognition the same scene can be construed with different trajector/landmark relations (Langacker 1987: 120–122, 217–222). While Newman (1996: 41) mainly considers the subject/object interpretation of the trajector/landmark relation, for the purposes of this article its motion interpretation is particularly relevant. In Figure 2 we see a very schematic representation of the spatio-temporal domain, where the arrow stands for the progression both in space and in time:

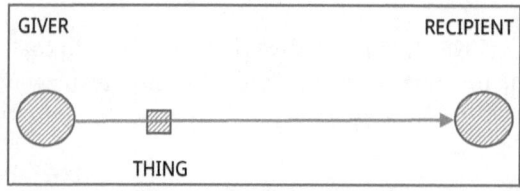

Figure 2: The spatio-temporal domain of 'give' (from Newman 1996: 42).

While the spatio-temporal domain shapes 'give' as a predicate expressing a change in location, the control domain actually models the change in possession of the THING. However, the term 'control' is preferred, since what passes from the hands of the GIVER to those of the RECIPIENT may be not really owned either by the former or by the latter (e.g., if my husband gives me the salt at the restaurant, it is neither his nor mine). From this viewpoint, 'give' denotes the change from a control sphere to another one, as the dashed rectangles in Figure 3 show:

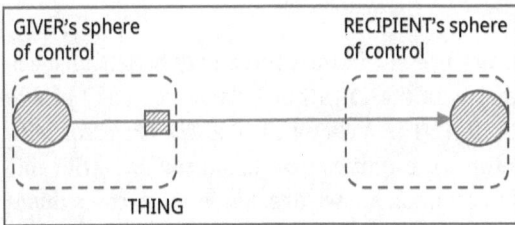

Figure 3: The control domain of 'give' (from Newman 1996: 47).

The force-dynamics domain is inspired by the semantic schema of the Force Dynamics (Talmy 1985, 1988) and adds to the representation of 'give' the idea of an energy flow, which arises from an 'energy source' and is exhausted in an 'energy sink' (Langacker 1991: 292–293). The energy flow can be variously conceived: in this case, it may represent, for instance, the physical movement of the three components, where the GIVER is the source, i.e., the initiator of the giving event, and the RECIPIENT the locus where it finishes. If we think of different domains as simultaneously combining by making up a matrix domain (Croft 1993), the same arrow that symbolizes the passage of time can also represent the flow of energy with the addition of two vertical lines standing for the starting and the end points of the energy flow and of dotted curved arrows to represent the participation of the profiled entities, as is shown in Figure 4 (next page); according to Newman (1996: 49), this participation is more active in the case of the GIVER as a 'willful' initiator (thicker lines) than for the RECIPIENT (finer lines).

Eventually, the so-called 'human interest' domain only conceptualizes the fact that an act of giving may have some effects on the RECIPIENT. According to Newman (1996: 51–52), on a scale ranging from benefactive effects to adversative ones, the act of giving is usually located towards the former. Of course, this is not always the case.

It is worth noting that all the domains are simultaneously present in the meaning of a lexically full verb. From this viewpoint, the semantic bleaching of the LV compared to the full counterpart can be conceived as the loss of the contribution of one or more domains to the matrix domain.

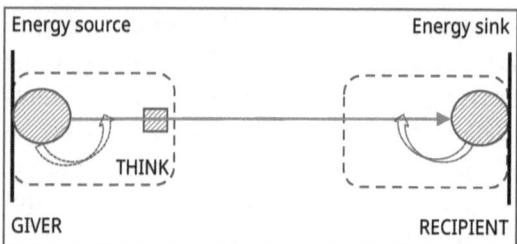

Figure 4: The force-dynamics domain of 'give' (from Newman 1996: 50).

Moreover, one or more of the entities present in the profile may be left unspecified, as happens, for instance, either with the THING in a clause such as *I give to the Catholic Church* or with the RECIPIENT in a clause such as *The professor gave the answers before the exam*. Sometimes the omitted participant can be retrievable either from the context or thanks to common knowledge, but in other cases this is not true, and we can think of particular constructions. Cognitive Grammar considers the parts that are filled in an actual construction as 'elaboration sites' (e-sites), shading them (like in Figures 2–4). Both the possibility of having a matrix more or less rich in domains and of profiling a decrease in the number of participants, as well as their increase (Section 3.1), foster flexibility in the uses of 'give'. In Newman's (1996) terms, this means figurative extensions.

3.2 Predicative noun actionality: reflecting on 'give' and boundedness

The notion of (un)boundedness arises from the comparison between the mass/count distinction within the nominal category and the aspectual oppositions within the verbal one (see *inter alia* Brinton 1991, 1998 and the bibliography provided therein). Indeed, both categories show the "human cognitive capacity of conceptualizing entities and event-situations as individuals or as [...] masses" (Paprotté 1988: 454). This is a matter of quantity conceptualization. Talmy (2000: 50) considers an unbounded quantity "as continuing on indefinitely", whereas a bounded quantity "is conceived to be demarcated as an individuated unit entity". The demarcation of a bounded quantity is due to the existence of boundaries. This definition perfectly fits the representation through two vertical lines of the starting and the end points of the energy flow that can be assumed as a characterizing feature in the meaning of 'give' (Figure 4).

It is worth noting that (un)boundedness does not completely overlap (a)telicity (Depraetere 1995). Atelic verbs are characterized by homogeneity. Homogeneous entities meet the principle of arbitrary divisibility formulated by Frege (1961[1884]: 66), whereby a part of a homogeneous continuum is an instance of the whole (any part of *walking* is *walking*). While states are homogenous down to instants, activities are homogeneous down to short intervals (Dowty 1979): the minimal interval is the part at which the event holds (e.g., to say that a walking event is under way, the first part of the walking event, i.e., the movement of lifting up the foot, is not enough, and more than two steps are needed; see Rothstein 2012: 77–78). When a minimal instance of the activity occurs, it is then maintained identical through increasingly bigger intervals of time, which is possible by virtue of the characteristic of cumulativity (Quine 1960: 91), or additivity (Carlson 1981: 50). On the other hand, telic events are not homogeneous, but heterogeneous: for instance, when a house is being built, there are very different subevents that are going on, until the endpoint is reached (and the house is ready). In this perspective, the difference between boundedness and telicity is that the former consists of a temporal boundary, while the latter of reaching the endpoint – or *télos*, or culmination –, which is inherent in telic events and obviously involves a temporal boundary, as well. This implies that with a homogeneous entity, usually unbounded, the outer, extrinsic boundary is a distinctive feature, whereas with heterogeneous entities, it is a redundant one. Since homogeneous entities are conceptualized as having no inherent boundaries, they can only be limited by imposing external ones. Talmy (2000: 51) defines this operation as 'bounding' or 'portion excerpting'. It can be variously realized.[4] As far as nominalizations are concerned, portion excerpting can be closely related to the morphology of the nouns: from this perspective, the suffix *-ata* (Section 2.1) is a clear bounding strategy in Italian. Similarly, the difference between *-ing* forms in English, such as *walking*, and Ø-derivation forms, such as *walk*, may be explained in terms of bounding (*inter alia* Brinton 1998: 48–51): *walking* is an unbounded nominalization like the verb *walk* is, whereas the Ø-derivation is a bounded nominalization, since it refers only to a single instance – that is to a portion – of the activity. Actually, nominalizations from activity verbs are one of the quite problematic areas for the *Aspect Preservation Hypothesis* formulated by Fábregas et al. (2012), which postulates the cross-categorial aspectual heritage. The fact that activities' unboundedness is not always preserved in nominalizations

---

[4] As for verbs, portion excerpting can be realized by degree adverbials (e.g., *walk for a while*) or prefixes, such as the prefix *po-* (e.g., RU *po-chodit* 'walk for a while', *po-begat* 'run for a while') and the perdurative prefix *pro-* (e.g., RU *proguliat' ves' den'* 'to go for a walk all day long') in Russian. The latter focuses on a bigger amount of the homogeneous continuum and requires the explicit specification of the period involved (Mehlig 1996).

has been shown also for French, for instance, for cases such as *promenade* 'walk' from the verb *se promener* 'walk' (Haas et al. 2008; Huyghe 2011).[5]

Another relevant point is the fact that the internal structure of a quantity may be either continuous – when it is seamless – or discrete – when it is conceptualized as having internal breaks, or interruptions (dividedness; cf. Talmy 2000: 55–58). From this perspective, activities such as *walk* are externally unbounded and internally continuous, whereas a verb such as *breathe* denotes an externally unbounded but internally discrete activity. Hence, verbs such as *breathe* may have both an activity and a semelfactive interpretation, a peculiarity that is termed 'naturally atomicity' by Rothstein (2008). In these cases, the nominalization precisely reveals this atomic internal structure, as *breath* does. Talmy (2000: 49) defines this discretizing operation as 'unit excerpting'. Indeed, this is an operation of singling out, namely of individuation of a single instance. As the unit intrinsically is bounded, it can also be considered as a further operation of bounding, according to Jackendoff (1991: 22–23). It can be variously realized.[6] The difference between the verb *breathe* and the LVC *take a breath* specifically consists in extracting a single instance from an unbounded discrete activity. As far as nominalizations are concerned, this means that, divisibility and additivity being equal, from unbounded continuous activities (such as the verb *walk*) only portions can be extracted (portion excerpting), while from unbounded discrete activities (such as *breathe*) individual members can be extracted (unit excerpting).

Eventually, according to the category of plexity – e.g., the "quantity's state of articulation into equivalent elements" (Talmy 2000: 48) – *take a breath* is uniplex, being a quantity that consists of only one element, like *(to) sigh*, whereas *breathe* is multiplex, consisting of more than one element, like *keep sighing*, which exploits a multiplexing strategy, i.e., the reverse of unit excerpting. Nevertheless, in addition to *breathe*, *take breaths* also exists, which is properly due to the multiplexing of *take a breath*: unboundedness, dividedness and multiplexing being equal, the difference between *take breaths* and *breathe* lies in the degree of blurring and fusion that discrete elements may exhibit, since *take breaths* allows one to conceptualize

---

[5] The different behavior of nouns with regards to (un)boundedness is detected by tests. Unbounded nominalizations co-occur with 'for-x-time' adverbs, like activity verbs (e.g., FR *l'écoute de la radio pendant trois heures* 'the listening of the radio for three hours'); on the contrary, bounded ones cannot, but they are compatible with 'of-x-time' adverbs, which only co-occur with nouns and detect bounded duration (e.g., FR **une promenade pendant une heure* 'a walk during an hour' vs. *une promenade d'une heure* 'a walk of an hour'); see Haas et al. (2008).

[6] As for verbs, the semelfactive suffix *-nu-* is a Russian strategy of unit excerpting (e.g., RU *gavknut'* 'to give a yap', from *gavkat'* 'to yap'). Sometimes, from the same activity both a unit and a portion can be extracted (e.g., RU *pogavkat'* 'to yap for a while' and *progavkat'* 'to yap for a certain period of time', from *gavkat'* 'to yap'; Mehlig 1996: 98).

individual breaths as discrete and not fused into an indistinct process, unlike what happens with *breathe*. Indeed, the selection of either *take a breath* or *take breaths* permits us to disambiguate between either a semelfactive or an iterative reading, which is not readily found with *breathe*, in the absence of contextual specifications.

In addition to the categories of plexity, boundedness, and dividedness, Talmy (2000: 61) also considers what he calls 'degree of extension', which has three main members (Figure 5):

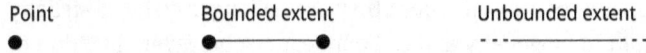

Figure 5: Talmy's (2000: 61) degree of extension.

From Figure 5 it is quite clear that uniplexity is actually the extreme pole of a continuum where the other pole is unboundedness. As for verbs, this continuum from unboundedness to punctuality primarily concerns a reduction in the extension in time. Considering that duration is the only relevant feature in predicative nouns – at least according to Gross and Kiefer (1995: 45; Section 2) – this approach seems to be particularly suitable also for dealing with nominalizations. Indeed, Simone (2003) presents a classification of Romance nominalizations along the continuum between verb and noun (Figure 6), which independently coincides with the continuum in Figure 5, albeit specular and starting from very different premises:

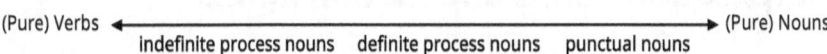

Figure 6: Nominalization classes in the continuum verb-noun (adapted from Simone 2003).

This classification is adopted by Ježek (2015: 147–151).[7] Nouns of indefinite process denote [+DYNAMIC], [+DURATIVE], and [-TELIC] events, such as Italian nominal infinitive *(il) bere* 'drinking' and *(il) nuotare* 'swimming' (and English *-ing* forms), which are characterized by the same aspectual features as the verbs from which they originate, i.e., activities. From the actionality perspective, atelicity implies unboundedness. On the other hand, in Ježek's (2015) classification, nouns of definite process denote two different kinds of events, both [+DYNAMIC] and [+DURATIVE], but [±TELIC],

---

7 Simone (2003) starts from two nominal deverbal forms of classical Arabic grammar, i.e., that of *maṣdar* (the form representing the semantics of the triconsonantal root in its most global way) and that of *'ismu al-marrati* (the form designating each individual instance of the process). Here we are not interested in Ježek's (2015) fourth class, i.e., state-denoting nouns, because we are dealing with PhINs and MNs, which are both characterized by the feature of dynamicity.

namely having a different internal structure: the first ones are homogeneous events, such as Italian -*ata* nominalizations – like *nuotata* 'swim' – (and English Ø-derivation forms), which denote a single instance of the event of swimming; conversely, the second type is constituted by heterogeneous events, such as *costruzione* 'construction', which needs culmination to be an accomplishment. In this case, both kinds of event are bounded: the atelic ones, through the superposition of outer boundaries; the telic ones, because they are intrinsically bounded. Bounding operations do not change the internal structure of predicates: bounded activities lose by definition their unboundedness, therefore they are no longer atelic, if atelicity is characterized by both homogeneity and unboundedness; however, they do not become certainly telic, if the *télos* is understood as culmination. In other terms, for definite – viz., bounded – predicates the feature of (a)telicity does not seem to be pertinent. The class of punctual nouns is also twofold, including both achievements – such as Italian *partenza* 'start, departure' – and semelfactive nouns – such as Italian *salto* 'jump'. The former are certainly [+DYNAMIC], [-DURATIVE] and [+TELIC], whereas the telicity of the latter is questionable, as they do not present any transition between one state and the next. However, semelfactives are 'intrinsically bounded' (Kiss 2011: 122).[8] Hence, both types of punctual nouns are bounded.

4 A case study: Latin *dare* 'give' with physical implication nouns and motion nouns

In this section, a case study of Latin will be considered. One of the advantages of analyzing Latin data is the possibility to study a very large corpus – although necessarily a closed one – which extends over a long period of time.[9] The data consid-

---

[8] As for verbs, according to Zaliznjak and Šmelev (2000: 118), semelfactive denote one 'quantum' of the activity described by the base. Concerning telicity, Bertinetto (1986: 273–279) denies that punctual verbs are telic, as the test 'in-x-time' is not applicable to them. Conversely, Van Valin and LaPolla (1997: 96) recognize the telicity at all the achievements, pointing out that "they are only compatible with *in*-phrases referring to an exceedingly short period of time, such as *in the blink of an eye, in an instant*" (see also Vendler 1957: 146–147).

[9] Closed corpora imply that what is not attested was not necessarily absent in the language. Hence, studies conducted on a quantitative basis have not always been found valid (see Baños 2019: 22 on the use of the frequency criterion for establishing the basic Latin LV for a given predicative noun). In this article, the data analysis will be qualitative. Texts considered for the study are literary in nature and cover the period from the Early to Imperial Latin (3rd c. BCE - 2nd c. CE); they are quoted according to the editions in Brepols' electronic corpus *Library of Latin Texts – Series A* (http://www.brepolis.net). In addition, the *New Testament* has been considered, following Merk's

ered concern PhINs (Section 4.1) and MNs (Section 4.2), which have been at least partially studied for Romance languages. The analysis is developed within the cognitive approach (Section 3.1.1). This choice allows us (a) to overcome a conception of LVCs as complex predicates exclusively focused on the argument structure and (b) to include both argument and event structure in a holistic view of the complex predicate, in which both components contribute to some extent to the LVC's semantics. This extent may be different, depending on how many features the LV inherits from the meaning of the full verb in its different uses. Moreover, the choice of this approach allows us to retain the terms of GIVER, THING and RECIPIENT, which constitute the profile of 'give' as a lexically full verb together with the relations holding between these entities. Therefore, a uniform treatment of different LVCs is possible, regardless of the semantic role of the constituents, namely, a consistent account of the flexibility of uses.

4.1 Physical implication nouns

PhINs are distinguished into hitting (Section 4.1.1) and sound nouns (Section 4.1.2), according to Moncó Taracena's (2011) suggestion of including both classes within the same construction ('Physical Implication Construction'), starting from Palancar's (2003) extension of the literal 'give' 'Dative Construction' uses to the co-occurrence of the same verb with hitting events (Section 3.1).

4.1.1 Hitting nouns

Hitting nouns usually select 'give' verbs in Romance languages, as noted, for instance, by Gross (2004b: 347) for French, Duarte et al. (2010) for Portuguese, Palancar (1999) and Moncó Taracena (2011) for Spanish (see also, Pompei and Piunno, this volume, for Italian). The same happens from a cross-linguistic viewpoint. Newman (1996: 201–210) includes hitting nouns within the class of 'sche-

---

edition (*Vulgate* Latin version). Text authors and titles are in Latin and not abbreviated, for ease of reference. Glosses follow the *Leipzig Glossing Rules*; for the sake of readability they are limited to basic morphological information (singular number, nominative case, and gender not indicated for nouns; active voice, indicative mood and present tense not indicated for verbs). In Latin, the quotation form is the singular nominative for nouns, the first-person singular of the present active (or deponent) indicative for verbs; however, verbs will be quoted in the present infinitive. English translations are from *The Loeb Classical Library*, and – as far as the *New Testament* is concerned – from the *New Revised Standard Version* (https://www.biblestudytools.com/).

matic interactions' (together with other uses, such as *give the car a wash, give someone a shove, give someone a hug/kiss*). Although considering it as one of the figurative uses of 'give', he recognizes the light nature of the verb in this case and notes that here 'give' "appears to contribute little more than the idea of an interaction between entities", whose nature is spelled out by "the more richly elaborated deverbal predicate" (Newman 1996: 201–202; see also Butt and Geuder 2001: 354; Section 3.1.1). However, according to the author this is mere appearance: he rejects this approach, together with the idea that the LV only provides the 'schema' for the Argument Transfer by the predicative noun (referring to Grimshaw and Mester 1988: 229–230). Conversely, in his opinion 'give' contributes several elements of meaning to the construction, namely (a) intentionality, (b) energy flow, and (c) a punctual, momentary sense (for which the indefinite article may be relevant in English constructions; cf. Newman 1996: 204). On the other hand, he thinks that in this type of meaning extensions 'give' "does not involve any literal or figurative path along which an entity moves" (Newman 1996: 201–202). However, if we consider exclusively hitting nouns, according to De Miguel (2008: 576–577) Spanish LV *dar* 'give' combine with eventive nouns such as *golpes* 'blows' exactly because of the sharing of the feature 'trajectory' (Section 3.1).

Actually, reasoning in terms of domain matrix, when co-occurring with hitting nouns, the LV 'give' seems to keep all the four domains considered for the lexically full counterpart (Section 3.1.1), albeit with different relevance. Indeed, intentionality can be linked to the control domain – where no transfer of possession, but only a metaphorical one, occurs in this case –, if intentional actions directed at other people are conceived as a metaphor for the transfer of a physical entity (Goldberg 1995: 149; Section 3.1). From this viewpoint, the GIVER is an Agent, like in the case of the lexically full counterpart (and in the case of hitting events expressed by a synthetic verb). In fact, the original adicity is preserved, but two relevant differences in the argument structure should be noted in this case, namely (a) the fact that the so-called RECIPIENT (i.e., the indirect object) is a Patient, having the semantic role of the second argument of hitting events, and (b) the fact that the position of the THING is occupied by a predicative noun. In truth, hitting nouns are usually non-deverbal predicative nouns, at least according to Latin data, which is a further language in which hitting nouns usually select *dare* 'give' (Pompei 2019). Indeed, using the classification of Gross and Kiefer (1995), they are either nouns having the event reading in their lexical representation – such as *alapa* 'slap', *colaphus* 'a blow with the fist, slap', *plaga* 'blow' – or nouns whose event interpretation is due to a conceptual shift to a dynamic reading – such as *palma* for 'slap', lit. 'the front part of the hand', with metonymy of the instrument for the effect; *verber* 'instrument for flogging', but also, by metonymy, 'blow delivered with a stick, rod, lash' (5); and *vulnus* for 'bite' lit. 'wound', through metonymy of the effect for the cause (6):

(5) *date   saeva   fero /   verbera   tergo*
    give:IMP.2PL savage:ACC.PL untamed:DAT blow:ACC.PL back:DAT
    'lay savage blows on his untamed back'   (Seneca, *Hercules furens* 1115–1118);

(6) *furit   ille   et   inania   duro /   vulnera   dat   ferro*
    rage:3SG that and vain:ACC.PL hard:DAT wound:ACC.PL give:3SG iron:DAT
    '[The serpent] is furious and bites vainly at the hard iron'
    (Ovidius, *Metamorphoses* 3. 83–84).

These examples are excerpts from poetic texts. In this creative register the subject of the imperative *date* 'give' in (5) is constituted by Hercules' arrows and quiver, which are incited by the chorus of the tragedy to participate in the funeral rite – made up of rhythmic blows – for his family extermination by the hero in the grip of madness. Of course, this is a very special scene. However, if we consider that (a) *date* 'give' is an imperative, which (at least partially) shifts the event control to the chorus expressing the order and that b) *ille* 'that' – i.e., the subject in (6) – is a serpent, these two examples actually weaken not only the intentionality, but also the agentivity that has been acknowledged to the GIVER in various approaches for the uses of 'give', both as a lexically full verb and as an LV (Sections 2.1, 3.1.1). It seems that the GIVER's agentivity can here only be conceived as an overlay that also includes the semantic roles of effector – i.e., entities not really endowed with intentionality – or even force – i.e., inanimate entities that can act and move independently –, according to Van Valin and LaPolla (1997: 118–122). Taken together, these observations weaken the control domain of *dare* 'give' with hitting nouns, not only with regard to the control sphere of the so-called RECIPIENT (which does not come into possession of anything in this case), but also of the GIVER. I represent this weakening in Figure 7 (below) by thinning the hatching of rectangles that symbolize control spheres.

As for the so-called 'human interest' domain, the indirect object being a Patient, it can be undoubtedly affected by the act of giving, but without any benefactive effects, unlike what happens with the lexically full verb (Newman 1996: 51–52). As a matter of fact, in these occurrences, the dative case can be considered as marking the RECIPIENT as a malefactive.[10]

---

10 See Newman (1996: 131) for the meaning of the case/PP marking the so-called RECIPIENT in the world languages, whose value depends on the different domains in the matrix: value of pos-

The affectedness of the Patient of hitting events is perfectly consistent with the prominence of the force-dynamics domain when *dare* 'give' co-occurs with hitting nouns. Indeed, from this perspective, the so-called RECIPIENT is the energy sink, viz., the locus where the energy flow transmitted by the hit/hits arrives and is discharged. Besides, the participation of the GIVER – namely the energy source, whether it is intentional or not – is certainly much greater than that of the RECIPIENT, which tends to be nil, since it merely suffers the blow/blows. For this reason, in Figure 7 the arrow representing the RECIPIENT's participation in receiving the THING that transfers energy is missing. On the other hand, in this case the hands of the GIVER are true 'active zones' (Langacker 1987: 271–274), namely entities directly involved in the interaction. GIVER's hands may wield the instrument by which the blow/blows are inflicted, or be themselves the instrument for hitting (7):

(7) tunc... colaphis eum ceciderunt. alii autem palmas in
    then   fist:AB.PL him beat:PF.3PL some then palma:ACC.PL on
    faciem ei dederunt
    face:ACC him give:PF.3PL
    'Then they... struck him; and some slapped him [on the face]'
    (Vulgata, *Matthaeus* 26. 67).

Whereas cross-linguistically, the THING can be marked as an instrumental case when the force-dynamics domain is pre-eminent, in Latin constructions with *dare* 'give' as an LV, the THING is always expressed by an accusative, denoting either the instrument that is availed to inflict the blow (e.g., (5), (7)), or directly the blow, implying the instrument as a shadow argument, in Pustejovsky's (1995) terms ((6), (8)):[11]

(8) unus adsistens ministrorum dedit alapam
    one stand.nearby:PART attendant:GEN.PL give:PF.3SG slap:ACC
    Iesu
    Jesus:DAT
    'one of the police standing nearby struck Jesus'   (Vulgata, *Ioannes* 18. 22–23).

---

sessor for the control domain; of benefactive for the 'human interest' domain; of instrument for the force-dynamics domain; of goal/locative for the spatio-temporal one. The same marker can be interpreted differently, according to the viewpoint and the prominence of a domain in the matrix.
11 On the other hand, the instrumental ablative of hitting nouns such as *colaphus* 'hit' (e.g., *colaphis* lit. 'with fists' in (7)) recurs frequently with verbs meaning 'hit', such as *caedo* (of which *ceciderunt* in (7) is an occurrence; see Pompei 2019).

When the hands are implied as instruments in hitting events (as usually happens), as they are body parts, the instrument is linked to the energy source by means of a meronymic relationship. Hands are the body part that really moves, i.e., the trajector, or Figure in Talmy's (2007) typology motion terms.[12] As (7) clearly shows, a meronymic relationship can also be established between the RECIPIENT (*ei* 'him') and the effectively affected part of the body (*in faciem* 'on the face'), viz., the 'active zone'. In this case, the prepositional phrase marks the landmark (*faciem* 'face') – viz., the Ground in Talmy's (2007) terms – as the Goal (*in* 'on') of the transfer, easily revealing the relevance – at least for 'schematic interactions' consisting of hitting events – of the spatio-temporal domain, i.e., the trajectory, as well.

Both the force-dynamics domain and the spatio-temporal one are absolutely relevant from the aspect viewpoint. Indeed, hitting nouns denote semelfactive events, which can be constituted by a single occurrence (8) or by multiple ones (5–7). Semelfactives are intrinsically bounded (Section 3.2): as Latin hitting nouns are not deverbal, the boundedness feature cannot be attributed to suffixes, such as Italian *-ata*; Latin being an article-free language, boundedness cannot be attributed either to the presence of the indefinite article in the singular noun construction. Semelfactives are also instantaneous, as already noted by Smith (1991: 46). Their boundedness is clearly consistent with the transfer of the energy flow from a starting to an end point. Their instantaneity involves the progression in time, and thus can be symbolized (Figure 7) by shortening the arrow representing it and bringing the components of the pattern closer together. Eventually, the discreteness of the internal structure of the event can be depicted in the representation of the THING.

In sum, the cognitive perspective is very useful to fully account for the complexity of LVCs, which is certainly not reducible to the sharing of a unique argument structure: only the inclusion of hitting events within the so-called 'Dative Construction' allows us to focus on the flow of energy that is transmitted from the Agent to the Patient and to conceive the latter as an endpoint, i.e., the energy sink. Such an approach permits us to represent the shortness of the 'transfer' as well. On the other hand, in this case the control domain is weakened, and there are no benefactive effects on the Recipient, as for the 'human interest' domain. Eventually, this approach accounts for the event structure well: being bounded, hitting nouns are perfectly compatible with a light use of the verb *dare* 'give' where the energy flow domain is pre-eminent, given its relevance in the verb boundedness.

---

[12] According to Talmy (2007: 70–71), Motion events consist of at least four basic components: Motion (meaning both motion and state), Figure (the entity that moves or is placed in a certain position), Ground (the entity with respect to which the Figure moves or is placed), and Path (hypernym for all the points on the path followed by the motion – origin (Source), trajectory (Path), goal (Goal) – and also for the position in which the Figure stands (Location)).

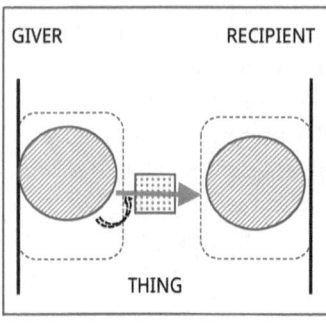

Figure 7: The domain matrix of the Latin LV *dare* 'give' with PhINs (hitting nouns).

4.1.2 Sound nouns

Among sound nouns, the relevant ones as PhINs are vocal sounds, i.e., those produced through the phonatory apparatus, especially the human one. In Romance languages, they very often select 'give' as basic LV, even though the generic LV 'do/make' can also be selected in some cases, at least in French and Italian (e.g., IT *dare / fare un grido* 'give a shout' in (2), and FR *faire un sifflement* 'make a whistle'). From a contrastive point of view, Moncó Taracena (2011: 130) speaks of 'energetic implication' and metaphorical transfer to explain the selection of French *donner* / Spanish *dar* 'give', highlighting that such LVCs frequently occur without any indirect object, although admitting it (e.g., SP *nos dio un grito* 'he gave us a shout'). As for Spanish, De Miguel (2008: 576–577) considers the LV *dar* 'give' and the noun *grito* 'shout' as combinable by reason of the muscular effort exiting from the body and the lexical feature 'trajectory' (Section 3.1). As far as Latin is concerned, vocal sounds have been studied as nouns constituting homogeneous object classes (Marini 2018; Section 2). They are nouns that denote laughter *(cachinnus, risus)*, weeping (e.g., *planctus, plangor, vagitus*), lament (e.g., *gemitus, lamenta, questus*), shouting *(clamor, eiulatus, ululatus)*, voice *(vox)*, and words *(dicta, verbum / verba)*. It is noteworthy that – like ancient grammarians – Marini (2018) distinguishes sound nouns into articulate and non-articulate, depending on whether they refer to verbal language or not. Indeed, laughter, crying, sobbing are usually part of non-verbal communication; instead, signifiers for 'word/words' are always used to allude to the linguistic dimension.

From the typological viewpoint, articulate sounds can be considered as 'interpersonal communication' extensions of the literal meaning of 'give', whereas non-articulate ones are labelled as 'emergence of entities' (Newman 1996: 136–157). The domain matrix of the former is in principle very similar to that of hitting nouns (Section 4.1.1): the original adicity of literal 'give' is usually preserved, only a metaphorical possession transfer occurs, and THING position is occupied by a predicative noun. However, in the case of interpersonal communication the RECIPIENT retains the Recipient semantic role, being the addressee of a speech act. This usually implies that this entity "plays more than the role of being just a passive bystander", from the control point of view, and that "the action is... for the benefit of the RECIPIENT", as far as the so-called 'human interest' is concerned (at least regarding the giving of an opinion, a piece of advice, etc.; see Newman 1996: 141–142). This also usually implies that the spatio-temporal and the force-dynamics domain are relevant, since the message is produced by the speaker as an energy source and covers a trajectory to get to the addressee, which is the energy sink. Together, these factors seem to make the figurative use of 'give' for interpersonal communication even akin to the literal use of the verb. Indeed, Butt and Geuder (2001: 354; Section 3.1.1) note that, in an expression such as *give someone one's regards*, the schema of abstract transfer is easily applicable, because the distinctiveness between what is denoted by the verb and by the object subsists. This is true even in cases where the noun does not express communication through an intermediary (like *one's* for *regards*). In the absence of an intermediary, the figurative extension can be considered an LVC, as the application of the coreference test reveals (*John gave Andrew's regards to Mary* vs. **John gave Andrew's speech to Mary*; Section 2). Last but not least, it is worth noting that the typological perspective clearly shows that the RECIPIENT is not equally relevant in every case: in some languages, such as Polish, the selection of 'give' is possible only when it is truly salient (e.g., POL *Marisya dała mi dobrą radę* 'Mary gave me good advice' vs. *Marisya wygłosiła / (*dała) mowę* 'Mary delivered / (*gave) a speech'; see Newman 1996: 143–144).

Latin data are very interesting from this perspective, since, on the one hand, they confirm that articulate sounds co-occur with the LV *dare* 'give' when there is the implication that the communication is directed toward a Recipient (otherwise, they select *facere* 'do/make'; see Pompei 2019). However, the actual realization of the Recipient is not at all necessary, perhaps because it can be inferred from the context, as happens in the following excerpts:

(9) talia   dicta   dabat
    such:ACC.PL word:ACC.PL give:IPF.3SG
    'Such words he said'   (Vergilius, *Aeneis* 5. 852);

(10) ingemuit-que   dedit-que   has   imo   pectore   voces
     moan:PF.3SG-and   give:PF.3SG-and   this:ACC.PL deep:AB breast:AB   word:ACC.PL
     'she sighed and from the heart's depth uttered these words'
                                                      (Vergilius, *Aeneis* 11. 840).

In (9), *dicta* '(one's) words' anaphorically takes up the previous four verses whereby Palinurus answers the God of Sleep, who has assumed the guise of his companion Phorbas; this resumption of the content of an earlier interpersonal communication is marked by *talia* 'such'. Therefore, *dicta* functions as an encapsulator of a propositional content. On the other hand, in (10) *voces* 'words' has a cataphoric value: in this passage Opis, one of the virgins of Diana's retinue, mourns Camilla, queen of the Volscians consecrated to the goddess, and to her she addresses the words that follow (although only ideally, because Camilla lies dead on the battlefield). It is noteworthy that in this case, in addition to the value of propositional content resumption, the phrase *imo pectore* 'from the bottom of her breast' clearly might also allude to the level of the signifier, i.e., of the sounds that are emitted. Indeed, the primary meaning of *vox* is 'voice', i.e., the (non-articulate) sound emitted by the phonatory apparatus, which can also function as articulate sound by metonymy. A similar function is performed by *ore* in (11), where a non-articulate sound noun (*ululatus* 'the utterance of drawn-out cries, howling, yelling') occurs, as well as by the prefix *ex-/e-* 'out of, from within', which precisely emphasizes the transfer from the inside to the outside, as in (12) the verb *edere* 'to eject, to emit' (made up by the prefix *e-* 'out of, from within' + *dare* 'give') does:

(11) ter   maestum   funeris   ignem /   lustravere   in
 three.times mournful:ACC funeral:GEN   fire:ACC circle:PF.3PL   on
 equis   ululatus-que   ore   dedere
 horse:AB.PL   yelling:ACC.PL-and mouth:AB   give:PF.3PL
 'thrice on horseback they circled the mournful funeral-fire and uttered the cries of wailing'   (Vergilius, *Aeneis* 11. 189–190);

(12) quas   hic   voces   apud Sophoclem   in   Trachiniis
 what:ACC.PL this   sound:ACC.PL   in   Sophocles:ACC   in   Trachiniae:AB.PL
 edit!
 emit:3SG
 'What cries he [Hercules] utters in the *Trachiniae* of Sophocles!'
                                        (Cicero, *Tusculanae Disputationes* 2. 20).

However, in most cases the emission of a sound is merely expressed through the basic LV *dare* 'give', without further specifications:

(13) vagitus   dedit   ille   miser
 wail:ACC.PL give:PF.3SG   that   hapless
 'The hapless babe broke forth in wailings'   (Ovidius, *Heroides* 11. 85).

What is evident in all these occurrences is the absence of the third argument involved by the argument structure of the lexically full verb. This fact is closely related to the substantial non-realization of the Recipient of the message in the case of articulate sound nouns, and to its non-relevance in the case of non-articulate ones. Indeed, once produced, the non-articulate sound can certainly be perceived by an Experiencer, but this is not codified in the argument structure of the LVC. From the cross-linguistic viewpoint, this means that in Latin the selection of 'give' is possible even when the RECIPIENT is scarcely or not at all salient, unlike what happens in other languages of the world (such as Polish; above). From the Latin linguistics perspective, this behavior of *dare* 'give' has been highlighted, for instance in the seminal work of Martín Rodriguez (1996: 57), who observes that this type of 'periphrastic constructions' almost never admits the dative, adding that the usual predicate structure of *dare* 'give' is thus 'broken', the dative being its 'most characteristic' argument. Actually, if the sound is perceived, the perception is not expressed by means of a dative, but by locatives denoting the Goal of the sound trajectory, as happens in the epic *tópos* of *clamor* rising to the stars:

(14) *Clamor ad astra datur*
shout to star:ACC.PL give:PASS.3SG
'Shout of triumph rose [to the stars]' (Silius Italicus, *Punica* 6. 252).

As noted above (Section 3.1.1), the Cognitive Grammar approach has the advantage of admitting both valency decreasing and a matrix more or less rich in domains. At the level of representation, the uncommon realization of the RECIPIENT can be rendered by means of a very weak shading of the relative e-site (Figure 8 below). The possibility of decreasing valency is closely linked to the argument structure of the predicative noun: on the one hand, the articulate sound nouns co-occurring with *dare* 'give' are not real interpersonal communication predicates, because they express saying rather than actually speaking to a Recipient; on the other hand, the non-articulate sound nouns actually never co-occur with the Experiencer they potentially admit, as also noted by Moncó Taracena (2011: 130; above) for Spanish. This implies the absence of a real – albeit abstract – transfer of possession, i.e., sharing of information. Hence, the domain of 'human interest' cannot be part of the domain matrix, and the control domain can at most relate to the GIVER, if it binds to the feature of intentionality. However, as happens with hitting nouns, also with sound ones the GIVER's agentivity must be conceived as including the semantic roles of effector – i.e., unintentional animate entities, such as a wailing baby (13) – or even force – i.e., inanimate entities that can act independently (Van Valin and LaPolla 1997: 118–122). In (15), for instance, the *stipes* is a log to whose duration – before it was completely consumed by fire – the Moire had linked the duration of Meleager's life; it was thrown on the fire by Meleager's own mother, Altea, in revenge for the death of her own brothers, killed by her son:

(15) Aut   dedit   aut   visus   gemitus   est   ille
     either   give:PF.3SG   or   see:PAST.PART   groan.ACC.PL   be.3SG that
     dedisse /   stipes
     give:PAST.INF   log
     'The brand either gave or seemed to give a groan'
     (Ovidius, *Metamorphoses* 8. 513–514).

In all these cases, GIVER's sphere of control mainly represents the physical region out from which the sound emerges. In other terms, GIVER's role seems to be basically that of emission impulse, producing the sound and causing its transmission outside of a 'container' – which is usually the same GIVER's body – to become perceptible. From the typological point view, this means that all Latin vocal sounds, including the articulate ones, better fit the pattern of 'emergence of entities' than that of 'interpersonal communication'. As happens in Latin with the prefix *ex-/e-* 'out of, from within', also cross-linguistically the sound emergence can be marked, for instance by a particle like *out* in English, as well as by a prefix, like *iz-* in Bulgarian, which expresses movement from the inside to the outside, and whose combination with 'give' involves "a comfortable "fit" of meaning" (Newman 1996: 148). This particular combinability concerns both the spatio-temporal and the force-dynamics domain. As for the former, the sound emergence involves a movement of some entity – the trajector, or Figure in Talmy's (2007) terms – out of a region which can be identified as some other entity – the landmark, or Ground in Talmy's (2007) terms. This is the central point, while the reaching of the RECIPIENT conceived as a Goal is really not relevant here, except for very peculiar cases, such as the hyperbole in (14). In Latin, this is perfectly expressed by a famous passage in which Lucretius describes the emission and articulation of *voces* 'sounds, words',[13] pointing out – by means of *ex-/e-*prefixed LV extensions (*exprimimus* 'we press' and *emittimus* 'we send… (forth)') – that the Source of the trajectory is within the body (*corpore nostro* 'from the inmost parts of our body'; cf. *imo pectore* 'from the heart's depth' in (10)) and the emission takes place through the mouth (*ore* 'through the mouth', cf. (11)), which marks the Path point at which the sound becomes perceptible outside (*foras* 'forth'). Hence, diffe-

---

[13] Cfr. Lucretius (*De rerum natura* 4. 549–552): *Hasce igitur penitus voces cum corpore nostro / exprimimus rectoque foras emittimus ore / mobilis articulat verborum daedala lingua, / formaturaque labrorum pro parte figurat* 'When therefore we press out these voices from the inmost parts of our body, and send them forth straight through the mouth, the quickly-moving tongue, cunning fashioner of words, joints and moulds the sounds, and the shaping of the lips does its part in giving them form'.

rent parts of the GIVER are identified as different points in the sound's trajectory. Therefore, with sound nouns there can be a meronymy relationship between the participants in the event and certain parts of the GIVER's body, just like in the case of hitting nouns (Section 4.1.1); on the other hand, unlike the case with hitting nouns, there is no meronymy relationship with the RECIPIENT. Actually, in the case of sound nouns LVCs, the initial part of the trajectory is focalized, namely that concerning the Source and the inside-outside transition. From the force-dynamics domain perspective, this means not only that the GIVER is the energy source, but also that the energy flow is exhausted almost immediately after the emission, whence the energy sink is not necessarily and preferably the RECIPIENT, but some point outside the GIVER. This can be represented (Figure 8) by a single vertical line, standing for the starting point of the energy flow, whereas no line for the endpoint is drawn. In addition, the short-dotted lines coming out of the arrowhead describe the immediacy of the cone of sound dispersion, which involves short duration.

Eventually, as far as the event structure is concerned, we may wonder whether the notion of boundedness is pertinent also in this case. In LVCs with 'give', sound nouns mainly occur in the plural. This can be considered as a non-blurred and non-fused discrete multiplex. Indeed, whether the sound has an articulate content or a non-articulate value – e.g., in the case of *voces* 'sounds, words' in (10) and (12), respectively –, the fact that the phonatory apparatus can produce one sound at a time in itself guarantees its discreteness, and hence its boundedness. This is true whether the subject of the LV is singular ((9)-(10), (12)-(13)) or plural, as in (11), where it is evident that each warrior emits, standing on horseback, his own funeral laments, in iterative form. In addition, when the plural is to be considered as anaphoric or cataphoric resumption of all the 'words' that constitute the propositional content of a whole message (e.g., *dicta* (9), *voces* (10)), it is effectively understood as a closed set, which ensures its boundedness. As for the singular *clamor* 'shout' in (14), it refers to the global view of the collective shouting rising to the heavens – in this case to express the joy the Roman troops feel when Regulus strikes the terrible Libyan serpent on the head with a spear; in other cases, the value is instead absolutely semelfactive.[14] In all the cases, the boundedness parameter is respected. Conversely, the unit excerpting operation is present only when the equivalence of the predicative noun with a verb expressing an externally unbounded but internally discrete activity is possible, as happens in the case of *ululatus* 'the utterance of drawn-out cries, howling, yelling' ((11), from the verb *ululare* 'utter drawn-out cries, howl, yell'), as well as of *vagitus* 'baby's cry' ((13),

---

[14] Cf., e.g., Silius Italicus, *Punica* 7. 325–326 (*ac dirum . . . / clamorem tum forte dabat* 'he uttered just then a frantic cry'), in which *clamor* 'shout' refers to the terrible cry that the hero Marasse lets out in his sleep, as if he were fighting and looking for his armor and sword.

from *vagire* 'utter cries by babies'), and of *gemitus* 'groan, moan' ((15), from *gemere* 'groan, moan'). In all these instances, the choice of the LVC allows one to conceptualize the cries, groans, and moans as individual, discrete entities, namely not fused into an indistinct crying, groaning, and moaning, unlike what happens with the synthetic verb form (Section 3.2). It is worth noting that all these nouns are derived from base verbs through the suffix *-tus*, which forms simple event nominals, viz., result nominals in Latin (on this suffix, cf. *inter alia* Fruyt 2011), as nouns meaning a single instance of an event are (Section 2.1). Sound nouns can also be considered as instances of punctual nouns, like hitting nouns, even though the former are not always truly instantaneous:[15] as soon as the energy flow comes out from the GIVER's inside to the outside, it dissipates and is almost immediately exhausted.

To sum up, the cognitive approach makes it easy to account for the possibility of decreasing the number of participants when Latin *dare* 'give' co-occurs with sound nouns, namely for the substantial absence of the RECIPIENT, which is effectively unrealized as a Recipient (articulate sound nouns) and absolutely not relevant as an Experiencer (non-articulate sound nouns). Likewise, the cognitive approach makes it possible to show that, in this case, the control domain (i.e., the transfer of possession) is very scarcely relevant and the so-called 'human interest' domain plays no role. On the other hand, the spatio-temporal domain remains fully active – given the transfer of sound from inside to outside the GIVER and its immediate dispersion –, as well as the force-dynamics domain, but with focus on the GIVER as energy source. Thus, the 'lightening' of *dare* 'give' exactly consists in the depletion of the domain matrix, in close connection with the decreasing of the number of participants.

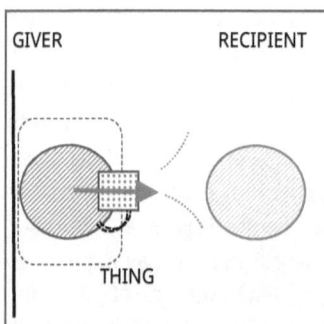

Figure 8: The domain matrix of the Latin LV *dare* 'give' with PhINs (sound nouns).

---

15 As regards verbs, Smith (1991: 46; Section 4.1.1) considers semelfactives as instantaneous, as well as Van Valin (2006: 157–158), albeit endowed of a slight duration, unlike achievements. Nesset (2013: 2) conceives semelfactives as a radial category attributing instantaneousness to prototypical instances. Kiss (2011: 122) explicitly includes the type of 'shouting out' within semelfactives.

4.2 Motion nouns

The analysis of MNs is particularly interesting. As for Romance languages, a difference in the selection of LVs contrasts the Iberian languages with the others ((3)-(4)), because the former select *dar* 'give', with the exception of long-time lasting motion activities (e.g., SP *hacer un viaje* 'have a trip', PT *fazer uma excursão* 'have an excursion'); actually, also Romanian can sometimes select *a da* 'give', in the case of short-time lasting motion (e.g., RM *a da o tură* 'take a stroll'; see Pompei and Piunno, this volume). On the other hand, French and Italian usually select *faire* and *fare* 'do/make', respectively, with this type of nouns. From a contrastive perspective, Moncó Taracena (2011: 131) considers the use of Spanish *dar* 'give' with PhINs to be the basis for the metaphorical expansion to LVCs with MNs such as *dar un paso* 'take a step'; while not dwelling on an explanation of how this happens, she points out that features such as directionality are present in the verb semantics. Conversely, as for Portuguese, Duarte et al. (2010: 29) explain the LVC *dar um passeio* 'take a walk' in actional terms, as specification by the MN of the LV's underspecified aspectual features ([-CHANGE], [-CAUSE], [+DURATIVE]), dynamicity being common to the LV and the predicative noun (Section 3.1). Beyond the different features considered, this means that in the former case the explanation is based on the verb semantics, while in the latter on that of the noun. The cognitive approach, on the contrary, allows the contribution of both LVC components to be accounted for, in terms of compatibility, and to highlight the effects occurring when compatibility is not met.

From the cross-linguistic viewpoint, the fact that a strong sense of directionality is inherent in the notion of giving is highlighted as well: in many languages 'give' may be marked to indicate its deictic value of moving away from or closer to the speaker (cf., e.g., in GM *hingeben* 'give away from speaker' vs. *hergeben* 'give to speaker'). Nevertheless, in some cases – as in Ik (Kuliak family, Uganda) – the 'give here' mark is mandatory, while the 'give away' one is optional "as though it ['give'] has as part of its meaning the notion "away from"" (Newman 1996: 23). This means that (a) literal 'give' is "a natural source for images of movement" and that (b) if the perspective of the GIVER is adopted, the "verb 'give' behaves as though it had an inherent orientation "away from the GIVER"" (Newman 1996: 223–224). In the case of reflexive occurrences of 'give', such as German *sich (nach...) begeben* 'go to', it seems that "one part of the self functions as an agent and another part as the patient" and "the agent part of the self "pushes" the patient into movement" (Newman 1996: 225). These are very relevant observations also for Latin data. On the other hand, Latin LVCs with *dare* 'give' and MNs are very similar to those found in the Iberian languages and also, partially, in Romanian. In fact, these languages belong to 'lateral areas' with respect to the core of Latin diffusion. From the historical linguistics viewpoint, this means that they are conservative languages, according to the norms established by Bartoli (cf., e.g., 1925).

4.2.1 Punctual nouns

We start the analysis of MNs from punctual ones, which are distinguished between semelfactives and achievements (Section 3.2). In Latin, the selection of *dare* 'give' is prevalent in both cases, although *facere* 'do/make' is also employed (see Pompei 2018, 2019).

Among semelfactive MNs, the behavior of *saltus* 'jump, leap, spring' is especially interesting. Some relevant differences are already clear from (16), not only with respect to the use of *dare* 'give' as a lexically full verb, but also as an LV in co-occurrence with both hitting nouns and sound ones:

(16) *Dixit   et   e   curru   saltum   dedit   ocius   arvis*
       say:PF.3SG and from car:AB leap:ACC give:PF.3SG swifter field:DAT.PL
       'He said, and leapt quickly from his car to the field' (Vergilius, *Aeneis* 12. 681).

The most obvious difference with other uses of *dare* 'give' is the fact that no transfer of possession of a THING takes place at all, not even an abstract one, from a GIVER to a RECIPIENT, either from the GIVER's inside to the outside. As a matter of fact, in (16) *arvis* 'to the field' is a dative, which is the case giving its name to the so-called 'Dative Construction' and the usual marker of the RECIPIENT in Latin: however, in this case its semantic role is neither of Recipient, nor of Experiencer, being a locative. This means that its occurrence is due to the predicative noun rather than to the argument structure of *dare* 'give'. In other words, 'give' adicity is not respected here, since the LV *dare* 'give' is not a three-slot verb, in this case as well as in co-occurrence with every MN. Therefore, *dare* 'give' as an LV with MNs is a clear instance of a valency-decreasing construction. On the other hand, MNs are usually nominalizations, so they might inherit the argument structure of the verb from which they derive.[16] Actually, the MN *saltus* 'jump, leap, spring' is derived from the base verb *salio* 'jump, leap', but through the suffix *-tus*, which

---

16 Cf. Spevak (2014: 32–33, 81–82, 245–246, 250–254) on the MNs argument structure in Latin and its heritage from the verb they derive from. Cf. also Martín Rodriguez (1996: 57), who notes that in Latin, in the absence of the dative, the 'periphrasis' adopts the construction required by the synthetic verb related to the object of *dare* 'give': exactly as happens in LVCs, according to Gross (1989: 113; Section 2).

forms nouns denoting a single instance of an event, i.e., having an individual reference and to be classified together with the result nominals, at least according to the tradition dating back to Grimshaw (1990; Section 4.1.2). From this perspective, *arvis* 'to the field' cannot be considered as instantiating an actual argument of the noun *saltus*, although participating in the event of jumping. Of course, in such a case also the existence of syntactic cohesion between the LV and the predicative noun can be taken into account; so that *arvis* 'to the field' could be considered as an argument of the whole LVC as well, double syntactic analysis being another distinctive feature of LVCs (Section 2.1). However, for Latin the possibility of moving arguments must always be evaluated in the light of the fact that it is a language with a high frequency of discontinuous phrases (Devine and Stephen 2006), hence the degree of cohesion is not easy to prove. On the other hand, in (16) there is certainly coreference between the subject of the form of *dare* 'give' (*dedit*) and the person who jumps, which confirms that this is an instance of LVC (Section 2). Furthermore, this means that the thematic role of the subject is in this case a Theme, i.e., a participant which is characterised as changing its position (Gruber 1965), rather than an Agent, as the subject of the fully lexical 'give' is. Nevertheless, this subject being volitional, it may fall under the overlay of the GIVER's agentivity from a functionalist approach to semantic roles (Section 4.1.1). Without going further into the argument structure – a very complex matter, not central for this article – the LVC of *dare* 'give' plus MNs has interesting characteristics also from the cognitive viewpoint.

As for the domain matrix, neither the control domain – relating to the transfer of possession of the THING – nor the 'human interest' domain – in the absence of a RECIPIENT that can have beneficial effects from the act of giving – are in this case pertinent. On the other hand, the spatio-temporal and the force-dynamics domains certainly are. Actually, the GIVER can be the 'energy source' who gives rise to the change in location (e.g., from the car to the field, in (16)), or at least, the starting point of the energy flow (17, below). On the other hand, the fact that the subject of the LV – viz., the GIVER – is the one who moves implies very interesting consequences regarding the spatio-temporal domain: in this case the GIVER is the trajector, i.e., the Figure in Talmy's (2007) typology motion terms. Conversely, in the case of hitting and sound nouns the trajector is usually constituted by the hands and the sound itself, respectively: when hands – or another body part – are the trajector, a meronymic relationship joins them with the Giver, while different parts of the GIVER's phonatory apparatus constitute different points of the trajectory, when the trajector is the sound. In both cases, in Talmy's (2007) typology motion terms, the GIVER is the Source of the motion, i.e., the starting point of the trajectory. Hence, in such cases there is a coincidence between the energy source and the trajectory one. On the other hand, this is not the case with MNs, as the example (16) clearly shows, since the Source of the motion is external to the GIVER (*e curru* 'from the car'). The motion Source is here marked by the preposition *e* 'from', having the same adverbial origin of the prefix *ex-/e-* 'out of, from within' (cf. *inter alia* Cuzzolin et al. 2006). For this reason, in Figure 9 (below) the arrow – which in this case represents only the spatio-temporal domain, i.e., the mere change in location and not that in possession – is drawn below the GIVER, i.e., externally. On the other hand, the vertical line represents the fact that the GIVER is usually the energy source (or, at least, the starting point of the energy flow), and the dotted curve arrow its consequent participation to the motion event. It is also worth noting that the energy flow basically serves to give rise to the event – namely, the THING –, in which it actually extinguishes (e.g., in the jump standing out in (16)). This means that the end of the event constitutes the energy sink, as represented by a vertical line in Figure 9. In other terms, if the energy is transferred from the GIVER to a RECIPIENT in the case of hitting nouns, and from the GIVER's inside to the outside in that of sound nouns, with MNs it is essentially kinetic energy, namely the energy that a body in motion possesses, the moving body being the same GIVER. Moreover, if the energy flow is what the movement consists of and it is effectively exhausted in the movement itself (e.g., in the jump), the RECIPIENT as an energy sink is not necessary. Indeed, a possible locative RECIPIENT with the function of landmark (e.g., *arvis* 'to the field' in (16)) may be interpreted either as a Goal in Talmy's (2007) terms (namely, as an added motion endpoint), or as a Ground – namely, the background against which the motion takes place. For this reason, in Figure 9 the RECIPIENT is placed after the vertical line, in addition to be rendered by means of a very weak shading of the relative e-site. In other cases, the very existence of a trajectory must be questioned:

(17) *sic onere   adsueto   vacuus dat   in aëre   saltus*
      so   weight:AB   usual:AB   empty   give:3SG   in air:AB leap:ACC.PL
      'so [the chariot of the Sun], deprived of its usual weight, makes leaps in the air'   (Ovidius, *Metamorphoses* 2. 165).

In (17) reference is made to the leaps in the sky of the Sun's chariot, due to the deprivation of its usual weight (and control), since it is driven by the young and light-weight Phaethon, the Sun's son, rather than by the Sun itself, who is the only one able to do it. In this instance, the Sun's chariot is the GIVER, as well as the Figure in Talmy's (2007) terms, viz., the trajector. However, there is no real trajectory, but only the jerking of the chariot in the sky at the very beginning of its daily path. In other words, in this case there is no Source of the movement, and the landmark – i.e., the sky – seems to be the Ground of the motion rather than its Goal. Therefore, from the spatio-temporal domain, there is neither the start nor the ending point of the motion.¹⁷ As for the force-dynamics domain, the chariot is not even the effective energy source, but only the starting point of the energy flow, given that its instability is due to an external reason: to explain the situation, the poet uses the metaphor of the ship at the mercy of the sea because of insufficient ballast. This means that the motion is unintentional and determined by an external thrust. The possibility that GIVER participation in energy flow may also be inactive is represented in Figure 9 by the thin lines of the dashed curved arrow.

Analyzing the passage in (17), Pinkster (2015: 75) notes that the synthetic verb *saltare* 'jump' would have signified "continuous jumping instead of incidental jumps". From the event structure perspective, the possibility of foregrounding the discreteness of the internal structure of jumping activity is obviously due to the unity excerpting device, which denotes semelfactive events, both uniplex (16) and multiplex (17). Since semelfactive events are 'intrinsically bounded' (Section 3.2), they are fully compatible with the LV *dare* 'give'. Of course, this is also true in the absence of an outer culmination. When a Goal is not added, *saltare* 'jump' only codifies the motion Manner, i.e., another possible component of motion predicates according to Talmy (2007).¹⁸ This is clear in (18):

(18) do-que   leves   saltus   udae-que   inmittor
     give:1SG-and slight:ACC.PL   leap:ACC.PL   wet:DAT-and   move:PASS.1SG
     harenae
     beach:DAT
     '[with the oars from starboard I land on the shore] and I make slight leaps and jump on the wet beach.'   (Ovidius, *Metamorphoses* 3. 598–599).

In these verses, the protagonist – Acoetes – is telling about when he approached by chance the shores of the island of Chios, heading towards Delos, and landed there. Even though a motion from the boat to the beach is described, the Manner to reach the latter by the Figure seems to be emphasized, namely jumping in an agile way; in fact, the Goal is specified separately (*udaeque inmittor harenae* lit. 'I reach the wet beach'). In such a case, it seems that the only domain actually constituting the

---

17 As a matter of fact, the passage in (17) also presents a so-called *varia lectio* from the philological viewpoint, viz., the possibility to read in the manuscripts that have transmitted the text either the PP *in aëre* (*in* + ablative), which denotes the Ground, or *in aëra* (*in* + accusative), which indicates the Goal ([the chariot of the Sun] makes leaps to the sky).
18 On the other hand, the adding of a Goal is mandatory to make telic the *Aktionsart* of the verb 'jump'. For instance, in Italian *saltare* 'jump' selects the auxiliary *avere* 'have' when it expresses motion Manner and *essere* 'be' when the Goal is expressed as well (Iacobini 2008: 109), as also happens with other verbs, among which *correre* 'run' (Section 4.2.2).

matrix of *dare* 'give' is the force-dynamics one. Therefore, in addition to the valency decreasing – in the absence of any form of Recipient – there is also a drastic reduction in the meaning with respect to the lexically full verb. For these reasons, in Figure 9 the arrow depicting the trajectory is dashed. These uses of the LV *dare* 'give' may be regarded as particularly 'light'. Indeed, it is for these kinds of uses that Pinkster (2015: 75) states that "the two-place expressions can be regarded as variations on a one-place frame", i.e., on the synthetic verb. In fact, Latinists have often perceived such passages as problematic, and have felt the need to account for their occurrence, as happened for the excerpt in (19), where the object of *dare* 'give' is *motus* (a *-tus* nominalization from *movere* 'move', here meaning 'dance moves'):

(19) haud   indecoros   motus   more   Tusco   dabant.
      not   ungraceful:ACC.PL move:ACC.PL   fashion:AB Tuscan:AB   give:IPF.3PL
      '[while dancing to the strains of the flautist] they performed not ungraceful evolutions in the Tuscan fashion.'   (Livius, *Ab urbe condita* 7. 2. 4).

In order to explain the occurrence of the LVC *motus... dabant* lit. 'moves... they gave' in (19), Pinkster (2015: 75) writes that the synthetic verb form "alone might indicate involuntary movement; this would exclude the addition of a manner adjunct (*indecore*), whereas the support verb construction has the advantage of allowing the adjective *indecoros*", so implying the volitionality. However, volitionality is by no means always present, as already noted (see 17). Furthermore, Alonso Fernández (2011: 133) observes that the gods can be considered as the effective Recipient of this dance, since the institution of the so-called *ludi scaenici* (public performances consisting of acting competitions) to prevent an epidemic is mentioned here. Nevertheless, it does not always seem necessary to think about someone's perception (nor to think about the existence of any RECIPIENT, as clearly seen in (18)): if anything, a movement may be perceived by an onlooker, who can be the spectator in the case of dance, but in the great majority of cases is a casual observer. As a matter of fact, from the cognitive point of view, the selection of *dare* 'give' in co-occurrence with the mere MN – viz., in monotransitive structures – is not to be considered as odd, either from the perspective of its distance from the meaning of the full lexical counterpart, or of the argument structure, or of the event structure. In fact, the reduction of domains, the valency decreasing, and the aspectual compatibility between the LV and the MNs selecting it are closely related: the absence (or, at least, the non-need) of the RECIPIENT is consistent with the simplification of the domain matrix, as well as with the short duration – in addition to boundedness – of the semelfactive motion events. In other words, the absence of other participants entails that the event only concerns the GIVER, in whose motion the flow of energy is exhausted, with no real transfer to other entities. In the case of MNs denoting semelfactive events, the motion tends to be instantaneous, and the possible trajectory to be very short. In the instances where only the motion Manner is expressed, without any Path (i.e., trajectory), it can also be noted that the short duration seems to be linked to the impulse of the initial phase, whose strength soon runs out if not renewed. Hence, there seems to be a focalization of the initial phase (e.g., cf. Pustejovsky's (1995: 72) 'event headedness' notion).

We can wonder whether these features of the use of *dare* 'give' – in particular, the event boundedness and its shortness, as well as the focalization of the initial phase – are present also when this LV co-occurs with achievements. Among the occurrences of achievement MNs that have particularly engaged philologists there are the passages in (20) and (21), from *De rerum natura* by Lucretius. In (20) the author speaks of the moment of death, when the soul and the body divide and return – in his model, inspired by Epicurean philosophy – to the atoms that constitute them:

(20) ... *cum   corpus   simul   atque   animi   natura*
         when   body   together and   mind:GEN   nature
     perempta /   in   sua   discessum
     destroy:PAST.PART.PL   in   their.own.ACC.PL   splitting.apart:ACC
     dederint   primordia   quaeque
     give:SUBJ.PF.3PL   primordial:ACC.PL   each:PL
     '[...] when body and mind, destroyed together, each back to its own primordials goes away.'   (Lucretius, *De rerum natura* 4. 44–45).

In (21), Lucretius speaks of the fact that even the walls that support the sky will collapse, under the impact of the external atoms:[19]

(21) *expugnata   dabunt   labem   putris-que*
     storm:PAST.PART.PL   give:FUT.3PL landslip:ACC   crumbled:ACC.PL-and
     ruinas.
     rubble:ACC.PL
     '[the ramparts of the mighty world] shall be taken by storm, and tumble to wrack and shivered fragments down.'   (Lucretius, *De rerum natura* 2. 1145).

---

[19] The passage in (21) is difficult to analyze also because of the coordination between *labem* 'landslip' and *putrisque ruinas*. Such a coordination can be considered as a zeugma, if we consider *ruinas* as a concrete noun, the noun phrase having the value of 'crumbled rubble'. At the same time, *dare ruinam* means 'ruin, collapse', like the synthetic verb *ruo*, with an effect of significance perfectly suited to the poetic context.

In (20), *discessus* is formed through the suffix *-tus* and properly means 'go away' (cf. verb *cedere*) 'in two different directions' (cf. prefix *dis-*), thus expressing the separation of the body and the soul. In (21), *labes* is a nominal formation from a root meaning the 'going down slipping and collapsing' (cf. verbs *labi* and *labare* 'slip, fall'). Therefore, in both cases the Manner and the Path are equally expressed, even if the spatio-temporal domain is not (only) a concrete one, but a change in state is involved. Actually, the trajectory consists of a transformation of the very essence of the body and soul, on the one hand, and of walls, on the other, until their complete disintegration into primordial elements (i.e., atoms) and into rubble, respectively. Even if this change cannot be conceptualized as a punctual event, having a certain temporal expansion, it is certainly bounded. Furthermore, in both instances the *télos* seem to be at the very beginning of the event, at the moment of the change of state from a situation of wholeness and integrity to one of disintegration: which means that the initial phase of the event is focused on. This implies that the pertinent domain is the force-dynamics one, even in the presence of a trajectory. In this case, the energy flow serves for the GIVER to enter in the new state. It is worth noting that it is not relevant if the energy source is external, as happens when the motion/change of state of the GIVER is not willful but is due to an external impulse (unlike what happens in Italian; Section 2.1). These Latin data confirm typological findings, namely, the inherent orientation of 'give' 'away from the GIVER' (Section 4.2). This interpretation can also easily be applied to passages such as (22):

(22) et   velut ab   arce   Ianiculo   passim   in   Romanum
     and   as   from citadel:AB Janiculum:AB dispersedly on   Roman:ACC
     agrum   impetus   dabant
     territory:ACC raid:ACC.PL give:IPF.3PL
     'from the Janiculum, as from a citadel, they made raids in all directions on the Roman territory'   (Livius, *Ad urbe condita* 2. 51. 4).

In (22), Livy speaks of Veientes – an Etruscan population that occupied Rome – who launched themselves into the Roman countryside making iterate incursions from the Janiculum. From the aspect point of view, the predicative noun *impetus* 'hostile movement' can be considered as an achievement. In fact, it is plural, so that reference is made to the iteration of the raids on the Roman territory; however, there is no pluralization of a semelfactive event because in this case the plural refers to assaults repeated at different times, rather than attributable to a single event. On the other hand, while in such occurrences a certain duration cannot be excluded, they are not instances of accomplishments: the noun *impetus* indicates just the initial impulse that characterizes the assault or the raid (cf. Ernout and Meillet 2001[1959]: *s.v. peto*). The conditions of use are very similar to those of *discessus* (20) and *labes* (21): the *télos* is on the change of state, from a situation of stasis to one of movement, as happens for verbs such as *start*. In this context, from the force-dynamics domain viewpoint, the energy flow is needed for the GIVER (Veientes) to start the motion, which is inherently orientated "away from the GIVER". Nevertheless, as for the spatio-temporal domain, the Source of the motion (*ab arce Ianiculo* 'from the Janiculum') is external to the GIVER, like in other cases (16). Likewise, also in this case, the locative RECIPIENT (*in Romanum agrum* 'on the Roman territory') is actually the Ground with respect to which the motion takes place 'in all direction' (*passim*): that is to say, the movement has a direction, but its attainment of a Goal is not needed.

To sum up, with punctual MNs it seems that the GIVER pushes himself/herself into the movement, as happens in case of reflexive occurrences of 'give', such as German *sich (nach...) begeben* 'go to' (above). As a matter of fact, from another typological perspective (Kemmer 1993: 55), physical actions – as motion events are – are prototypical instances of the middle category, which implies the focalization of the unique participant, who is affected by the same motion he/she makes, regardless of its voluntary participation. Hence, the behavior of *dare* 'give' with punctual MNs can be considered as middle from the diathetic point of view. On the other hand, as far as the *Aktionsart* is concerned, the hypothesis of the occurrence of this LV exclusively with bounded predicative nouns is confirmed both in the case of semelfactive MNs, and in that of achievement ones, since boundedness is implied by telicity (Section 3.2). The use of *dare* 'give' is particularly 'light' in these instances, both because of the valency decreasing and the substantial reduction of the matrix domain to the force-dynamics one. Only the event structure seems to be the same as in the semantically full verb, in terms of dynamicity and compatibility with bounded entities.

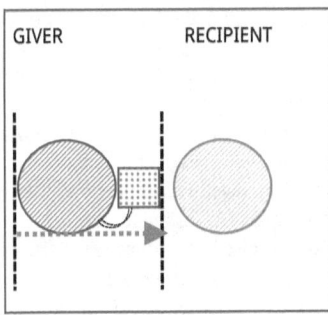

Figure 9: The domain matrix of the Latin LV *dare* 'give' with MNs.

4.2.2 Definite and indefinite process nouns

In co-occurrence with definite and indefinite process MNs, LVs different from *dare* 'give' – first of all *facere* 'do/make' (Pompei 2018, 2019) – are undoubtedly preferred. However, some interesting observations can also be made regarding the (rare) selection of *dare* 'give'. For instance, in (23) the noun *cursus* 'run' occurs together with this LV:

(23) Sic   cursum   in   medios   rapidus   dedit
     So   run:ACC into fray:ACC.PL fast   give:PF.3SG
     'So he rushed quickly into the fray'   (Vergilius, *Aeneis* 10. 870).

In this passage, Virgil is talking about Mezentius, who has just learned that his son has died instead of him and rushes towards the battlefield at full gallop, with the intention of avenging him. The predicate *cursus* 'run' is a classic nominalization from a Manner motion verb (*currere* 'run') expressing an activity – namely, an indefinite process MN – that can become an accomplishment, when the presence of a Goal telicizes it. Hence, *cursum in medios... dedit* lit. 'a run into the fray... he gave' might be considered as an accomplishment – i.e., a definite process MN –, since telicity implies boundedness. However, this is not necessarily the right interpretation. Another possible one is that Mezentius 'makes a run until the fray', i.e., up until the place where the fight rages, having left to clean up his wounds in the water of the Tiber River. Indeed, the noun *cursus* is also a nominalization in *-tus*. Hence, the selection of *dare* 'give' would be simply linked to the boundedness due to the portion excerpting of the activity of running, more than to the final boundary constituting a *télos*. This interpretation is the same as the meaning of the Spanish LVC *dar(se) una corrida* (e.g., in *dar(se) una corrida hasta la plaza* 'make a run until the square'), which is a middle meaning (Pompei and Piunno, this volume). In other words, this could be the same use found in the current Iberian languages and which is very peculiar among the Romance ones.[20] From this perspective, the presence of

---

[20] Cf. also the Old Italian *dà una corsa fino in piazza* 'he makes a run until the square', taken from a 16th century comedy (*La Sibilla* by Antonfrancesco Grazini) and cited as an example by the 4th edition of the *Vocabolario degli Accademici della Crusca* (1729–1738), together with the definition of *Correre sollecitamente senza fermarsi* 'Running fast without stopping'. As for the Iberian languages, the event expressed by *dar* 'give' with definite process MNs may also be 'perdurative' (Section 3.2), thus having a certain extension, though not long-lasting (e.g., SP *dar un paseo todo el día* 'take a walk all the day'). This probably means that in the Iberian languages the selection of *dar* 'give' as LV is lexicalized with some MNs, whereas in Latin it seems to be constrained by the shortness of the event, in addition to the boundedness.

an effective Goal has no real influence on the bounded interpretation, as we have already seen concerning *saltus* (Section 4.2.1). Boundedness being equal, while the trajectory – hence the spatio-temporal domain – is relevant in the interpretation as an accomplishment, this seems not to be the case with that as a bounded activity (unless for what pertains to the time extension, albeit short (*rapidus* 'fast')). On the other hand, the force-dynamics domain seems to be present in both interpretations, but more relevantly in the latter: indeed, the *cursus* here is a short-lasting event, for which the energy source is the necessary impulse to start the motion, whose ending coincides with the energy sink.

On the other hand, the LV *dare* 'give' never seems to be selected in Latin by real indefinite process MNs, namely, in the absence of boundedness mechanisms. Conversely, *facere* 'do/make' is selected in this case, as shown, for instance, by *iter facere* 'march' (Pompei 2018, 2019). The interesting instance in (24) can be considered as an exception:

(24) *Qua   venti   incubuere,   fugam   dant   nubila   caelo*
     where   wind:PL   assail:PF.3PL   escape:ACC   give:3PL   cloud:PL   sky:AB
     'where the winds assail, the clouds take flight in the sky'

     (Vergilius, *Aeneis* 12. 367).

The MN *fuga* 'escape, getaway' is a nominal formation from the same root as the verb *fugere* 'run away (from), flee (from)'. As a matter of fact, the verb can mean both an achievement and an activity: fleeing involves a change of state, i.e., entering the movement leaving a place suddenly, but the process of escaping might persist. In the former case ('run away from'), both the motion Manner ('run') and the Path ('away from') are expressed, whereas in the latter only the Manner ('flee'). The selection of different LVs makes it possible to separate these different phases. Therefore, an LVC such as *esse in fuga* 'be in escape' focuses on the activity, i.e., on the indefinite process, while *dare* 'give' is selected to focus on the initial phase, consistently with the encoding of an inherently oriented motion "away from the GIVER". Actually, in (24) *caelo* 'in the sky' is just the Ground. In this case, the effect with respect to the unbounded MN seems to be an inchoative one, due to the incompatibility between the unboundedness of the noun and the actionality of the LV. If so, this is a case of event augmentation, which yields inchoative effects, whereas the other cases considered here seem to be of event modification, in the terms of Butt and Geuder (2001: 358–361; Section 3.1.1).

In brief, *dare* 'give' does not usually co-occur with indefinite MNs. When this happens, some bounding mechanism takes place, such as telicization, portion excerption, or inchoative effect.

5 Conclusions

At the very birth of the notion of LV, the semantic emptiness of the verb was mainly emphasized, reducing it to a mere support of grammatical features. At the same time, the concept of noun predicativeness was explored, and was identified not only in the encoding of the predicative lexical meaning, but also in establishing the argument structure. Even though the idea that LVCs can be considered as complex predicates has gradually begun to emerge, both the concordance of lexical features of a certain LV with a certain predicative noun and the mechanisms of argument sharing have been mainly investigated. On the other hand, the event structure of LVCs has been scarcely studied. In this article, an attempt has been made to provide a holistic view of the different levels that are involved in reconsidering the semantic LV contribution to LVCs. A cognitive approach has been adopted, which makes a uniform treatment of different types of LVC possible. From this perspective, firstly the semantic bleaching of the LV with respect to the lexically full counterpart can be explained, in terms of reduction of domains within the domain matrix. Moreover, at least some theoretical difficulties concerning the argument structure can be overcome, since the valency decreasing of the number of participants is admitted. Finally, the event structure of the LVC can be taken into account as result of the contribution of both components.

This paper focuses on Latin LVCs having the pattern [V+N], where the LV is *dare* 'give' and the noun either a PhIN (hitting noun or sound one) or a MN (punctual noun, definite process noun or indefinite one). This case study assays the validity of a semantic path suggested to explain the 'odd' use of the LV *dar* 'give' in the Iberian languages, which is much more widespread than in other Romance languages. The findings show that there is an extensive use of the LV *dare* 'give' in Latin as well. Moreover, the mutual weight of the LV and the predicative noun differs as the LVCs vary. In particular, a gradual emptying of the domain matrix occurs. Indeed, the beneficial effects of the 'human interest' domain expected in Newman's (1996) typological perspective are never present in the matrix, in co-occurrence with any of the noun types considered. As regards the control domain, it is weakened when *dare* 'give' co-occurs with hitting nouns, as no transfer of possession, but only a metaphorical one, takes place; it is very scarcely relevant with sound nouns, and not pertinent however in the case of MNs. On the other hand, the spatio-temporal domain, which refers to change in location, is fully pertinent in the case of hitting and sound nouns, whereas it is not always relevant in the case of MNs, given that the encoding of the Manner prevails over that of the Path, in Talmy's (2007) terms. Finally, the force-dynamics domain is the only domain really relevant in any case.

The argument structure is closely related to the emptying of domains. Thanks to the adoption of the cognitive approach, it is possible to use the same labels of GIVER, THING and RECIPIENT – which constitute the profile of 'give' as a lexically full verb – to deal with the different LVCs uniformly. The adicity is the same as the lexically full verb in the case of hitting nouns, viz., the construction is ditransitive, as the RECIPIENT is always present while having the semantic role of Patient. On the other hand, with sound nouns the RECIPIENT is substantially absent, since it is effectively unrealized as a Recipient (articulate sound nouns) and absolutely not relevant as an Experiencer (non-articulate sound nouns). In the case of MNs, there is never a RECIPIENT governed by the LV, while there may be a Goal or Ground, depending on the predicative noun or the whole LVC. Therefore, there is a valency decreasing, with a passage to a monotransitive construction. Furthermore, with all types of nouns considered, the THING always consists of the predicative noun, so it cannot be an argument. As for GIVER, in the case of PhINs, its agentivity can only be conceived as an overlay that also includes the semantic roles of effector and force in Van Valin and LaPolla's (1997) terms, hence the volitionality of the subject is questioned in the case of Latin LV *dare* 'give'. With MNs, the GIVER is certainly a Theme in Gruber's (1965) terms, being the entity that moves. These changes in the adicity and in semantic roles of the LVC subject are undoubtedly indicative of increasing predicativeness of the noun as the verb loses domains in the domain matrix.

As far as the event structure is concerned, a boundedness constraint seems to be respected in all LVCs. The LV *dare* 'give' is perfectly compatible with PhINs and some punctual MNs, since they are semelfactive, and hence intrinsically bounded. Compatibility is also assured with achievement MNs, boundedness being implied by telicity. In the case of atelic nouns, boundedness is not questioned if MNs are definite processes, as a result of telicization or a portion excerpting strategy. Conversely, the LV *dare* 'give' cannot usually co-occur with indefinite process MNs: if this happens, it gives rise to an inchoative effect. Compatibility with bounded nouns is closely related to the boundaries imposed by the spatio-temporal domain of the verb *dare* 'give'. In the absence of such a domain, compatibility with bounded nouns is due to the dominance of the force-dynamics domain, since the energy flow is exhausted in the event itself. In fact, the energy flow serves the GIVER to enter the event. This initial impulse related to the energy flow promotes the inchoative value that the LV *dare* 'give' acquires with indefinite process MNs. Moreover, the orientation 'away from the GIVER' of the motion due to the energy flow develops a middle value, focusing on the unique participant, who is affected by the same motion he/she makes. Actually, motion events are prototypical instances of the middle category, in Kemmer's (1993) terms. Such an explanation may also be valid for the use of the LV *dar* 'give' with MNs in the Iberian languages.

Abbreviations

1	first person
2	second person
3	third person
ACC	Accusative
AB	Ablative
DAT	Dative
FUT	Future
GEN	Genitive
IMP	Imperative
INF	Infinitive
IPF	Imperfect
PART	Participle
PASS	Passive
PAST	Past
PF	Perfect
PL	Plural
SG	Singular
SUBJ	Subjunctive

References

Alonso Fernández, Zoa. 2011. *La danza en época romana: una aproximación filológica y lingüística*. PhD dissertation. Madrid: Universidad Complutense de Madrid.
Alsina, Alex. 1996. *The Role of Argument Structure in Grammar*. Stanford: CSLI Publications.
Alsina, Alex, Joan Bresnan & Peter Sells (eds.), 1997. *Complex predicates*. Stanford: CSLI Publications.
Apresjan, Jurij. 2009. The theory of lexical functions: An update. In David Beck, Kim Gerdes, Jasmina Milićević & Alain Polguère (eds.), *Proceedings of the Fourth International Conference on Meaning-Text Theory*, 1–14. Montréal: Observatoire de linguistique Sens-Texte (OLST).
Baños, José Miguel. 2019. Las construcciones con verbo soporte en latín: una perspectiva diacrónica. In Colette Bodelot & Olga Spevak (eds.), *Les constructions à verbe support en latin*, 21–52. Clermont Ferrand: Presses Universitaires Blaise Pascal.
Bartoli, Matteo-Giulio. 1925. *Introduzione alla neolinguistica: principi, scopi, metodi*. Genève: Olschki.
Bertinetto, Pier Marco. 1986. *Tempo, Aspetto e Azione nel verbo italiano. Il sistema dell'indicativo*. Firenze: Accademia della Crusca.
Borer, Hagit. 2013. *Structuring Sense*: *Taking Form*. Vol. 3. Oxford: Oxford University Press.

Brinton, Laurel J. 1991. The mass/count distinction and Aktionsart. The grammar of iteratives and habituals. *Belgian Journal of Linguistics* 6. 47–69.
Brinton, Laurel J. 1998. Aspectuality and countability: a cross-categorial analogy. *English Language and Linguistics* 2(1). 37–63.
Butt, Miriam. 1995. *The Structure of Complex Predicates in Urdu*. Stanford: CSLI Publications.
Butt, Miriam. 1998. Constraining argument merger through aspect. In Erhard Hinrichs, Andreas Kathol & Tsuneko Nakazawa (eds.), *Complex Predicates in Nonderivational Syntax*. Syntax and Semantics. Vol. 30, 73–113. New York: Academic Press.
Butt, Miriam. 2010. The light verb jungle: still hacking away. In Mengistu Amberber, Brett Baker & Mark Harvey (eds.), *Complex Predicates: Cross-linguistic Perspectives on Event Structure*, 48–78. Cambridge: Cambridge University Press.
Butt, Miriam & Wilhelm Geuder. 2001. On the (semi)lexical status of Light Verbs. In Norbert Corver & Henk van Riemsdijk (eds.), *Semilexical Categories: On the Content of Function Words and the Function of Content Words*, 323–370. Berlin/New York: Mouton de Gruyter.
Carlson, Lauri. 1981. Aspect and quantification. In Philip Tedeschi & Annie Zaenen (eds.), *Tense and Aspect*. Syntax and Semantics. Vol. 14, 31–64. New York: Academic Press.
Chomsky, Noam. 1981. *Lectures on Government and Binding*. Dordrecht: Foris Pubblications.
Croft, William. 1993. The role of domains in the interpretation of metaphors and metonymies. *Cognitive Linguistics* 4(4). 335–370.
Cuzzolin, Pierluigi, Ignazio Putzu & Paolo Ramat. 2006. The Indo-European adverb in diachronic and typological perspective. *Indogermanische Forschungen*. 111. 1–38.
De Miguel, Elena. 2006. Tensión y equilibrio semántico entre nombres y verbos: el reparto de la tarea de predicar. In Milka Villayandre (ed.), *Actas del XXXV Simposio de la Sociedad Española de Lingüística*, 1289–1313. León: Ediciones del Dpto. de Filología Hispánica y Clásica – Universidad de León.
De Miguel, Elena. 2008. Construcciones con verbos de apoyo en español. De cómo entran los nombres en la órbita de los verbos. In Inés Olza Moreno, Manuel Casado Velarde & Ramón González Ruiz (eds.), *Actas del XXXVII simposio internacional de la Sociedad Española de Lingüística*, 567–578. Pamplona: Servicio de Publicaciones de la Universidad de Navarra.
De Miguel, Elena. 2011. En qué consiste ser verbo de apoyo. In M.ª Victoria Escandell Vidal, Manuel Leonetti & Cristina Sánchez López (eds.), *60 problemas de gramática*, 139–146. Madrid: Akal.
Depraetere, Ilse. 1995. On the necessity of distinguishing between (un)boundedness and (a)telicity. *Linguistics and Philosophy* 18. 1–19.
Devine, Andrew M. & Laurence D. Stephens. 2006. *Latin Word Order. Structured Meaning and Information*. Oxford: Oxford University Press.
Dowty, David. 1979. *Word Meaning and Montague Grammar*. Dordrecht: Reidel.
Duarte, Inês, Anabela Gonçalves, Matilde Miguel, Amália Mendes, Iris Hendrickx, Fátima Oliveira, Luís Filipe Cunha, Maria de Fátima Henriques da Silva & Maria da Purificação Silvano. 2010. Light verbs features in European Portuguese. In Pier Marco Bertinetto, Anna Korhonen, Alessandro Lenci, Alissa Melinger, Sabine Schulte im Walde & Aline Villavicencio (eds.), *The Identification and Representation of Verb Features*, 27–31. Pisa: Università di Pisa.
Ernout, Alfred & Antoine Meillet. 2001[1959]. *Dictionnaire étimologique de la langue latine. Historie des mots*. 4th ed. Paris: Klincksieck.
Fábregas, Antonio, Rafael Marín & Louise McNally. 2012. From psych verbs to nouns. In Violeta Demonte & Louise McNally (eds). *Telicity, Change, and State: A Cross-Categorial View of Event Structure*, 162–184. Oxford: Oxford University Press.

Folli, Raffaella & Heidi Harley. 2013. The syntax of argument structure: Evidence from Italian complex predicates. *Journal of Linguistics* 49. 93–125.

Frege, Gottlob. 1961[1884]. *Die Grundlagen der Arithmetik*. Darmstadt: Wissenschaftliche Buchgesellschaft.

Fruyt, Michèle. 2011. Word formation in Classical Latin. In James Clackson (ed.), *A Companion to the Latin Language*, 157–175. Hoboken: Wiley-Blackwell.

Gaeta, Livio. 2000. On the interaction between morphology and semantics: the Italian suffix *-ata*. *Acta Linguistica Hungarica* 47(1–4). 205–229.

Gaeta, Livio. 2002. *Quando i verbi compaiono come nomi*. Milano: FrancoAngeli.

Giry-Schneider, Jacqueline. 1986. Les noms construits avec *faire*: compléments ou prédicats? *Langue Française* 69. 49–63.

Giry-Schneider, Jacqueline. 1987. *Les prédicats nominaux en français: les phrases à verbe support*. Genève/Paris: Droz.

Goldberg, Adele. 1995. *Constructions: a Construction Grammar Approach to Argument Structure*. Chicago: University of Chicago Press.

Grimshaw, Jane. 1990. *Argument Structure*. Cambridge, MA: The MIT Press.

Grimshaw, Jane & Armin Mester. 1988. Light verbs and Θ-marking. *Linguistic Inquiry* 19(2). 205–232.

Gross, Gaston. 1989. *Les constructions converses du français*. Genève/Paris: Droz.

Gross, Gaston. 1996. *Les expressions figées en français*. Paris: Ophry.

Gross, Gaston. 2004a. Introduction. In Gaston Gross & Sophie De Pontonx (eds.), *Verbes supports. Nouvel état des lieux* 27(2). 167–169. [=Special issue of *Lingvisticae Investigationes*].

Gross, Gaston. 2004b. Pour un Bescherelle des prédicats nominaux. In Gaston Gross & Sophie De Pontonx (eds.), *Verbes supports. Nouvel état des lieux* 27(2). 343–358. [=Special issue of *Lingvisticae Investigationes*].

Gross, Gaston & Ferenc Kiefer. 1995. La structure événementielle des substantifs. *Folia Linguistica* 29(1–2). 44–65.

Gross, Maurice. 1981. Les bases empiriques de la notion de prédicat sémantique. *Langages* 63. 7–52.

Gruber, Jeffrey S. 1965. *Studies in Lexical Relations*. PhD dissertation. Cambridge, MA: Massachusetts Institute of Technology.

Haas, Pauline, Richard Huyghe & Rafael Marín. 2008. Du verbe au nom: calques et décalages aspectuels. In Jacques Durand, Benoît Habert & Bernard Lacks (eds.), *Congrès mondial de linguistique française 2008* (CMLF 2008), 2051–2065. Paris: Institut de Linguistique Française.

Hilpert, Martin. 2014. *Construction Grammar and its Application to English*. Edinburgh: Edinburgh University Press.

Hook, Peter E. 1991. The emergence of perfective aspect in Indo-Aryan languages. In Elizabeth Traugott & Bernd Heine (eds.), *Approaches to Grammaticalization*. Vol. 2, 59–89. Amsterdam: Benjamins.

Huyghe, Richard. 2011. (A)telicity and the mass/count distinction: the case of French activity nominalizations. *Recherches linguistiques de Vincennes* 40. 101–126.

Iacobini, Claudio. 2008. Presenza e uso dei verbi sintagmatici nel parlato dell'italiano. In Monica Cini (ed.) *I verbi sintagmatici in italiano e nelle varietà dialettali*, 103–120. Frankfurt: Peter Lang.

Jackendoff, Ray. 1991. Parts and boundaries. *Cognition* 41. 9–45.

Jespersen, Otto. 1942. *A Modern English Grammar on Historical Principles*. Vol. 6. *Morphology*, London: George Allen and Unwin Ltd.

Ježek, Elisabetta. 2004. Types et degrés de verbes supports en italien. In Gaston Gross & Sophie De Pontonx (eds.), *Verbes supports. Nouvel état des lieux* 27(2). 185–201. [=Special issue of *Lingvisticae Investigationes*].

Ježek, Elisabetta. 2011. Verbes supports et composition sémantique. *Cahier de Lexicologie* 1(98). 29–44.
Ježek, Elisabetta. 2015. *The Lexicon. An Introduction*. Oxford: Oxford University Press.
Ježek, Elisabetta. This volume. A semantic co-compositional account of verb-noun Light Verb Constructions in Italian. 221–238.
Kemmer, Suzanne E. 1993. *The Middle Voice*. Amsterdam: Benjamins.
Kiss, Katalin. 2011. Remarks on semelfactive verbs in English and Hungarian. *Argumentum* 7. 121–128.
La Fauci, Nunzio & Ignazio Mirto. 2003. *Fare. Elementi di sintassi*. Pisa: Edizioni ETS.
Langer, Stefan. 2004. A linguistic test battery for support verb construction. In Gaston Gross & Sophie De Pontonx (eds.), *Verbes supports. Nouvel état des lieux* 27(2). 171–183. [=Special issue of *Lingvisticae Investigationes*].
Langacker, Ronald W. 1987. *Foundations of cognitive grammar*. Vol. 1. Stanford: Stanford University Press.
Langacker, Ronald W. 1991. *Foundations of cognitive grammar*. Vol. 2. Stanford: Stanford University Press.
Marini, Emanuela. 2018. La théorie des "classes d'objets" et son application au vocabulaire latin des <phénomènes vocaux>. In Jesús de la Villa & Anna Pompei (eds.), *Classical Languages and Linguistics. Lenguas clásicas y lingüística*. 103–126. Madrid: UAM Ediciones.
Martín Rodriguez, Antonio Mª. 1996. *Dare*, auxiliaire lexical en latin. In Michèle Fruyt & Claude Moussy (eds.), *Structures lexicales du latin*. 49–64. Paris: Presses de l'Université Paris-Sorbonne.
Mehlig, Hans Robert. 1996. Some analogies between the morphology of nouns and the morphology of aspect in Russian. *Folia Linguistica* 30(1–2). 87–109.
Michaelis, Laura A. 2004. Type-shifting in Construction Grammar: an Integrated Approach to Aspectual Coercion. *Cognitive Linguistics* 15(1). 1–67.
Moncó Taracena, Sofía. 2011. Étude constrastive des verbs *dar* (espagnol) et *faire* (français). In *Méthodes et analyses comparatives en Sciences du langage. Actes de la 3eme edition des Journées d'Etudes Toulousaines*, 125–134. Toulouse: Université de Toulouse.
Nesset, Tore. 2013. The history of the Russian semelfactive: the development of a radical category. *Journal of Slavic Linguistics* 21(1). 123–169.
Newman, John. 1996. *Give: A Cognitive Linguistic Study*. Berlin/New York: Mouton de Gruyter.
Palancar, Enrique L. 1999. What do we give in Spanish when we hit? A constructionist account of hitting expressions. *Cognitive Linguistics* 10(1). 57–91.
Palancar, Enrique L. 2003. La polisemia dei verbi *dar, pegar* e *meter* in spagnolo. In Silvia Luraghi & Livio Gaeta (eds), *Introduzione alla linguistica cognitiva*, 197–212. Roma: Carocci.
Paprotté, Wolf. 1988. A discourse perspective on tense and aspect in standard Modern Greek and English. In Brigida Rudzka-Ostyn (ed.), *Topics in Cognitive Linguistics*, 447–505. Amsterdam: Benjamins
Parsons, Terence. 1990. *Event in the Semantics of English. Study in Subatomic Semantics*. Cambridge, MA: The MIT Press.
Perek, Florent. 2015. *Argument Structure in Usage-Based Construction Grammar*. Amsterdam: Benjamins.
Perek, Florent & Martin Hilpert. 2014. Constructional tolerance: are Argument Structure Constructions equally powerful across languages? *Constructions and Frames* 6(2). 266–304.
Pinkster, Harm. 2015. *Oxford Latin Syntax*. Vol. 1. Oxford: Oxford University Press.
Pompei, Anna. 2018. *Facere saltum* ou *dare saltum*? Verbes supports et noms de mouvement. In Colette Bodelot & Olga Spevak (eds.), *Les constructions à verbs support en latin*, 169–186. Clermont-Ferrand: Presses Universitaires Blaise Pascal.
Pompei, Anna. 2019. *Dare, facere* e i nomi di implicazione fisica e di movimento in latino. In Anna Pompei & Lunella Mereu (eds.), *Verbi supporto. Fenomeni e teorie*, 111–153. München: LINCOM.

Pompei, Anna & Valentina Piunno. This volume. Light Verb Constructions in Romance languages. An attempt to explain systematic irregularity. 99–147.
Pustejovsky, James. 1991a. The Generative Lexicon. *Computational Linguistics* 17(4). 409–441.
Pustejovsky, James. 1991b. The syntax of Event Structure. *Cognition* 41. 47–81.
Pustejovsky, James. 1995. *The Generative Lexicon*. Cambridge, MA: The MIT Press.
Quine, Willard Van Orman. 1960. *Word and Object*. New York: Wiley.
Rothstein, Susan. 2008. Telicity and atomicity. In Susan Rothstein (ed.), *Theoretical and Crosslinguistic Approaches to the Semantics of Aspect*, 43–78. Amsterdam: Benjamins.
Rothstein, Susan. 2012. Another look at accomplishments and incrementality. In Violeta Demonte & Louise McNally (eds.), *Telicity, Change and State*, 60–102. Oxford: Oxford University Press.
Samek-Lodovici, Vieri. 2003. The internal structure of arguments and its role in complex predicate formation. *Natural Language & Linguistic Theory* 21. 835–881.
Sanromán Vilas, Begoña. 2011. The unbearable lightness of light verbs. Are they semantically empty verbs? In Igor Boguslavsky & Leo Wanner (eds.), *Proceedings of the 5th International Conference on Meaning-Text Theory*, 253–263. Barcelona: Observatoire de linguistique Sens-Texte (OLST).
Simone, Raffaele. 2003. Maṣdar, 'ismu al-marrati et la frontière verbe/nom. In Jose Luis Giron Alconchel (ed.), *Estudios ofrecidos al profesor J. Bustos Tovar*, 901–918. Madrid: Universidad Complutense.
Smith, Carlota. S. 1991. *The Parameter of Aspect*. Dordrecht: Kluwer.
Spevak, Olga. 2014. *The Noun Phrase in Classical Latin Prose*. Leiden: Brill.
Talmy, Leonard. 1985. Force dynamics in language and thought. In William Eilfort, Paul Kroeber & Karen Peterson (eds.), *Papers from the Parasession on Causatives and Agentivity at the 21st Regional Meeting*, 293–337. Chicago: Chicago Linguistic Society.
Talmy, Leonard. 1988. Force dynamics in language and cognition. *Cognitive Science* 12. 49–100.
Talmy, Leonard. 2000. *Toward a Cognitive Semantics*. Vol. 1: *Concept Structuring System*. Cambridge, MA: The MIT Press.
Talmy, Leonard. 2007. Lexical typologies. In Timothy Shopen (ed.), *Language Typology and Syntactic Description*. Vol. 3, 66–168. 2nd edn. Cambridge: Cambridge University Press.
Tovena, Lucia M. & Marta Donazzan. 2017. Italian -*ata* event nouns and the *nomen vicis* interpretation. *Italian Journal of Linguistics* 29(1). 75–100.
Van Valin, Robert D. J. 2006. Some universals of verb semantics. In Ricardo Marail & Juana Gil (eds.), *Linguistic Universals*, 155–178. Cambridge: Cambridge University Press.
Van Valin, Robert D. J. & Randy J. LaPolla. 1997. *Syntax: Structure, Meaning and Function*. Cambridge: Cambridge University Press.
Vendler, Zeno. 1957. Verbs and times. *The Philosophical Review* 66. 143–160.
Vivès, Robert. 1984. L'Aspect dans les constructions nominales prédicatives: *avoir, prendre*, verbe support et extension aspectuelle. *Lingvisticae Investigationes* 3(1). 161–185.
Zaliznjak, Anna A. & Aleksej D. Šmelev. 2000. *Vvedenie v russkuju aspektologiju*. [Introduction in the Russian aspectology]. Moscow: Jazyki russkoj kul'tury.

Roberta Mastrofini
6 When lightness meets lexical aspect
A corpus-based account of English Light Verb Extensions

Abstract: Since Jespersen's definition of the concept (1942: 117–118), studies on Lightness have profusely developed in many languages. Recent contributions have focused on the hypothesis that Lightness is not uniquely a property of general verbs or Verb+Noun constructions, but that there are different instances of Light Verb patterns exhibiting different degrees of cohesion between the elements involved. In other words, various verbs can become 'light' in specific syntagmatic environments implying an eventive or deverbal nominal element. This suggests the existence of a gradient of lightness, which implies other constructions than the ones officially recognized by the previous literature on the topic. In keeping with this approach, this paper focuses on Light Verb Extensions. Like prototypical Light Verb Constructions, they stem from the combination of a verb and an eventive or deverbal noun; unlike prototypical Light Verb Constructions, they exploit fully lexical verbs that, under certain syntagmatic conditions, are turned into aspectual devices (e.g., *to cultivate a virtue, to embrace a concept, to deliver a speech*). This contribution presents a corpus-based account of such constructions in English, recognizing different aspectual configurations conveyed by the Light Verb Extension patterns, in which the predicate, devoid of its literal meaning, plays a crucial role in determining them. According to these findings, the criteria used so far to identify Lightness should include the aspectual dimension of the construction, thus confirming the idea that this phenomenon should be dealt with in a broader perspective.

Keywords: Lightness, Light Verb Extensions, Aspectual configuration, corpus-based analysis, Sketch Engine

1 Introduction: Light Verb Constructions

The term *lightness* was first coined by Jespersen in relation to English verbal constructions formed by "an insignificant verb, to which the marks of person and tense are attached, before the really important idea" (Jespersen, 1942: 117–118). In other words, lightness was first detected as a property of general English predicates (i.e. *to make, to have, to give, to take*) when found in combination with a *nomen actionis* (Nickel, 1968) or, following a more recent definition, an eventive or deverbal noun (Gross and Kiefer, 1995; Kiefer, 1998), as in the case of *to make a call, to give a talk, to take a walk, to have a row*. These examples represent a verbal construction in which the verb is devoid of its literal meaning through a process of "predicate bleaching" (Hook, 1974; Szabolsci, 1986). As a consequence, the verb turns into a mere syntactic device, while the noun undertakes the main aspectual-semantic content of the construction (i.e. *to make a call* means 'to call'; *to give a talk* means 'to talk', and so forth).

Since then, the so-called Light Verb Constructions (hence, LVCs) have been an extensively debated topic in the literature, and have been the object of research in a number of different languages, such as German (cf. Helbig, 1979, 1984; Hoffmann, 1996), Spanish (cf. Blanco Escoda, 2000; Bosque, 2004; De Miguel, 2008), Italian (cf. Alba Salas, 2002; Gaeta, 2002; La Fauci and Mirto, 2003; Mastrofini, 2004; Ježek, 2004), English (cf. Wierzbicka, 1982, 1988; Dixon, 1991; Kearns, 2002; Butt, 2010; Tu and Roth, 2011; Mastrofini, 2013), Japanese (cf. Grimshaw and Mester, 1988; Dubinsky, 1997; Miyamoto, 1999), and French (cf. Vivès, 1998; Giry-Schneider, 1987; Gross G., 1996, 1999).

2 State of the art

There have been many varied approaches to the study of LVCs, ranging from morphology (Helbig 1979, 1984) to syntax (Grimshaw and Mester, 1988; Kearns, 2002), and semantics (Wierzbicka, 1982, 1988), just to name but a few. Nevertheless, many aspects seem to be unsolved. The first question concerns the methodology: using a single level of analysis (morphological *vs.* syntactic *vs.* semantic) has shed some light on the properties of the verb or of the noun, but failed in considering the phenomena of interface underlying the construction as a whole. Secondly, the criteria used to determine what is an LVC from what is not one are not universally recognized in the literature. The most exhaustive taxonomy of parameters was developed by French scholars (Giry-Schneider, 1978, 1987; Gross M., 1996; Vivès, 1998; Gross G., 1994, 1996, 1999) within the works carried out by the L.A.D.L. (*Laboratoire d'Automatique Documentaire et Linguistique*) and the L.L.I. (*Laboratoire de Linguistique Informatique*). It includes both syntactic and semantic parameters according to which an LVC behaves differently from other formally similar V+N constructions. The main ones are:

- the impossibility of nominalizing the verbal component[1] (**The giving of a cry*; **The making of a call*), or for the nominal component to be the focus of a WH-question (**Which cry did she give?*);

---

[1] As a matter of fact, the nominalization of an LV is accepted in some Romance language constructions in which the nominal element is not preceded by a Determiner. For example, the Italian and

- the impossibility of making the object the surface subject of a passive (*A row was had by Sarah and John; *A cry was given by me);
- the possibility of extracting the object through clefting (It is a cry she gave; it is a call she made), and cancelling the verb without a significant semantic loss (John gave a speech → John's speech).

Following this approach, a prototypical LVC like *to make a call* would not undergo nominalization and passivization, but would accept clefting and the deletion of the predicate, as exemplified in the following Table 1.

Table 1: Identification criteria applied to English prototypical LVCs.

	CRITERION	LVC
1.	Nominalization	–
2.	WH-question	–
3.	Passivization	–
4.	Clefting	+
5.	Verb deletion	+

As a matter of fact, apart from the first parameter which seems to be paramount for any LVC considered,[2] the others are applicable only to some LVCs and not to others, as emerged in more recent studies (Kearns, 2002; Butt, 2010; Mastrofini, 2019; among others). Kearns (2002) suggests a distinction between Truly Light Verbs and Vague Action Verbs, which allows for the passivization in *an inspection was made*; *the cry given by Mark scared me* is also acceptable since the object is definite and not indefinite.

Considering what Butt (2010) calls "Complex Predicates",[3] that is a monophrasal and a multiword predicate (e.g. *to take into account, to fall in love, to look*

French LVCs *prendere coscienza/ prendre conscience* – 'to take conscience, to realize' – admit the nominalization of the Verb (e.g. *La presa di coscienza/ la prise de conscience*). Nevertheless, this variation is not registered in English instances.

2 "Les transformations morphologiques (nominalisations, adjectivations, verbalisations) sont le fait des prédicats. Les verbs supports ne peuvent faire l'objet d'un changement de catégorie" (Gross G., 1996: 55). «Morphological changes (i.e. nominalization, adjectivization, and verbalization) are typical of fully lexical predicates. Light verbs cannot undergo any category shift». The translation is mine.

3 "The term *complex predicate* designates a construction that involves two or more predicational elements (e.g., nouns, verbs and adjectives) which predicate as a single unit, i.e., their arguments map onto a monoclausal syntactic structure" (Butt, 2010: 49).

forward to), the extraction of the object is not possible. Moreover, several studies (Gross M., 1981; Cicalese, 1999; Ježek, 2011; Mastrofini, 2019) detected lightness in full lexical predicates when found in specific syntagmatic environments, that is in combination with an eventive or deverbal noun. This construction has been named Light Verb Extension (hence, LVE), since it shares semantic and syntactic similarities with traditional LVCs. Like LVCs, LVEs contain a bleached predicate, and the noun carries the semantic content of the pattern. Unlike LVCs, the verb functions as an aspectual device (e.g. *to nourish resentment*; *to fuel growth*; *to entertain illusion*; *to break a relationship*).

In the following section, I will provide a more detailed account of LVEs, which is the topic of my investigation.

3 Light Verb Extensions

An LVE (e.g. *to cultivate virtue, to deliver a speech, to raise awareness*) is represented by the combination of a lexical[4] verb and an eventive or deverbal noun. While the verb, thanks to its combination with a nominal representing an event, loses most of its semantic configuration, and serves as an aspectual device, the eventive noun, namely a nominal item that implies a process having duration and phases (cf. Gross and Kiefer 1995, Kiefer 1998), carries the semantics of the pattern, as in prototypical LVCs. This is made possible since any verb involved in an LVE construction undergoes a process of bleaching through the interaction with the semantic configuration underlying the nominal element it combines with. In other words, the lightness of the pattern is contextually licensed.

LVEs have not received much attention so far. A few studies have been conducted on French (Gross M., 1981) and Italian (D'Agostino, 1995; D'Agostino and Elia, 1998; Cicalese, 1999; Ježek, 2011); to the best of my knowledge, only two were recently published on English (Mastrofini, 2019, 2021). They were first mentioned in Gross M. (1981), in which the author reports a number of examples (1) in which a full predicate is devoid of its literal meaning, although it participates in conveying the aspectual configuration of the construction:

(1) a. L'argent   a   de l'influence sur Max   (French)
       Money   have.3SG   some influence on Max
       'Money has some influence on Max'   (English)

---

[4] The term 'lexical' is here used in opposition to 'light', namely to denote any predicate conveying a full meaning (e.g. *to adopt, to cultivate, to follow, to run*, etc.).

b. L'argent prend de l'influence sur Max (French)
   Money exert.3SG some influence on Max
   'Money exerts some influence on Max' (English)
c. L'argent conserve de l'influence sur Max (French)
   Money keep.3SG some influence on Max
   'Money keeps some influence on Max' (English)
d. L'argent perd de l'influence sur Max (French)
   Money lose.3SG some influence on Max
   "Money loses some influence on Max" (English)

With respect to the example (1a), the sentences (1b) to (1d) make use of a lexical predicate whose function is that of marking the aspect of the event. More specifically, example (1b) represents an inchoative event ("Money starts having an influence on Max"); example (1c) depicts a continuative event ("Money continues to have an influence on Max"); example (1d) denotes a transformative event ("Money stops having an influence on Max").[5] In all these cases, the original full meaning of the predicate is bleached, and the verb serves as an aspectual device.

After Gross (1981), the interest in LVEs has emerged in a few Italian contributions. D'Agostino (1995) underlines the fact that any lexical verb can be light (or, even better, used 'lightly') if combined with an eventive noun, and provides some examples of Italian LVEs, such as *elaborare un progetto* ('to work out a project'), *perpetrare una truffa* ('to perpetrate a fraud'), *assegnare un premio* ('to award a prize'), *sudarsi un risultato* ('to strive for a goal'), etc. I argue that the vast majority of these constructions undergo nominalization, both in Italian and in English, and are, therefore, to be considered instances of collocations and not of LVEs.[6] Ježek (2011) carries out a more fine-grained analysis from an aspectual-semantic perspective, and groups Italian LVEs according to a number of components or dimen-

---

5 The aspectual classes used in the present contribution refer to Bertinetto et al. (1995). Bertinetto et al. classify verbs into 6 aspectual categories: Statives, Continuatives, Resultatives, Transformatives, Inchoatives, and Iteratives. The first four classes correspond to Vendler's (1967) States, Activities, Accomplishments, and Achievements, respectively. More specifically, Statives denote unchanging situations (e.g. *to be, to own*); Continuatives depict dynamic events that go on in time (e.g. *to speak, to walk*). Resultatives and Transformatives refer to telic events: while in the former the resulting State is brought about by a Process (e.g. *to build, to burn*), in the latter there is a shift from an initial State to a final one (e.g. *to arrive, to die*). Moreover, according to Bertinetto et al.'s taxonomy, Inchoatives denote the beginning of a process (e.g. *to fall asleep, to start speaking*), while Iteratives imply the repetition of the same event (e.g. *to clap, to sip*).
6 For example, *l'elaborazione di un progetto* ('the workout of a project'); *l'assegnazione di un premio* ('the award of a prize').

sions they seem to convey, such as Aspect (A), Modality (Mod), Intensity (I), Quantity (Q), Register (R), Connotation (C), Figurative Sense (FS) (see Table 2).

Table 2: Aspectual-semantic dimensions of Italian LVEs (adapted from Ježek 2011: 6).

Dimension	Example	English Translation
A	*intavolare una discussione*	*to start a discussion*
Mod	*azzardare una risposta*	*to hazard a guess*
I	*sferrare un colpo*	*to land a blow*
Q	*abbondare in critiche*	*to receive plenty of criticism*
R	*arrecare disturbo*	*to cause disturbance*
C	*commettere un errore*	*to commit a mistake*
FS	*lanciare un segnale*	*to launch a signal*

I argue that the aspectual component is always represented in the LVEs identified by Ježek (2011), and that features such as Modality or Quantity may be additionally present. For example, even though *to land a blow* contains a certain degree of strength (which the author called "intensity"), it also marks the aspect of the action as Transformative. In the same way, *to hazard a guess* conveys a Transformative aspect, together with a degree of epistemic modality. Moreover, the last example (*to launch a signal*), although metaphorical, expresses Inchoativity with respect to the correspondant LVC *to give a signal*. As explained later on in this paper, aspect is the crucial topic which distinguishes LVEs from LVCs, and characterizes the first as examples of contextually-driven Lightness. As for English, a recent study by Mastrofini (2019) analyzes English LVEs starting from a corpus of 104 instances, and accounts for their syntactic and semantic behaviour using Pustejovsky's (1994) *Generative Lexicon* Model as an analytic tool. The results show that the semantic loss of the lexical predicate when participating in an LVE is licensed at a syntagmatic level, and re-defines the Argument Structure and the aspectual configuration of the pattern.

The following Section 4 illustrates the methodology according to which I built my corpus of English LVEs, and the results of my inquiry. Section 5 analyzes and discusses the aspectual dimension connected with the retrieved examples.

4 Methodology and results

I started from the istances of LVEs retrieved in previous contributions (Gross, 1981; Elia et al., 1985; D'Agostino, 1995; D'Agostino and Elia, 1998; Cicalese, 1999; Mastrofini, 2005; Ježek, 2011); I translated them into English, and checked their use in online (www.wordreference.com, www.dictionary.com) and paper dictionaries (Collins Cobuild *English Language*, MacMillan *English Dictionary*, Oxford *English Dictionary*). I then searched for their occurrence in Sketch Engine (www.sketch-engine.eu), which collects several corpora in many different languages. To carry out my research I selected English Web 2018 (enTenTen18), which is an English corpus made up of texts collected from the Internet, for a total of 21,926,740,748 billion words and more than 25 billion tokens.

My analysis resulted in retrieving 444 LVE types, for a total of 3,089,294 instances. The following Table 3 illustrates my results: Column 1 presents the list of predicates used as LVEs in alphabetical order; Column 2 reports the nominal part of the pattern, that is the direct objects the verbs in Column 1 combine with to create LVEs; Column 3 provides the number of istances found in the corpus for each verb.

Table 3: English LVEs in Sketch Engine.

Verb	Objects	# of instances in the corpus
absorb	blow, culture, damage, knowledge, lesson, shock	10,799
accumulate	evidence, experience, fatigue, knowledge, stress, wisdom	20,662
adopt	approach, attitude, behaviour, change, concept, culture, decision, diet, habit, idea, innovation, interpretation, language, perspective, policy, proposal, recommendation, reform, resolution, solution, statement, strategy, view	208,233
break	agreement, commandment, connection, contact, curse, marriage, promise, relationship, silence, spell, trust	70,972
breed	contempt, corruption, cynicism, discontent, hatred, resentment, success, violence	5,124
chase	dream, perfection, suspect, win	6,557
commit	abuse, assault, attack, error, excess, infraction, massacre, mistake, offence, outrage, rape, transgression, violation, violence	84,947
conclude	agreement, alliance, argument, arrangement, bargain, celebration, consultation, deal, debate, discourse, discussion, examination, inquiry, interview, investigation, mission, negotiation, pact, presentation, speech, report, statement, talk, transaction, treaty, war	42,827
consummate	acquisition, agreement, arrangement, assault, bargain, conquest, deal, exchange, massacre, purchase, redemption, revolution, sale, sacrifice, salvation, transaction, transgression, vengeance	2,743
cultivate	appreciation, awareness, compassion, consciousness, creativity, culture, curiosity, disposition, empathy, friendship, gratitude, habit, humility, intimacy, kindness, love, loyalty, mindfulness, passion, patience, peace, relation, relationship, reputation, resilience, self-awareness, skill, talent, taste, understanding, virtue, wisdom	31,326
cut	cost, deal, emission, loss, pollution, production, waste	89,587

Table 3 (continued)

Verb	Objects	# of instances in the corpus
deal	blow, damage, death, defeat, punishment	41,480
deliver	advice, blow, education, efficiency, experience, growth, improvement, information, innovation, instruction, judgement, lecture, opinion, outcome, performance, power, presentation, result, solution, speech, statement, support, talk, work	319,045
embrace	approach, belief, challenge, change, concept, creativity, culture, failure, faith, freedom, idea, innovation, life, lifestyle, love, movement, mission, notion, opportunity, perspective, practice, responsibility, revolution, thinking, transformation, uncertainty, view	65,989
entertain	affection, ambition, appeal, apprehension, belief, claim, complaint, conception, contempt, conviction, delusion, desire, doubt, expectation, fantasy, fear, feeling, hope, idea, illusion, jealousy, motion, notion, opinion, prejudice, regard, request, respect, sentiment, suspicion, thought, wish	26,316
establish	communication, connection, contact, control, credibility, culture, goal, link, practice, record, relation, relationship, reputation, trust	204,395
follow	advice, diet, direction, instructions, order, meeting, procedure, recommendation, rules, treatment	480,331
fuel	addiction, ambition, anger, anxiety, concern, consumption, corruption, creativity, curiosity, debate, demand, desire, development, discontent, efficiency, enthusiasm, expansion, fear, growth, hatred, imagination, increase, innovation, instability, obsession, optimism, passion, perception, protest, rage, resentment, revolution, suspicion, tension, terrorism, transformation, violence	39,402
gain	ability, acceptance, access, acclaim, admission, advantage, appreciation, approval, attention, awareness, confidence, control, credibility, education, employment, experience, knowledge, influence, insight, interest, possession, power, promotion, reputation, respect, strength, success, support, trust, understanding, victory, wisdom	665,630
gush	admiration, adoration, adulation, compliments, enthusiasm, flattery, gratitude, praise, sentimentality	392
heap	accusation, blame, contempt, criticism, curse, denunciation, disgrace, embarrassment, guilt, injustice, persecution, praise, pressure, reproach, scorn, shame	7,019
hurl	abuse, accusation, criticism, curse, defiance, denunciation, insult, reproach	
land	blow, conversion, deal, degradation, gamble, interview, kick, nomination, penalty, shot, win	10,038
nourish	creativity, faith, hatred, hope, imagination	995
nurse	ambition, anger, grievance, grudge, hatred, resentment	1,274

Table 3 (continued)

Verb	Objects	# of instances in the corpus
raise	alarm, argument, awareness, challenge, claim, complaint, concern, consciousness, demand, doubt, expectation, hope, objection, question, risk, stake, suspicion	548,927
reap	acclaim, advantage, destruction, enjoyment, glory, happiness, praise, revenge, rewards, satisfaction, sorrow, success, vengeance	19,796
shower	affection, adoration, adulation, blessings, compliment, kindness, love, mercy, praise	2,636
slap	ban, fine, injunction, sanction	1,396
win	acclaim, approval, argument, independence, praise, promotion, recognition, respect, support, victory	75,531

5 Analysis and discussion

I classified the LVE instances retrieved in the English Web 2018 corpus according to the aspectual configuration they convey. The aspectual configuration refers to the entire pattern: it is the combination between the Verb and the nominal element which triggers the aspectual interpretation, even in cases of Nouns that undergo a Type Coercion[7], as for *to cultivate patience* ot *to gain knowledge*. Even though abstract nouns like *patience* and *knowledge* do not convey aspect in themselves, they are forced into an aspectual reading by the V+N construction in which they are involved, with the continuative meaning of "to go on being patient" and "to learn", respectively. Out of the 444 types, 134 are classified as Continuative, 53 as Iterative, 162 as Transformative, 95 as Inchoative, following Bertinetto et al.'s (1995) taxonomy. No examples of Stative and Resultative constructions were detected.

Continuative constructions are represented by the following LVEs:
- **to breed** *contempt/corruption/criticism/discontent/hatred/resentment/success/violence*
- **to chase** *dream/perfection/suspect/win*
- **to cultivate** *appreciation/awareness/compassion/consciousness/creativity/culture/curiosity/disposition/empathy/friendship/gratitude/habit/humility/intimacy/kindness/love/loyalty/mindfulness/passion/patience/*

---

[7] Type Coercion is defined as "the mechanism to allow an NP, or any expression, in general, to change its type (and hence its denotation) depending on the context" (Pustejovsky, 1994: 106).

peace/relation/relationship/reputation/resilience/self-awareness/skill/talent/taste/understanding/virtue/wisdom
- **to entertain**
affection/ambition/appeal/apprehension/belief/claim/complaint/conception/contempt/conviction/delusion/desire/doubt/expectation/fantasy/fear/feeling/hope/idea/illusion/jealousy/motion/notion/opinion/prejudice/regard/request/respect/sentiment/suspicion/thought/wish
- **to follow**
advice/diet/direction/instructions/order/meeting/procedure/recommendation/rules/treatment
- **to fuel**
addiction/ambition/anger/anxiety/concern/consumption/corruption/creativity/curiosity/debate/demand/desire/development/discontent/efficiency/enthusiasm/expansion/fear/growth/hatred/imagination/increase/innovation/instability/obsession/optimism/passion/perception/protest/rage/resentment/revolution/suspicion/tension/terrorism/transformation/violence
- **to nourish** creativity/faith/hatred/hope/imagination
- **to nurse** ambition/anger/grievance/grudge/hatred/resentment.

As described in Bertinetto et al.'s (1995), Continuative constructions denote durative and dynamic events that do not imply any *telos*, namely the reaching of an ending point. Two instances for this aspectual category are *to cultivate appreciation* (8,002 tokens found in the corpus) and *to fuel growth* (12,110 tokens found in the corpus). Let's consider the following examples:

(2) Weekly, I am delighted at the opportunity **to cultivate an appreciation** for the perpetually underpowered "UnderCurrents" column.

(3) These rising demands among the hospitals expected to **fuel the growth** of the image guided therapy system market.

Both examples see the combination of the verbs *to cultivate* and *to fuel* with an eventive noun. With respect to the correspondent synthetic verbs (i.e. *to appreciate* and *to grow*, respectively), these constructions mark the durative aspect of the event. Therefore, they may be modified using durative adverbials such as "for x time", as shown in the following example excerpted from the corpus:

(4) All the signs point to a general decline in business activity unless there is some kind of technological breakthrough equivalent to the computer revolution that **fueled growth for decades.**

Iterative constructions are represented by the following LVEs:
- ***to accumulate*** *evidence/experience/fatigue/knowledge/stress/wisdom*
- ***to heap***
  accusation/blame/contempt/criticism/curse/denunciation/disgrace/embarrassment/guilt/injustice/persecution/pressure/reproach/scorn/shame
- ***to gush***
  admiration/adoration/adulation/compliments/enthusiasm/flattery/gratitude/praise/sentimentality
- ***to reap***
  acclaim/advantage/destruction/enjoyment/glory/happiness/praise/revenge/rewards/satisfaction/sorrow/success/vengeance
- ***to shower*** *affection/adoration/adulation/blessings/compliment/kindness/love/mercy/praise.*

As described in Bertinetto et al.'s (1995), Iterative constructions, like Continuatives, denote dynamic events that do not imply any *telos*, but the repetition of the same event. The most representative instances for this aspectual category are *to accumulate evidence* (6,279 tokens found in the corpus) and *to reap rewards* (17,494 tokens found in the corpus).

Let's consider the following examples:

(5) Did you **accumulate** some **evidence**, or is this an intuitive belief?

(6) This approach may be the most effective way to **reap the rewards** of both worlds.

Both examples see the combination of the verbs *to accumulate* and *to reap* with an eventive noun, thus providing a metaphorical reading of the concepts of "accumulating" and "reaping". Like Continuative constructions, they may be modified using durative adverbials such as "for x time", even though both examples allow a number of sub-events that repeat themselves; one may accumulate a piece of evidence "in x time" or "after x time", but one accumulates evidence (as an uncountable noun) "for x time":

(7) We [. . .] have been **accumulating evidence for years** that resistance genes are primarily designed for communication between differing bacteria and other chemical messaging even with other organisms such as plants and even animals.

In other words, Iterative constructions are made up of a series of Transformative micro-events: each of them is concluded and iterated in time.

Transformative constructions are represented by the following LVEs:

- **to break**
  agreement/commandment/connection/contact/curse/marriage/promise/relationship/silence/spell/trust
- **to commit**
  abuse/assault/attack/error/excess/infraction/massacre/mistake/offence/outrage/rape/transgression/violation/violence
- **to conclude**
  agreement/alliance/argument/arrangement/bargain/celebration/consultation/deal/debate/discourse/ discussion/examination/inquiry/interview/investigation/mission/negotiation/pact/presentation/speech/report/statement/talk/transaction,/treaty/war
- **to consummate**
  acquisition/agreement/arrangement/assault/bargain/conquest/deal/exchange/massacre/purchase/redemption/revolution/sale/sacrifice/salvation/transaction/transgression/vengeance
- **to cut** cost/deal/emission/loss/pollution/production/waste
- **to deal** blow/damage/death/defeat/punishment
- **to deliver**
  advice/blow/education/efficiency/experience/growth/improvement/information/innovation/instruction/judgement/lecture/opinion/outcome/performance/power/presentation/result/solution/speech/statement/support/talk/work
- **to gain**
  ability/acceptance/access/acclaim/admission/advantage/appreciation/approval/attention/awareness/confidence/control/credibility/education/employment/experience/knowledge/influence/insight/interest/possession/power/promotion/reputation/respect/strength/success/support/trust/understanding/victory/wisdom
- **to land** blow/conversion/deal/degradation,/gamble/interview/kick/nomination/penalty/shot/win
- **to slap** ban/fine/injunction/sanction
- **to win**
  acclaim/approval/argument/independence/praise/promotion/recognition/respect/support/victory.

As described in Bertinetto et al.'s (1995), Transformative constructions denote a quick shift from an initial to a final State. Therefore, they represent telic events with no prior process involved between the two States (the lack of a process differentiates Transformative constructions from Resultative ones, as in Vendler's (1967) opposition between Achievement and Accomplishment verbs). The most representative instances for this aspectual category are *to deliver results* (47,223 tokens found in the corpus) and *to gain experience* (81,096 tokens found in the corpus).

Let's consider the following examples:

(8) The Dario mobile app **delivers** accurate **results** in real-time and actionable insights so you always know where you stand and what to do next.

(9) Using this form of cooperation, we have **gained** necessary **experience** during implementation of projects.

Both examples see the combination of the verbs *to deliver* and *to gain* with abstract concepts which refer to events. With respect to the correspondant LVCs (i.e. *to give results* and *to have experience*, respectively), these constructions underline in a more precise way the final step of the action. Therefore, they may be modified using punctual or telic expressions such as "in x time".

Inchoative constructions are represented by the following LVEs:
- **to absorb** blow/culture/damage/knowledge/lesson/shock
- **to adopt**
approach/attitude/behaviour/change/concept/culture/decision/diet/habit/idea/innovation/interpretation/language/perspective/policy/proposal/recommendation/reform/resolution/solution/statement/strategy,/view
- **to embrace**
approach/belief/challenge/change/concept/creativity/culture/failure/faith/freedom/idea/innovation/life/lifestyle/love/movement/mission/notion/opportunity/perspective/practice/responsibility/revolution/thinking/transformation/uncertainty/view
- **to establish**
communication/connection/contact/control/credibility/culture/goal/link/practice/record/relation/relationship/reputation/trust
- **to hurl** abuse/accusation/criticism/curse/defiance/denunciation/insult/reproach
- **to raise**
alarm/argument/awareness/challenge/claim/complaint/concern/consciousness/demand/doubt/expectation/hope/objection/question/risk/stake/suspicion.

As described in Bertinetto et al.'s (1995), Inchoative constructions depict the beginning phase of an action or a State. They are considered somehow telic, since they single out that phase, and present it as it were concluded. The most representative instances for this aspectual category are *to adopt an approach* (47,964 tokens found in the corpus) and *to establish a relationship* (48,878 tokens found in the corpus).

Let's consider the following examples:

(10) Mapletree Bay Point **adopted** a holistic **approach** based on a minimalistic functional philosophy.

(11) Most of this research confirms the crucial importance of **establishing** a good therapeutic **relationship**.

Both examples see the combination of the verbs *to adopt* and *to establish* with an eventive noun. With respect to the correspondant synthetic verbs (i.e. *to approach* and *to relate*, respectively), these constructions focus on the starting phase of the event, and represent it as isolated from the rest. This is why they may be modified using punctual adverbials such as "in x time" or "immediately":

(12) Such ornament can be seen to have evolved directly from the script embellishments of the early Cathach of Saint Columba, thus **establishing a relationship in time** subsequent to that work".

In all the examples excerpted from the corpus, the aspectual configuration of the constructions is given by a mechanism of *Co-Composition* (Pustejovsky, 2012), which permits the interaction between the semantic configurations underlying the verbal and the nominal elements of the pattern. More specifically, Co-Composition results in a process of Qualia Unification[8] in which the semantics of the predicate and the noun interact. For example, applying Pustejovsky's (1994) Model, the representation of the inchoative LVE *to adopt an attitude* will be the following:

(13) **to adopt an attitude**
Argument Structure: T-Arg [+human]; T-Arg [+abstract]
Event Structure: PROCESS (e_n)
Qualia Structure: Constitutive = e_1
  Formal = Process
  Telic = to have an attitude
  Agentive = [+ cognitive process] [+ human]

The example in (13) is characterized by an event structure which is similar to that of Processes, even if the focus here is on the beginning of that Process, as indicated by the Constitutive Quale (e_1). The lexical structure underlying the verb *to adopt* in

---

[8] For a thorough analysis of the Qualia Structure of LVEs see Mastrofini, 2021.

its original and prototypical meaning incorporates a semantic constraint regarding the Object ([+animate]), as in *to adopt a child*. As exemplified in (13), the eventive noun entering the LVE affects the lexical representation of the construction, and forces the predicate into a new syntagmatic environment in which the nominal item licenses both the Agentive and Telic Qualia. This mechanism multiplies the syntagmatic contexts in which the verb may be used, and assigns a different weight to the two components: whereas the eventive noun gives semantic salience to the pattern, the predicate is lightened to convey aspectual information about it. Therefore, unlike prototypical LVCs, the verb entering an LVE is not merely a grammatical device, but it participates in licensing aspect. The following Table 4 summarizes the identification parameters, with the addition of the criterion which specifies the aspectual component.

Table 4: Identification criteria applied to English LVEs.

	CRITERION	LVE
1.	Nominalization	–
2.	WH-question	–
3.	Passivization	±
4.	Clefting	+
5.	V Deletion	–
6.	Aspectual configuration	V+N

6 Conclusion

This paper presented a corpus-based analysis of a recent phenomenon of contextually-triggered Lightness, called Light Verb Extension. Like prototypical LVCs, LVEs stem from the combination of a verb and an eventive or deverbal noun; unlike prototypical LVCs, they exploit fully lexical verbs that, under certain syntagmatic conditions, are turned into aspectual devices. LVEs have been scarcely investigated in English so far. My contribution wanted to analyze this interesting phenomenon, adopting a synchronic perspective and a corpus-based approach, which demonstrated how pervasive LVES are in contemporary English.

My inquiry retrieved 444 LVEs types in English, for a total of more than 3 million tokens. LVEs are characterized by different aspectual configurations (i.e. Continuative, Iterative, Transformative, Inchoative). As a matter of fact, aspect is the crucial element that distinguishes these V+N patterns from prototypical ones, thus implying a reformulation of the parameters adopted in the literature to detect LVCs.

Duly, although partially bleached from a semantic viewpoint, any predicate used as an Extension participates in conveying the aspectual configuration of the construction as a whole, through a phenomenon of *Co-composition* licensed at a syntagmatic level by the interaction of the verbal and the nominal components.

References

Alba-Salas, Josep. 2002. *Light Verb Constructions in Romance: a Syntactic Analysis*. PhD dissertation. Ithaca, NY: Cornell University.

Bertinetto, Pier Marco, Valentina Bianchi, Östen Dahl & Mario Squartini (eds.), 1995, *Temporal Reference, Aspect and Actionality*. Torino: Rosenberg & Sellier.

Blanco Escoda, Xavier. 2000. Verbos soporte y clases de predicados en español. *Lingüistica española actual* 22(1). 1–12.

Bosque, Ignacio. 2004. On the weight of light verb predicates. In Julia Herschenson, Enrique Mallén & Karen Zagona (eds.), *Features and Interfaces in Romance*, 23–38. Amsterdam: Benjamins.

Butt, Miriam. 2010. The light verb jungle: still hacking away. In Mengistu Amberber, Mark Harvey & Brett Baker (eds.), *Complex Predicates: Cross-linguistic Perspectives on Event Structure*, 48–78. Cambridge: Cambridge University Press.

Cicalese, Anna. 1999. Le estensioni di verbo supporto. Uno studio introduttivo. *Studi Italiani di Linguistica Teorica e Applicata* 28(3). 447–487.

D'Agostino, Emilio. 1995. *Tra sintassi e semantica. Descrizione e metodi di elaborazione automatica della lingua d'uso*, Napoli: ESI.

D'Agostino, Emilio & Annibale Elia. 1998. Il significato delle frasi: un continuum dalle frasi semplici alle forme polirematiche. In Federico Albano Leoni, Daniele Gambarara, Franco Lo Piparo, Raffaele Simone & Stefano Gensini (eds.), *Ai limiti del linguaggio*, 287–310. Bari-Roma: Laterza.

De Miguel, Elena. 2008. Construcciones con verbos de apoyo en espanol. De como entran los nombres en la orbita de los verbos. In Ines Olza Moreno, Manuel Casado Velarde & Ramon Gonzalez Ruiz (eds.), *Actas del XXXVII simposio internacional de la Sociedad Espanola de Linguistica*, 567–578. Pamplona: Servicio de Publicaciones de la Universidad de Navarra.

Dixon, Robert M.W. 1991. *A new Approach to English Grammar on Semantic Principles*. Oxford: Clarendon.

Dubinsky, Stanley. 1997. Syntactic underspecification and light verb phenomena in Japanese. *Linguistics* 35. 627–672.

Elia, Annibale, Emilio D'Agostino & Maurizio Martinelli. 1985. Tre componenti della sintassi italiana: frasi semplici, frasi a verbo supporto e frasi idiomatiche. In Annalisa Franchi de Bellis & Leonardo Maria Savoia (eds.), *Sintassi e morfologia della lingua italiana d'uso. Teorie e applicazioni descrittive*, 311–325. Roma: Bulzoni.

Gaeta, Livio. 2002. *Quando i verbi compaiono come nomi*. Milano: FrancoAngeli.

Giry-Schneider, Jacqueline. 1978. *Les nominalisations en français. L'opérateur FAIRE dans le lexique*. Genève/Paris: Droz.

Giry-Schneider, Jacqueline. 1987. *Les prédicats nominaux en français: les phrases à verbe support*. Genève/Paris: Droz.

Grimshaw, Jane & Armin Mester. 1988. Light Verbs and Θ-marking. *Linguistic Inquiry* 19(2). 205–232.

Gross, Gaston. 1994. Classes d'objets et description des verbes. *Langages* 115. 15–30.

Gross, Gaston. 1996. Prédicats nominaux et compatibilité aspectuelle. *Langages*. 121. 54–73.
Gross, Gaston. 1999. Verbes supports et conjugaison nominale. *Revue d'Etudes francophones* 9. 70–92.
Gross, Gaston & Ferenc Kiefer. 1995. La structure événementielle des substantifs. *Folia Linguistica* 29. 29–43.
Gross, Maurice. 1981. Les bases empiriques de la notion de prédicat sémantique. *Langages* 63. 8–50.
Gross, Maurice. 1996. Les verbs supports d'adjectifs et le passif. *Langages* 121. 8–18.
Helbig, Gerhard & Wolfgang Schenkel. 1979. *Wörterbuch zur Valenz und Distribution deutscher Verben*. Tübingen: Niemeyer.
Helbig, Gerhard. 1984. *Studien zur deutschen Syntax*. Leipzig: Enzyklopädie.
Hoffmann, Roland. 1996. Funktionsverbgefüge im Lateinischen. In Alfred Bammesberger & Friedrich Heberlein (eds.), *Akten des VIII internationalen Kolloquiums zur lateinischen Linguistik*, 200–212. Heidelberg: Winter.
Hook, Peter E. 1974. *The Compound Verb in Hindi*. Ann Arbor: The University of Michigan, Center for South and Southeast Asian Studies.
Jespersen, Otto. 1942. *A Modern English Grammar on Historical Principles*. Vol. 6: *Morphology*. London: Allen & Unwin.
Ježek, Elisabetta. 2004. Type et degrés de verbes supports en italien. In Gaston Gross & Sophie De Pontonx (eds.), *Verbes supports: Nouvel état des lieux* 27(2). 185–201. [=Special issue of *Lingvisticae Investigationes*].
Ježek, Elisabetta. 2011. Verbes support et composition semantique. *Cahiers de Lexicologie* 1. 29–44.
Kearns, Kate. 2002. *Light verbs in English*. Unpublished manuscript. Cambridge, MA: Massachusetts Institute of Technology.
Kiefer, Ferenc. 1998. Les substantifs déverbaux événementiels. *Langages* 131. 56–63.
La Fauci, Nunzio & Ignazio M. Mirto. 2003. *Fare. Elementi di sintassi*. Pisa: Edizioni ETS.
Mastrofini, Roberta. 2004. Classi di costruzioni a verbo supporto in italiano: implicazioni semantico-sintattiche nel paradigma V+N. *Studi Italiani di Linguistica Teorica e Applicata* 33(3). 371–398.
Mastrofini, Roberta. 2005. On the nature of Italian light verb extensions. In Pierrette Bouillon & Kyoko Kanzaki (eds.), *Proceedings of the Third International Workshop on Generative Approaches to the Lexicon, Geneva, 19–21 May 2005*, 149–158. Ginevra: University of Ginevra.
Mastrofini, Roberta. 2013. *Classi di verbi inglesi tra pesantezza e leggerezza*. Roma: Aracne.
Mastrofini, Roberta. 2019. Le estensioni di verbo supporto in inglese: teoria e applicazione. In Anna Pompei & Lunella Mereu (eds.), *Verbi supporto: fenomeni e teorie*, 23–45. Monaco: LINCOM.
Mastrofini, Roberta. 2021. On English light verb extensions: analysis, classification, and types. *Rassegna Italiana di Linguistica Applicata (RILA)* 1–2. 279–301.
Miyamoto, Tadao. 1999. *The Light Verb Construction in Japanese: the Role of the Verbal Noun*, Benjamins.
Nickel, Gerhard. 1968. Complex verbal structures in English. *International Review of Applied Linguistics (IRAL)* 6(1). 1–21.
Pustejovsky, James. 1994. *The Generative Lexicon*. Cambridge, MA: The MIT Press.
Pustejovsky, James. 2012. Co-compositionality in Grammar. In Markus Werning, Wolfram Hinzen & Edouard Machery (eds.), *The Oxford Handbook of Compositionality*, 371–385, Oxford: Oxford University Press.
Szabolsci, Anna. 1986. Indefinites in complex predicates. *Theoretical Linguistic Research* 2. 47–83.
Tu, Yuancheng & Dan Roth. 2011. Learning English light verb constructions: contextual or statistical. In *Proceedings of the Workshop on Multiword Expressions: from Parsing and Generation to the Real World*, 31–39. Portland, Oregon, USA.

Vendler, Zeno. 1967. *Linguistics in Philosophy*. Ithaca, NY: Cornell University Press.
Vivès, Robert. 1998. *Les mots pur le dire*: vers la constitution d'une classe de predicats. *Langages* 131. 64–76.
Wierzbicka, Anna. 1982. Why can you *have a drink* when you can't **have an eat*? *Language* 58 (4). 753–799.
Wierzbicka, Anna. 1988. *The Semantics of Grammar.* Amsterdam: Benjamins.

Section 3: **The verb fullness**

Elisabetta Ježek
7 Semantic Co-composition in Light Verb Constructions

Abstract: Light Verb Constructions (LVCs) such as Italian *prendere una decisione* 'to make a decision' and *fare una passeggiata* 'to go for a walk' have been widely studied from different theoretical perspectives, while still remaining a highly debated topic in linguistics. Traditional approaches maintain that in LVCs the verb is devoid of meaning and has no predicative role; the predication resides in the noun. These approaches no longer represent state-of-the-art research on LVCs. More recent approaches (see, *inter alia*, Butt 2010) claim that LVCs represent a type of complex predicate in which each element contributes to the joint predication. In this study, we propose an additional approach, called co-compositional, which rules out the traditional model of semantically empty Light Verbs in LVCs, and is compatible with the complex predicate account, in which it can be easily integrated. The proposal is based on two theoretical tools; first, a revised version of the dichotomic distinction between predicative and referring expressions proposed *inter alia* in the work of Searle (1969) and Bossong (1992); second, an enriched theory of semantic composition (called *co-composition,* see Pustejovsky 1995, 2012) according to which, in verb-argument combinations, verb and noun influence each other's meanings in subtle ways. The goal of the contribution is to corroborate our claim with empirical data and propose a representation of the collaborative way in which noun and verb contribute to determine the overall meaning of an LVC. For the discussion, we will focus on Italian LVCs with Light Verbs *prendere* 'take' and *fare* 'to make, to do'.

Keywords: co-composition, semantic representation of Light Verb Constructions, Italian, corpus-based data

---

Acknowledgments: We acknowledge two anonymous reviewers for their helpful comments and suggestions.

https://doi.org/10.1515/9783110747997-008

1 Background and motivation

Traditionally, Light Verb Constructions (LVCs) are defined as constructions in which a Light Verb (i.e., a verb with a general meaning, such as *do*, *make*) combines with a noun that expresses an eventuality;[1] the meaning of the resulting expression is somewhat similar to that of single predicates,[2] as in Italian *prendere una decisione* 'make a decision' (somewhat equivalent to *decidere* 'to decide') and *fare una passeggiata* 'go for a walk' (somewhat equivalent to *passeggiare* 'to stroll').

LVCs have been widely studied from different theoretical perspectives, while still remaining a highly debated topic in linguistics. Traditional approaches maintain that in LVCs the verb is devoid of meaning; it conveys tense, aspect and modality (TAM) features and has no predicative role; the predication resides in the noun. These approaches have been challenged by several studies (cf. *inter alia* Bosque 2001, Mastrofini 2004, De Miguel 2008; Ježek 2011), and do not represent state-of-the-art research on LVCs. Other approaches (see, *inter alia*, Butt 2010) claim that LVCs represent a type of complex predicate, in which each element contributes to the joint predication; according to this account, the arguments of the complex predicate map onto a mono-clausal syntactic structure.

In this study, we would like to propose an additional approach called co-compositional, that rules out the traditional model of Light Verbs in LVCs as semantically empty, and is compatible with the complex predicate account, in which it can be easily integrated. Our proposal is based on the assumption that words are semantically flexible and that, when they combine, they influence each other meanings (Recanati 2012); we assume that this holds for verbs, nouns, adjectives, and other lexical categories. Of particular note in the case of LVCs, we assume that nouns may act functionally and contribute to determining the meaning of the verb they co-occur with (Pustejovsky 1995, 2012). Under this view, LVCs are constructions in which both the verb and the noun act as functors, albeit in different ways. Specifically, in our account, a noun referring to an eventuality (such as *decisione* 'decision', *passeggiata* 'walk') combines with a Light Verb that, together with that specific noun, *predicates* the occurrence of the eventuality (or its existence if the eventuality denotes a state). In our account, the verb plays the main predicative role and selects the nominal object argument, which provides the referring expression on which the predication applies; however, the noun also acts as a functor, as its meaning includes predicative components at a sub-lexical level, which are

---

[1] See Section 2 for a definition of the notion of *eventuality*, as expressed by nouns.
[2] Single predicates are not always available, as in *fare la spesa* ('do the grocery shopping), which has led scholars to view LVCs as a type of analytic (Ježek 2016) or complex (Butt 2010) predicate.

activated in V-N combinations. The result is an analytic lexicalization that acts as a complex predicative expression, in which both the verb and the noun contribute to the predication, albeit at different levels (lexical and sub-lexical respectively).

Our account is based on two theoretical tools: first, a revised version of the dichotomic distinction between predicative and referring expressions proposed *inter alia* in Searle (1969) from a philosophical and pragmatic perspective, and in Bossong (1992) from a cognitive one; second, an enriched theory of semantic composition (Pustejovsky 1995, Jackendoff 1977), called *co-composition* (Pustejovsky 2012) according to which in verb-argument combinations not only verbs but also arguments act functionally to determine the resulting meaning of the expression.

The goal of our contribution is to corroborate our claims with empirical data from corpora and dictionaries, and to propose a representation of a small number of LVCs as a proof of concept of how the object argument contributes to determine the meaning that the verb acquires in the LVC. For the discussion, we will focus on Italian LVCs with *prendere* 'take' and *fare* 'to make, to do', particularly LVCs denoting an activity intentionally performed by a human.

The structure of the article is as follows. First we will review the notions of verb, noun, eventuality, and the distinction between predicating and referring expression, highlighting the inadequacy of the view that conceives them as dichotomic notions (Section 2). In Section 3, we will introduce the principle of semantic co-composition, and in Section 4, we will illustrate the methodology we adopt to inform and corroborate our analysis with empirical data. In Section 5, we will discuss the results of our investigation, and in Section 6, we will provide a representation of a selection of examples as a proof of concept of how co-composition can be applied to the analysis of LVCs. In Section 7, we will present some concluding observations and suggest directions for further research.

2 Verbs, nouns, eventualities and predication: a revised approach

According to common knowledge, a verb is a word that typically denotes an *eventuality* (in Emmon Bach's terms),[3] i.e., a state that holds or an event that happens. An eventuality includes participants, i.e., entities that take part in the eventuality; they are expressed linguistically as complements of the verb. Through the use of verbs, we "predicate" *properties* of the participants, as in "The sun is shining" or

---

3 See Bach (1986).

relations between the participants, as in "The sun dried my t-shirt", where the relation between the participants (*the sun* and *my T-shirt*) is causal (the sun caused my t-shirt to dry). Meaning (or denotation) and predication are two distinct levels of analysis. The *meaning* of a word is its informational content whereas the *predication* is the function it plays in the context of use, and entails the property of selecting arguments.[4]

Verbs act as predicates most of the time; sometimes, however, depending on the context in which they are used, they may play either the role of a predicate or that of an auxiliary (thus not a predicate).[5] Compare the example of Italian *avere* 'to have' in (1a), where the verb acts as a stative predicate of possession, with (1b), where the verb acts as an auxiliary:

(1) a. Luca *ha* due macchine.
       'Luca has two cars'
    b. Luca *ha* comprato due macchine.
       'Luca has bought two cars'

Verbs do not act as predicates in copular constructions. A verb serves as a copula when the function of predication is performed by another element, for example, a noun (2a) or an adjective (2b,c):[6]

(2) a. Luca *è* un ingegnere.
       'Luca is an engineer'
    b. Luca *sembra* stanco.
       'Luca seems tired'
    c. Luca *è diventato* aggressivo
       'Luca has become aggressive'

In (2) the verbs connect the subject with the non-verbal predicate (nominal or adjectival). Generally, the non-verbal predicate attributes a quality (or property) to the subject. Copular verbs such as *sembrare* 'seem' and *diventare* 'become' are generally assumed to have a 'weak' or 'light' meaning, unlike *essere* 'to be' in its copular

---

[4] There are, of course, correlations between the meaning of a word and its ability to predicate; we will not, however, discuss them here.
[5] The term "context" can be interpreted in at least the following ways: word co-occurrence context, syntactic context, semantic context, and pragmatic context. For our current purposes, in this section, where the argumentation is mainly based on corpus linguistics sources, we will use the word "context" to indicate the linguistic surrounding of a keyword in context.
[6] See the overview in Ježek, 2011.

uses. Some scholars, however, prefer to distinguish between the copula (*essere* 'to be') and the so-called copular (or copulative) verbs such as *sembrare* and *diventare* because, while it is assumed that the copula is semantically a mere joining element (a "bridge" between the subject and the semantic content of the nominal constituent) as in (2a), copular verbs as in (2b) and (2c) are assumed to contribute to the semantics of the construction and thus perform a function that is both copulative and predicative, as in (3):

(3) Luca è diventato ingegnere / sembra un ingegnere.
 'Luca has become an engineer / seems an engineer'

Turning now to nouns, although their most typical denotation is a concrete or abstract entity, nouns may also denote an eventuality. In traditional grammar, nouns denoting eventualities are known as *action nouns*. This label is primarily applied to nouns morphologically derived from verbs through suffixation (deverbal nouns), such as Engl. *training* (from *to train*) or *examination* (from *to examine*) (Comrie 1976). Deverbal nouns, however, do not exhaust the class of nouns that denote an eventuality: morphologically simple nouns such as *walk, party, lunch, war, crime,* and *trip* in (4) also qualify as action nouns:

(4) a. We went for an evening *walk*.
 b. The *party* is over.
 c. *Lunch* is ready.
 d. The *war* lasted three years.
 e. The *crimes* occurred on his property.
 f. How was your *trip* to Istanbul?

A useful test to establish whether a noun denotes an eventuality consists in verifying whether it can answer the following question: "What happened?" Nouns denoting eventualities respond positively to this question ("A crime") – except for state-denoting nouns – whereas nouns denoting entities do not ("*A table").

Nouns may denote an eventuality, but they present the eventuality in fundamentally different ways from verbs; for example, they do not, as a rule, provide information about the time at which the eventuality takes place. With a noun such as *run* (as in *go for a run*) for example, there is no way to specify that one is talking about the run which was done yesterday or the one that will be done tomorrow (as when the event is expressed by the verb: *I was running, I ran, I will run,* and so forth). Most importantly, with nouns, the eventuality is presented as something to which we can *refer* to and at which we may even point, as in the case of *sunset* in *Just look at that sunset*),⁷ whereas with verbs, the eventuality is presented as a change that occurs to something at some point or interval in time (*The sun is setting*) or a state in which something participates (*The sun is shining*).

The notions of *reference* and *predication* have received several interpretations in linguistics and in the philosophy of language. John Searle interprets them as "acts that we perform by uttering words", i.e., as *speech acts* (Searle 1969). According to him, "by means of referring, we identify objects in the world" (Searle 1969: 28], whereas "through predicating, we ascribe properties to them" (Searle 1969: 102). Georg Bossong takes instead a cognitive perspective and claims that the concepts of *predication* and *reference* are two fundamental activities of human reasoning, and thus universal modalities of conceiving things and organizing our thought. He observes: "The basic features of noun and verb are directly derived from the basic activities of the mind: to conceive entities, i.e., the objects of our thoughts; and to judge about these entities, i.e., to make statements and utterances. The fundamental categories of every conceivable human language are but the reflex of the fundamental categories of our thought" (Bossong 1992: 13). Finally, Ježek (2016: 106) argues that reference and predication are not, strictly speaking, two notions but rather two different ways of imposing form on notions; one and the same event can be either predicated of a participant, as *burn* of *house* in "The house was burning", or be referred to as a participant (*fire*) of another event (*spread*), as in "The fire is spreading through the house".

To our knowledge, regardless of the interpretation, predication and reference have predominantly been conceived in dichotomic terms. In this paper, we contend that from a lexical semantic point of view, this assumption should be reconsidered and re-evaluated in light of the fact that referring expressions may include one or more predicative components in their semantic sub-structure that do not appear in the semantic "surface" structure; these components may be activated in semantic composition, thereby licensing complex predicative constructions in which more than one element contributes to the overall predication, albeit in different ways, as we will show below.

---

7 The example is taken from Lyons (1977: 444).

3 Semantic Co-composition in Light Verb Constructions

As referenced above, we couch our study of LVCs within an approach to lexical semantics according to which when words combine, they influence each other's meanings. In particular, we maintain that in verb-argument combinations, arguments are not only selected by predicates – as in the traditional compositional account – but may also act functionally and concur to determine the meaning that the verb acquires in the context of use. We resort to the principle of semantic *co-composition* (Pustejovsky 2012) to formalize this assumption. We also adopt a rich lexical semantic representation for the meaning of nouns that may include one or more predicative components at a sub-lexical level, corresponding to the actions typically performed with the *denotatum* (*bake* for *bread*, *read* for *book*, and so forth). We employ the notion of *Qualia role* to represent these components.[8]

The principle of *co-composition* has been introduced to account for the shortcomings in the capability of the principle of composition to account for the flexibility of meaning exhibited by words in context. As is widely known, the principle of composition is the basic principle used in logic and formal semantics to explain how word meanings combine within the sentence. According to this principle, the meaning of a complex linguistic expression is systematically determined by the composition of the meanings of its component parts and the way they are put together, provided that the restrictions imposed by the constituents themselves are satisfied. An example is the restriction based on which the noun *chair* in its literal meaning cannot be the subject of the verb *talk* (as in **that chair is still talking*) in that *talk* poses the restriction that its subject be a human. Specifically, the principle states that "given an expression E formed by the words X, Y, Z, the meaning ME is the composition of MX + MY + MZ" (Partee 1995).

The compositionality principle is generally assumed to be a fundamental property of natural languages, and perhaps an indicator of how we build thoughts in our mind out of simpler concepts. There is, however, good linguistic evidence that suggests that taking the meaning of the expression as the "sum" of the meaning of its parts is not sufficient to account for what complex expressions are actually able to denote. On the one hand, there are several complex expressions, which either carry more meaning than what is expressed (as in *black tie dinner* meaning 'a

---

[8] See Pustejovsky and Ježek (2012) for a corpus-informed introduction to the system of lexical representation based on *Qualia Roles*, used in Pustekovsky's work to represent the meanings of words and their contextual variation. For the purposes of our discussion, we define a *Quale* as a portion of a word's meaning.

dinner where the participants are assumed to wear a black tie') or mean something different from what is said (as in idiomatic expressions such as *show someone the door*). Furthermore, there is the problem of polysemy; given a word with multiple acknowledged meanings, how would the appropriate meaning be selected in context? How is the disambiguation of the senses of a polysemous word achieved in a strict compositional language? How does the adjective *next* for example acquire the spatial meaning in combination with *table* and the temporal meaning in combination with *train*? Strictly speaking, the principle of compositionality in its traditional formulation holds only for monosemous words, and does not address the problem of how polysemous words are disambiguated.

From a theoretical perspective, the problems raised above have traditionally been addressed by claiming that all the meanings that words display in actual use are stored in the lexicon as part of the information encoded by the word. On such a view, polysemous words encode a list of pre-defined meanings and a list of lexical restrictions, which specify the contexts in which the different meanings may be activated. According to this model, the selection of the relevant meaning occurs at the syntagmatic level (i.e., in the context of use), in agreement with these restrictions. This is the standard way dictionaries are put together. New approaches to lexical meaning suggest however that "sense-enumerative lexicons" as described above are uneconomic (they require long lists of meanings for each word), incomplete (words in context can potentially take on an infinite number of meanings), and inadequate (the boundaries between meanings are not rigid and tend to overlap). They contend that words are better conceived as flexible and permeable entities, and that the meaning of each word is expected to vary from occurrence to occurrence as a function of the interaction with the other words it combines with, and of the situation of utterance (Recanati 2012). The outcome of this interaction (referred to as *modulation*, *adjustment*, or *fitting* in the literature) generates the meaning of the sentence. These latter theories, therefore, claim that the syntagmatic dimension prevails in the definition of the lexical meaning, not as the level at which meanings are selected (as in the case of sense enumeration theories) but as the level at which meanings are generated by foregrounding the compatible information stored in the lexical representation of the co-occurring words. A dynamic approach – as the one described above – requires a revision of how the process of meaning composition works. This is where the principle of *co-composition* comes into play as a mechanism that in addition to the compositionality principle and together with other principles) is assumed to be active in the semantic processes of adjustment that occur when word meanings combine.

The principle of co-composition has recently been used to account for the distinction between arguments and adjuncts in Ježek (2022) and the variation in the semantics of *esserci* in Ježek and Mereu (2021). In this paper, we will apply it to the semantic analysis of agentive LVCs with *prendere* and *fare* in Italian. After examining data of LVCs with *prendere* and *fare* in corpora and dictionaries in Section 5, in Section 6 we provide a proof of concept of how it can be used to account for the overall meaning of the LVCs under investigation.

4 Methodology

As referenced above, in our study we use data to inform and verify our theoretical insights. To this end, we analyse the meanings that *prendere* and *fare* exhibit in different kinds of texts and dictionaries. Specifically, we use two corpora preloaded in the Sketch Engine corpus query tool[9] – the Italian section of the *Europarl7* corpus and the *ItTenTen16* corpus, and two electronic dictionaries available online, Sabatini and Coletti[10] and Treccani.[11]

Europarl is a parallel corpus created from the European Parliament proceedings in the official languages in the EU from the period January 2007 and November 2011, and later expanded to May 2012, with the goal of generating aligned text for statistical translation systems. *Europarl7* Italian currently contains about 50 million words.[12] This corpus contains documents related to the European Parliament's activities and Committees. Our second corpus, Italian Web 2016 (ItTenTen16), is an Italian corpus downloaded from the web in the period of May to August 2016, and contains about 5 billion words. It is a very large corpus, and the type of texts it contains is more varied with respect to *Europarl*.

To query both corpora we use the *Concordance* function of the Sketch Engine, which provides us with an overview of the contexts in which *prendere* and *fare* are used, and the *Word Sketch* function, which returns a combinatorial profile for each verb, i.e., lists of collocates classified based on their syntactic relation, for example Object, Subject or Modifier. The Word Sketch function provides two measures for each collocate, *frequency* and *typicality score*. Frequency indicates how often the collocate is found with the target word, whereas the *typicality score* indicates how strong the collocation with the target word is. A low score means that the words in the collocation frequently combine with many other words besides the target. The

---

[9] The Sketch Engine is a sophisticated tool to query corpora automatically. More will be said about its functions later in the text.
[10] https://dizionari.corriere.it/dizionario_italiano/
[11] https://www.treccani.it/vocabolario/
[12] Corpus data and more information can be found on the official website http://www.statmt.org/europarl/

ability to group occurrences based on their specific grammatical function greatly facilitates the research, and allows us to overcome the limits of manual concordance inspection.

As regards dictionaries, we choose two dictionaries that are available online and that are regarded as very qualified lexicographic sources for Italian. *Sabatini-Coletti online* is a dictionary that specifically addresses how words are used in sentences and texts, and *Treccani vocabolario online* is part of a large effort to compile, update, publish and disseminate lexicographic and encyclopedic works for the Italian language. We query both dictionaries manually by examining their verb entries and focusing on the sense distinctions and the grouping of usage examples in the different senses. Although manual inspection is a time-consuming activity, it is fruitful as it adds introspective data and judgments to our analysis – in the form of lexicographic choices – that corpus data does not provide.

5 Results from the analysis of corpus data and dictionaries entries

The first observation from our corpus analysis regards the frequency per million (number of hits per million tokens) of *prendere* and *fare* in the two corpora. In Europarl7 Italian corpus the frequency per million of *prendere* is 621.23 (equivalent to 0.06212% in the entire corpus whose size is 59.177.399 tokens). This frequency is higher than the frequency per million of *prendere* in the ItTenTen16 corpus (477.62, equivalent to 0.048% in the entire corpus whose size is 5.864.495.700 tokens). The opposite is true for *fare*. *Fare* has a frequency per million of 2.706,76 equivalent to 0.2707% in the Europarl7 corpus, and a frequency per million of 3.308.1 equivalent to 0.3308% in the ItTenTen16 corpus. To sum up, *fare* is much more frequent than *prendere* in both corpora; *prendere* is more frequent in Europarl7 and *fare* is more frequent in ItTenTen16.

A second observation is qualitative. If we extract the list of the 100 most typical[13] V-Obj pairs of *prendere* in the corpus using the Word Sketch function, and manually classify the Objects as eventuality-denoting or entity-denoting, we see that their distribution is almost equal (see Table 1: 56 vs. 41 in Europarl7 and 53 vs 47 in ItTenTen2016). This shows that *prendere* is equally used in LVCs (*prendere una decisione* 'take a decision) and in constructions that are not LVCs (*prendere il*

---

[13] By "most typical" V-Obj pairs we mean the V-Obj pairs with the highest typicality score, as defined above.

Table 1: 100 most frequent Nouns in Object position with *prendere* and *fare* in Europarl7 and ItTenTen16 corpora, classified as eventuality-denoting or entity-denoting.

	eventuality-denoting N		entity-denoting N		Errors	
	prendere	*fare*	*prendere*	*fare*	*prendere*	*fare*
Europarl7 IT	56	65	41	34	3	1
ItTenTen20	53	64	47	36		

treno 'take the train). If we apply the same methodology to *fare*, we obtain different results: among the 100 most typical Objects of *fare*, eventuality-denoting nouns are the majority in both corpora (65/99 in Europarl7 and 64/100 in ItTenTen2016). This shows that both verbs are very frequently used as Light Verbs in LVCs and that with *fare* the LVCs use is predominant over the other uses.

Examples of eventuality-denoting and entity-denoting noun types for *prendere* and *fare* can be found in Table 2:

Table 2: Examples of eventuality-denoting and entity-denoting nouns with *prendere* and *fare* in Europarl7 and ItTenTen16.

	eventuality-denoting N	entity-denoting N
prendere	*decisione* 'decision', *iniziativa* 'initiative', *provvedimento* 'action', *impegno* 'commitment'	*aereo* 'plane', *treno* 'train', *sole* 'sun', *caffè* 'coffee', *pillola* 'pill', *palla* 'ball'
fare	*attenzione* 'attention', *domanda* 'question', *scelta* 'choice', *richiesta* 'request'	*nome* 'name', *esempio* 'example'

Let us now turn to the analysis of the entries for *prendere* and *fare* in the two Italian monolingual dictionaries Treccani and Sabatini Coletti.[14] We begin with *prendere*. Both dictionaries identify the literal meaning of 'grasp' as its core meaning. Following the traditional lexicographic conventions, this literal meaning is presented as the first meaning in the entry and defined as follows:[15]

(5)   **1.** "grasp something or someone with one's hands or arms, to hold it in a certain position, lift it from the ground or other surface, and move it according to one's intentions"
   Treccani

---

[14] In the following we provide a synthesis of the information contained in the two dictionaries.
[15] We report the English translation equivalents.

(6) **1.** "grasp, squeeze someone or something with your hands or with a tool, to lift it, to take possession of it or to move it: *prendere il cappello* 'grab the hat'" *Sabatini Coletti*

18 meanings for the entry *prendere* are reported in Treccani, whereas Sabatini Coletti reports 24. Both sources identify sub-meanings. For example, Treccani meaning 1 includes a sub-meaning that specifies that alternative tools can be used instead of hands or arms, as when the "grip" guided by the hands is mediated by the use of a tool, as in *con le tenaglie* 'with pincers'; Sabatini Coletti includes this latter use in the meaning definition ("with a tool"). Sabatini Coletti meaning 1 interestingly states that "the specific meaning of the verb is often determined by the argument with which it is linked to": *prendere il treno* 'take the train', *prendere un caffè* 'take a coffee, *prendere troppe medicine* 'take too many drugs', and so forth. This observation is in line with and supports our co-composition account, and suggests it can be extended to constructions in which the verb co-occurs with entity-denoting nouns.

Treccani meaning 2 gathers a number of senses that gradually depart from the core meaning. Among these we find "get, obtain something to use it for specific needs" as in the example *prendere del denaro per ogni evenienza* 'take some money just in case'. This sense no longer necessarily evokes the use of hands.[16] Other meanings witness the absence of intentionality: *prendere un premio* 'receive a prize'. In these uses, the subject is no longer an Agent but a Beneficiary or an Experiencer. The concept of "grip" determined by the use of the hands is totally missing: it is the object that "reaches" the subject, who has no control over the action.

It is interesting to note that the basic meaning of *prendere* is not "light", and has instead a rich intension (intentionality, physical contact, direction from the object to the subject), which is gradually "modulated" into less literal uses.

As regards the uses we are most interested in, namely the combination of *prendere* with eventuality-denoting nouns, neither dictionary encodes them separately from the combinations of *prendere* with entity-denoting nouns.

Turning now to *fare*, we can see that unlike *prendere* the two dictionaries disagree on the first meaning they propose for the entry. Sabatini-Coletti follows the *literal-meaning-first* convention and presents "construct, prepare" as the first meaning of *fare*: all the examples that illustrate this meaning contain entity-denoting nouns as Objects. On the other hand, Treccani meaning 1 refrains from providing a definition of the denotation; it describes *fare* as a verb of generic meaning, that "can express any action; the action is better specified by the complement",

---

[16] A reviewer has noticed that a literal interpretation is not excluded in this case.

again supporting our co-composition approach. All the examples of complements that follow are eventuality-denoting nouns. See the definitions below:[17]

(7) **1.** "verb of generic meaning: it can express any action, material or not, better specified by the complement: *fare un passo* 'a step', *un gesto* 'a gesture', *un movimento* 'a movement', *un salto* 'a leap', *una risata* 'a laugh', *un urlo* 'a scream', *un sospiro* 'a sigh', *uno sbadiglio* 'a yawn' []".
Treccani

(8) **1.** "construct, build something; pack, prepare something: *fare un ponte* (a bridge), *un vestito* (a dress), *il pane* (bread); *cooking*, preparing a dish: *fare il pesce ai bambini* (the fish for the children)"
Sabatini Coletti

Interestingly, the second meaning of Treccani ("compose, construct, build, put together and similar": *fare un armadio* 'a wardrobe', *un vestito* 'a dress', *un libro* 'a book', *una canzone* 'a song') corresponds to the first meaning of Sabatini Coletti, and the second meaning of Sabatini Coletti ("perform an action": *fare un gesto* 'a gesture', *un passo* 'a step', *il bagno* 'a bath', *un viaggio* 'a trip', *gli auguri a qualcuno* 'the wishes to someone') corresponds to the first meaning of Treccani. In other words, both dictionaries register the uses of *fare* with an eventuality-denoting noun as distinct from and in contrast with those with an entity-denoting noun (a situation we did not find with *prendere*), and differ in the priority assigned to them in the entry. Globally, 18 meanings are reported in Sabatini Coletti (excluding copular and pronominal uses) and 12 in Treccani. Examining the entries, we can observe the effort of lexicographers to cluster uses that share common synonyms as the main strategy to tell the meanings apart.

Summing up, the organization of the entries for *prendere* and *fare* in dictionaries reflects what we found in corpora. The presence in dictionaries of a separate meaning for *fare* in LVCs reflects corpus data that show that this use is predominant over other uses of the verb, whereas the absence of a separate meaning for *prendere* in LVCs is in line with the empirical evidence that *fare* is more frequent in LVCs than *prendere*. Importantly, both dictionaries explicitly state that the meaning of the two verbs varies depending on the complement they combine with. This statement overtly supports our claim that verb and noun meaning co-compose.

---

[17] We again report the English equivalents.

6 Co-compositional analysis of LVCs with *prendere* and *fare*

After examining the semantic behaviour of *prendere* and *fare* in corpora and dictionaries, in this section we focus on a selection of examples and present an analysis that derives the interpretation that the verbs acquire in LVCs through the application of the principle of co-composition described in Section 3. The examples are meant as a proof of concept to show that in co-composition, both the verb and the noun contribute to the overall predication in the LVCs, albeit at different levels, lexically and sub-lexically respectively. This analysis supports the hypothesis that LVCs are complex predicates and refines this view by providing a representation of how the verb and the noun interact both at a functional and at a semantic level. For the purposes of our discussion, we focus on examples in which the LVC denotes an activity intentionally performed by a human.

As referenced in Section 3, we assume that nouns include in their sub-lexical structure the predicates that are typically employed to talk about their *denotatum*. We represent this information as one of the noun's *Qualia roles*. The Qualia role relevant to our discussion is the *Agentive Quale* (AQ). This role encodes the predicate that brings into being the *denotatum* of the noun.[18] In the case of eventuality-denoting nouns, it reports the occurrence/coming into being of the eventuality, and it varies depending on the type of eventuality: for example, with the noun *decision* we assume that the predicate is CONCEIVE (9a), with the noun *commitment* that it is TAKE ON (9b), and so forth. Let us examine a few examples with *prendere* and *fare* in (9) and (10):

(9) a. *Luca ha preso una decisione*
'Luca took a decision'
b. *Luca ha preso un impegno*
'Luca made a commitment'

(10) a. *Maria ha fatto un sospiro*
'Maria made a sigh.'
b. *Maria ha fatto una passeggiata*
'Maria made a walk.'

---

18 The predicate in the Agentive Qualia role answers the question: "How did *x* come into being, what brought it about"?

In our analysis, the semantics of the verbs in (9) and (10) are not empty, nor are the verbs devoid of predication. On the contrary, in combination with the eventuality-denoting noun, the verbs *prendere* and *fare* predicate the specific act that brings about the eventuality denoted by the noun (CONCEIVE in (9a), TAKE ON in (9b), EMIT in (10a), CARRY OUT, PERFORM in 10b)). We assume that this piece of information is originally present in the lexical sub-structure of the noun (as a value of its *Agentive Quale*) and unifies with the verb meaning through the co-composition process.

Let us represent the process described above. The process takes place in three steps:

(11) Semantic co-composition:
  a) the semantics of the noun and the verb come into contact.[19]
  b) the predicate encoded in the noun's semantic sub-structure as a value of its *Agentive Quale* is activated in the composition and is transferred to the verb;
  c) the predicate in the *Agentive Quale* of the noun and the semantics of the verb unify and give rise to an enriched (or specified) meaning of the verb in context.

This is represented in (12) and (13), where <= indicates the co-composition.

(12) *prendere una decisione* 'to take a decision'
  a) prendere + [decisione$_{AQ<concepire>}$[20]] >
  b) [prendere$_{<concepire>}$] <= [decisione$_{AQ<concepire>}$] >
  c) [prendere$_{<concepire>}$ + decisione].

(13) *prendere un impegno* 'to take on a commitment'
  a) prendere + [impegno$_{AQ<assumere>}$[21]] >
  b) [prendere$_{<assumere>}$] <= [impegno$_{AQ<assumere>}$] >
  c) [prendere$_{<assumere>}$ + impegno].

Also with *fare*, the activated Quale in the examples in (14) and (15) is the Agentive, whose values are predicates that lexicalize the different ways in which the eventuality denoted by the object is created:

---

[19] For reasons of space, we will not discuss how the selection mechanism underlying this step works. See Pustejovsky (2012) for a comprehensive analysis.
[20] 'conceive'.
[21] 'take on'.

(14) *fare un sospiro* 'to sigh'
  a) fare + [sospiro$_{AQ<emettere>}$] >
  b) [fare$_{<emettere>}$ + <= sospiro$_{AQ\ <emettere>}$²²] >
  c) [fare$_{<emettere>}$ + sospiro].

(15) *fare una passeggiata* 'to take a walk'
  a) fare + [passeggiata$_{AQ<effettuare>}$²³] >
  b) [fare$_{<effettuare>}$] + <= passeggiata$_{AQ<effettuare>}$] >
  c) [fare$_{<effettuare>}$ + passeggiata].

According to our proposal, thanks to its rich lexical sub-structure, the noun is able to act functionally on the verbal semantics, specify the denotation of the verb in context, and, together with the verb, contribute to the overall predication.

7 Concluding observations and further research

In this contribution, we presented an analysis of LVCs in which the verb plays the predicative role and the noun contributes functionally to the predication by supplying the predicative information it contains at the sub-lexical level. We have resorted to the principle of semantic co-composition to represent the way in which this unification phenomenon occurs. Our proposal can be easily integrated into the complex-predicate account of LVCs, since it acknowledges the role of the noun in the overall predication, albeit at a sub-lexical level.

Our proposal is reinforced by a preliminary analysis of the semantics of *prendere* and *fare* in corpora and dictionaries. Corpus data shows that in the most typical 100 V-Obj pairs, *prendere* co-occurs with almost identical frequency with entity nouns and eventuality-denoting nouns, whereas *fare* combines more frequently with eventuality-denoting nouns. Quite remarkably, both dictionaries explicitly state that the complement is highly relevant in determining the verb's meaning, thereby supporting our hypothesis.

Our proposal leaves a number of problems open that can be addressed in future studies. One of the main problems is related to the recognized limits of the Qualia roles in accounting for the wide variety of semantic relations activated by nouns. The notion of *conventionalized attribute*, that is, a property or an event that is conventionally associated with an entity and is not strictly part of the four tradi-

---

22 'emit'.
23 'carry out', 'perform'.

tional Qualia Roles (*Agentive, Telic, Constitutive* and *Formal*), may provide a means for overcoming this difficulty and encoding default information that can be used in semantic composition.[24] A second problem is related to the fact that it is reasonable to assume that all complements, not only the Object, are active in semantic composition. Further studies shall explore the role of the Subject and other complements, if present, in the co-composition process.

References

Bach, Emmon. 1986. The algebra of events. *Linguistics and Philosophy* 9. 5–16.
Bosque, Ignacio. 2001. On the weight of light predicates. In Julia Herschenson, Enrique Mallén & Karen Zagona (eds.), *Features and Interfaces in Romance. Essays in honor of Heles Contreras*, 23–38. Amsterdam: Benjamins.
Bossong, Georg. 1992. Reflections on the history of the study of universals: The example of the 'Partes Orationis'. In Michel Kefer & Johan van der Auwera (eds.), *Meaning and Grammar. Crosslinguistic Perspectives*, 3–16. Berlin/New York: Mouton de Gruyter.
Butt, Miriam. 2010. The light verb jungle: still hacking away. In Mengistu Amberber, Brett Baker & Mark Harvey (eds.), *Complex Predicates: Crosslinguistic Perspectives on Event Structure*, 48–78. Cambridge, Cambridge University Press.
Comrie, Bernard. 1976. The syntax of action nominals: A cross-language study. *Lingua* 40(2). 177–201.
De Miguel, Elena. 2008. Construcciones con verbos de apoyo en español, De cómo entran los nombres en la órbita de los verbos. In Inés Olza Moreno, Manuel Casado Velarde & Ramón González Ruiz (eds.), *Actas del XXXVII Simposio Internacional de la Sociedad Española de Lingüística*, 567–578. Pamplona: Servicio de Publicaciones de la Universidad de Navarra.
Jackendoff, Ray. 1977. *The Architecture of the Language Faculty*. Cambridge, MA: The MIT Press.
Ježek, Elisabetta. 2011. Verbes supports et composition sémantique. *Cahiers de Lexicologie* 1. 29–43.
Ježek, Elisabetta. 2016. *The Lexicon: An Introduction*. Oxford: Oxford University Press.
Ježek, Elisabetta & Lunella Mereu. 2021. The Syntax and Semantics of Locative there-sentences in Italian. *Italian Journal of Linguistics* 33(2). 183–209.
Ježek, Elisabetta. 2022. La teoria della struttura argomentale: problemi sintattici e proposte semantiche. *Storie e Linguaggi* 8(1). 47–66.
Lyons, John. 1977. *Semantics*. Vol. 2. Cambridge: Cambridge University Press.
Mastrofini, Roberta. 2004. Classi di costruzioni a verbo supporto in italiano: implicazioni semantico-sintattiche nel paradigma V + N. *Studi Italiani di Linguistica Teorica e Applicata* 33(3). 371–398.
Partee, Barbara. 1995. Lexical semantics and compositionality. In Lila R. Gleitman & Mark Liberman (eds.), *Invitation to Cognitive Science. Part I: Language*, 311–360. 2nd edn. Cambridge, MA: The MIT Press.

---

[24] For example, one might assume that the predicate *bark* (which does not correspond to any of four Qualia roles of the noun *dog*) is a conventionalized attribute based on the observation that the expression "I heard the dog" means 'I heard the barking of the dog' (Pustejovsky and Ježek 2012).

Pustejovsky, James. 1995. *The Generative Lexicon*. Cambridge, MA: The MIT Press.
Pustejovsky, James. 2012. Co-compositionality in grammar. In Markus Werning, Wolfram Hinzen & Edouard Machery (eds.), *Oxford Handbook of Compositionality*, 371–384. Oxford: Oxford University Press.
Pustejovsky, James & Elisabetta Ježek. 2012. Introducing Qualia Structure. Unpublished manuscript, available at http://gl-tutorials.org/wp-content/uploads/2015/12/GL-QualiaStructure.pdf
Recanati, François. 2012. Compositionality, flexibility and context-dependence. In Markus Werning, Wolfram Hinzen & Edouard Machery (eds.), *The Oxford Handbook of Compositionality*, 175–91. Oxford: Oxford University Press.
Searle, John. 1969. *Speech Acts: An Essay in the Philosophy of Language*. Cambridge: Cambridge University Press.

Marcos García Salido and Marcos Garcia

8 On the unpredictability of Support Verbs
A distributional study of Spanish *tomar*

Abstract: There is an ongoing debate on whether Support Verb choice is semantically motivated and, therefore, predictable or it depends on the lexical identity of the predicate noun with which it combines. This paper addresses the question by studying the combinatorial properties of Spanish *tomar* 'take', a verb highly productive in this type of construction. Three key aspects will be analysed, namely: (i) whether *tomar* shares the combinatorial properties of verbs of similar semantics (and, in this respect, particular attention will be paid to *coger* 'grab'); (ii) on what grounds a unique core or basic meaning can be identified for this verb; and (iii) whether this core meaning can predict its uses as a Support Verb.

Keywords: Support Verb Construction, collocation, semantic motivation, predictability

1 Introduction

Support Verb Constructions (SVC) are usually considered complex predicates made up of a predicate noun, i.e. a noun with argument slots, and a verb that contributes very little to the lexical content of the whole, either because it is devoid of lexical content or because it is redundant with the sense expressed by the noun (for instance, *take a walk*, where *take* is devoid of the notion of 'physically grabbing' or *tell lies*, where *lie* entails an act of telling; see Alonso Ramos 2004 and references therein). SVCs have often been viewed as a type of collocations (see Alonso Ramos 2004; or Mel'čuk 2004, among others):[1] i.e., from a semantic perspective, lexical combinations that, on the one hand, are compositional, and, on the other, are not strictly predictable from the meanings of their parts. Collocations are a pervasive phenomenon in all languages and this is one of the reasons why some scholars

---

1 Although not everyone shares this view (cf. Simone 2007).

Acknowledgements: This study was funded by MICINN (PID2019-109683GB-C21), by a Ramón y Cajal grant (RYC2019-028473-I), and by the Galician Government (ERDF 2014-2020: Call ED431G 2019/04, and ED431F 2021/01). The authors wish to thank the two anonymous reviewers for their valuable comments and suggestions.

have characterised lexical co-occurrence as an unpredictable (Mel'čuk 1997) or a semi-productive phenomenon (Pawley and Syder 1983).

SVCs conform to a widespread definition of collocation: from an onomasiological perspective, collocations are compositional lexical combinations where a lexical unit—the *collocate*—is chosen depending on the lexical identity of the other—the *base* (Mel'čuk 2012).[2] In the particular case of SVCs, the noun guides the choice of the verb. For instance, to express the undertaking of the activities denoted by the Spanish semantically similar nouns *paseo* 'walk' and *excursión* 'trip' the verb *dar* must be used with the former and *hacer* with the latter.

As said, collocations—and SVCs among them—have been regarded as unpredictable lexical combinations, but there seems to be an ongoing debate questioning this view. In general, one can distinguish two fundamental approaches that cross over different theoretical frameworks:

A) The first one claims that a big repertoire of multiwords is somehow specified in the lexicon. This is the view of scholars such as Sinclair (1991) or Wray (2002), who contend that language users rely on extensive repertoires of prefabricated sequences. In a similar vein, Bybee and Eddington (2006) argue for the representation of exemplars of linguistic sequences in speakers' memory. Finally, the traditional approach to collocations within the Meaning-Text Theory (MTT) could also be grouped here.[3] Its treatment of phraseological units is perhaps more detailed, since a distinction is made between non-compositional phrasemes, stored as lexical units in the lexicon, and collocations or compositional *quasi-phrasemes*, which should be specified in the *syntactics* of each collocation base, along with other non-predictable combinations, such as several morphological features, government patterns, etc.[4]

B) The second approach emphasises the semantic motivation of collocations. Some scholars within the MTT framework (Apresjan 2009; Sanromán 2011,

---

[2] Hausmann (1989: 1010) proposes a similar definition more on the semasiological side. According to him, it is the meaning ("identité sémantique") of the collocate that is determined by the base.
[3] The Meaning-Text Theory was put forward by Igor Mel'čuk and Konstantin Zholkovsky in the mid-nineteen-sixties. Broadly speaking, it aims to build formal models that describe the observable correspondences between the infinite set of meanings and the infinite set of texts of natural language. The framework has been very productive in semantics, lexicology, lexicography, or computational linguistics, and scholars within it have devoted considerable attention to the phenomenon of collocations. The interested reader is referred to Mel'čuk (1981) for further details.
[4] According to Mel'čuk, the *syntactics* is a component of linguistic signs, along with the saussurean *signified* and *signifier*, that accounts for "the set of all combinatorial properties, or features, of [a given sign], that are determined neither by its signified nor by its signifier" (Mel'čuk 2006: 384).

2014) have proposed motivations for the combinatorial patterns of collocates, and particularly of Support Verbs (SVs), on the assumption that idiomaticity of collocations "has been somewhat exaggerated" (Apresjan 2009: 7).[5] Similarly, within a pustejovskyan framework, authors such as De Miguel (2008) or Radulescu (2009) have set out to explain, through the notions of *underspecification* and *co-composition*, not only the polysemy of forms acting as SVs, but also their combinatorics. Accounting for the semantic motivation of SV choice necessarily entails questioning the emptiness of SVs. In the practice, however, the meanings proposed to provide an account both of SV and full senses of a given verb are necessarily either underspecified (De Miguel 2008) or quite an abstract version of the alleged basic meaning of the full sense (see Sanromán's [2011: 261] for the definition of *tomar* and the features inherited by its support versions).

All in all, there is inconclusive evidence as to the amount of meaning provided by verbs in SVCs, apart from grammatical features and certain diathesis-like indications (e.g. *X da un consejo a Y / Y recibe un consejo [de X]* 'X gives advice to Y/ Y takes advice [from X]'), especially because usually a certain amount of redundancy or "semantic agreement" (in terms of Apresjan and Glovinskaja 2007) is posited between the meanings of the SV and the predicate noun. In this respect, Alonso Ramos (2017) reviews some studies that identify some degree of overlapping between nouns and their respective SVs: e.g., *commit* combines with nouns entailing errors with potentially negative consequences, such as *mistake*; achievement nouns, such as Spanish *susto* 'scare' or *disgusto* 'displeasure', collocate with the verb *llevarse* 'take', which likewise denotes an achievement, etc. However, Alonso Ramos herself points out that, even though certain semantic-based generalisations are possible, the existence of numerous counterexamples demands an exhaustive lexicographic account of SVCs and collocations in general.

The aim of this paper is to show, through a distributional study of the verb *tomar*, that an approach of the type of A above is necessary to account for the combinatorial patterns of SVs. More specifically, we address the questions:

a) whether verbs sharing an alleged basic meaning display similar distributions, which would be expected if one is to assume that combinatorial patterns are motivated purely on semantic grounds;

---

[5] A precedent within this very framework could be the formulation of the Principle of Lexical Inheritance by Mel'čuk and Wanner (1994), an attempt to generalise lexical co-occurrence restrictions for classes of lexemes sharing common semantic features. See also Barrios (2009) for an application of this principle to the study of Spanish collocations.

b) whether it is possible to delimit a unique "basic" or "ground" meaning for a highly frequent and polysemous verb such as *tomar* and on what grounds this can be done;
c) and whether this core meaning can predict the combinatorial features of *tomar* in SVCs.

In what follows, we tried to answer these questions. In the next section, we provide a general description of Spanish *tomar*. The methodology and data we used are explained in Section 3. Section 4 presents the results of the study. Lastly, in Section 5, we discuss the implications of these results for the three questions above.

2 Lexicographic descriptions of *tomar*

The verb *tomar* is one of the most frequent of Spanish, it is highly polysemous and very productive as an SV (Koike 2011: 83). According to several dictionaries, its core or basic sense is approximately 'to grab something gently with the hand and hold it' (see, for instance, CLAVE, GDUEsA or DUE, s. v. *tomar*). Two of these dictionaries (CLAVE and GDUEsA) claim to have ordered the senses of each lemma according to their frequency.[6] In both of them, the above-mentioned sense appears as the first one. A preliminary examination of a large corpus of Spanish (the esTenTen11, including American and European Spanish with a size of 9.5 billion tokens; Kilgarriff and Renau 2013), however, challenges this picture. Through the Sketch Engine interface, we extracted the word-sketch for the verb *tomar*.[7] The syntactic objects co-occurring most frequently with this verb are, in decreasing order of frequency, *decisión* 'decision' (35.5 occurrences per million words), *medida* 'measure' (18.8 opmw), *conciencia* 'consciousness' (8.7 opmw), *parte* 'part' (6.8 opmw), *nota* 'note' (5 opmw), *conocimiento* 'knowledge' (4 opmw), *posesión* 'possession' (3.8 opmw), *foto* 'photo' (3.6 opmw), *contacto* 'contact' (3.6 opmw) and *tiempo* 'time' (3.2 opmw). The fact that these lemmas are the ones that occur most frequently as objects of *tomar* suggests that this verb acts mainly as a SV, rather than as a verb denoting a physical

---

[6] Only the GDUEsA states explicitly to have been based on a 20 million-word corpus, the CUMBRE corpus. In fact, at the moment of its publication, the GDUEsA was announced as the first corpus-based dictionary of Spanish (CLAVE and DUE were published previously).
[7] Word-sketches are lists of collocates for a given lemma. The collocates are presented according to their syntactic function, established based on Sketch Engine formal grammars, and can be sorted by several metrics. In our case, we chose frequency. For further information, the reader is directed to: https://www.sketchengine.eu/guide/word-sketch-collocations-and-word-combinations/

activity, at least in written discourse,[8] the one represented in the corpus (*tomar [una decisión]* 'make a decision', *tomar medida[s]* 'take measures', *tomar conciencia* 'become aware', etc.).[9] This fact is not surprising nor exclusive of Spanish. Sinclair (1991) already detected that delexical senses (i.e., senses allegedly semantically bleached regarding a full, autonomous one) were more frequent in corpora.

However, if frequency is not evidence nor condition as to the *basicness* of a given meaning, in what sense is then the physical grabbing meaning central to the verb *tomar*? Lexicographic descriptions often treat the support versions of a given verb as extensions of the chosen central meaning. Thus, in the DUE there are explicit references to support senses, which are conceived of as extensions of the 'physically grab' meaning. Along with it, an alternative definition is given that modifies this physical sense by stating "Coger cualquier cosa aunque no sea con la mano" 'To grab something even though without the hand'. Additionally, some of the synonyms provided, such as *adoptar* 'to adopt', commute well with the SV *tomar* (e.g. *adoptar medidas, adoptar acciones, adoptar una decisión*).[10] Likewise, the DUE provides a very abstract sense "pasar a tener" 'start to have' that the author explicitly relates to the physical one. The cases of CLAVE and the GDUEsA are less clear since both include senses that could be attributed to the SV *tomar* ("Adoptar o emplear" 'To adopt or employ' in CLAVE, again "Pasar a tener" in the GDUEsA), but after the physical one —i.e. as supposedly less frequent senses— and with no explicit link.

A study of *tomar* in additional sources seems necessary to establish the prominence of the 'physical grabbing' sense in relation to other senses of the form, particularly those occurring in SVCs. The next two sections are devoted to such a task.

3 Data sources and methodology

We have examined data from three different sources to establish whether the pre-eminence given to the 'grab physically' sense of *tomar* in the above-reviewed dictionaries has an actual basis on usage data.

---

8 Although, as noted by one anonymous reviewer, TenTen corpora contain written data that approximates speech, such as chats, blogs, etc.
9 Even the nouns *nota* and *foto*, in the company of *tomar* are most naturally interpreted as result nouns and, as a consequence, the entire expression as a SVC (*tomar nota[s]* 'take note[s]', *tomar foto[s]* 'take pictures/fotos').
10 As one of the reviewers has pointed out, these variants or synonyms of SVs are what M. Gross (1981) termed *extensions des verbes supports*.

In the first place, we will examine a distributional model. Distributional models represent the words of a given vocabulary by assigning them a vector, the dimensions of which represent the contexts where the word at issue occurs. Usually, those contexts are other words within a given text span. The coordinates of such a vector represent the association between the word in question and its contexts in terms of some association measure (co-occurrence counts, mutual information, etc.) (Erk 2012; Levy et al. 2015). Vectors that are close in space can thus be interpreted as words with similar distributions and bearing a variety of semantic relations between them —synonymy, hypo/hypernymy, etc.[11] Besides these models, in which each possible context is represented by one dimension, yielding high-dimensional vectors, others manage to "embed" word distribution representations into vectors with less dimensions (hence the term *word-embeddings*). In the present paper, we use one of such low-dimensional models: *word2vec* skip-gram (Mikolov et al. 2013), a distributional semantics approach that learns word vectors using a language modeling objective implemented on a feed-forward neural network. Despite the advances of vector space models in natural language processing, the results of *word2vec* are still competitive in both intrinsic and extrinsic evaluations (Vulić et al. 2020; Lenci et al. 2022). The *word2vec* model has been trained in a *ca.* 1.5 billion corpus of Spanish, compiled from several sources (see Cardellino [2016] for a detailed specification of the corpora used for training the model).

In the second place, we have analysed conversation data. Considering that large corpora are mostly made up of written discourse and it could be contended that the discourse genre speakers engage in more often is everyday conversation, we have also examined the use of *tomar* in a conversation corpus taking a more qualitative approach. In addition to the primary nature of conversation as a linguistic activity, it also seems to be a more propitious locus for conveying less abstract meanings than written discourse. It is, therefore, reasonable to test the hypothesis that the physical sense of *tomar* is more frequent in everyday conversation than in written discourse —thence its basic or central position with respect to the set of senses conveyed by this verb. As a data source, we have used the Val.Es.Co corpus, one of the few sources representative of the conversational genre in Spanish available to the research community. It contains the transcriptions of 46 spontaneous conversations recorded mostly in secret, amounting to a total of 73,344 tokens. The corpus

---

[11] It is important to bear in mind that, although the coordinates of each vector result from co-occurrence data —i.e., from syntagmatic relations—, vectors close in a vectorial space are in paradigmatic relationships. That is, "neighbour" vectors can be substituted for one another in a given context.

is tagged and lemmatised with FreeLing (Padró and Stanilovsky 2012) and can be accessed and queried online. From this corpus, we have extracted all the instances of the lemma *tomar* (71 cases; 968 opmw) and have classified them manually after examining the corresponding concordances.

Finally, since it could be argued that basic senses are those acquired at early stages of linguistic activity, we have also analysed the use of *tomar* in conversation with children. Here, we have examined the occurrences of *tomar* in the BecaCESNo corpus. This corpus contains transcripts of 81 hours of conversation between children and adults, amounting to a total of 522,904 tokens. The ages of the children range between three and a half, and twelve years. The occurrences of *tomar* in this corpus amount to 238 (i.e., 455 opmw).

4 Results

4.1 *Tomar* (and *coger*) in a word-embeddings model

As stated above, the word-embeddings model used here is a collection of numerical vectors representing a word form or *type* and ultimately based on the distribution of the tokens corresponding to the type in question. According to their coordinates, some vectors occupy a space nearer or farther to another vector —the closeness being ultimately the result of shared contexts. For the present study, we have extracted the word forms with vectors closest to those of the different inflectional variants of *tomar* (i.e., the word forms with vectors closest to those of *tomo* 'I take', *tomas* 'you take', *toma* 'he/she/it takes', *tomamos* 'we take', etc). Thus, we have obtained lists of types ordered by their relative closeness to a given type of *tomar* (e.g. for *toma: tomar, toman, tomó. . ., adopta. . ., asume*, etc.). A substantial part of such lists are further types of *tomar* (e.g. the vector of *toma* is close to those of *tomar, tomaba*, etc.), since their distributions are similar, as one would expect.

In Table 1, we present the data corresponding to the lists containing the 50 closest vectors to the inflectional variants of *tomar* (i.e., each inflectional variant heads a list of 50 other types). Additionally, for the sake of comparison, we have done the same with the data corresponding to *coger*, a verb that shares with *tomar* the meaning of 'physically grabbing' and some of its SV values (e.g., *coger/tomar apuntes* 'to take notes'). For the sake of brevity, we have grouped the inflectional variants of each verb under its conventional lemma. The ranking in the table results from the number of times a type of a given verb other than the queried one (i.e. *coger* or *tomar*) appears as a spatially close vector: the more forms of a verb appear in the lists of close vectors, the higher that verb has been ranked.

Table 1: Recurrent verbs within the 50 forms most similar to *tomar* and *coger*.

TOMAR	COGER
adoptar 'to adopt' (52)	*agarrar* 'to grab' (21)
hacer 'to do, to make' (27)	*tirar* 'to pull, to throw away' (19)
dar 'to give' (20)	*soltar* 'to lose, to let go' (16); *meter* 'to put into' (16)
tener 'to have' (19)	*echar* 'to kick out, to put in' (12)
llevar 'to carry, to bear' (16); *asumir* 'to accept, to assume' (16)	*pillar* 'to catch, to get' (10)

The summary of the most recurring "neighbours"[12] of the two verbs suggests relatively different distributional patterns for the alleged synonyms.[13] Although these neighbouring vectors themselves represent polysemous word forms and assigning them a given meaning can be criticised as arbitrary, the results seem to indicate that *tomar* in Spanish occurs mostly with SV senses, whereas *coger* is predominantly a verb denoting the action of grabbing something physically. Two of the five most recurring neighbours of *coger* can convey such a notion: *agarrar* and *pillar*. At least in European Spanish, *pillar* can express in addition other meanings shared by *coger* (*No lo pillo/cojo* 'I don't understand'; *pillar/coger el bus, el tren*, etc. 'to catch the bus, the train, etc.'). Another recurrent neighbour —*soltar*— can be thought of as an antonym conveying the idea of 'letting something go'. Finally, the semantic relation between the remaining three verbs and *coger* is more difficult to grasp: they can express the idea of letting something go that has been previously taken (*tirar, echar, meter?*) or grabbing something and then pull (*tirar*). Be that as it may, it could be claimed with relative certainty that *coger* is mainly associated with the idea of 'physical grabbing', even in a model trained on written discourse, which is not the case for *tomar*.

As for the claim that *tomar* is predominantly a delexical verb, it finds support in the most recurring verbal forms sharing its distribution. This group of verbs has very little in common if we attend to their alleged basic meanings. Thus, whilst *adoptar* and *asumir* have to do with the idea of 'starting to have something', *dar* is normally conceived as the prototype of transfer verbs, *hacer* is a verb of creation, *tener* is a stative verb of possession and *llevar* can denote the activity of 'bearing something', but it also can take patient-like subjects in a stative reading (e.g., *Llevaba mucho tiempo esperando* 'He had waited for a long time', lit.: 'He carried a

---

[12] That is, neighbours in a vectorial space. In other words, *neighbours* are types with close vectors, which is indicative of a paradigmatic relation, i.e. substitutability in a given context.
[13] It must be noted that *coger* does occur among the sets of neighbours of *tomar*, but in the ranking of the most recurring ones it would have occupied the eleventh place. On the contrary, *tomar* does not occur among the sets of neighbours of *coger*.

long time waiting'). What most of the verbs in the list do have in common is their frequent use as SVs (*dar, hacer, llevar, tener* and *tomar* are listed in Koike [2001: 83–84] as frequent "neuter functional verbs") and it can be hypothesised[14] that this is the reason for the proximity of their vectors to that of *tener*, given the disparity of their full or basic senses.

If instead of considering the 50 closest vectors to each inflected variant of *tomar*, we take into account only the first one (after discarding types of *tomar*), the picture stays more or less the same in the case of *coger*: types corresponding to the lemma *agarrar* 'to grab' are the most recurring equivalents (11 cases), followed by those of *tirar* 'to throw/to pull' (2). The rest of the verbs occur only once. In the case of *tomar*, however, although *adoptar* 'to adopt' is still the most recurrent equivalent (18 instances), *beber* 'to drink' is the next more frequent one (3 instances), followed by *hacer* (twice). The remaining forms occur only once each. This can be suggestive of the fact that, among the physical senses of *tomar*, the one of 'ingestion' occurs in corpora more frequently than the 'grabbing' one.[15]

4.2 *Tomar* in everyday conversation and in a children's corpus

A summary of the uses[16] of *tomar* in the conversation corpus is provided in Table 2.

Table 2: Distribution of the senses of *tomar* in everyday conversation (Val.Es.Co).

USES	Frequency (Frequency per million words)
'to ingest'	38 (518.1)
'to physically grab'	10 (136.3)
SVC	8 (109.1)
phrasemes	10 (136.3)
Other	5 (68.2)

---

14 It should be remembered that the word-embeddings model used here does not give us direct access to the contexts of occurrence of the word forms themselves: it is only a vectorial representation of such data.
15 In European Spanish, *tomar* can express the act of ingestion of solids or liquids. In American Spanish it seems to have a more specialised sense when used without an explicit direct object: 'to drink alcohol' (see *DUE*, s. v. *tomar*).
16 The label *use* is employed here for the sake of brevity and encompasses the set of different values grouped in Tables 2 and 3: pairings of a certain signifier with a given sense (*tomar* 'to grab' vs. *tomar* 'to ingest'), instances of *tomar* used as an SV in different collocations, instances of tomar as a part of phrasemes, etc.

Contrary to the predominance of support versions of *tomar* in the word-embeddings model (ultimately derived from written discourse data), its physical senses seem to be more prominent in everyday conversation, even though SVCs are recurrent as well. Out of the former, the most recurrent is the ingestion sense, as illustrated in the following examples:

(1) entonces   luego   después de   comer   dice   ¿nos=vamos   a
    so   then   after   of   eating says   1SG.REFL=go=1PL to
    <u>toma=r</u>   <u>café?</u>/
    take=INF   coffee
    'so after lunch she says: shall we go have a coffee?'   (Val.Es.Co, 0030)

As for the 'physically grabbing' sense, it is remarkable that its ten occurrences are all in the imperative mood:

(2) <u>toma→</u>/// ya   tiene=s   esto   [...] colóca=te   eso
    take   already have=2SG   this   put=2SG.REFL that
    'take, you already have that? put it on'   (Val.Es.Co, 0009)

This is in contrast with the distribution of *coger* with the same sense in the same corpus. With *coger*, the 'grab' sense occurs 36 times (490 opmw) in 12 different tenses, mostly in the present indicative (12 instances; 163.6 opmw). As for the SVCs, we have classified as such combinations of *tomar* with only three nouns: *apunte(s)* 'note(s)' (4 instances; 54.5 opmw), *medidas* 'measures' (3 occurrences; 41 opmw) and *iniciativa* 'initiative' (1 occurrence; 13 opmw). The remaining cases are either less recurring senses of *tomar* or occurrences of the verb as part of non-compositional phrases, such as *tomar por el pito del sereno* 'to disrespect somebody' or *toma y daca* 'quid pro quo'.

Lastly, we have analysed the occurrences of the verb *tomar* in speech produced by or directed to children (BecaCESNo corpus). The distribution of the senses expressed by *tomar* bears some similarities with what we found in the Val.Es.Co corpus, as can be seen in Table 3.

This time, the most recurrent sense in the corpus is that of grabbing physically, but again, this sense is exclusively conveyed by the imperative.[17] The second most common sense in the children's corpus is 'to ingest something'. The third use is the

---

17 It must be kept in mind that both the conversation and the children's corpora are representative of Peninsular Spanish. The restriction of the grabbing meaning to the imperative of *tomar*, seemingly yielding to the unrestricted conveying of this meaning by *coger*, probably does not apply to American Spanish, where *coger* is largely used as a taboo word with the sense 'to have sex'.

Table 3: Distribution of the senses of *tomar* in a children's corpus (BecaCESNo).

USES	Frequency (Frequency per million words
'to physically grab'	124 (237.1)
'to ingest'	62 (118.6)
discourse marker	14 (26.8)
'to be exposed'	7 (13.4)
Other	31 (59.3)

one characterised as *discourse marker* and, like other discourse markers, the form is itself polysemous, rather than conveying a unified sense. Sometimes, it is used to express surprise on the part of the speaker (3). However, there are instances difficult to distinguish from the imperative of the 'grabbing' sense: for instance, when there is no transfer of a physical object, but *toma* accompanies the description of a physical or verbal aggression or punishment, as in (4).[18]

(3) *MAD: no ve=s que ha querido pone=r ella la mesa!
       no see=2SG that has wanted put=INF she the table
       'don't you see that she has wanted to set the table?'
   *RAQ: la=ha=s puesto tú?
       3SG.ACC=have=2SG put you
       'have you set it?'
   *RAQ: toma ya!
       'wow!'   (BecaCESNo, 06f05)

(4) *CHI: y luego el otro que le=pega=ba patadas al payaso
       and then the other that 3SG.DAT=hit=IPFV3SG kicks to.the clown
       toma.
       take
       'and then the other kicked the clown. So there!'
                                                           (BecaCESNo, 05m03)

The last two categories in the table are cases of *tomar* in collocations where it conveys the meaning 'X is exposed to Y' (*tomar el sol* 'to sunbathe', *tomar el fresco* 'to get fresh air'; 7 occurrences), and other less recurring uses.

---

18 This instance has been included within the category "Other", due to its ambiguous interpretation, along with other ambiguous and/or non-recurring cases.

5 Discussion and conclusions

Whereas, according to the lexicographic review of Section 2, there seems to be a consensus on considering 'to physically grab' as the basic meaning of *tomar*, the results of the distributional data presented in this paper lead to a certain reconsideration of this idea. If we judge only after the results of the embeddings model, frequency cannot be the determining factor for establishing that the notion of grabbing physically is the core meaning of this verb. However, it could still be argued that the large corpora on which such models are trained are strongly biased towards written varieties and do not reflect the everyday linguistic experience of speakers, casual conversation being a much more central genre. To that, one could add that physical senses are more likely in conversation, where speakers share a situational context with which they can interact physically. The examination of everyday conversation has provided only partial evidence for this idea: while it is true that the physical senses of *tomar* are equally or more frequent than its support instances in conversation (including conversation with children), the reverse does not apply to *coger*, which shows up as an eminently physical verb even in the model trained in corpora representative of written discourse.

Even though we only had the results of the word-embeddings model, the high frequency of *tomar* as a SV should be treated with a caveat when determining its core meaning. In fact, researchers have been reluctant to acknowledge the basic character of frequent senses if these are delexical or not full ones. Already three decades ago, Sinclair (1991) noted the high corpus frequency of delexical senses of frequent word forms.[19] Notwithstanding, he resisted considering such delexical senses as basic, hypothesising that "[t]he 'core' meaning of a word—the one that first comes to mind for most people—will not normally be a delexical one. A likely hypothesis is that the 'core' meaning is the most frequent independent sense" (Sinclair 1991: 113). Thus, for Sinclair, delexical meanings like the ones conveyed by SVs seem, then, to be context-dependent[20] and frequency only starts playing a role in determining the "coreness" of the meaning of a lexical unit once the delexical senses have been discarded. A different issue, which we will come to later, is the role of such core meanings in explaining or predicting delexical senses (or, in particular, the senses associated with SVs).

If the core meaning of *tomar* is the most frequent sense outside of its values as an SV, our data suggest at least two possibilities. The grabbing sense is recurrent

---

19 Alonso Ramos (2012) observed a similar phenomenon with the Spanish adjective *ligero* 'light'.
20 An idea that is not new by any means. The existence of meanings contingent on the presence of other lexical items is precisely a definitory trait of collocations in Hausmann (1989) or the MTT and, within the latter, it has informed the lexicographic treatment of SVs (see Alonso Ramos 2007).

in terms of token frequency, but it does not seem productive in terms of type frequency, being limited to the imperative mood—at least in the samples of Peninsular Spanish examined here. The ingestion sense, also very recurrent in conversation, appears as a suitable candidate in this respect, but further experimental evidence on the competence of native speakers is needed to determine whether this is the case.

Irrespective of opting for one or another sense as the basic meaning of *tomar*, if we wanted to account for all the possible collocate values of this verb based only on one meaning, such concrete senses seem not ideal candidates. In fact, the scholars who intend to explain the meanings of delexical verbs starting from an alleged core meaning posit very general or underspecified meanings, which only become more specific in context by such mechanisms as co-composition (De Miguel 2008). We saw before an example of this approach in the attempt to link the core meaning of *tomar* and its delexical senses by positing the general meaning 'to start to have' in the DUE. A similar attempt is the definition of the discussed verb provided in Sanromán (2011: 261): "direction [. . .] towards the self". Probably, one can successfully explain the two physical senses referred to above on the grounds of such a meaning via co-composition: if the second argument of the verb is a physical object, the verb will be understood as expressing the act of grabbing with the hand; if it is an ingestible object (food, drink, medicine, etc.), the verb will be understood as the act of ingesting something, etc. In the case of understanding support senses, the co-composition mechanism looks particularly adequate, since it is the noun what mainly determines the sense of the resulting SVC. However, as Alonso Ramos (2017) or Van Valin (2013) point out, underspecification and co-composition are mechanisms used for explaining decoding processes, but they fail to model linguistic production. Thus, an underspecified version of *tomar* or *coger* cannot account for the fact that in Spanish one can say *tomar/coger cariño a algo* 'grow affectionate of something', but one must say *tomar una decisión* lit. 'take a decision', rather than **coger una decisión*.[21] Similarly, if one insists on predicting SV values from a given core meaning, the quite different patterns for *tomar* and *coger* evinced by the examination of a distributional model in Section 4.1 are unexpected. The only viable alternative seems to be to admit that the co-occurrence possibilities of SV — and other collocates, as well— are stored in the lexicon.

---

[21] One could be tempted to add the feature of volition to the subject of *tomar* and thus distinguish it from *coger* in collocations such as *coger cariño*, which select non-volitional subjects. However, this would have the undesired effect of preventing possible uses of *tomar*, such as *tomarle cariño a algo* 'grow affectionate to something', *tomar un aspecto/cariz X* 'take an X appearance', which either do not admit or do not need a volitional subject.

One could argue that an account whereby every collocation must be specified in the lexicon cannot explain linguistic creativity, whereas one based on the mechanisms of underspecification and co-composition can—although it over-generates undesired results. However, as Bybee and Eddington (2006) have demonstrated, speakers produce new combinations based on the similarity with stored exemplars of multiword sequences (see also Keuleers [2008] for an account of memory-based pluralisation patterns in Dutch), and some SVCs with *tomar* are so frequent in discourse that they seem ideal candidates to be stored in speakers' minds. Thus, it appears more reasonable that speakers create new SVCs with *tomar* on the model of frequent combinations, such as *tomar una decisión* —as said before, *decisión* is the most frequent object of *tomar* in the esTenTen11 corpus—, rather than claiming that they start from the grabbing sense of the verb or from an underspecified sense constructed mostly for theoretical purposes. Ultimately, speakers have in their input—and likely in their lexica—different meanings and different contexts associated with the signifier *tomar* from which to innovate. It is difficult to see an unavoidable need to postulate a single invariant from which to derive all the instances of the verb.

Moreover, it has been observed that a high frequency of use leads to the independence of the members of a paradigm from said paradigm (Bybee and Thompson 1987). Thus, it could be questioned that speakers link every instance of *tomar* in a SVC to an alleged basic meaning of the verb. In this vein, García Salido (2017) discusses the case of some causative collocations with *meter* 'to put into' (*meter miedo* 'to cause fear', *meter prisa* 'to cause haste'), where the verb seems to convey some meanings it had at a certain moment of the History of Spanish (either 'to put' or 'to produce'), but that it has lost in the present day. The link between the meaning of *meter* in the surviving collocations and the extinct meanings of the verb could have existed in the moment of their creation —or even caused their appearance—, but it has since been broken without the loss of the collocations in question, probably due to recurrence of these collocations.

In sum, this paper has investigated the meaning and distribution of Spanish *tomar* using two different approaches: namely, the analysis of a distributional model trained on big data and the qualitative analysis of conversational data of adult speakers and children. The emerging picture questions the validity of using very general semantic descriptions to predict the use of the studied verb and the necessity of connecting SVs with other meanings expressed by the same signifier. Alternatively, we have argued for the need of a representation of the combinatorial patterns of lexical units in the lexicon.

References

Alonso Ramos, Margarita. 1997. Coocurrencia léxica y descripción lexicográfica del verbo DAR: hacia un tratamiento de los verbos soportes. *Zeitschrift für Romanische Philologie* 113(3). 380–417.
Alonso Ramos, Margarita. 2004. *Las construcciones con verbo de apoyo*. Madrid: Visor.
Alonso Ramos, Margarita. 2012. Explorando la frecuencia léxica para el Diccionario de colocaciones del español. In Tomás Eduardo Jiménez Juliá, Belén López Meirama, Victoria Vázquez Rozas & Alexandre Veiga Rodríguez (eds.), *Cum corde et in nova grammatica*, 19–40. Santiago: Universidade de Santiago de Compostela.
Alonso Ramos, Margarita. 2017. Can collocations be deduced? A lexically-driven analysis from the perspective of language production. In Sergi Torner Castells & Elisendal Bernal Gallen (eds.), *Collocations and other lexical combinations in Spanish. Theoretical, lexicographical and applied approaches*, 21–40. London: Routledge.
Apresjan, Juri D. 2009. The theory of lexical functions: an update. In David Beck, Kim Gerdes, Jasmina Milićević & Alain Polguère (eds.), *Proceedings of the Fourth International Conference on Meaning-Text Theory*, 1–14. Montréal: Observatoire de linguistique Sens-Texte (OLST).
Apresjan, Juri & Marina Glovinskaja. 2007. Two projects: English ECD and Russian production dictionary. In Kim Gerdes, Tilmann Reuther & Leo Wanner (eds.), *Proceedings of the Third International Conference on Meaning-Text Theory* 69. 31–46. [Special issue of *Wiener Slawistischer Almanac*].
Barrios, María Auxiliadora. 2009. Domain, domain features of lexical functions, and generation of values by analogy according to the MTT approach. In David Beck, Kim Gerdes, Jasmina Milićević & Alain Polguère (eds.), *Proceedings of the Fourth International Conference on Meaning-Text Theory*, 45–53. Montreal: Observatoire de linguistique Sens-Texte (OLST).
Bybee, Joan & David Eddington. 2006. A usage-based approach to Spanish verbs of becoming. *Language* 82(2). 323–355.
Bybee, Joan & Sandra A. Thompson. 1997. Three frequency effects in syntax. *Proceedings of the Annual Meeting of the Berkeley Linguistics Society* 23. 378–388.
Cardellino, Cristian Adrián. 2016. *Spanish Billion Words Corpus and Embeddings*. http://crscardellino.ar/SBWCE/
De Miguel, Elena. 2008. Construcciones con verbos de apoyo en español. De cómo entran los nombres en la órbita de los verbos. In Inés Olza Moreno, Manuel Casado Velarde & Ramón González Ruiz (eds.), *Actas del XXXVII Simposio Internacional de la Sociedad Española de Lingüística*, 567–577. Pamplona: Servicio de Publicaciones de la Universidad de Navarra.
Erk, Katrin. 2012. Vector space models of word meaning and phrase meaning: A survey. *Language and Linguistic Compass* 10. 635–653.
García Salido, Marcos. 2017. Diacronía de colocaciones causativas con los verbos *meter, causar, producir* y *provocar*. *Hispanic Research Journal* 18(3). 181–196.
Gross, Maurice. 1981. Les bases empiriques de la notion de prédicat sémantique. *Langages* 63. 7–52.
Hausmann, Franz J. 1989. Le dictionnaire de collocations. In Franz J. Hausmann, Oskar Reichmann, Herbert E. Wiegand & Ladislav Zgusta (eds.), *Wörterbücher. Dictionaries. Dictionnaires: ein internationales Handbuch zur Lexikographie*, 1010–1019. Berlin/New York: Mouton De Gruyter.
Keuleers, Emmanuel. 2008. Memory-Based Learning of Inflectional Morphology. PhD dissertation. Antwerp: University of Antwerp.
Koike, Kazumi. 2001. *Colocaciones léxicas en el español actual*. Alcalá: Universidad de Alcalá.

Lenci, Alessandro, Magnus Sahlgren, Patrick Jeuniaux, Amaru Cuba Gyllensten & Martina Miliani. 2022. A comprehensive comparative evaluation and analysis of Distributional Semantic Models. *Language Resources and Evaluation* 56, 1269–1313.

Levy, Omer, Yoav Goldberg & Ido Dagan. 2015. Improving distributional similarity with lessons learned from word embeddings. *Transactions of the Association for Computational Linguistics* 3. 211–225.

Mel'čuk, Igor. 1981. Meaning-Text Models: A recent trend in Soviet linguistics. *Annual Review of Anthropology* 10. 27–62.

Mel'čuk, Igor. 1997. Vers une Linguistique Sens-Texte. Inaugural lecture at the Collège de France. http://olst.ling.umontreal.ca/pdf/MelcukColldeFr.pdf

Mel'čuk, Igor. 2004. Verbes supports sans peine. In Gaston Gross & Sophie De Pontonx (eds.), *Verbes supports. Nouvel état des lieux* 27(2). 203-217 [=Special Issue of *Lingvisticae Investigationes*].

Mel'čuk, Igor. 2006. *Aspects of the Theory of Morphology*. Berlin/New York: Mouton De Gruyter.

Mel'čuk, Igor. 2012. Phraseology in the language, in the dictionary, and in the computer. *Yearbook of Phraseology* 3. 31–56.

Mel'čuk, Igor & Leo Wanner. 1994. Lexical co-occurrence and lexical inheritance. Emotion lexemes in German: A lexicographic case study. *Lexikos* 4. 86–161.

Mikolov, Tomas, Greg Corrado, Kai Chen & Jeffrey Dean. 2013. Vector space. *Arxiv*. 1–12.

Padró, Lluis & Evgeny Stanilovsky. 2012. FreeLing 3.0: Towards Wider Multilinguality. In Nicoletta Calzolari, Khalid Choukri, Thierry Declerck, Mehemet Uğur Doğan, Bente Maegaard, Joseph Mariani, Asuncion Moreno, Jan Odijk & Stelios Piperidis (eds.), *Proceedings of the Language Resources and Evaluation Conference (LREC 2012)*, 2473–2479. Istanbul: European Language Resources Association (ELRA).

Pawley, Andrew & Frances Hodgetts Syder. 1983. Two puzzles for linguistic theory: nativelike selection and nativelike fluency. In Jack C. Richards & R. W. Schmidt (eds.), *Language and Communication*, 191–226. London: Longman.

Radulescu, Romana-Anca. 2009. Sobre cuánto puede dar de sí el verbo dar en fraseologismos españoles y rumanos. In Elena De Miguel Aparicio, Santiago U. Sánchez Jiménez, Ana Serradilla Castaño, Romana Anca Radulescu, Olga Batuikova (eds.), *Fronteras de un diccionario*, 469–500. San Millán: Cilengua.

Sanromán Vilas, Begoña. 2011. The unbearable lightness of light verbs. Are they semantically empty verbs? In I. Boguslavsky & L. Wanner (eds.), *Proceedings of the 5th International Conference on Meaning-Text Theory*, 253–263. Barcelona: Observatoire de linguistique Sens-Texte (OLST).

Sanromán Vilas, Begoña. 2014. La alternancia DAR/HACER en construcciones con verbo de apoyo y nombre de comunicación. *Borealis* 3(2). 185–222.

Simone, Raffaele. 2007. Constructions and categories in verbal and signed languages. In Elena Pizzuto, Paola Pietrandrea & Raffaele Simone (eds.), *Verbal and signed languages: comparing structures, constructs, and methodologies*, 199–250. Berlin/New York: Mouton de Gruyter.

Sinclair, John. 1991. *Corpus, concordance, collocation. Describing English language*. Oxford: Oxford University Press.

Van Valin Robert D. 2013. Lexical representation, co-composition, and linking syntax and semantics. *Text, Speech and Language Technology* 46. 67–107.

Vulić, Ivan, Edoardo Maria Ponti, Robert Litschko, Goran Glavaš & Anna Korhonen. 2020. Probing pretrained language models for lexical semantics. In Bonnie Webber, Trevor Cohn, Yulan He & Yang Liu (eds.), *Proceedings of the 2020 Conference on Empirical Methods in Natural Language Processing (EMNLP)*, 7222–7240, Online. Association for Computational Linguistics.

Wray, Alison. 2002. *Formulaic Language and the Lexicon*. Cambridge: Cambridge University Press.

Corpora

BecaCESNo = Benedet, Maria, Celis Cruz, Maria Carrasco & Catherine Snow. N. d. *Corpus BecaCESNo*. http://childes.talkbank.org/browser/index.php?url=Spanish/BecaCESNo/ (accessed in July 2016).
esTenTen11 = Kilgarriff, Adam & Irene Renau. 2013. esTenTen, a Vast Web Corpus of Peninsular and American Spanish. *Procedia* 95. 12–19. https://www.sketchengine.eu/estenten-spanish-corpus/ (accessed in July 2016).
Val.Es.Co 2.0 = Cabedo, Adrián & Salvador Pons (eds.), N. d. *Corpus Val.Es.Co 2.0*. http://www.valesco.es (accessed in July 2016).

Dictionaries

CLAVE = Maldonado, Concepcion. 1996. *Clave. Diccionario del uso del español actual*. Madrid: SM.
DUE = Moliner, Maria. 1998. *Diccionario del uso del español*. Madrid: Gredos.
GDUEsA = Sánchez, Aquilino. 2001. *Gran diccionario del español actual*. Madrid: SGEL.

Noemi De Pasquale
9 *Making a move* towards Ancient Greek Light Verb Constructions

Abstract: This paper investigates some Light Verb Constructions expressing motion in Ancient Greek, with a specific focus on the comparison with their synthetic counterparts. By means of a corpus-based analysis, this study aims to show that the patterns at issue exhibit a number of different functions and meanings, mostly related to the actional properties of the event. In this paper, after a general overview of Ancient Greek Light Verb Constructions from a crosslinguistic perspective, which also addresses some terminological issues, the methodology of data collection is shown. The discussion of data concerns 1) the main types of Light Verb Constructions related to the motion domain, 2) the most common Light Verbs and *nomina actionis* occurring in this pattern, as well as 3) the semantics of the construction as a whole.

Keywords: Light Verb Construction, motion, Ancient Greek

1 Light Verb Constructions: an overview

Light Verb Constructions (henceforth LVCs) are traditionally described as complex predicates composed of a semantically bleached – or light – verb and a predicative action-denoting noun (e.g. English *take a walk*; Italian *fare festa* 'celebrate, party'; Latin *mentionem facere* 'mention, commemorate'). From a lexical point of view, the predicative noun seems to apply some restrictions to the verb, as shown, for instance, by the Italian examples *fare una scelta* vs. **prendere una scelta* 'make a choice'. LVCs often have synthetic counterparts (e.g. Eng. *make a claim* > *claim*; It. *fare una telefonata* 'make a call' > *telefonare* 'call'; Fr. *faire une promenade* 'take a walk' > *se promener* 'walk') and, by virtue of their syntax and semantics, they represent a challenge for linguistic studies, as shown by the increasing number of contributions on this topic (cf., *inter alia*, Butt 2010; Baños 2012; Osborne and Gross 2012).

Starting with some terminology, the English label *Light Verb* was first coined by Jespersen (1942), who stressed the semantic "emptiness", or underspecification, of verbs like *make, do, take, give, have, be* compared to "full" verbs such as *eat, sing, love, walk*. The French term *verbe support* (cf. It. *verbo supporto* or *verbo operatore*, Sp. *verbo de apoyo* or *verbo soporte*) – originated in the Laboratoire d'Automatique Documentaire et Linguistique (LADL) of the Université Paris VII, directed by Maurice Gross – refers to neutral verbs which serve as a grammatical support of the noun they co-occur with, providing it with TAM (tense, aspect, mood) features, thus acting as verbalizers of the whole construction, and contributing to the joint predication. The German term *Funktionsverbgefüge* provided by Polenz (1963) highlights the functional nature of such verbs, which require a nominal part in order to fulfil the predication.

From a superficial point of view, LVCs can participate in different syntactic schemas. The most common is V + N, i.e. a transitive verb taking a nominal complement (i.e. a direct object) which can either be preceded by an article (e.g. Eng. *have a rest*; It. *fare una scelta* 'make a choice'; Fr. *faire une promenade* 'take a walk'; Sp. *dar una explicación* 'give an explanation') or not (e.g. Eng. *have fun*; It. *prendere sonno* 'fall asleep'; Fr. *avoir peur* 'be afraid'; Sp. *coger frío* 'get cold'). The presence or absence of the determiner between the verb and the noun mirrors different degrees of lexicalization of the construction. In addiction to the V + N template, LVCs can consist of the following patterns:

- V + PREP + N (e.g. Eng. *take into account*);
- V + ADJ (e.g. Eng. *get cold*);
- V + ADV (e.g. Eng. *get well*).

As previously stated, the most common LVCs are verb-noun combinations in which a high frequency verb displaying generic meanings combines with an event-denoting noun (Butt 2010: 50).

Light Verbs are traditionally described as being semantically "empty". However, despite this traditional view, according to some scholars (Butt 2010: 48), "the verbs are clearly not entirely devoid of semantic predicative content either: there is a clear difference between *take a bath* and *give a bath*. The verbs thus seem to neither retain their full semantic predicational content, nor are they semantically completely empty".

Furthermore it seems worth stressing that one and the same verb can perform both the light and the full (lexical) use, depending on the noun with which it combines. Let us consider the two Italian examples *fare una scelta* 'make a choice' vs. *fare una torta* 'make a cake'. The first one shows a light use of the verb *fare* 'do, make', which combines with the action-denoting noun for 'choice'; in the second example the same verb is employed in its "full" predicative meaning 'make, create' and selects the concrete noun *torta* 'cake'. In the light of such premises, recent studies (cf., *inter alia*, De Miguel 2008; Ježek 2011) have shown that:

- the Light Verb provides the construction with a meaning that cannot be completely derived from the noun;

- the same Light Verb can receive different interpretations according to the noun with which it co-occurs (e.g. It. *fare un sospiro* 'make a sigh' < *fare* 'heave' vs. *fare pressione* 'make pressure' < *fare* 'apply').[1]

It is thus possible to hypothesize that a semantically generic verb, by virtue of its high combinability, acquires different meanings depending on the contexts in which it appears.

As far as the predicative nouns participating in LVCs are concerned, they mainly express actions, states or events. In Ježek (2011) the umbrella term employed to indicate nouns of this type is *nomina actionis*, i.e. nouns denoting temporal entities, independently of their aspectual (action, state or event) and morphological properties (deverbal or not deverbal). The *nomen actionis* applies lexical restrictions on the Light Verb in that not every root can indifferently appear within the construction (e.g. Eng. *I take a shower* vs. **I do a shower*). It goes without saying that, as for the combinations with Light Verbs allowed by the predicative noun, there are significant interlinguistic differences (e.g. It. *fare un sonnellino*, Sp. *echar una siesta* 'take a nap'; It. *fare un esempio*, Sp. *poner un ejemplo* 'give an example'; It. *fare una domanda*, Fr. *poser une question* 'ask a question').

Generally speaking, by virtue of their phrasal structure, LVCs share some properties with idioms. However, the two types of construction differ with respect to the noun semantics. In fact, while in LVCs the noun keeps its original transparent meaning, in idioms it develops opaque nuances derived from its literal sense by means of metaphorical or metonymical shifts (cf. *prendere una decisione* 'make a decision', *annullare una decisione* 'revoke a decision' vs. *prendere piede* 'become established, get a foothold').[2]

The nouns involved in LVCs can display different degrees of referentiality. The lower the referentiality of the noun, the higher the lexicalization of the LVCs (Heid 1994). This is, for instance, the case for the Italian LVC *prendere sonno* 'fall asleep', in which the lack of article between the verb and the noun is evidence in favour of a high level of tightness.

From a diachronic perspective, Light Verbs are said to have developed from their "heavy" counterparts through semantic bleaching, a process in which the

---

1 Concerning the influence of the noun semantics on the Light Verb, according to Ježek (2011: 29), « (. . .) le sens d'un verbe général est modulé/specifié par le sens du nom avec lequel il entre en contact sur le plan syntagmatique » "the meaning of a general verb is specified by the meaning of the noun it interacts with on the syntagmatic level".

2 As stated by Wittenberg (2016: 88), compared to LVCs, «idioms (. . .) are just one step further out on the scale from fully transparent to fully opaque sentential expressions».

verb loses some or all of its original semantic content. In some contributions on the topic (cf., *inter alia*, Hopper and Traugott 1993), Light Verbs are described as part of a grammaticalization cline proceeding from a full lexical verb towards conjugation ("heavy" verb → light verb → auxiliary verb → clitic → affix → conjugation). Nevertheless, some scholars (cf., *inter alia*, Butt and Lahiri 2002) claim that Light Verbs are not part of the continuum that is often posited, but that instead Light Verb and full verb usages must be drawn from the same underlying lexical entry.

In addition to primary Light Verbs, such as *have, be, make, do, give, take*, languages have a set of so-called *extensions* (Gross 1998), which are variants of the primary support verbs carrying further semantic and pragmatic information, ranging from aspectual nuances to quantity and register, as shown by the grid proposed in Ježek (2011: 3). As far as Ancient Greek is concerned, the present analysis has been restricted to LVCs involving primary Light Verbs, such as 'do' or 'have'. In the following section the methodology of data collection and coding is presented.

2 Methodology and data

My analysis of the main LVCs expressing motion in Ancient Greek has been led on a corpus of five texts dating back to the 5th and the 4th century BC. The sample in question embraces both prose and poetry, in the form of two main literary genres, i.e. history and drama. As for the former, three texts have been scrutinized, namely Herodotus' *Histories* (book 1), Thucydides' *History of the Peloponnesian war* (book 1), and Xenophon's *Anabasis* (book 1). With regard to the dramatic genre, the choice has fallen upon Euripides' *Bacchae* and Aristophanes' *Thesmophoriazusae*.

The five texts belonging to the corpus constitute the core of the data set. After an extensive reading aiming to identify the most frequent LVCs related to the motion domain, the research tool provided by the *Perseus 4.0*[3] has been exploited in order to check the employment of such constructions within other Ancient Greek texts from the Classical period. The English translations have been extracted from *Perseus 4.0* and adjusted when necessary.

All the occurrences have been coded based on a coding grid taking into account both the morphosyntactic (i.e. verbs, adnominal, satellites) and the semantic information (i.e. Figure, Motion, Ground, Path, Manner, cf. Talmy 2000).

---

3 http://www.perseus.tufts.edu/hopper/

3 Light Verb Constructions in Ancient Greek

Despite the great interest recently devoted to the study of LVCs in modern spoken languages, a systematic analysis of the patterns at issue in Ancient Greek is still lacking in the relevant literature.[4]

Nevertheless, LVCs are attested throughout the whole history of the Ancient Greek language. However, compared to other ancient languages such as Latin, in which patterns such as *bellum gero* or *proelium facio* 'make war' occur massively (Baños 2012), Ancient Greek shows a clear preference towards synthetic forms (Jiménez López 2012).

Consistently with the general typological tendency, the most common pattern of LVCs is V + N (a transitive verb selecting a nominal complement as its direct object). The most frequent Light Verb attested in this kind of combinations is *poiéo*: 'make', which can co-occur with different nouns expressing both actions and states (e.g. *apókrisis* 'answer', *lógos* 'discourse', *naumakhía* 'sea-fight', *orgé:* 'anger').[5]

By virtue of its intrinsic dynamism resulting, at the linguistic level, in a number of action-denoting nouns, the motion domain proves particularly suitable for an analysis of the LVCs in Ancient Greek. In the following section, the main syntactic templates, Light Verbs and *nomina actionis* involved in LVCs expressing displacement are investigated.

3.1 Syntactic templates

The data analysis has revealed that Ancient Greek LVCs employed for motion encoding fit into two main syntactic templates. In the first one (V + N), a transitive Light Verb combines with a predicative noun in the accusative case. This pattern is exemplified in (1), in which the verb *poiéo*: 'do, make' governs the noun for 'acquisition, possession', preceded by the definite article. The literal translation of the LVC at issue would be 'making the acquisition of the wealth'.

(1) οἱ   παρὰ   θάλασσαν   ἄνθρωποι   μᾶλλον   ἤδη
    hoi   parà   thálassan   ánthro:poi   mâllon   é:de:
    ART.NOM.M.PL beside sea(F).ACC.SG man(M).NOM.PL More already

---

[4] The main exception to this claim is represented by Jiménez López (2012) and Tronci (2015, 2016).
[5] This pattern corresponds to the *DO-type* identified in Tronci's (2015) study on Ancient Greek constructions in which the verb *ékho:* 'have' combines with psychological nouns.

τὴν   κτῆσιν   τῶν   χρημάτων
tèn   Ktê:sin   tôn   khre:máto:n
ART.ACC.F.SG acquisition(F).ACC.SG ART.GEN.PL good(N).GEN.PL
ποιούμενοι   Βεβαιότερον   ᾤκουν
poioúmenoi   Bebaióteron   ó:ikoun
do.PTCP.PRES.MP.NOM.M.PL   more_firm.ACC.N.SG   inhabit.IMPF.3PL

'The coast populations now began to apply themselves more closely to the acquisition of wealth, and their life became more settled'

(Thucydides *History of the Peloponnesian War* 1.8.3)

The second pattern (V + Adj) consists of a stative Light Verb combining with an adjective in the nominative case. This syntactic schema is shown in (2), in which the LVC is employed to encode the motion of the Figure away from a Source.

(2) ἔκτοπος   ἔστω
    éktopos   ésto:
    away_from_a_place.NOM.M.SG be.IMP.PRES.3SG
    'Let him get out of the way indoors'   (Euripides *Bacchae* 69)

3.2 Light Verbs

As already stated for Ancient Greek LVCs in general, for the motion domain too the first Light Verb by usage is *poiéo:* 'make, do'. It is attested especially in prose (i.e. within the historical texts), and it proves highly versatile, in that it can select the highest number of different predicative nouns expressing motion.

(3) Κῦρος   ὁδὸν   ἐποίεε
    Kû:ros   hodòn   Epoíee
    Cyrus(M).NOM.SG journey(F).ACC.SG   make.IMPF.3SG
    'Cyrus made the journey'   (Herodotus *The histories* 1.211.1b)

The second Light Verb by usage is *ékho:* 'have, hold'. Differently from *poiéo:* 'make, do' it is more common in poetry than in prose. In (4) it selects the noun for 'return'.

(4) νόστον   ἄθλιον   πάλιν   σχήσουσι
    nóston   áthlion   pálin   skhé:sousi
    return(M).ACC.SG miserable.ACC.M.SG back   have.FUT.3PL
    'they will have a miserable return'   (Euripides *Bacchae* 1337)

Two more verbs behave as Light Verbs in the corpus under analysis, namely *híste:mi* 'make to stand, set up' and *títhe:mi* 'set, put, place'.⁶ Both verbs occur more frequently in the dramatic texts and combine with few *nomina actionis* compared with *poiéo:* 'make, do'. Examples (5) and (6) respectively show one context of use for each of the verbs at issue.

(5) οἵαν   μ'   ἄρ'   ἔθου   Λώβαν
    hoían   m'   ár'   éthou   ló:ban
    such_as.ACC.F.SG 1SG.ACC PTC   put.AOR.2SG outrage(F).ACC.SG
    'What a ruin have you brought (*lit.* put) upon me'   (Sophocles *Trachiniae* 996)

(6) πρῶτον   εὐκύκλου   χορείας   εὐφυᾶ
    prôton   eukúklou   khoreías   euphuâ
    first   well_rounded.GEN.F.SG   dance(F).GEN.SG   well_grown.ACC.F.SG
    στῆσαι   βάσιν
    stêsai   básin
    make_stand.INF. AOR step(F).ACC.SG
    'First we (have to) set the graceful rhythmic step of the round dance'
    (Aristophanes *Thesmophoriazusae* 968)

An important feature of Ancient Greek LVCs, already noticed in Ittzés' (2007) work on Sanskrit, Latin and Greek periphrastic constructions involving the verb 'do', is the massive use of the middle voice. According to some scholars (cf., *inter alia*, La Fauci 1979; Cock 1981), it could be exploited to mark the use of the verb as a support (or Light) Verb, as opposed to its causative employment. In the case of LVCs, the middle voice would thus work as an antipassive detransitivizing the construction, emphasizing the Agent role of the subject (stressing its interest in the action), and relegating the predicative noun to the role of *chômeur* object by exploiting its non-referentiality (Marini 2010: 148, 177).⁷

An effective example of the distribution of the two voices (active and middle) according to the different function covered by the verb is provided by the comparison between (7) and (8), where the verb *poiéo:* 'make, do' co-occurs with the noun *odós* 'road, street, journey, travel'.

---

6 According to Cock (1981: 24), the employment of *títhe:mi* 'set, put, place' within the LVC is anterior to that of *poiéo:* 'make, do', which is as a matter of fact completely absent in Homer.
7 According to Marini (2010: 158), who follows the Relational Grammar theory, the recourse to the middle voice as a morphosyntactic marker of the light use of a verb is an ancient phenomenon, dating back to the Mycenean phase of the Ancient Greek language.

(7) πρῶτον μὲν τὴν ὁδὸν στενοτέραν
    prôton Mèn tè:n hodòn stenotéran
    first PTC ART.ACC.F.SG journey(F).ACC.SG narrower.ACC.F.SG
    Ποιήσας
    poié:sas
    do.PTCP.AOR.NOM.M.SG
    'first he made the road narrower' (Demosthenes *Against Callicles* 22)

(8) τὴν ὁδὸν Ποιευμένους πρὸς
    tè:n hodòn Poieuménous pròs
    ART.ACC.F.SG journey(F).ACC.SG do.PTCP.PRES.MP.ACC.M.PL towards
    Ζέφυρον ἄνεμον
    Zéphuron ánemon
    westerly_wind(M).ACC.SG wind(M).ACC.SG
    'making the journey towards the west' (Herodotus *The histories.* 2.32.5)[8]

In line with what previously stated, when the noun at issue is employed in its concrete meaning of 'road, street', the verb occurs in the active voice and performs its full lexical use ('make' = 'create') (7). Conversely, the verb takes the middle voice when the noun has its action-denoting meaning of 'journey, travel' (8).

3.3 Nomina actionis

As for the nouns occurring in LVCs, two main types have been found in the corpus. The first group includes nouns denoting both concrete entities and actions, as the previously mentioned *hodós* 'of Place, way, road; as an Action, travelling, journeying' (Liddell, Scott and Jones: s.v. ὁδός), or *stólos* 'equipment, armament; journey, travel', which occurs in (9) with *poiéo:* 'make, do' in the expected middle voice.

(9) ὥσπερ πάλιν τὸν Στόλον Κύρου
    hó:sper pálin tòn Stolon Kúrou
    as back ART.ACC.M.SG journey(M).ACC.SG Cyrus(M).GEN.SG
    ποιουμένου
    poiouménou
    do.PTCP.PRES.MP.GEN.M.SG
    'just as if Cyrus were going home again' (Xenophon *Anabasis* 1.3.16)

---

[8] It is worth mentioning that in Ancient Greek winds were often used to refer to directions.

A peculiar feature of the Ancient Greek language is that these nouns can take directional prefixes, exactly like motion verbs, see for instance from *hodós* > *éxodos* 'going out', *eísodos* 'entering, entrance', *prósodos* 'going to, approach', *káthodos* 'descent'.

The second group of *nomina actionis* in the corpus under analysis consists of deverbal nouns derived from different types of motion verbs. Such nouns, analogously to those belonging to the first group, can occur either in their bare form or prefixed. Among the non-prefixed ones, the most frequent are *básis* 'stepping, step; rhythmical or metrical movement'; *nóstos* 'return home; travel, journey'; *plóos* 'sailing, voyage'; *poreía* 'mode of walking or running, gait; journey; march'; *strateía* 'expedition, campaign'. In (10) *strateía* occurs in the plural number with the usual *poiéo:* in the middle voice.

(10) οὐδ'   αὖ   αὐτοὶ   ἀπὸ   τῆς   ἴσης
     oud'   aû   autoì   apò   tês   íse:s
     NEG   again   DEM.NOM.M.PL   from   ART.GEN.F.SG   equal.GEN.F.SG
     κοινὰς   στρατείας   ἐποιοῦντο
     koinàs   strateías   Epoioûnto
     common.ACC.F.PL   expedition(F).ACC.PL   do.IMPF.MP.3PL
     'they did not make common expeditions for combination of equals'
                    (Thucydides *History of the Peloponnesian War* 1.15.2)

The most frequent deverbal nouns taking directional satellites in the data set at issue are *diábasis* 'crossing over, passage; act of crossing'; *diálusis* 'separating, parting'; *ékploos* 'sailing out, leaving port'; *katadromé:* 'inroad, raid'; *katafugé:* 'place of refuge; retreat'. Examples from (11) to (13) show the employment of some of such prefixed nouns within the LVC.

(11) ἐπ'   ὧν   τὴν   διά-βασιν   ἐποιεῦντο
     ep'   Hôn   tè:n   diá-basin   epoieûnto
     upon   REL.GEN.PL ART.ACC.F.SG   through-step(F).ACC.SG   do.IMPF.MP.3PL
     οἱ   Βαβυλώνιοι
     hoi   Babuló:nioi
     ART.NOM.M.PL Babilonian.NOM.M.PL
     'on which the Babylonians crossed'   (Herodotus *The histories.* 1.186.3)

(12) οἱ   Σάμιοι   ἐξαπιναίως
    hoi   Sámioi   exapinaío:s
    ART.NOM.M.PL Samian.NOM.M.PL suddenly
    ἔκ-πλουν   ποιησάμενοι
    ék-ploun   poie:sámenoi
    out_of-sailing_out(M).ACC.SG do.PTCP.AOR.MP.NOM.M.PL
    'the Samians made a sudden sally'
    (Thucydides *History of the Peloponnesian War* 1.117.1a)

(13) πρός   τε   τὴν   Δεκέλειαν   κατα-δρομὰς
    prós   te   tè:n   Dekéleian   kata-dromàs
    towards PTC ART.ACC.F.SG Decelea(F).ACC.SG down-run(F).ACC.PL
    ποιουμένων
    poiouméno:n
    do.PTCP.PRES.MP.GEN.M.PL
    'making excursions to Decelea'
    (Thucydides *History of the Peloponnesian War* 7.27.5)

As the examples provided so far have shown, most Ancient Greek verbs expressing motion can be replaced by their analytic counterparts, i.e. by a LVC, independently of the motion component they express. Deverbal nouns involved in LVCs expressing motion derive, as a matter of fact, from different verb classes encoding the main conceptual components of motion, namely:
– basic motion verbs, i.e. verbs which encode motion itself, without defining either the trajectory followed by the Figure, or the mode of motion it performs, like *baíno:* 'go, come' → *básis* 'stepping, step';
– caused motion verbs, i.e. verbs describing motion events in which an Agent causes an entity to change location by acting on it, like *bállo:* 'throw, cast' → *metabolé:* 'change, transition, migration';
– Manner verbs, i.e. verbs which encode the mode of motion performed by the Figure, like *pléo:* 'sail' → *ékploos* 'sailing out, leaving port';
– Path + Manner verbs, i.e. verbs which combine the information about the trajectory followed by the Figure and the Manner (i.e. the type of motion), like *feúgo:* 'flee, escape' → *katafugé:* 'place of refuge, retreat'.

3.4 Functions and semantics

The comparison between the LVCs in the data set and their synthetic counterparts occurring in the same text has shed new light on the possible functions and meanings of LVCs.

To begin with, in some contexts, LVCs can be synonyms of the predicative verbs from which they derive, i.e. the author can resort to the LVCs for, so to speak, arbitrary stylistic reasons, such as avoiding repetition, as in examples (14: *ekpleûsai*) and (15: *ékploun*), which are taken from the same passage of the same text.

(14) ξυν-εβούλευε   μὲν πλὴν πεντακοσίων   ἄνεμον
     xun-eboúleue   mèn plè:n pentakosío:n Ánemon
     with-advise.IMPF.3SG PTC except five_hundred wind(M).ACC.SG
     τηρήσασι   τοῖς   ἄλλοις   ἐκ-πλεῦσαι
     te:ré:sasi   toîs   állois   ek-pleûsai
     watch_over.PTCP.AOR.DAT.PL ART.DAT.PL other.DAT.PL out_of-sail.INF.AOR
     'advised all except five hundred to watch for a wind, and sail out of the place'
     (Thucydides *History of the Peloponnesian War* 1.65.1a)

(15) ἔκ-πλουν   ποιεῖται   λαθὼν
     ék-ploun   poieîtai   lathò:n
     out_of-sailing(M).ACC.SG do.PRES.MP.3SG hide.PTCP.AOR.NOM.M.SG
     τὴν   φυλακὴν   τῶν   Ἀθηναίων
     tè:n   phulakè:n   tô:n   Athe:naío:n
     ART.ACC.F.SG guard(F).ACC.SG ART.GEN.PL   Athenian.GEN.M.PL
     'he eluded the guardships of the Athenians and sailed out'
     (Thucydides *History of the Peloponnesian War* 1.65.1b)

Another possible function of LVCs is the encoding of an additional actional nuance stressing the occasional character of the action, as in (16), where the noun for 'expedition' is employed with reference to a specific march against a specific city, while in (17) the corresponding motion verb encodes the act of marching in general.

(16) ἀπεῖπον   αὐτῷ   πορεύεσθαι   μετὰ δυνάμεως
     apeîpon   autôi   poreúesthai   metà dunámeo:s
     prohibit.AOR.3PL   3SG.DAT   march.INF.PRES.MP   with army(F).GEN.SG
     ἐντὸς   Πυλῶν
     entòs   Pulôn
     within   Pylos(M).GEN.PL
     'they forbade his marching south of Thermopylae with an army'
     (Polibius *Histories* 2.52.8)

(17) ἐκ   τῶν   Συρακουσῶν   ἐποιεῖτο   τὴν
    ek   tôn   Surakousôn   epoieîto   tè:n
    out_of ART.GEN.PL Syracuse.GEN.PL do.IMPF.MP.3SG   ART.ACC.F.SG
    πορείαν   ἐπὶ   τὴν   προειρημένην
    poreían   epì   tè:n   proeire:méne:n
    expedition(F).ACC.SG upon   ART.ACC.F.SG before_say.PTCP.PF.PASS.ACC.F.SG
    πόλιν
    pólin
    city(F).ACC.SG
    'he made an expedition from Syracuse against that city'
                                            (Polibius *Histories* 1.11.8)

In some contexts, the predicative noun involved in the LVC is semantically richer than the verb from which it derives. This is the case of *básis* 'stepping, step' in (18) = (6), which refers to a rhythmic movement (Liddell, Scott and Jones: s.v. βάσις), while the corresponding verb *baíno:* 'come, go' (which is preceded by the Median satellite *katá* 'downwards' in example 19) simply encodes a basic displacement of the Figure.[9]

(18) πρῶτον   εὐκύκλου   χορείας   εὐφυᾶ
    prôton   eukúklou   khoreías   euphuâ
    first   well_rounded.GEN.F.SG dance(F).GEN.SG well_grown.ACC.F.SG
    στῆσαι   βάσιν
    stêsai   básin
    make_stand.INF.AOR step(F).ACC.SG
    'First we (have to) set the graceful rhythmic step of the round dance'
                                       (Aristophanes *Thesmophoriazusae* 968)

(19) εἶτα κατα-βαίνω   λάθρᾳ
    eîta kata-baíno: láthrai
    then down-go.PRES.1SG secretely
    'and I was going down noiselessly' (Aristophanes *Thesmophoriazusae* 482)

The last couple of examples taken from the same author shows another function performed by the LVCs as opposed to their synthetic counterparts. While in (20) the syntactic templates forces the speaker to express the bare return of the Figure,

---

[9] In Talmy's (2000) terminology, Median is one of the subcomponent of Path, i.e. the intermediate portion of the trajectory followed by the moving Figure.

without providing further details, the structure of (21) = (4), i.e. Light Verb + predicative noun, allows to specify the qualitative connotation of the action by means of an adjective. As stated by Cock (1981: 27), in fact, «la construction périphrastique offre du point de vue sémantique et syntaxique plus de possibilités d'emploi que le verbe simple: elle permet de distinguer le caractère défini et indéfini et le nombre; en outre, elle facilite l'emploi d'une subordonnée relative» "the periphrastic construction provides more usage options from a semantic and syntactic point of view compared to the simple verb: it allows to distinguish the definite or indefinite character and the number; furthermore it facilitates the insertion of a relative clause".

(20) μόνος δὲ νοστῶ
 mónos dè nostô
 alone.NOM.M.SG PTC return.PRES.1SG
 'I come back alone' (Euripides *Helen* 428)

(21) νόστον ἄθλιον πάλιν σχήσουσι
 nóston áthlion pálin skhé:sousi
 return(M).ACC.SG miserable.ACC.M.SG back have.FUT.3PL
 'they will have a miserable return' (Euripides *Bacchae* 1337)

4 Conclusions

To sum up, the data concerning the employment of LVCs for motion encoding in the texts under analysis have shown that: (a) the most common syntactic pattern entails a transitive Light Verb selecting a predicative noun in the accusative case superficially behaving as its direct object; (b) the Light Verb showing the highest degree of combinability is *poiéo:* 'do'; (c) Light Verbs usually appear in the middle voice employed as an antipassive marker; (d) as for the *nomina actionis* involved in LVCs, they may fall into two main types, i.e. non-deverbal nouns (both prefixed and non-prefixed) expressing either concrete entities or actions, and deverbal nouns (both prefixed and non-prefixed) denoting actions and events; (e) Ancient Greek LVCs expressing motion exhibit a number of meanings and functions, ranging from stylistic variation, to qualitative connotation of the action encoded by the noun.

Our analysis has provided an accurate descriptive deepening of Ancient Greek LVCs expressing motion. The Ancient Greek data can be used to shed new light on the typological features of these complex predicates, as well as on their functional distribution compared to the corresponding synthetic verbs.

Abbreviations

1	first person
2	second person
3	third person
ACC	Accusative
AOR	Aorist
ART	Article
DAT	Dative
DEM	Demonstrative
F	Feminine
FUT	Future
GEN	Genitive
IMP	Imperative
IMPF	Imperfect
INF	Infinitive
M	Masculine
MP	Middle-Passive
N	Neuter
NEG	Negation
NOM	Nominative
PASS	Passive
PF	Perfect
PL	Plural
PRES	Present
PTC	Particle
PTCP	Participle
REL	Relative
SG	Singular

References

Baños, José Miguel. 2012. Verbos soporte e incorporación sintáctica en latín: el ejemplo de ludos facere". *Revista de Estudios Latinos* 12. 37–57.

Butt, Miriam. 2010. The Light Verb jungle: still hacking away. In Mengistu Amberber, Brett Baker & Mark Harvey (eds.), *Complex predicates: Cross-linguistic Perspectives on Event Structure*, 48–78. Cambridge: Cambridge University Press.

Butt, Miriam & Aditi Lahiri. 2002. Historical Stability vs. Historical Change. http://ling.uni-konstanz.de/pages/home/butt/main/papers/stability.pdf.

Cock, A.J.C.M. 1981. Ποιεῖσθαι: ποιεῖν. Sur les critères déterminant le choix entre l'actif ποιεῖν et le moyen ποιεῖσθαι. *Mnemosyne* 34(1). 1–62.

De Miguel, Elena. 2008. Construcciones con verbos de apoyo en español, De cómo entran los nombres en la órbita de los verbos. In Inés Olza Moreno, Manuel Casado Velarde & Ramón González

Ruiz (eds.), *Actas del XXXVII Simposio Internacional de la Sociedad Española de Lingüística*, 567–578. Pamplona: Servicio de Publicaciones de la Universidad de Navarra.

Gross, Maurice. 1998. La fonction semantique des verbes supports. *Travaux de Linguistique: Revue Internationale de Linguistique Française* 37(1). 25–46.

Heid, Ulrich. 1994. On ways words work together – topics in lexical combinatorics. In Willy Martin, Willem Meijs, Margreet Moerland, Elsemiek ten Pas, Piet van Sterkenburg & Piek Vossen (eds.), *Euralex 1994, Proceedings*, 226–257. Amsterdam: European Association for Lexicography.

Hopper, Paul J. & Elizabeth Traugott. 1993. *Grammaticalization*. Cambridge: Cambridge University Press.

Ittzés, Máté. 2007. Remarks on the periphrastic constructions with the verb 'to make, to do' in Sanskrit, Greek and Latin. In Dezső Csaba (ed.), *Indian Languages and Texts Through the Ages. Essays of Hungarian Indologists in Honour of Prof. Csaba Töttössy*, 1–40. New Delhi: Manohar.

La Fauci, Nunzio. 1979. *Costruzioni con verbo operatore in testi italiani antichi. Esplorazioni sintattiche.* Pisa: Giardini.

Liddell, Henry George, Robert Scott & Henry Stuart Jones. 1940. *A Greek-English Lexicon*. Oxford: Clarendon.

Jespersen, Otto. 1942. *A Modern English Grammar on Historical Principles*. Vol. 6: *Morphology*. London: George Allen and Unwin Ltd.

Ježek, Elisabetta. 2011. Verbes Supports et Composition Sémantique. *Cahier de Lexicologie* 1. 98. 29–44.

Ježek, Elisabetta. 2005. *Lessico. Classi di parole, strutture, combinazioni*. Bologna: il Mulino.

Ježek, Elisabetta. 2004. Types et degrés de verbes supports en italien. In Gaston Gross & Sophie De Pontonx. *Verbes supports. Nouvel état des lieux* 27(2). 185–201. [=Special Issue of *Linguisticae Investigationes*].

Jiménez López, Dolores. 2012. Construcciones con verbo de apoyo, verbo simple y nombre predicativo: un ejemplo en griego antiguo. *Minerva* 25. 85–107.

Marini, Emanuela. 2010. L'antipassivo in greco antico: poiésthai come verbo supporto in Aristotele. *Journal of Latin Linguistics* 11(1). 147–180.

Osborne, Timothy & Thomas Gross. 2012. Constructions are catenae: Construction Grammar meets Dependency Grammar. *Cognitive Linguistics* 23. 1. 163–214.

Polenz, Peter von. 1963. *Funktionsverben im heutigen Deutsch. Sprache in der rationalisierten Welt*. Düsseldorf: Schwann.

Pompei, Anna. 2010. Space coding in verb-particle constructions and prefixed verbs. In Giovanna Marotta, Alessandro Lenci, Linda Meini & Francesco Rovai (eds.), *Space in language*, 401–418. Pisa: Edizioni ETS.

Simone, Raffaele. 2007. Categories and constructions in verbal and signed languages. In Raffaele Simone, Elena Pizzuto, & Paola Pietrandrea (eds.), *Verbal and Signed Languages. Structures, Constructs and Methodologies*, 197–252. Berlin/New York: Mouton de Gruyter.

Skopeteas, Stavros. 2008. Encoding spatial relations: language typology and diachronic change in Greek. *Language Typology and Universals* 61. 54–66.

Talmy, Leonard. 2000. *Toward a cognitive semantics*. Vol. 2: *Typology and process in concept structuring*. Cambridge, MA: The MIT Press.

Tronci, Liana. 2015. At the lexicon-syntax interface: Ancient Greek constructions with ἔχειν and locative prepositional phrases, talk presented at the *12th International Conference on Greek Linguistics*. Freie Universität Berlin (16–19 September 2015).

Tronci, Liana. 2016. Sur le syntagme prépositionnel en N du grec ancien: syntaxe et lexique de ses combinaisons avec le verbe ékhein 'avoir'. In Christiane Marque-Pucheu, Fryni Kakoyianni-Doa, Peter Machonis & Harald Ulland (eds.), *À la recherche de la prédication: autour des syntagmes prépositionnels*, 141–158. Amsterdam: Benjamins.

Wittenberg, Eva. 2016. *With Light Verb constructions from syntax to concepts*. Potsdam: Universitätsverlag Potsdam.

Section 4: **The verb emptiness**

Johanna Mattissen
10 Light Verbs and 'light nouns' in polysynthetic languages

Abstract: This chapter argues that Light Verbs in polysynthetic languages of the compositional type are parallel in form and function to non-polysynthetic ones. They mostly occur synthesized with their lexical carriers and are at an intermediate stage on a lexicalisation path, or on a grammaticalisation path to verbal classifiers, aspectoid, valency and modal functions. The article also argues for the existence of 'light nouns' as a category on a lexicalisation or grammaticalisation cline towards adpositions and conjunctions in non-polysynthetic languages and relational and instrumental markers, classifiers and valency operators in polysynthetic ones.

Keywords: Light Verb, light noun, polysynthetic language, lexicalisation, grammaticalisation, classifier, aspectoid, valency, modal, relational marker

1 Introduction

Light Verbs (LVs) are a well-known phenomenon of languages of the isolating or analytic, fusional and agglutinative morphological types. The question that has not been studied to date is whether they also exist in polysynthetic languages, because of the propensity of polysynthetic languages of encoding, in complex wordforms, information in non-root bound morphemes (Mattissen 2003) that are not easily classified as either derivational or inflectional, grammatical or lexical. As the analysis of polysynthetic languages of the compositional type (cf. Mattissen 2017) shows, forms of verbal origin on a cline to lexicalisation or grammaticalisation do exist. They are, as a rule, integrated into a complex word form. Their parallels to Light Verbs are discussed in this study.

As some subtypes of polysynthetic languages do not exhibit a strong noun-verb-distinction, and there are bound morphemes that may have a nominal source (Mattissen 2004, 2006), a second question poses itself that has never been thrown up, whether also 'light nouns' can be identified as nouns grammaticalising into functional elements. This issue is discussed in Section 7.

After a quick look at polysynthesis in Section 2 we will delimit LVs from other multiverb constructions in Section 3, and compare potential Light Verb Constructions (LVCs) in polysynthetic languages to LVCs in non-polysynthetic languages in order to work out their parallels (Section 4) and their functions with regard to lexicalisation (Section 5) and grammaticalisation into classifiers, markers of aspectoid categories (e.g. progressive, completive, resultative, repetitive, habitual), valency and modality (Section 6).

2 Polysynthesis

Polysynthesis is a heterogeneous phenomenon of productive morphological complexity which I have defined along different parameters (Mattissen 2003, 2004, 2006, 2017). One main parameter is the word formational type, i.e. whether the complex verb form allows only one lexical root (affixal type) or more than one (compositional type), along with non-root bound morphemes with lexical and grammatical meanings/functions. Non-root bound morphemes, especially local ones, are a necessary condition for polysynthesis.

The search for constructions in polysynthetic languages fulfilling the definition of LV as exposed in Section 3 leads to polysynthetic languages of Australia, North Asia, and North and South America that are all of the compositional type. I want to argue here that LVs can indeed be found in such languages, e.g. Ket, Ainu, Caddoan, Panoan, Papuan and Gunwinjguan languages.

In languages of the affixal type, for instance Eskimoan, Wakashan, Salishan languages, Purepecha, Abkhaz, and Tiwi, LVs do not exist. Some of these languages use verbalizers instead, i.e. non-root bound morphemes (Mattissen 2017).

3 Delimitation of Light Verbs

LVs are verbs identical in form to full lexical verbs occurring in a Light Verb Construction (LVC). Such a construction consists of a main lexical-semantic carrier and a main functional/inflectional carrier, the latter being the LV. The LV is not completely devoid of meaning (cf. Butt 2003: 6), but contributes to the semantics, actional class and participant frame of the LVC.

The lexical carrier of an LVC may be of various lexical categories, most frequently nouns or verbs. In European and Asian non-polysynthetic languages, construction types with N/NP + LV and PP + LV are best known, e.g.:

(1) German
 Luft holen (air fetch) "breathe, suck in air"
 einen Antrag stellen (an application put.up) "apply"
 zur Verfügung stehen (to.the disposal stand) "be at s.o.'s disposal"

Other combinations are possible, however:

(2) zu erwarten stehen   (to await stand)   "be due"   (V + LV)
     unentschieden stehen (undecided stand)   "be a draw/even"   (ADJ + LV)
     zack-zack machen   (chop-chop make)   "work chop, chop" (ideophone + LV)

Farsi (Karimi-Doostan 2008), Kalam (Pawley 1993) and some Northern Australian (McGregor 2002) languages are known as non-polysynthetic languages in which LVCs are the dominant syntactic pattern, and the number of basic verbs is restricted.

When LVCs consist of a verbal lexical carrier and an LV, they come close to other constructions formed from two verb forms: verb serialisation, verb root serialisation, converb, auxiliary and coverb constructions (cf. Bisang 1995, Harris 2008). These types are distinguished in terms of form, juncture type, clause status and further features, which I present here as an overview in Table 1:

Table 1: Overview of multiverb construction types.

Construction type	form	juncture, clause status	features
LVC*	one verb form inflected for TAM+Person with minor lexical contribution, one uninflected or non-predicate-inflected form contributing lexical content + argument frame	asyndetic, monoclausal, can adopt all forms of the inflectional paradigm	no independent verbal occurrence of uninflectable form as a rule, no meaning preservation of the inflected form standing on its own, closed class of LVs
Verb root serialisation	two (or more) lexical verb roots in one word form with shared inflection	complex verb form, monoclausal	independent occurrence of both/all verbs
Verb serialisation	two (or more) symmetrically inflected verbal predicate forms	asyndetic, monoclausal or multiclausal	independent occurrence of both/all verbs
Coverb (e.g. Chinese)	two symmetrically inflected verb forms, one in participant relational function to the other	monoclausal	relational form polysemous or quasi-homophonous to a free verb, closed class of coverbs
Converb construction	at least two asymmetrically inflected verb forms, one being dependent on and in scope of categories of the other	syndetic, monoclausal or multiclausal	independent occurrence of all verbs

Table 1 (continued)

Construction type	form	juncture, clause status	features
Auxiliary construction	one form inflected for TAM+Person without lexical contribution, one non-finite verb form; fully grammaticalised	periphrastic verb form within an inflectional TAM paradigm, monoclausal	independent occurrence of both or independent occurrence of neither, closed class of auxiliaries with very few members

*called coverb (!), vector verb, preverb in the Caucasus, India, Australia (Butt 2003)

LVCs can thus be delimited due to their combination of a fairly uninflected lexical carrier and an inflected functional carrier which inflects for the whole verbal paradigm (cf. Harris 2008: 220), and which form the predicate together (Butt 2003: 2).

Nevertheless, transitions from one type in Table 1 to the other are not only possible but frequent cross-linguistically and diachronically, e.g. from verb serialisation to coverb (Bisang 1995: 145).

A transition to an LVC is possible from a monoclausal structure with shared participants and scope of negation: one of the verbs reduces or shifts its lexical contribution, becoming more functional, one loses its inflectability (Butt 2003:17 for Sanskrit). In Wichita and Kiowa, for instance, there are lexical verb roots (e.g. 'dance' in (3)) which may not form a verb form on their own but must be in verb root serialisation with another verb (Rood 1976: 72, Watkins 1984: 225).

(3) Kiowa (Watkins 1984: 225)
à-c'à·-tʰó·-yà
1s-dance-move.about-IMPF
"I'm dancing"

Although Butt (2003: 18) supports the claim that LVCs are diachronically stable, Harris (2008), Evans (2003: 547) and Werner (1997: 213, 59), among others, present evidence for a development from an LV to inflection via the loss of recognisability as a root.

From a typological viewpoint, LVCs can thus be a transitional phenomenon either on a lexicalisation path from a 'sum-of-parts' syntagm to an opaque (analytic) lexeme or on a grammaticalisation path from a syntagm of full lexemes along the cline in Figure 1.

verb → light verb → auxiliary → clitic → affix → conjugation class marker.

Figure 1: Grammaticalisation cline (based on Hopper and Traugott 2003: 111).

From the LV stage onwards, the elements of the construction may fuse into one word unit, as for instance in Udi (Harris 2008), Japanese and Kalam (Pawley 1993).

From a semantic perspective, LVCs should be discussed in the light of collocations and idioms, which space constraints do not permit here. The formal and functional sides of LVCs are treated and illustrated with relevant examples in Sections 4, 5 and 6.

4 Light Verbs in polysynthetic languages

Within the polysynthetic languages mentioned in Section 2, candidates for LVCs generally occur in a synthetic form, which fits the overall morphological organisation of the language. Constructions qualifying for an LVC were chosen according to the following criteria developed in Section 3:
– the status and semantic contribution of the potential lexical and functional carrier elements
– a single set of inflection on and no syndetic markers between the two carriers
– the membership in a closed class of (one of) the carriers and
– signs of grammaticalisation or lexicalisation of the construction.

On this basis, languages with Light Verbs and lexical carriers of different categories could be identified. A formal comparison of the polysynthetic and the non-polysynthetic LVCs is presented in Table 2.

Table 2: Formal types of Light Verb Constructions.

Form of LVC	Polysynthetic languages	Non-polysynthetic languages	
		LV in synthetic construction	LV in analytic construction
V + V (or V + Adj)	Ket, Nivkh, Kiowa, Wichita, Murrinhpatha, Marrithiyel, Ngan'gityemerri, Bininj Gun-wok, Arabana	Japanese, Kalam, Igbo, Imonda, Udi	Farsi, Hindi, Kalam, Warlpiri, German
V + N(P) (or V + Adj)	Ket*, Kiowa, Bininj Gun-wok, Nivkh	Japanese, Udi, Basque	Farsi, Hindi, German, English, Chechen, Basque, Kalam, Laz, Japanese

Table 2 (continued)

Form of LVC	Polysynthetic languages	Non-polysynthetic languages	
		LV in synthetic construction	LV in analytic construction
V + PP			German, English, Farsi, Basque
V + particle/ adverb	Ainu*, Arabana*, Bininj Gun-wok*, Murrinhpatha	Udi	Chechen, Jaminjung, Kalam
V + ideophone/ borrowing	Bininj Gun-wok*	Japanese, Udi	Japanese, Warlpiri, Jaminjung, Gooniyandi, Farsi, Chechen, German, Basque

The languages marked with an asterisk are those exhibiting the few examples of analytic LVCs in polysynthetic languages. In Ainu (4) and Ket (5), the same or cognate LVs occur in analytic and synthetic constructions.

(4) Ainu (Tamura 2000: 45f)
    a. *san   etupsi   tomo   k-osma*
       shelf nose inside/middle 1s-crash
       "I bumped into the edge of the shelf"
    b. *u-tom-osma*
       RECI-inside-crash
       "they bumped into each other"

(5) Ket (Werner 1997: 169)
    l'ɔvet bayaʀan / l'ɔvetbayaʀan
    work begin.1s.PRS
    "I begin to work"

Examples (4) and (6) show that polysynthetic languages allow, with the exception of PPs, the same range of categories of lexical carriers:

(6) Kiowa (Watkins 1984: 225, 226)
    a. *à-dè̖·-hê̖·m-à*
       1s-sleep-die-IMPF
       "I'm sleepy"
    b. *mɔ́n-yáygɔ́*
       hand-foot.hit   with "foot-hit = kick"
       "wave at s.o."

c. Bininj Gun-wok (Evans 2003: 587)
derrengkerd yime-ng
axe.sound 3P.say-PST.PTV
(sound of an axe squeaking)
d. *bandi-ga-ni walkabout*
3a>3p-take-PL
"they'd take them walkabout"

In Ket ((5), (9), (11)) and Murrinhpatha (10) (see Sections 5, 6.1), the LVC is the dominant syntactic pattern of the language, as in non-polysynthetic Kalam and Farsi. However, none of the languages in Table 2 is characterised by the LVC type indicated alone.

Synthetic LVCs in non-polysynthetic languages constitute a transitional stage, e.g. between an analytic LVC and the next stage in grammaticalisation or lexicalisation, or even a transitional stage between non-polysynthetic and polysynthetic structure (cf. Mattissen 2004, 2006).

Japanese is a case in point. This agglutinating language has both analytic LVCs (as in (7a)) and noun incorporation into the LV *suru* 'do' (7b), which exists as an independent full verb as well. In addition, it has verb root serialisation with LVs encoding aspectoid categories and valency which are still formally identical to full verbs (7c).

(7) Japanese (Mattissen 2003:278)
 a. *Ainu-go=no   benkyô=o   **su**-ru*
    A.-language=GEN study=ACC do-NPST
    "s.o. studies the Ainu language"
 b. *Ainu-go=o   benkyô-**su**-ru*
    A.-language=ACC study-do-NPST
    "s.o. studies the Ainu language"
 c. *hanasi-**kakeru*** (speak-attach)   "begin to speak"
    *warai-**dasu*** (laugh-put_out)   "start laughing"
    *yomi-**kaesu*** (read-return)   "read again"

Some lexicalised verb-root serial combinations exist, too, e.g. *hanasi-kakeru* 'address s.o.' or *warai-dasu* 'burst out laughing'.

A comparison of V + V constructions in polysynthetic languages of the compositional type shows that they are either verb root serialisations in which each verb root contributes its full lexical content ('sum-of-parts' meaning, as in (8)), in particular combinations of action + motion, action + manner of action, action + degree, action + its evaluation, action + its result (cf. Mattissen 2003: ch. 6).

(8) Gunwinjguan (Evans 2003: 536)
    a. *ga-ganj-**ngu**-nihmi-**re***
       3-meat-eat-IVF-go.NPST
       "he goes along eating meat"
    b. Tunica (Haas 1941:72)
       na'ra-ya'ka-po'-wī-hč
       rise-come-look-3ms-when
       "when he got up, came and had a look . . ."

Or they can be considered LVCs (as in (9)) with one root being the lexical carrier, the other taking over the functional load (as 'chop' does).

(9) Ket (Drossard 2002:230)
    d-al'-d-a-d-do
    3s.M.S-beat-DETV-PRS-1sO-chop
    "he beats me up"

A transition from verb root serialisation to an LVC is possible: when one verbal root begins to alter its lexical contribution to the V + V construction, the LV stage sets in. From the LVC stage onwards, further development is possible, too, and in either of two directions: lexicalisation with creation of new lexical items, or grammaticalisation. So, a construction may be called an LVC as long as lexicalisation or grammaticalisation have not advanced to a stage where the items involved have lost their status as roots.

So far, LVCs in non-polysynthetic and polysynthetic languages show substantial parallels. A crucial point in which polysynthetic LVCs differ from non-polysynthetic ones is the locus of inflection. As a polysynthetic complex verb form is inflected as a whole, it may be difficult to determine which of the roots is the inflectional carrier. Usually, however, the positions of the root and inflection either suggest a coalescence of an uninflected and an inflected root at an earlier stage of the language, e.g. in Murrinhpatha (10), where the lexical carrier follows an inflected portmanteau form. Or they allow the identification of the main verb slot, as in Ket, where the verbal template is such that the serial root, i.e. the lexical root, takes a slot among the inflectional prefixes, as in (11b), when a Light Verb is present.

(10) Murrinhpatha (Nordlinger 2015: 494)
    ***bangam**-let*
    3sS.bash.NFUT-stick
    "he stuck it together (with sth.)"

(11) Ket   (Drossard 2002: 249f)
   a. *d-aŋ-s'-ej*
      1sS-3pO-PRS-kill
      "I am killing them now"   no LV
   b. *d-ej-aŋ-a-vet*
      1sS-kill-3pO-PRS-do
      "I kill them again and again"   LV ousts lexical verb

In addition to the formal point of view, LVCs in non-polysynthetic and polysynthetic languages must be compared in functional perspective in order to decide whether they can be considered the "same" category. Table 3 already presents an overview of the different functions expressed by LVCs in both types (the asterisk indicates the existence of analytic LVCs in Ket as shown in (5)). The functions will be discussed and contrasted in detail in the ensuing sections of this paper: lexeme formation will be treated in Section 5, and grammatical functions of LVCs in Section 6.

Table 3: Functions of Light Verb Constructions.

Function of LVC	Polysynthetic languages	Non-polysynthetic languages	
		Synthetic	Analytic
lexeme formation	Ket*, Ainu, Kiowa, Wichita, Arabana, Nivkh	Japanese, Igbo, Kalam	Farsi, German, Laz, Chechen, Kalam, Warlpiri
classification of V	Iroquoian, Ket, Kiowa, Murrinhpatha		Jaminjung
aspectoid/stage of a state of affairs	Kiowa, Wichita, Ket, Nivkh, Ainu, Yagua, Yanomami, Arabana, Ngan'gityemerri	Japanese, Igbo, Udi	German, Chechen, Farsi, Hindi, Marathi, Kalam, Diyari, Gooniyandi, Yoruba, Warlpiri, Tamil, Thai, Chinese
valency orientation	Ket, Wichita, Bininj Gun-wok, Kiowa, Yagua, Ngan'gityemerri, Murrinhpatha	Japanese, Udi, Sakao	Gooniyandi, Warlpiri, German, Kalam, Tamil, Fon, Thai, Chinese, Ulithian, Puluwat, Marathi
modality negation	Nivkh, Kiowa, Wichita, Yagua, Yanomami	Japanese	Laz, Thai

5 Light Verbs in lexicalisation

Polysynthetic LVCs with nominal or verbal lexical carriers are prone to lexicalisation. At the outset, we find noun incorporation or verb root serialisation with 'sum-of-parts' semantics, as in (12), (13) and (14).

(12) Ket (Werner 1997: 58)
 dɔ́nʼ-**bèt**
 knife-make
 "make a knife"

(13) Gunwinjguan (Evans 2003: 536)
 ga-ganj-**ngu**-nihmi-**re**
 3-meat-eat-IVF-go.NPST
 "he goes along eating meat"

(14) Wichita (Rood 1976: 70)
 ti-riye:cks-**iyari**-c
 3.IND-sleep-move.randomly-ITER
 "he is sleep-walking"

The first step towards lexicalisation is the LV stage, where there is no longer a sum-of-parts meaning (e.g. in Ainu (15)) and where a smaller number of verbs recurs in a large array of combinations (as *maŋg-* 'strong-' and *biŋr-* 'cheap' in Nivkh (16)).

(15) Ainu (Tamura 2000: 45f)
 *aske **uk*** (hand take) "invite"
 *ramu **ye*** (mind/soul tell) "praise"
 *ramu **suye*** (mind/soul wag) "comfort"
 *tomo **oytak*** (inside/middle talk) "soothe"

(16) Nivkh (Mattissen 2003: 188)
 va-maŋg- (fight-strong-) "pugnacious"
 to-biŋr- (cry-cheap-) "tearful"

For polysynthetic Cayuga, Sasse (2002:215) shows the different stages from productive root incorporation into the full verb 'be in a liquid' (as in (17a)) via a monolithic verb form in which the LV 'be in a liquid' still incorporates but does not contribute much meaning, as in (17b), to a monolithic opaque verb form in (17c). In (17c), *-ahs-*

is a cranberry morpheme in the incorporee position and the semantic reference of -*o*- to a liquid is plausible but not transparent to the native speakers.

(17) Cayuga (Sasse 2002: 215)
    a. *hę-k-at-ahsí't-o-h*
       TRSL-3snA-SRFL-foot-be_in_liquid-CAUS
       "I'll put my feet into the water"
    b. *-at-rihst-o-h*
       -SRFL-metal-be_in_liquid-CAUS
       "trap" (lit. "put metal in water for self")
    c. *-ahs-o-h* "paint"

Whereas Cayuga still has a rich inventory of full verbs, Ket possesses no more than 50 to 60 full verbs (Werner 1997: 163) and is thus further advanced on the cline towards lexicalisation. The full verbs in Ket appear together with noun incorporation, verb root serialisation and non-root bound morphemes. The resulting constructions are transparent to different degrees because of the inflecting verb reducing its concrete or specific meaning, as does -*kìt* 'smear' in (18). It is not only compatible with mass nouns, but also with nouns for liquids and even for individual solid objects which cannot literally be smeared. This growing opacity is a correlate of lexicalisation.

(18) Ket (Drossard 2002: 237f, 248, Werner 1997: 58)

t-haj-ivet	(1s-oar-make)	"I am rowing"
án'iŋ-bet	(idea-make)	"think"
d-ul'-t-a-i-bet	(1s-water-out-PRS-3sO-make)	"I spit"
kí't-kìt	(fat-smear)	"smear with fat"
hít-kìt	(glue-smear)	"glue"
d-ul'-ta-kit	(water-smear)	"moisten"
³*tu:n'-git*	(comb(N)-smear)	"comb"
en-ba-s'-uk	(memory-1s-PRS-fly)	"I forget"

This pattern pervades the language and makes it reminiscent of non-polysynthetic Kalam (cf. (19) with *nŋ* 'perceive') and Farsi with their analytic and descriptive ways of presenting states of affairs.

(19) Kalam (Drossard 2002: 245, Lane 2007: 109)
    a. *d nŋ* (take perceive) "feel"
       pk nŋ (hit perceive) "nudge"
       wdn nŋ (eye perceive) "see"

b. *yp   nabŋ   **d-p***
   1sO   shame   get-PTV.3s
   "I am ashamed"

In sum, there are clear parallels in lexicalisation patterns between polysynthetic and non-polysynthetic languages.

6 Light Verbs in grammaticalisation

This section analyses the grammatical functions of LVCs in polysynthetic languages and compares them to LVCs in non-polysynthetic ones to work out any parallels between the morphological types. In order for a grammatical function to be recognized as such, the LV must show signs of a beginning grammaticalisation, for instance a relaxation of selectional restrictions and a reduction of its semantic contribution. The different semantic paths open for grammaticalisation of LVs in non-polysynthetic languages will be examined here in polysynthetic languages: verbal classifiers (6.1), aspectoid markers (6.2), valency (6.3) and modal (6.4) morphemes.

6.1 Classification

Verbal classification is typical of Australian languages (both non-polysynthetic and polysynthetic), but also of Ket.

In Ngan'gityemerri there are 31 forms (Reid 2011: 228) and in Murrinhpatha 38 inflecting classifier verbs that contribute a meta-classification (McGregor 2002) of the action expressed by the lexical carrier, for instance with respect to the instrument used. Part of such forms do not bear a significant meaning of their own (Nordlinger 2017). They are clearly functional carriers and can be considered to be LVs (Nordlinger 2017). Lexical carriers combine with various LVs to modulate the meaning of the state of affairs (as in (20), (21)), with the LV in boldface):

(20) Murrinhpatha   (Nordlinger 2015:494, see also (10))
   a. ***bangarn**-tal*
      3sS.bash.NFUT-chop
      "he chopped it with an axe"
   b. ***pan**-tal*
      3sS.slash.NFUT-chop
      "he sliced it with a knife"

c. **mungarn**-tal
   3sS.break.NFUT-chop
   "he broke it with his hands"
d. **banga**-melmel
   3sS.bash.NFUT-flatten
   "he flattened it with a hammer"

(21) Ket   (Drossard 2002: 247f)
    ka-s-ti-**Rus**   (3s.take-PRS-1sO-take_away)   "s/he leads me away"
    d-usk-a-v-**us**   (1s.open-PRS-3snO-take_away)   "I am opening it"
    to-**tet**   (seize-hit)   "seize"
    t'el-**tet**   (push-hit)   "push"

Only eleven of the 38 Murrinhpatha inflecting verbs can be used as a predicate without a lexical carrier (Nordlinger 2017), the others are already further advanced on the grammaticalisation cline towards affixes marking TAM and person.

Classification in non-polysynthetic languages, e.g. in Jaminjung, functions according to the same principle (cf. Schultze-Berndt 2015), only the lexical and the functional carrier are two separate word forms.

6.2 Aspectoids and stage of a state of affairs

The domain of aspectoid markers (progressive, completive, resultative, habitual etc.) and stage of a state of affairs ('begin', 'end' etc.) is a well-studied area within the field of grammaticalisation. The source for markers in non-polysynthetic languages are (among others) frequently motion and postural verbs (e.g. 'go'-futures, 'sit'- or 'lie'-progressives; Bybee et al. 1994). In polysynthetic languages, verb root serial source constructions with a motion, postural or other verb can be found, in which the postural or motion verb has taken on a grammatical function, lost semantic features and combines with more and more verbs. This can be identified as the LV stage.

In Kiowa (22), a form originating in a verb root 'go' encodes continuative into the future, and one originating in a verb root 'be' a resultative; in Ngan'gityemerri (23), a form originating in a verb root 'sit' marks a progressive.

(22) Kiowa (Watkins 1984: 180, 152)
    a. hègɔ́   yá̰-kɔ́y-tò̰-mɔ̀·gɔ̀-ɔ̀mdè-**hɔ̀**
       now   2/3s.A>1su.PL-Kiowa-speak-adept-become-going
       "I am getting better at speaking Kiowa"
    b. tʰêm-**dɔ̀**·
       break-be
       "be broken"

(23) Ngan'gityemerri (Reid 2011: 232)
    yini-pefi-tye   peyipa   nyinyi   yini-wurrkama-tye
    2s.sit-DUR-PST   papers   2s   2s.sit-work-PST
    "you sat around a while (and you were) working on your papers"

Note the compatibility of postural 'stand' in Wichita (24) with dynamic 'follow': 'stand' has given up selectional restrictions and does not contribute its full semantics anymore, which is a correlate of grammaticalisation. The LV 'become' is used for the inchoative in (25).

(24) Wichita (Rood 1976: 73)
    ti-táta'-**ariki**
    3.IND-follow-stand
    "he's coming behind"

(25) Arabana (Hercus 1994: 141)
    a. kudnala-**wityi**- (sleep-become) "fall asleep"
       tharka-**wityi**- (stand-become) "get into upright position"
    b. paya-**wityi**- (bird-become) "turn into a bird" (N+V)

In Ket, 'do' and 'make' as LVs encode the iterative, another aspectoid category. The comparison of (11a) and (11b) shows that 'do' takes the main root position (R1 in Werner's 1997 terms), urging the lexical verb 'kill' into the serial position.

When the LV loses its connection to its source (the full verb) through a change in form or because the root is no longer extant, it cannot be considered a LV any more and its grammaticalisation has reached the affixal stage. This is the case in Yagua (Payne 1990) for instance. In the example below, the presumed source verbs appear in a verb root serialisation in full form and LV in (26a), whereas in (26b) we find the suffix -siy 'out of, perfective, ABL, upon departure from' grammaticalised from this source.

(26) Yagua (Payne 1990: 223)
    a. *siiy-maasiy*
       run-exit
       "rush out"
    b. *sa-suuta-siy*
       3s-wash-upon_departure
       "he washed just prior to leaving"

In Nivkh, morphemes from different sources constitute a heterogeneous paradigm of stage and aspectoid markers, among them converb constructions, reduplication and suffixes. For instance, *tataḍ* 'whole' seems to have given rise to the bound morpheme *-data-* ~ *-tata-* 'in the state of being V-ed/keeping V-ed' via verb root serialisation, but the connection between the verb and the morpheme is no longer transparent (Mattissen 2003:79).

(27) Nivkh (Mattissen 2003:200)
    a. *hə-baχ*   *qʻav-**data**-gu-t*   *hə-ʈʻaχ-tox*   *si-ta.*
       that-stone   hot-SCON-CAUS-CV:3p   that-water-ALL   put-ENU:3p
       "they put that stone into that water hot (in heated condition)"

A quick glance at non-polysynthetic languages shows parallel developments. Remember that in Japanese, the serialised verb root/converb combines with inflected posture/motion LVs with an aspectoid function, as in (7c). In Kalam, some aspectoid LVs appear in analytic constructions, e.g. *d-* in (28a), others in synthetic constructions (e.g. *-ju-* in (28b); Pawley 1993: 117f), suggesting a transition in construction type which points to a grammaticalization.

(28) Kalam (Lane 2007: 110, 113)
    a. *kmn*   *ak*   *pak*   *ñb*   ***d**-p-al*
       mammal_game   this   hit   eat   complete-PERF-3p
       "they have hunted (struck and eaten) out the game mammals"
    b. *mñi*   *ag-d-**ju**-p-in*
       now   say-get-withdraw-PERF-1s
       "now I have finished reporting"

The examples in this section show that polysynthetic languages follow the general grammaticalisation path both in form and function via an LV stage.

6.3 Valency and orientation

A third large domain of grammaticalised LVs in non-polysynthetic languages is operation on valency. In non-polysynthetic German, a frequent type of LVC combines both valency and aspectoid features in the functional carrier. Several recurring LVs form a loose kind of paradigm, as displayed in Table 4.

Table 4: German aspectoid/valency Light Verbs.

Valency Aspectoid	Intransitive	Transitive/causative
Inchoative	*geraten* "get into", *kommen* "come"	*bringen* "bring/take", *stellen* "put", *geben* "give", *nehmen* "take"
Durative	*sein* "be", *stehen* "stand"	*haben* "have"

One and the same noun/NP or PP does not usually combine with a LV from all cells – there are generally pairs or triplets with the same lexical carrier.

(29) German
    a. *in Gebrauch **kommen*** ↔ *in Gebrauch **nehmen***
       in usage come   in usage take
       "come to be used"   "put into use"
       ↕   ↕
    b. *in Gebrauch **sein*** ↔ *in Gebrauch **haben***
       in usage be   in usage have
       "be used"   "usually use"
    c. *unter Schutz **stehen***   *unter Schutz **stellen***
       under protection stand   under protection put
       "be under protection"   "protect"

Now, Ket uses different synthetic LVs for intransitivisation, i.e. valency reduction:

(30) Ket   (Drossard 2002: 251f)
    a. *eet'k* "show" → *asl'ineŋ   eet'k-a-R-a-**n***
                           boat   show-3sS-DET-PST-become
                           "the boat appeared"
    b. *da-s'iraqa-d-da* → *s'iraqa-d-**dij***
       3sfS-learn-1sO-CAUS   learn-1sS-grow
       "she teaches me"   "I learn"

c. *t-kav-i-t* → *kavä-**tij***
   1sS-tear-EV-CAUS.3sO   3snS.tear-fall
   "I'm tearing it"   "it is torn"
d. *d-ul'tav-d-aq* → *ul'tav-**ut***
   1sS-release-1s>3sn-go   3snS.release-end
   "I am untying it"   "it is getting loose"

Wichita integrates 'make' for marking a causative of statives, and Bininj Gun-wok incorporates a construction into 'go' for an anticausative and into *-we-* 'throw' or *-wo-* 'give' to form a causative.

(31) Wichita   (Rood 1976: 63)
   ti-tariwi:-rhi-rʔ-i-s
   ti-tariwi:k-ri-raʔi-ʔi-s
   3.IND-round-PL-make-be-IMPF
   "he is making them round"

(32) Bininj Gun-wok   (Evans 2003: 536, 540f)
   a. *ba-rrang-marrhm-i-**wam***
      3P-door-open(TR)-IVF-go.PST.PTV
      "the door opened up"
   b. *bi-djordm-ih-**we**-ng*   (3>3-grow.up-IVF-throw-PST.PTV)   "she raised him up"
      *gabandi-djoukga-ih-**we***   (3a>3p-cross-IVF-throw.PST.PTV)   "they take them across"
      *ba-manka-yh-**wo**-ng*   (3>3-fall-IVF-give-PST.PTV)   "he let it fall"
      *bindi-yawoyh-ngime-**wo**-ng*   (3a>3p-again-enter-IVF-give-PST.PTV)   "they put them into them again"

So, in the domain of change-of-valency LV, polysynthetic and non-polysynthetic languages show parallels as well.

6.4 Modality and polarity

Two further significant categories are also encoded by LVs: modality and polarity. In non-polysynthetic languages, these categories are expressed by a range of different forms, e.g. modality by modal verbs, word formation (e.g. *-able*), syntagmatic constructions as well as LVs and affixes, and polarity by adverbs, particles as well as LVs and affixes. Modal and polar LVs may be analytic or synthetic forms (cf. (33)).

(33) Japanese
    a. *yom-a-nakereba*   *naranai*
        read-stem.marker-if.not   does.not.become
        'somebody must read'
    b. *yom-a-na-i*
        read-stem.marker-NEG-NPST
        'somebody does not read'

Japanese *na-* still exists as a free verb 'not exist', but as a negation marker fuses with a specific stem of the lexical carrier verb while still bearing the inflection of its own paradigm, which makes it a functional carrier.

As for polysynthetic languages, modal and polar LVs can be found in Yagua and Nivkh. In Yagua, grammaticalisation is already far advanced to a clitic postbase (Payne 1990: 228): *-rquy* POT < *niryuy* 'love, desire'. In Nivkh, however, the synchronic situation allows us to identify LVs as a transitional stage on a grammaticalisation path. The language has positive and negative modal verbs and three different ways of encoding modality, displayed in Table 5: complement-taking modal verbs, light modal verbs in root serialisation and suffixes.

Table 5: Nivkh polar modality (Amur variety and East Sakhalin variety of Nivkh).

Probable source verb	Complement-taking verb	LV in root serialisation	suffix
	j-ali-ḑ "cannot master/cope with"		
	j-aʁñ-ḑ "want" (Amur)	*-aʁñi-d* "want" (East Sakh.)	
	j-əyzu-ḑ "ignore"		*-yzu- ~ -xsu- ~ -ksu-* NEG.EXP/HAB
kerḑ "refuse"		*-ger-ḑ ~ -ker-ḑ* "not willing to"	
molo-ḑ "steep"			*-molo-* "not want"

These different construction types are shown in the following examples:

(34) Nivkh   (Mattissen 2003: 189f)
    a. *ñi j-əjm-nə-ḑ-aʁñ-ḑ*   complement clause of 'want': *j-əjm-nə-ḑ*
       1s 3SU-know-FUT-IND/NML-want-IND/NML
       "I want to know it"

b. *ñi ra-i-n-aʙñi-d*   LV -*aʙñi*-d
   1s drink-FUT-PTCL-want-IND/NML
   "I want to drink sth."

c. *it-molo-ḑ-ra*   suffix -*molo*-
   say-not_want-IND/NML-HILI
   "he did not want to say anything/speak"

Deontic modality is fully productive and formed *ad hoc*, the LVs take the position of the second root in serialisation, and the first (lexical) verb root is not subject to any restrictions. The grammaticalisation stages of the LV have the following correlates:

(i) Serialising modal verbs cannot be constructed in an analytic way.
(ii) Inflection for causative, tense, etc. follows the first (non-modal) root whereas, in non-modal verb root serialisation, inflection follows the second root.
(iii) The modality markers have lost their free verb status to different degrees.
(iv) They have developed their own allomorphy.
(v) They have in part lost phonological substance.

A good example of the formal change going hand in hand with a semantic one is shown in (35) with different stages still extant side by side. Semantics evolve from 'ignore' (35a) via 'not know how to V' (35b) and negative experiential 'have never V-ed' (35c) to negative habitual 'not be used to' (35d), sometimes even close to a simple negation 'not' without an aspectoid component (35e).

(35) Nivkh   (Mattissen 2003: 194)

a. *hə-ñivx*   *pʻ-oʙla-əyzu-yət-ra*
   that-person   REFL-child-ignore-CPL-HILI
   "he did not know his child at all"

b. *ṭʻi napa ur-gu-r*   *kʻerqo-ḑ-əyzu-ḑ-ra*
   2s still   good-CAUS-CV:2s   ice_fish-IND/NML-ignore-IND/NML-HILI
   "you still don't know how to do ice fishing well"

c. *imŋ əyřagin tol-dox*   *məy-ksu-ḑ-yu*
   3p never   body_of_water-ALL   descend-NEG.EXP-IND/NML-PL
   "they have never gone down to the water"

d. *əyrku*   *ñivy-gu*   *ṭʻaj-χavu-t*   *ra-ysu-ta.*
   former_times person-PL tea-heat-CV:3p drink-NEG.HAB-ENU:3p
   "in the past, the Nivkh did not heat tea and drink it"

e. *jaŋ arak-ra-xsu-nt*
   3s vodka-drink-NEG.HAB-IND/NML
   "he does not drink vodka"

This section has shown further parallels between non-polysynthetic Japanese and polysynthetic Nivkh where modal and negational LVCs are concerned. As modality and negation have various forms of expression cross-linguistically on different stages of grammaticalisation, a comparison is more difficult.

7 'Light nouns'

Up to date, light forms have only been discussed of verbs and never of other lexical categories. Nouns, however, can be found on a cline as well when they gradually reduce their semantic contribution to the construction they are a part of (cf. Mattissen 2004).

On the one hand, nouns undergo lexicalisation from a full noun to a cranberry morpheme (e.g. (17)) or a derivative (e.g. German *Zeug* 'things' in *Flugzeug* 'plane' (lit. 'fly-thing'), *Waschzeug* 'toiletries' (lit. 'washing-things'), *Klebzeug* 'goop' (lit. 'gluing-thing')). On the other, nouns grammaticalise into classifiers, instrumental markers, local relators, adpositions, applicatives, causatives, nominalisers, complementisers or conjunctions. In the transitional phase, the forms constitute a special delimited category that is different from both a full noun and an affix. They are functional carriers and are combined with a lexical carrier in an analytic or a synthetic construction. On this basis, it is argued here that relevant forms may be regarded as 'light nouns', in analogy to Light Verbs.

Such 'light nouns' are found in both non-polysynthetic and polysynthetic languages of the compositional type, and in the latter type start out from noun incorporation. However, whereas 'light nouns' in non-polysynthetic constructions tend to be grammaticalised into adpositions and complementisers or conjunctions, 'light nouns' in polysynthetic constructions tend to be grammaticalised into classifiers, instrumental markers, applicative and causative markers. Nevertheless, adposition-like markers ("relators") occur as well.

7.1 'Light nouns' in non-polysynthetic languages

Pertinent examples of 'light nouns' in non-polysynthetic languages are pre-stages of adpositions (e.g. (36a)), complementisers and conjunctions (e.g. (36b)). In German, the 'light noun' *Hilfe* 'help' is still recognisable as noun and still triggers the genitive of the complement (*eines Fadens* in (36a)), not the dative or accusative as older prepositions do, but its semantic change (it is used with inanimate referents that cannot actively 'help') and the fact that *mithilfe* may already be written as one word show that it is being grammaticalised to a preposition.

Japanese has the complementiser *koto* which is still formally identical to the full noun *koto* 'thing' and still bears case marking in its complementising function, i.e. it still is a functional carrier, but has already become part of the complementiser paradigm. In this paradigm, the complementisers *koto*, *no* (NML), *to* (QUO) and *yô* (Similative) are used to distinguish complements of different evidentiality types (cf. (36b-d)).

(36) a. German
   mit Hilfe / mithilfe (eines Fadens) 'with the help of, by (a thread)'
   b. Japanese   (Mattissen 1995: 4.5.3.1.1)
   *Matsushita-san=ga   jishoku-shi-ta   **koto=o**   kii-ta.*
   M.-Mr/Ms=NOM   stepdown-do-PST   thing=ACC   hear-PST
   "I heard (about the fact) that Mr/Ms M. stepped down."
   c. *Matsushita-san=ga   jishoku-shi-ta   **no=o**   kii-ta.*
   M.-Mr/Ms=NOM   stepdown-do-PST   NML=ACC   hear-PST
   "I heard (with my own ears) that Mr/Ms M. stepped down."
   d. *Matsushita-san=ga   jishoku-shi-ta   **to**   kii-ta.*
   M.-Mr/Ms=NOM   stepdown-do-PST   QUO   hear-PST
   "I heard (from someone) that Mr/Ms M. stepped down."

Adpositions, complementisers and conjunctions play a minor role in polysynthetic languages because they are function words encoding syntactic relations, which in polysynthetic languages are preferably encoded via complex – polysynthetic – word forms.

7.2 'Light nouns' in polysynthetic languages

Incorporated nouns in polysynthetic languages can lose their nominal status and/ or their connection to a full noun, and their semantic contribution to the construction may become less concrete and more functional, so that the incorporating verb becomes the sole main lexical carrier. In this stage, the (de)nominal element is in a transitional phase in which it reminiscent of a LV in a polysynthetic language.

In polysynthetic Greenlandic, the "dummy root" *pi-* has a carrier function. It cannot be traced back to a noun but takes the position only a noun root can appear in in a polysynthetic form, and it bears the verbalisers, which cannot form free verb forms on their own otherwise.

(37) Greenlandic (Fortescue 1984: 320–324)
    a. *Hansi   illu-qar-puq*
       H.   house-VBL:exist-IND.3s
       "Hansi has a house"
    b. *Hansi   illu-mik   **pi**-qar-puq*
       H.   house-INS dummy-VBL:exist-IND.3s
       "Hansi has a house"

In Haida, there are forms from nouns with mostly body part semantics that serve as instrumental markers which may be treated as 'light nouns':

(38) Haida (Swanton 1911: 221–226)

instrumental lexical affix		lexical root
st!a-	'by kicking'	'foot'
sL!-	'with the fingers'	'hand'
k!ut-	'with the lips'	'lips'
xAñ-	'with the face'	'face'
χi-	'with the arms'	'arm, wing'
Lu-	'by canoe'	'canoe'

'Light nouns' with a relational function similar to adpositions exist in Nivkh. They are relational nouns that appear in N+N(+case) constructions or in N+N+incorporating verb constructions, for instance *vəj* 'bottom' in (39a, b), *erq* 'side; in/from the direction' and *qʻomi* 'flank; next to' (in (39d, e)). Their appearance as free noun forms in texts (e.g. in (39c)) varies.

(39) Nivkh (Gruzdeva 1997: 144; Jakobson 1971: 78; Savel'eva/Taksami 1970: 150)
    a. *utkuoʁla   tər-vəj-uin   pʻləv-ḍ*
       boy   table-under-LOC hide-IND/NML
       "the boy hid under the table"
    b. *ño-vəj-si-ḍ*
       barn-under-put-IND/NML
       "s.o. puts sth. under the barn"
    c. *ñi   qʻomi   qʻo-ḍ-ra*
       1s   flank   hurt-IND/NML-HILI
       "my flank hurts"
    d. *kʻu   qʻotr-qʻomi-ra-ḍ-ra*
       arrow bear-flank-strike-IND/NML-HILI
       "the arrow hit the bear's flank"

e. əvñ   mu-χomi-si-ja
    oar   boat-flank-put-IMP.S
    "Put the oar next to the boat!"

Because of the nominal character of the forms, they enter into N + N constructions of which they are the head and bear case, and they appear in the incorporee position within a complex verb form (as in (39b, d, e); Mattissen 2003: 1.3.1, 3.3.1). Case markers, on the other hand, cannot be combined with each other and are prohibited from complex-internal position in Nivkh, they are right-margin markers only. Also, there are no free adpositions in Nivkh (Mattissen 2003: 3.8.1, 2023). So, the relational nouns are best regarded as 'light nouns', forming a closed class, but not being fully grammaticalised to case (yet). In distinction to full nouns, they have lost or reduced their occurrence as free forms and their semantic features, e.g. because they are compatible with inanimates, which do not have body parts, and can be used in more and more contexts.

The development from noun incorporation via a 'light noun' stage to a verbal classifier can be illustrated with Gunwinjgu and Caddo examples. When in a noun incorporation construction the incorporee has no referential properties (e.g. is inaccessible to subsequent anaphora; cf. Mattissen (2023)), Gunwinjgu allows a verb-external noun in the same clause with (nearly) synonymous (40a) or – one step further – hyponymic semantics (40b) to the incorporee. The verb-external noun may even be the full noun formally identical to the incorporee. The incorporee then has become a 'light noun'.

(40) Gunwinjgu   (Mithun 1984: 867)
   a. bene-ṟed-naŋ   ṟed-gereŋeni
      3d-camp-saw   camp-new
      "they saw a freshly made camp"
   b. bene-dulg-naŋ   mangaralaljmayn
      3d-tree-saw   cashew.nut
      "they saw a cashew tree"

As a further step on the cline towards a verbal classifier, a one-to-many relation between the 'light noun' incorporee and a verb external noun arises, laying the foundation for classification: one and the same incorporee co-occurs with more and more nouns of different semantic domains (cf. Mattissen (2023)). Example (41) shows the root of Caddo $\check{c}^{\prime}ah\text{-}uh$, the free form of 'eye', as an incorporee with different verb-external nouns.

(41) Caddo (Mithun 1984: 865)
 a. *kassiʔ háh-ʔi-čʔá-sswíʔ-saʔ*
  bead PROG-prefix-eye-string-PROG
  "she is stringing beads"
 b. *kaʔás háh-ʔi-čʔah-ʔíʔ-saʔ*
  plum PROG-prefix-eye-grow-PROG
  "plums are growing"

The noun root is still recognisable, but has taken on a classificational function and as such fits the category of 'light noun'. For the full path from different valency types of noun incorporation towards classificatory verbs see Mattissen (2006, 2023).

In Murrinhpatha (Southern Daly), Marrithiyel (Western Daly) and Ngan'gityemerri, incorporated body part nouns are on a grammaticalisation cline towards applicative markers, but still recognisable as nouns. In (42), this is true of 'hand' which has become a source applicative; the grammaticalisation is manifest in the semantics in (42b), as in spoken language you cannot listen to the hands.

(42) Murrinhpatha (Nordlinger 2017: 799, 800)
 a. *dirran-ngi-ma-thith=dim*
  3sS.28.NFUT-1sO-hand-stare=3sS.sit.NFUT
  "she is staring at my hands"
 b. *bim-pun-ma-yepup*
  1sS.hear.NFUT-3pO-hand/APPL-listen
  "I heard it from them"

In Ngan'gityemerri, the 'light noun' *muy* 'eye' already had a comitative applicative function in the 1930s (cf. (43a)) and has developed into the comitative applicative maker -*mi* (43b) since. The phonological reduction and the constructional change tied to the grammaticalisation could be witnessed from 1930s to date (Nordlinger 2017:801).

(43) Ngan'gityemerri (Reid 1990: 139)
 a. *wab yenim-muy* → b. *yenim-mi-wab*
  sit 3sS.go.PRS-eye/APPL   3sS.go.PRS-APPL-sit
  "he sits with him"   "he sits with him"

In Marrithiyel, it is also the 'light noun' -*mi* 'eye' that has acquired a comitative applicative function, whereas the 'light noun' -*ma* 'belly' has taken on the function of a causative of emotion.

(44) Marrithiyel (Nordlinger 2017: 801)
gumun-ngi-ma-tjarr mana yigin-wa mubungandi
3sS.R.paint-1sO-belly/APPL-sad.PRS brother 1s-PURP poor.fellow
'It makes me feel sad for my brother, poor bugger.'

Evidence for the grammaticalisation are the structural changes: whereas an incorporated body part noun appears either before or after the verb stem, in the applicative use the morpheme can only appear in pre-stem position (Nordlinger 2017:801).

In all the stages in which nouns still keep their form and nominal properties, such as inflection, or their usual position in incorporation, but have lost or reduced their semantic contribution to the entire construction, they are considered 'light nouns' here because of the parallels to LVs, which, too, keep their form and inflection while not contributing their (full) lexical semantics any longer. In addition, 'light nouns' and LVs both take over functions in the domains of valence-changing operations and classification.

This seems to be all the more true for the languages with verbal classifiers in which morphemes occur in the LV position (cf. Section 6.1) that are formally identical or very similar to nouns (in boldprint in (45)), e.g. in Murrinhpatha:

(45) Murrinhpatha (Nordlinger 2017:788)
   a. ku tumtum **mam**-lerrkperrk
       nounclass:ANIM egg 1sS.hands(8).NFUT-crush
       "I crushed the egg in my hand."
   b. nanthi karlay kanhi-ka
       nounclass:THING fishing.net this-TOP
       nguma-dharday-deyida-nu-neme
       1dS.hands(8).FUT-descend-again-FUT-PAUCAL.MASC
       "We will drop this fishing net down again."

The forms *mam-* and *nguma-* serve as verbal classifiers in the same way as the forms in (20) do (cf. Nordlinger 2017).

8 Resume

In the preceding, LVs have been worked out to exist in polysynthetic languages as well. LVs in polysynthetic languages occur mostly in a synthetic formation with their lexical carriers and are best seen as a stage on a lexicalisation or grammaticalisation path. They are completely parallel in form and function to LVs in non-polysynthetic languages, which partly also exhibit synthetic LVCs. Both non-polysynthetic and polysynthetic LVCs grammaticalise into verbal classifiers, aspectoid markers, valency and modal functions, and in these domains form paradigms with markers of different morpho-syntactic statuses. The characteristic morphosyntactic features of compositional polysynthesis thus do not block LVs.

In addition, it has been argued to recognise 'light nouns' as stages on a lexicalisation or grammaticalisation cline from nouns to derivatives or opaque stem elements on the one hand and a range of grammatical morphemes on the other. 'Light nouns' have gradually reduced their lexical contribution to the construction they are part of. In polysynthetic languages, they are incorporated into verbs and are on a lexicalisation or a grammaticalisation cline towards classifiers, instrumental markers, applicative and causative markers. In this, they differ from 'light nouns' in non-polysynthetic languages, which tend to be grammaticalised into adpositions, complementisers and conjunctions, that is function words that play a minor role in polysynthetic languages. However, 'light nouns' functioning as adposition-like relational morphemes do occur in polysynthetic languages, as well.

Light Verbs and 'light nouns' have in common to take over functions in valence-changing and classification. Besides, the present study has also pointed out parallels between polysynthetic languages and Japanese, which has been identified as difficult to delimit from polysynthetic languages in several points (cf. Mattissen 2003, 2004).

Abbreviations

3d>3sn	3rd person dual acting on 3rd singular neuter
A	actor
ABL	ablative
ACC	accusative
ADJ	adjective
ALL	allative
ANIM	animate
APP	applicative
CAUS	causative
CPL	completive
CV	converb
DET	determiner
DETV	determinative
DUR	durative
ENU	enumerative
EV	epenthetic vowel
EXP	experiential
FUT	future

GEN	genitive
HAB	habitual
HILI	highlighting focus
IMP	imperative
IMPF	imperfective
IND	indicative
INS	instrumental
ITER	iterative
IVF	incorporating verb form
LV (C)	Light Verb (Construction)
NEG	negation
NFUT	non-future
NML	nominalisation
NOM	nominative
NPST	non-past
O	object
PERF	perfect
PL	plural
POT	potential
PROG	progressive
PRS	present
PST	past
PTCL	participle
PTV	perfective
PURP	purposive
QUO	quotative
RECI	reciprocal
REFL	reflexive
S	subject
SCON	stative continuative
SRFL	semireflexive
TOP	topic
TRSL	translocative
u	undergoer
VBL	verbaliser

References

Bisang, Walter. 1995. Verb serialization and converbs – differences and similarities. In Martin Haspelmath & Ekkehard König (eds.), *Converbs in Cross-Linguistic Perspective*, 37–188. Berlin/New York: Mouton de Gruyter.

Butt, Miriam. 2003. The light verb jungle. *Harvard Working Papers in Linguistics* 9. 1–49.

Bybee, Joan, Revere Perkins & William Pagliuca. 1994. *The Evolution of Grammar. Tense, Aspect, and Modality in the Languages of the World*. Chicago: University of Chicago Press.

Drossard, Werner. 2002. Paleosiberian Ket as a polysynthetic language (with special reference to complex verbs). In Nicholas Evans & Hans-Jürgen Sasse (eds.), *Problems of Polysynthesis*, 223–56. Berlin: Akademie.
Evans, Nicholas. 2003. *Bininj Gun-wok*. 2 vols. Canberra: Pacific Linguistics.
Evans, Nicholas, Marianne Mithun & Michael Fortescue (eds.), 2017. *Handbook of Polysynthesis*. Oxford: Oxford University Press.
Fortescue, Michael. 1984. *West Greenlandic*. London: Croom Helm.
Gruzdeva, Ekaterina. 1997. Nivxskij jazyk. In Aleksandr P. Volodin (ed.), *Jazyki mira. Paleoaziatskie jazyki*, 139–154. Moscow: Indrik.
Haas, Mary R. 1941. *Tunica*. Extract from Franz Boas (ed.), *Handbook of American Indian Languages* IV. New York: Augustin Publ.
Harris, Alice C. 2008. Light verbs as classifiers in Udi. *Diachronica* 25(2). 213–241.
Hercus, Luise A. 1994. *A Grammar of the Arabana-Wangkangurru Language*. Canberra: Australian National University.
Hopper, Paul J. & Elizabeth Traugott. 2003. *Grammaticalization*. 2nd ed. Cambridge: Cambridge University Press.
Jakobson, Roman. 1971. Notes on Gilyak. In Roman Jakobson, *Selected Writings* II, 72–97. The Hague/Paris: Mouton.
Karimi-Doostan, Gholamhossein. 2008. Event structure of verbal nouns and light verbs. In Simin Karimi, Vida Samiian & Donald Stilo (eds.), *Aspects of Iranian Linguistics*, 209–226. Newcastle: Cambridge Scholars Publishing.
Lane, Jonathan. 2007. *Kalam serial verb constructions*. Canberra: Pacific Linguistics.
Mattissen, Johanna. 1995. *Das Nomen im Japanischen: Abgrenzung und Subklassifizierung*. (Arbeiten des Sonderforschungsbereichs 282 "Theorie des Lexikons" Nr. 65). Düsseldorf: Heinrich-Heine-Universität Düsseldorf.
Mattissen, Johanna. 2003. *Dependent-Head Synthesis in Nivkh. A Contribution to a Typology of Polysynthesis*. Amsterdam: Benjamins.
Mattissen, Johanna. 2004. The missing link between different types of polysynthetic languages. *Chicago Linguistic Society* 38(2). 386–399.
Mattissen, Johanna. 2006. The ontology and diachrony of polysynthesis. In Dieter Wunderlich (ed.), *Advances in the Theory of the Lexicon*, 287–353. Berlin/New York: Mouton de Gruyter.
Mattissen, Johanna. 2017. Subtypes of polysynthesis. In Nicholas Evans, Marianne Mithun, & Michael Fortescue (eds.), *The Oxford Handbook of Polysynthesis*, 70–98. Oxford: Oxford University Press.
Mattissen, Johanna. 2023. Incorporation. In Peter Ackema, Sabrina Bendjaballah, Eulàlia Bonet & Antonio Fábregas (eds.), *The Wiley Blackwell Companion to Morphology*. Hoboken: Wiley-Blackwell.
McGregor, William B. 2002. *Verb classification in Australian languages*. Berlin/New York: Mouton de Gruyter.
Mithun, Marianne. 1984. The evolution of noun incorporation. *Language* 60(4). 847–893.
Nordlinger, Rachel. 2015. Inflection in Murrinh-Patha. In Matthew Baerman (ed.), *The Oxford Handbook of Inflection*, 491–519. Oxford: Oxford University Press.
Nordlinger, Rachel. 2017. The languages of the Daly River region (Northern Australia). In Nicholas Evans, Marianne Mithun & Michael Fortescue (eds.), *The Oxford Handbook of Polysynthesis*, 782–807. Oxford: Oxford University Press.
Payne, Doris L. 1990. Morphological characteristics of Lowland South American languages. In Doris L. Payne (ed.), *Amazonian Linguistics. Studies in Lowland South American Languages*, 213–41. Austin: University of Texas Press.

Pawley, Andrew. 1993. A language which defies description by ordinary means. In William A. Foley (ed.), *The Role of Theory in Language Description*, 87–129. Berlin/New York: Mouton de Gruyter.

Reid, Nicholas J. 1990. *Ngan'gityemerri: A language of the Daly River Region, Northern Territory of Australia*. Canberra: ANU dissertation.

Reid, Nicholas J. 2011. *Ngan'gityemerri*. München: LINCOM.

Rood, David S. 1976. *Wichita Grammar*. New York: Garland.

Sasse, Hans-Jürgen. 2002. Lexicological and lexicographic problems of word families in Cayuga. In Nicholas D. Evans & Hans-Jürgen Sasse (eds), *Problems of Polysynthesis*, 203–221. Berlin: Akademie.

Savel'eva, Valentina N. & Čuner M. Taksami. 1970. *Nivxsko-Russkij Slovar'*. [Nivkh-Russian Dictionary] Moscow: Sovetskaja Enciklopedija.

Schultze-Berndt, Eva. 2015. Complex verbs, simple alternations: valency and verb classes in Jaminjung. In Andrej Malchukovj & Bernard Comrie (eds.), *Valency Classes in the World's Languages: Case Studies from Austronesia, the Pacific, the Americas, and Theoretical Outlook*. Vol. 2, 1117–1162. Berlin/Boston: De Gruyter Mouton.

Swanton, John R. 1911. Haida. In Franz Boas (ed.), *Handbook of American Indian Languages*. Part 1, 205–282. (Bureau of American Ethnology Bulletin 40). Washington: Government Printing Office.

Tamura, Suzuko. 2000. *The Ainu Language*. Tokyo: Sanseido.

Watkins, Laurel J. 1984. *A Grammar of Kiowa*. Lincoln: University of Nebraska Press.

Werner, Heinrich. 1997. *Die ketische Sprache*. Wiesbaden: Harrassowitz.

Lu Lu and Chu-Ren Huang

11 A diachronic insight into the aspectual meaning in Light Verb Constructions

A case study in Mandarin Chinese

Abstract: This study takes a diachronic perspective to look at the different aspectual encodings in Light Verb Constructions. By using the Light Verb Constructions in Mandarin Chinese as examples, we observe and generalise the patterns of aspectual encodings in GIVE group Light Verbs, including *jiyu, yuyi,* and *jiayi,* with the basic meaning of 'give.' Assuming that Light Verbs typically follow the grammaticalisation path from independent lexical verbs to grammatical morphemes, we propose that the various realisations of aspectuality can be explained by the different grammaticalisation stages of the three verbs: the verb *jiayi* is the most grammaticalised followed by *yuyi* and *jiyu*. Their grammaticalisation status is evidenced by the light/independent verb usages of the three verbs in a synchronic corpus of Mandarin Chinese. This corpus-based study on Mandarin LVCs within the framework of Construction Grammar complements the discussion on the lightness of Light Verbs across languages.

Keywords: Light Verb Constructions, Mandarin Chinese, aspectual encoding, GIVE Light Verbs, corpus data, diachrony and synchrony, grammaticalisation

1 Introduction

The term *Light Verb* (henceforth, LV), coined by Jespersen (1942), refers to verbs such as *have* and *give* in complex predicates;[1] for example, *have a bath* and *give a push*, where the main semantic content is provided not by the verb, but by the action nominal[2] (AN, thereafter) *bath* and *push*, respectively. Therefore, the meaning of Light Verb Constructions (LVCs, hereafter) differs from usual predicate structures or direct aggregation of its semantic components (e.g. in *have a bath*, its meaning is different from the combined literal meaning of *have* 'to possess' and *bath*). As

---

[1] The scope of the complex predicate is limited to an LV pairing with an action nominal, cf. Brinton and Akimoto (1999: 2) and Sundquist (2018).
[2] The working definition of action nominal in this study follows Comrie (1976: 178): It specifically refers to the nominal complements that encode an event, the argument structure of which is similar to the corresponding verbs.

a crucial type of complex predicate, it poses a number of challenges in semantic annotation and understanding.

The light semantic content in LVs can be found in many languages, for instance, Japanese (e.g. Grimshaw and Mester 1988), Hindi (e.g. Mohanan 1994), Urdu (e.g. Butt 1995), French (e.g. Giry-Schneider 1978), Persian (e.g. Golshaie 2016), Swedish (Sundquist 2018), Irish (e.g. Nolan 2014), and Malayalam (e.g. Jayasselan 1983). For example, the Japanese *suru* functions as an LV with little semantic content in (1), which contrasts with its use as a regular two-place independent verb (thus 'heavy'; henceforth IV) in (2).

(1) Taroo ga   eigo   no   benkyoo o   suru
    Taroo NOM English GEN   study   ACC LV
    'Taroo studies English.'   (Miyamoto 1997: ii)

(2) Taroo ga   gorufu o   suru
    Taroo NOM golf   ACC do
    'Taroo plays golf.'   (Miyamoto 1997: ii)

An increase in linguistic exploration across languages has brought into question the semantic bleaching of LVs. In Urdu, for example, LVs seem to condition the meaning and morphosyntactic choices of the whole construction in (3). Although the LVs *par* 'fall' and *ḍaal* 'put' both occur with *ciik^h* 'scream' in Urdu, the LV in (3a), which involves an involuntary action, is preceded by an unmarked nominative subject. However, the LV *ḍaal* 'put' in (3b), which denotes a conscious control over the action, requires the marked ergative case on the subject argument. Based on this observation, Butt (1995) argues that it is the particular LV *ḍaal* 'put' that contributes to the meaning of conscious choices of a given action, which further assigns a marked ergative case to the subject in (3b). This suggests that the so-called 'LV' is not completely 'light,' nor fully devoid of its meaning.

(3) a. vo   ciik^h paṛ-aa
       pron=NOM scream   fall-PRF.M.SG
       'He began screaming suddenly (despite himself).'
    b. us=ne   ciik^h ḍaal-aa
       pron=ERG scream   put-PRF.M.SG
       'He screamed violently (on purpose).'   (Butt 1995: 110)

In addition to this feature, what is typologically recognised in the literature is the closely related historical association between LVs and their IV counterparts (see Butt 2003, 2010; Butt and Lahiri 2002, amongst others). However, the question concerning whether LVs originated from their corresponding IVs is not without contention. In this study, as is often posited (see Hopper and Traugott 1993; Hook 1991, amongst others), LVs are assumed to enter the grammaticalisation[3] cline and are prone to be further grammaticalised into an auxiliary, as shown in (4).

(4) IV[4]> (vector verb/LV) > auxiliary> clitic>affix
(based on Hopper and Traugott 1993: 108)

The association of semantic content between the LV and its corresponding IV is illustrated in (5). In Persian, the term *xordan* is used in the literal sense as 'eat' in (5a), whereas the meaning shown in (5b) is 'bleached.' Golshaie (2016) further examined the family of *xordan* constructions with corpus data. Although the meaning of *xordan*-LVCs seem unrelated to 'eating' and can be as varied as 'swear' and 'regret/grief,' Golshaie argues that those LVCs still retain some central characteristics of the heavy verb meaning 'eat,' and can arguably be seen as an extension of the core sense 'eat' (see also Family 2014). For example, the meaning 'swear' was motivated by the use of *xordan* 'to eat': in Ancient Iran, people suspected of lying were forced to drink a chemical substance to prove that they were not lying. This example demonstrates the influence (or 'inheritance,' see its interpretation in Section 2.1) of historical information on the current usages of LVs.

(5) a. Heavy verb:
       Maryam   sib   râ   xor-d.
       Maryam   apple   ACC   eat-PST.3SG
       'Marya ate the apple.'
    b. LV:
       Maryam   xeili   ghosse   xor-d.
       Maryam   very   grief   eat-PST.3SG
       'Maryam grieved very much.'   (Golshaie 2016: 22)

LVCs, as a cross-linguistic phenomenon, are also observed in Chinese (e.g. Lin 2001; Butt 2003; Feng 2005). In Mandarin Chinese, verbs such as *jinxing* 'carry out' and *jiayi* 'give' are regarded as LVs (Zhu 1982, 1985), and they can be further categorised

---

[3] In our study, grammaticalisation is understood as the movements from a lexical item to a grammatical morpheme, which is defined by Kuryłowicz (1965: 69): "Grammaticalisation consists in the increase of the range of a morpheme advancing from a lexical to a grammatical or from a less grammatical to a more grammatical status, e.g. from a derivative formant to an inflectional one."
[4] The term IV in our study roughly corresponds to the notion of 'full verb' in Hopper and Traugott (1993).

into DO and GIVE groups based on their basic verb sense. In this study, we will analyse GIVE LVs, including *jiyu* 'give', *yuyi* 'give', and *jiayi* 'give', all meaning 'give' (see Sections 3 and 4). Similar to other languages illustrated above, Xu et al. (2020) showed that some Mandarin LVs are interchangeable in certain contexts, giving weight to the hypothesis that they lack the ability to contribute to the meaning of the sentence. On the other hand, in other contexts, the same Mandarin LVs cannot be switched. For example, *jiayi* tends to take accomplishment events, the feature of which is not observed in other LVs. This finding underlines the fact that LVs still have some unique lexical meaning.

In what follows, we will use *jiyu* of the GIVE group to illustrate the prototype construction, which is assumed to be the most frequent example of a given category (Schmid 2000). As shown from the data retrieved from the ToRCH 2009 corpus (Xu 2014 see Section 3.1), in Contemporary Mandarin,[5] the GIVE LV *jiyu* in (6a) is followed by the AN complement *guanzhu* 'attention,' and jointly, the two items form a complex predicate, which roughly has the same meaning as the corresponding verbal form of AN, i.e., *guanzhu* 'attend.'

(6) a. Laoshi   dui   ruoxiao   xuesheng jiyu-le   gengduo guanzhu.
       teacher   to   vulnerable student   LV-ASP   more   attention
       'Teachers paid more attention to vulnerable students.'   (ToRCH 2009)[6]
    b. Laoshi   gengduo guanzhu   ruoxiao   xuesheng.
       teacher   more   attend.to vulnerable student
       'Teachers attend more to vulnerable students.'

The undergoer argument *ruoxiao xuesheng* 'vulnerable students,' introduced by the preposition *dui* 'to,' is placed pre-verbally as an oblique argument. This is different from the prototypical order of constituents in Mandarin Chinese, where an undergoer argument is usually located at the postverbal position. The paraphrase

---

[5] The periodisation in this study follows Sun (1996): *shanggu hanyu* 'Old Chinese' (500 B.C-A.D. 200), *zhonggu hanyu* 'Middle Chinese' (201-1000), *jindai hanyu* 'Early Mandarin' (1001-1900), and *xiandai hanyu* 'Modern mandarin' (1901-present). Furthermore, we adopt 'Classical Chinese' as a cover term to refer to both Old Chinese and Middle Chinese. We refer to the language retrieved from the ToRCH 2009 corpus as *dangdai hanyu* 'Contemporary Chinese.' Contemporary Chinese is used to refer to the current version of Mandarin (or Modern Chinese) after the year 2000. Note that the periods described above are intended to give a rough idea only, and do not imply a clean division; they are adopted simply for better illustration and discussion.

[6] The sources of examples used in this article are identified in brackets immediately following the translation in the last line. Additionally, if no source follows, the sentences are conceived by the author and judged by the ten Mandarin native speakers (see Section 3.1), as exemplified by example (7).

of (6a) in example (6b) shows the prototypical word order in Mandarin Chinese with the undergoer argument placed after the verb *guanzhu*. In this study, the term LVC refers to the complex predicate (i.e. the LV and the AN) and its participants; the prototypical construction with a preposed oblique constituent, as can be seen in (6a), is also known as the 'oblique construction.'

An interesting property associated with Mandarin LVCs, in particular with the verb *jiayi*, is that not all LVCs can take aspectual markers (see Hu and Fan 1995; Diao 2004; Kuo 2011). For example, in the one-million-word ToRCH 2009 Corpus (see Section 3.1 for a brief description), none of *jiayi*-LVCs can take an aspectual marker in Mandarin Chinese. That is to say, the aspectual marker *-le* has to be removed from the *jiayi*-LVC in (7), whereas it can remain in the *jiyu*-LVCs in example (6a). This seems to imply that LVs in Mandarin Chinese, similar to the Urdu *ḍaal*-LVC, do maintain some inherent semantic content to date.

(7) Women dui zhege wenti jiayi(*-le) kaolü.
    we   to   this   issue   LV-ASP   consider
    'We thought carefully about this issue.'

In light of this observation, we attempt to describe and examine the meaning implied in Mandarin LVCs with naturally occurring corpus data in this study. In Section 2, we will present the tenets of the particular strand of Construction Grammar adopted in this study, including the notion of construction, the emergence of constructional meaning, and the usage-based grammarians' view on language change and diachronic inheritance. Corpus methodology and observations of the GIVE LVCs will be detailed in Section 3, based on which a hypothesis, regarding the different degrees of aspectuality among the three GIVE LVCs, is presented at the end of the section. A thorough examination of the empirical evidence from corpora, in support of the hypothesis, will be shown in Section 4. This paper concludes with a cross-linguistic discussion on the semantic 'heaviness' of LVCs in Section 5.

2 Constructional framework

In this section, we will introduce some of the main assumptions associated with usage-based construction grammar, which is the main framework of this study. Specifically, we will show the interpretation of construction, the emergence of constructional meaning, and the constructionists' view of language change and development.

2.1 The notion of construction

Prior to our examination of the corpus data concerning LVCs, we will present the tenets of the particular strands of Construction Grammar (Goldberg 1995, 2006; Bybee 2010) adopted in this paper.

Although the interpretation of '(grammatical) construction' varies in constructionist circles, construction is widely viewed as a form meaning pairing. In particular, Goldberg (2006: 5) defines constructions as a linguistic pattern, some aspects of whose form or function 'is not strictly predictable from its component parts or from other constructions recognized to exist.' Furthermore, Goldberg claims that occurrences with sufficient frequency can also be seen as constructions. In the current study, we will adopt Goldberg's (2006) understanding of construction because it is in line with the usage-based idea of language development, which shows that constructions are formed due to repeated entrenchment in the cognitive system.

Constructions are structured and represented in a taxonomic network, wherein each construction is a node that is established in a continuum from the most schematic to the most substantial (Croft 2001: 25). The network makes sense of the association between what is predictable and what is arbitrary, which often entails motivation. In Construction Grammar, motivation can be used to explain why it is natural for a lexical unit to mean what it means, or why it makes sense that a specific meaning is realised by a particular lexical item and not others. The link between constructions can be captured by the concept of 'inheritance,' a central notion in many versions of Construction Grammar. In Goldberg's (1995: 67) system, motivation can be used to explain why formally similar constructions are also semantically similar (namely, the semantic and formal overlaps of a construction), because "the inheritance network lets us capture generalisations across constructions while at the same time allowing for subregularities and exceptions" (Goldberg 1995: 67). The crucial characteristic in this hierarchical network, espoused by some versions of Construction Grammar (e.g. Lakoff 1987; Goldberg 1995, 2006), is the 'default inheritance', where each node inherits diachronic and synchronic properties from its dominating nodes. The inheritance mechanism is crucial for solving the aspectual issue of Mandarin LVCs presented in Section 1. This is because the inheritance relation, especially the one from diachronic features, enables us to capture the non-conflicting information of LVCs between diachrony and synchrony, whose relationship will be detailed in Section 2.3.

2.2 Constructional meaning

Another issue that pertains to the notion of construction, especially one whose meaning is not lexicalized by any of its components, is how the constructional meaning comes into being. In Goldberg's (1995, 2006) analysis of argument structure constructions, she hypothesised that constructional meaning originates with the meaning of the verbs that frequently occur in a given syntactic pattern. For instance, since the most frequent (50%) verb in the ditransitive construction is *give* (according to Perek's (2009) study on the spoken part of the British component of the International Corpus of English), the syntactic form, as a consequence, denotes the meaning 'X CAUSE Y TO HAVE Z', which exactly reflects the meaning of *give*. That is to say, there is a verb to lexicalise the schematic meaning of the construction. However, in Perek and Lemmens' (2010) case study of the English *at*-constructions (e.g. *look at* and *shout at*), they observed that there is a discrepancy between the meaning of the most frequently occurring *look at* construction denoting a visual meaning and the schematic meaning of 'directed action,' which is generalised from all *at*-constructions. Hence, they argue that the schematic constructional meaning more plausibly emerges from the shared commonalities abstracting over a number of instances.

As for the meaning in a specific construction, Michaelis (1998, 2004) distinguishes the meaning contributed by the verbs from the one by the constructions, and further argues that the meaning specified by the verb will yield to the constructional meaning if the two are in conflict. In Michaelis's analysis of aspectual meaning, she found that the aspectual meanings encoded by the lexical item and by the whole construction are not compatible in (8). For instance, the stative aspectual meaning denoted by the state verb *live* occurs in the morphosyntax of a schematic progressive construction typically denoted by an event verb.

(8) I am living on Pearl Street. (Michaelis 2004: 30)

To reconcile this incompatibility, where different values are assigned to a given attribute, a coercion mechanism is assumed, by which constructional requirements are favoured over lexical constraints. The governing rule, according to Michaelis (2004: 25), is referred to as the override principle, as quoted in (9).

(9) The override principle:
If a lexical item is semantically incompatible with its morphosyntactic context, the meaning of the lexical item conforms to the meaning of the structure in which it is embedded. Michaelis (2004: 25)

In consideration of the ideas in Perek and Lemmens (2010) and Michaelis (1998, 2004), we assume that constructional meaning may not always be associated with its componential lexical meaning. Instead, it emerges from the abstract generalisations of a number of instances, and it is favoured over the lexical meaning if the constructional and the lexical meanings are not compatible in a given context.

2.3 Constructionists' view on language change

To better capture the motivation and inheritance among constructions, usage-based constructional grammarians take advantage of historical data. They assert that change occurs as language is used (Bybee 2010; Bybee, Perkins and Pagliuca 1994; Croft 2000; Heine and Kuteva 2002, 2007; Lehmann 1985, among others), that is, language evolves through the natural process of daily use, and therefore change is not abrupt, but instead it is continuous and gradual. In this paper, we adopt this view. Specifically, instead of arising overnight, language change actually evolves in an incremental way, in which new constructions build on early ones (e.g., Heine and Reh 1984; Heine and Kuteva 2002, 2007; Lehmann 1985; Tomasello 2003; Bybee and Hopper 2001; Bybee 2010, 2013; Traugott 1989; Traugott and Koening 1991; Goldberg and Ackerman 2001; Petré 2016). Language renovation, according to Heine and Reh (1984), more often takes place before the existing material has disappeared, and therefore the old form "tends to be retained in some way or other" (Heine and Reh 1984: 70).

Building upon this, Bybee (1998, 2007, 2010, 2013, 2015) believes that language structures are not strictly bounded nor fixed, but can be viewed as emergent. That is, language expressions are recreated based on experience or repetition and they are recorded in memory. Those memories are linked with one another in an ongoing way. As a result, it is possible to explain synchronic properties based on how language structures have developed. Bybee clearly addresses the inseparability of synchronic analysis from diachronic change: "the diachronic dimension is important [...] because the diachrony determines a great deal about synchronic distributions and meanings of forms" (Bybee 2010: 166, see also Bybee 1988; Goldberg and Ackerman 2001). As exemplified by Bybee (2010), the reason that the English negator *not* comes after (not before) the first auxiliary verb or copula verb (e.g. *do not, is not*) can be ascribed to grammaticalisation: *not* is derived from the negative morpheme *nā/nō* and a noun in direct object position *wiht* 'someone, something.' At the time when VO was the word order in English, the negative element followed the verb. This suggests that historical information can be passed down from earlier stages, and as a result, the newer linguistic formations are "heavily influenced by both immediate and long-range experience with language" (Bybee and Hopper 2001: 19).

Torrent (2015) takes the network of constructions into account in his analysis of the *para* infinitive family of constructions in Brazilian Portuguese; he argues that constructions change over time via grammaticalisation. He found that the inheritance from the Modified Purpose Construction (see example (10)) to the Imminent Time Construction (see example (13)) parallels a grammaticalisation process.

(10) Modified Purpose Construction
El   prestes   staua   pera   filhar   o   testemuyho (13th century)
he.NOM   ready   be.PST.3SG   for   take.INF the   testimony
'He was ready to testify.'   Torrent (2015: 197)

(11) Diaboos que   estavã   prestes pera tomar   as   almas
     devils   who   be.PST.3PL   ready   for   take.INF the   souls
     'Devils who were ready/about to take their souls.' (13th Century)
                                                             Torrent (2015: 197)

(12) Imminent Purpose Construction
     quando   tinha   apertada a   azcuma estava   prestes
     when   have.PST.3SG tight   the spear   be.PST.3SG   ready
     pera   errar
     for   miss.INF
     'When he held the spear tight, he was about to miss the target.' (15th Century)
                                                             Torrent (2015: 198)

(13) Imminent Time Construction
     Dom   Nuno   foi   ferido   no   rostro   e   esteve
     Dom   Nuno   be.PST.3SG   hurt.PART   in.the   face   and   be.PST.3SG
     pera se   vencer.
     for   self.3SG   win.INF
     'Dom Nuno was injured in the face and was about to be defeated.' (15th Century)
                                                             Torrent (2015: 198)

Specifically, in this process, *prestes* 'ready' fills the Adjective-Phrase position in the Modified Purpose Construction, which can only be interpreted according to its lexical meaning, see (10). However, the *prestes* in the context of example (11) gives rise to two different interpretations: the devils were ready to, or they were just about to take the souls. Conversely, the readiness reading was impossible in the 15th century; for example, in (12) where it is unlikely to be interpreted that the horseback rider is preparing to intentionally miss the target. Finally, the adjective is no longer present and the meaning of imminence occurs in (13). The emergence of the newly acquired construction is in line with the grammaticalisation process from a lexical construction to a more grammatical one.

The above assumption regarding the explanatory power of grammaticalisation is also substantiated by studies on Classical Chinese. Sun (2006) observes that synchronically speaking, grammaticalisation can be used to account for the variations of a given linguistic item in synchronic data. In his investigation of *de* (glossed as

DE₂ in this study and written as 得 in Chinese) in Modern Mandarin, Sun found that almost all of the uses that emerged during different historical periods have survived into Modern Mandarin. For example, *de*, as a lexical verb meaning 'have' in Modern Mandarin (e.g. *de gouloubing* 'have rickets') was actually derived from the meaning of 'obtain' used more than 2000 years ago (e.g. *de tianxia* 'obtain the world'). Additionally, the epistemic meaning of *de* as an affix in Modern Chinese (e.g. *kan-de-jian* look-DE-see 'can see') is suspected to have originated from the meaning of possibility as a verb in Classical Chinese (e.g. from *ji fu de cheng*, which literally translates to 'several axes possibly succeed' we obtain the meaning 'How many (strikes of) axes can do (it)?'). He further observes that the different grammatical status of *de* in Modern Mandarin (i.e. as a verb and an affix with different meanings) may result from different stages of grammaticalisation (for more illustration, see Sun (1996, Chapter 5)).

Throughout all of the aforementioned studies there is the assumption that the historical development of constructions can be used to account for their synchronic properties. In arguing that each construction must be motivated, Goldberg (2005: 17–18) appeals to grammaticalisation as one of the potential principles in order to better account for a particular form-meaning correspondence. As such, the following analysis will build on these foundations, which are expected to support the explanatory adequacy of grammaticalisation.

3 Corpus observation and proposal

Following the basic assumptions introduced in Section 2, we will present a corpus-based approach to investigate the aspectual properties in the GIVE LVCs introduced in Section 1. Based on the observation from corpus data, we take a diachronic perspective and put forward a hypothesis to justify the aspectual features of the three verbs.

3.1 Research methodology

In accordance with the cognitive commitment of the usage-based approach, we will use corpus data as the primary source to examine the syntactic and semantic changes of Mandarin LVCs.[7] As such, the ToRCH 2009 (Texts of Recent

---

7 In Mandarin Chinese, while spoken and written varieties have a lot in common, some lexical items and sentence structures may tend to occur in one variety of Mandarin Chinese rather than

Chinese[8]) Corpus (Xu 2013), a well-balanced written corpus of over one million words (1,087,619 words or 1,703,635 Chinese characters[9]) in Mandarin Chinese, was used. Patterned after the Brown Corpus (Francis and Kucera 1979), the ToRCH 2009 Corpus, which collects texts published in 2009 (± 1 year), covers four broad text categories: press, general prose, learned writing, and fiction. The broad collection of data is meant to represent usages from all text types. Similar to the Brown corpus, the ToRCH 2009 Corpus also consists of 500 samples of approximately 2,000 words each. This corpus is readily accessible both online[10] and offline. Queries of the LVs in question were entered into the search interface of the ToRCH 2009 Corpus, which returned 109 occurrences of *jiyu-*, 70 occurrences of *yuyi-*, and 67 occurrences of *jiayi-*constructions.

Although the descriptions and analyses of LVCs largely rely on the ToRCH 2009 data, we will also, briefly, consult the CCL (Centre for Chinese Linguistics) corpus of Modern Chinese[11] (Zhan et al. 2019; size: 581,794,456 characters or, roughly, 125 million Chinese words, as of 03/03/2021) and Google search engine. In cases where the frequencies from the one-million-word ToRCH 2009 Corpus are too low (e.g. less than five occurrences per million words) to generate a valid output, we will consult the CCL corpus and query results from Google. That said, we take examples from Google search with caution as it is often unclear whether the author is a native language user, or whether the occurrence is actually the result of typos. It should be noted that different sources of data should not impact the quality of data as all website data sources in this research have been verified by ten language consultants who are native speakers of Mandarin Chinese via an informal acceptability judgement survey. Specifically, following Bader and Häussler's (2010) practice, all participants in my study were asked to judge whether a given sentence was acceptable[12] or not (i.e. the binary judgement). If a sentence is judged

---

the other. In the case of the LVCs being considered, they tend to occur in the formal, written variety, so the corpora used for this study all contain written texts in Mandarin Chinese.

8 'Recent Chinese' here can be seen as *dangdai hanyu* 'Contemporary Chinese,' the most recent version of Mandarin Chinese in this study.

9 Note that characters and words are different units in written Chinese. While most Chinese corpora use character as the basic unit, the ToRCH 2009 Corpus, in order to conform to the size of the one-million-word Brown corpus, adopts word counting. Unlike the word space of written English, written Chinese words are composed of multiple characters without explicit word boundary markers. As such, all the texts in the ToRCH 2009 Corpus underwent word segmentation.

10 Access is available at http://114.251.154.212/cqp/ (accessed on March 20, 2021).

11 The corpus is available online at http://ccl.pku.edu.cn:8080/ccl_corpus/

12 In our study, acceptability is different from grammaticality. Grammaticality concerns the innate knowledge of a language, whereas acceptability is about the actual language use, i.e. acceptability is 'speaker-oriented and depends on what speaker will consider appropriate' (Bauer 2014: 84). It

acceptable over 80% of the time, it will remain unmarked. Otherwise, a question mark '?' will be assigned to the sentence when the acceptability value is between 60% to 80%. The sentence will be labelled with an asterisk '*' if the value drops to 60% or below. Note, however, that in order to maintain the underpinnings of the usage-based approach taken in the Goldbergian strand of Construction Grammar (cf. Thompson 2002; Boas 2003; Bybee 2006, inter alias), invented examples gained from introspection by native speakers have been kept to a minimum. However, on some occasions, original examples from corpora may be presented in conjunction with manipulated or invented (non-)acceptable versions to provide clearer illustration or argumentation.

3.2 Corpus generalization and hypothesis

In Mandarin Chinese, it is generally agreed that the dichotomy of the perfective and imperfective aspects is widely accepted, and the perfective markers -*le* and -*guo* and the imperfective markers -*zhe* and *zai*- are used to mark aspect morphologically (see e.g. Smith 1991; Li and Thompson 1989; Xiao and McEnery 2004)[13]. The two imperfective markers -*zhe* and *zai*- do not entail a boundary (i.e. the presence or absence of a final temporal/spatial endpoint, following Jackendoff (1990)), whilst the beginning or final boundaries are grammatically marked by -*le* and -*guo*. Whether a verb can occur with a particular marker depends on the compatibility regarding the meaning of the marker, the verb, and the context (e.g. temporal adjuncts). For example, the LV *jiayi* rarely takes the two imperfective markers because *jiayi* (with the abstract meaning of 'give') encodes a boundary per se that is in conflict with the imperfective markers. However, this does not explain why one of the GIVE LVs *jiayi* never takes a perfective marker in naturally-occurring language data, although it can take one in theory. We will look at this issue in detail for the remainder of the study.

The grammatical encoding of aspectuality varies in the three GIVE LVCs. In the ToRCH 2009 Corpus, *jiyu*-LVCs can take the perfective aspect markers, such as -*le*, immediately after the LV, whereas *jiayi*-LVCs cannot, see (14) and (15).

---

may have some overlap with grammaticality, which is one of the factors that determine whether a sentence is acceptable or not (Bard, Robertson, and Sorace 1996).
13 Li (2012) adopted a broader view and included the prepositions *gei* and *dao* to encode aspectuality, such as boundedness. However, we focus on the four markers -*le*, -*guo*, *zhe*-, and -*zai* in this study, because 1) they are widely agreed upon as aspectual markers in the literature of the Mandarin aspectual system and 2) they encode aspectuality grammatically.

(14) Laoshi   dui   ruoxiao   xuesheng jiyu-le   gengduo guanzhu.
     teacher to   vulnerable   student   LV-ASP   more   attention
     'Teachers paid more attention to vulnerable students.'   (ToRCH 2009)

(15) Weisheng   bumen   dui   zhe-pi   yaopin   jiayi   (*-le)   yange
     health   department   to   this-batch   medicine LV   -ASP   strict
     guanli.
     regulation
     'The health department strictly regulated this batch of medicines.'
                                                                    (ToRCH 2009)

These differences have been observed in Hu and Fan (1995), Diao (2004), and Kuo (2011). To account for this, Kuo proposed that *jiayi* was not a verb, but a preverbal affix in Mandarin Chinese. This analysis proved to also be applicable to other LVs in the GIVE group, that is, *jiyu* 'give' and *yuyi* 'give.' However, our investigation into the ToRCH 2009 Corpus offers some counterexamples. Firstly, Kuo's claim that *jiayi* was a preverbal affix was supported by the fact that *jiayi* and the following 'complement' could not be separated by numeral-classifier modification (e.g. *san-ge* three-CLF), as illustrated in (16).

(16) Zhangsan [dui zhe-ge   anzi] jiayi (*san-ge)   diaocha
     Zhangsan to   this-CLF   case   LV   three-CLF   investigate
     'Zhangsan gave three investigations into this case.'   (Kuo 2011: 141)

Although there is no occurrence of a *jiayi*-construction whose complements are modified by numeral-classifiers, the corpus data do show some cases where the complement can be modified by adjectives or adverbs; this can be seen in the adjectival modification *renzhen* 'careful' in (17).

(17) Laoshi   dui   zhe-ge   ti'an   jiayi   renzhen   kaolü.
     teacher   to   this-CLF   proposal   LV   careful   consideration
     'The teacher gave careful consideration to this proposal.'   (ToRCH 2009)

This example suggests that the complement does contain some nominal properties. Therefore, it is not appropriate to claim that *kaolü* is the main verb, and consequently, it does not sound grammatically correct to treat the LV as a preverbal affix. As such, the LV in this study is argued to be a verb that bears morphological changes, and the complement is a noun.

Furthermore, the corpus data do not support the application of Kuo's proposal to the other two GIVE-LVCs, in particular to *jiyu*, as shown in Table 1. While the

ToRCH 2009 Corpus investigation subscribes to the generalisation that aspectual markers cannot co-occur with *jiayi*, statistical results show that 15.6% (17/109) of *jiyu* usage is attached to the aspect marker -*le*, and such co-occurrence is only found once in *yuyi*-LVCs. Similar properties can be seen in the larger CCL Corpus. Table 1 exhibits the token frequencies of each LV concerning the occurrence of aspectual markers in the ToRCH 2009 and CCL corpora.

Table 1: The aspectual properties evidenced in the ToRCH 2009 and CCL corpora.

	-le		-guo		-zhe		zai-	
	ToRCH	CCL	ToRCH	CCL	ToRCH	CCL	ToRCH	CCL
jiyu	17	4624	–	31	–	5	–	8
yuyi	1	119	–	–	–	–	–	3
jiayi	–	–	–	–	–	–	–	12

[Note: the '–' symbol means not found.]

The aspectual properties of the three GIVE LVs in Table 1 can be generalised as follows: 1) only perfective aspects, in particular -*le*, can occur in GIVE LVs; 2) the perfective -*le* can mostly be seen in *jiyu*-LVCs, rarely in *yuyi*-LVCs, and is not attested in *jiayi*-LVCs; 3) as for the imperfective markers, they seldom occur with any of the LVs.

According to constructional grammarians (e.g. Michaelis 2004; Perek and Lemmens 2010), the aspectual information, as reviewed in Section 2.2, is co-provided by the verb and the construction. This is assumed to be true in the GIVE LVCs. Hence, we hypothesise that if an LVC encodes aspectual information entirely by the construction, it would not be surprising to see that the aspectual meaning is no longer encoded by the verb. Therefore, it typically does not require the realisation of an aspectual marker to show its aspectual value. According to the corpus data concerning different aspectual properties pertaining to the three GIVE verbs, we further claim that *jiayi* is hypothesised to be the most grammaticalised amongst the three GIVE LVs. This means that its construction is assumed to include more grammatical information than other LVs in the GIVE group. In other words, the perfective meaning encoded in the construction of *jiayi* is sufficient to embody perfectivity in its own right, so the perfective value internally conveyed in the construction pertinent to *jiayi*-LVCs makes it incompatible with any other means of perfective encodings, such as perfective aspectual markers. On the contrary, in less grammaticalised verbs such as *jiyu*, the perfective aspectual information is not sufficiently encoded in the construction, thus requiring the verb to provide more aspectual values in order to embody aspectual information when necessary. This results in the morphological realisations of the perfective markers -*le* or -*guo* in *jiyu*-LVCs.

If the above hypothesis is correct, we expect to find some empirical evidence to support the different grammaticalisation stages of the three verbs, which will be the focus of the next section.

4 Empirical evidence from corpora

In Section 4, we will mostly draw upon the synchronic data retrieved from corpora, while making some necessary reference to diachronic data. This is because synchrony and diachrony are neither abrupt nor discontinuous. Therefore, synchronic analysis cannot be separated from the diachronic evolution of the language.

4.1 The syntactic structures of the three GIVE verbs

As previously noted, an LV is always assumed to have an identical form as an independent lexical verb in a language (see Section 1). If LVs evolve from their IV counterparts (Hopper and Traugott 1993; Hook 1991, amongst others), it would be likely to see some syntactic and semantic properties that have close associations with (i.e. are inherited from, see Section 2.1 for the notion of inheritance) their corresponding IVs. If an LV still retains some of its uses as an IV, it is seen as not fully converted into an LV, which, in other words, means that it is at an earlier stage (or bears a lower degree) of grammaticalisation. In this sense, a close inspection of the data in a synchronic corpus would enable us to see the different stages of grammaticalisation of the three GIVE LVs; namely, *jiyu* is believed to be at the earliest stage followed by *yuyi* and *jiayi*.

Although grammaticalisation is better understood over a long period of time, our investigation into the analysis of the GIVE group will begin with the data retrieved from a synchronic corpus (i.e. ToRCH 2009 Corpus), with occasional consultations to previous studies, earlier texts, and online corpora of Classical Chinese (from 500 B.C. to A.D. 1000). The reason is twofold: firstly, examples from the Contemporary Chinese corpus of ToRCH 2009, although not of very great size, are sufficient to show the distinct syntactic environments of each GIVE verb both as an IV and as an LV. Secondly, following the postulation concerning the continuity between diachronic and synchronic phases (see Section 2.3), it is expected to find some intermediate stages of grammaticalisation in the synchronic corpus of ToRCH 2009. Therefore, for the remainder of this section, we will look at the syntactic patterns of the three GIVE verbs functioning as an IV and as an LV.

When used as IVs, *jiyu*, *yuyi*, and *jiayi* all mean 'give' or 'cause to receive' in the literal sense. Prototypically, the given thing is expressed by a genuine noun, and the three GIVE verbs usually require the giver, the recipient, and the given in semantic representations. In Contemporary Mandarin, a full realisation of the three participants in an independent verb construction (IVC) can be found in *jiyu* in particular, and all of these participants can be realised as core arguments (namely, subject, direct object, and indirect object).

4.1.1 *Jiyu*-LVCs

Functioning independently, *jiyu* can be used in ditransitive constructions. In example (18a), the recipient *xuesheng* 'student' and the theme *jihui* 'opportunity' are both realised as core arguments in the ditransitive structure. Apart from the three-place argument realisation, *jiyu* can also be a two-place verb. For instance, only the giver *laoshi* 'teacher' and the given *kending-de pingyu* 'positive comments' are realised in the first half of the sentence in (18b), whereas the givee *xuesheng* 'students' is not syntactically realised, though it can be inferred from the context.

(18) a. Xuexiao **jiyu** xuesheng kua xueke, kua zhuanye de jihui.
school give student cross discipline cross major DE opportunity
'The school gave students inter-disciplinary and inter-major opportunities.'
(ToRCH 2009)

b. Laoshi **jiyu** kendingde pingyu, guli xuesheng jinbu.
teacher give positive comment encourage student progress
'Teachers gave positive comments to students and encouraged them to keep up in their study.' (ToRCH 2009)

c. Ta zai shenghuoshang **jiyu** ta wuweibuzhide zhaogu.
he on life LV her meticulous care
'He cared for her meticulously in life.' (ToRCH 2009)

d. Zhuanjia xuezhe **jiyu**-le chongfen kending.
expert scholar LV-PRF adequate affirmative
'Experts and scholars have given adequate affirmation (of something).' (ToRCH 2009)

e. Guojia dui huanbao.de qiye **jiyu** zhichi.
country to environmental company LV support
'The country support environmentally-friendly companies.' (ToRCH 2009)

f. Xialuoke **jiyu** zhaiwuren Andongniao yi kuanrong-de quanshuo
   Shylock LV debtor Antonio with sympathetic persuasion
   'Shylock sympathetically persuaded the debtor Antonio.' (ToRCH 2009)

As an LV, *jiyu* takes an AN, from which the predicational content is derived, such as examples from (18c) to (18e). Like its IV counterparts in (18a) and (18b), *jiyu* retains the same argument realisations in LVCs. The LV *jiyu* can occur in ditransitive constituency as shown in (18c) where the theme and the AN occupy the positions that are generally filled by the indirect object *ta* and the direct object *wuweibuzhi-de zhaogu*, respectively, in an IVC. Alternatively, it occurs in a two-place predicate structure, in which the undergoer argument is omitted but can be inferred from the context, as shown in example (18d).

However, *jiyu*, as an LV, can also be used in oblique constructions. For example, in (18e) the theme *huanbao-de qiye* 'environmentally-friendly companies' is dislocated pre-verbally as an oblique argument and introduced by the preposition *dui* 'to,' instead of being placed after the verb, similar to the one in (18c). This results in an OV word order.

The oblique argument can also be realised by the AN, as in (18f). In this case, the oblique encodes the action of 'persuasion' and its manner. The oblique is placed post-verbally after the undergoer argument, hence keeping the prototypical VO order in Modern Mandarin. In (18f), the AN *kuanrong-de quanshuo* 'sympathetic persuasion' is realised as an oblique and is introduced by the preposition *yi*, which is close to the preposition 'with' in English, see the glossing in (18f). The insertion of *yi* in the *jiyu* construction is popular in Old Chinese (see e.g. Sun (1996) for the history of *yi*), the use of which gives (18f) an archaic and formal reading. This is also supported by the acceptability judgement survey amongst our ten native speakers of Mandarin Chinese. They all agree (100%) that *yi* can be removed from (18f) in Contemporary Mandarin, resulting in the same syntactic structure as (18c).

4.1.2 *Yuyi*-LVCs

The major syntactic difference between *yuyi* and *jiyu* lies in the ditransitive structure. This syntactic structure,[14] regardless of if *yuyi* acts as an LV or an IV, is not

---

14 *Yuyi* is actually made up of two characters *yu* 'give' and *yi* 'with,' which has evolved into one word *yuyi* over time. Between the two characters, only *yu* has lexical contributions to the meaning

attested in contemporary Mandarin Chinese corpora, such as the ToRCH 2009 Corpus. The contrived examples (i.e. not naturally found in a corpus) in (19a) and (19b) demonstrate that it is ungrammatical to use *yuyi* in ditransitive constructions.

(19) a. *Xuexiao **yuyi** wu xuewei zhe zhengshu.
school give no degree people certificate
'The school gave non-degree holders certificates.'
b. *Ben wen **yuyi** kaocha gai xianxiang.
this paper LV examine this phenomenon
'This paper examined this phenomenon.
c. Boshi, xiuye qiman, wu xuewei zhe, **yuyi** zhengshu.
doctor schooling finish no degree people give certificate
'Doctoral students, who have finished the coursework but who have not obtained the degree, will be given certificates.' (ToRCH 2009)
d. Ben wen dui gai xianxiang **yuyi** kaocha.
this paper to this phenomenon LV examine
'This paper examined this phenomenon.'
(lit. 'This paper gave an examination to this phenomenon.') (ToRCH 2009)
e. Shehui dongdangbuan, zhengfu caiqu xingdong, **yuyi** jiejue.
society unstable government take actions LV solve
'The society was unstable, (so) the government took actions to solve (the issues of social instability).' (ToRCH 2009)

Nevertheless, similar to *jiyu* constructions, *yuyi* can also function as an IV and take a genuine noun in a two-place predication structure. For example, *yuyi* in (19c) is an IV and takes the given role *zhengshu* 'certificate.' Similar to *jiyu*, the verb *yuyi*, when in an LVC, can realise the theme role as an oblique argument, for instance, *gai xianxiang* 'this phenomenon' in (19d). Additionally, the undergoer role may be

---

of the whole word, and thus *yi* can be removed in some cases. Note that, although *yuyi* and *yu* encode the same meaning, the former is largely preferred in modern Chinese. This also implies that *yu*, if used in modern Chinese, would give the text an archaic flavour. Since ditransitive structures can only occur in four-character idioms (or *chengyu* in Chinese) that contain *yu*, it is not surprising to find that expressions such as (i) have an archaic tone.

(i) yu ren koushi
give people cause.for.gossip
'give people the cause for gossip'

As for *yuyi* as a whole unit, it cannot be used in ditransitive structures, see the following illustration in the body of the text.

predisposed to be unrealised in most cases. For instance in (19e), the theme of *jiejue* 'solve' is not expressed syntactically but can be determined from the context.

4.1.3 *Jiayi*-LVCs

The syntactic contexts of *jiayi* are even more restricted. In Contemporary Mandarin Chinese, *jiayi* cannot function as an IV to take a genuine noun. This use, however, is readily available in Classical Chinese. Similar to *yuyi*, *jiayi* is also composed of two characters, *jia* 'add' and *yi* 'with,' which integrated into one word *jiayi* over a long period of evolution. (The details on how *jia* 'add' and *yi* 'by/with' were fused into a single word *jiayi* are beyond the scope of this paper; readers are advised to see Liu (2011) for more). In Classical Chinese, *jia* can be used independently as a verb. In the Classical Chinese subsection of the CCL corpus, we found *jia*, as an IV, occurring in both ditransitive and oblique constructions. In example (20a), *jia* (IV) is directly followed by *bing* 'military force' and *wo* 'me' in the ditransitive construction. The oblique construction of *jia* is shown in the two clauses in (20b). Although the givee role *wo* 'me' precedes the given in the first half of the sentence and the givee argument *ren* 'people' follows the given role in the second half of the sentence in (20b), the two givee arguments, introduced by the preposition *yu* 'on/to,' are both demoted to oblique positions in this Classical Chinese sentence.

(20) a. Zhuhou jie he, wu wang he er du bude
  duke all congratulate I go congratulate but only not
  tong, ci bi **jia** bing wo, wei zhi naihe?
  receive this must add military.force me to 3 what.to.do
  'Other dukes all congratulated (him), so did I, but he did not receive me. This means that he must be going to dispatch troops on me. How am I going to cope with it?' (Classical Chinese, CCL corpus)
 b. Zigong yan wo bu yu ren jia yu wo zhi shi, wo
  Zigong said I not want people add on me de thing I
  yi bu yu ci jia zhi yu ren
  also not want this add 3 on people
  'Zigong said, for the thing that I do not want other people to impose on me, I also would not like it to be imposed on others.' (Classical Chinese, CCL corpus)
 c. Yantaohui dui zhe yi lilun jiayi shenshi.
  seminar to this one theory LV examine
  'The seminar examined this theory.' (ToRCH 2009)

d. Ta   yi   shengbing wei   you   jiayi   jujue.
   he   use   illness   as   excuse   LV   decline
   'He used his illness as an excuse to decline (this invitation).'

(ToRCH 2009)

Nevertheless, the above constructions have become obsolete, and the undergoer argument has to be fronted as an oblique argument in Modern Chinese in *jiayi* (LV) constructions. This is exemplified in (20c), wherein the theme *zheyi lilun* 'this theory' is displaced in front of the LV *jiayi*. Similar to the other LVs, the undergoer argument can also be omitted if it can be readily recovered from the context, see (20d).

Having described the various syntactic patterns of the three GIVE verbs in both contemporary and Classical Chinese, we will summarise the IV and LV usages of the three GIVE verbs in the next section and, based on this, justify the distinct encodings of aspectual information.

4.2 An account of different aspectual properties

The various synchronic data in Section 4.1 indicates that a mixture of IVCs and LVCs is widely manifested in the Contemporary *jiyu* constructions, but such mixture is rarely seen in *yuyi* constructions and does not occur in *jiayi* constructions. Since it is assumed that LVCs develop from IVs to grammatical morphemes, our hypothesis that all three verbs are still in the process of grammaticalization is supported. That is, the three LVs are at different stages of grammaticalization: *jiayi* is the closest to the grammatical end of the cline, followed by *yuyi* and *jiyu*.

The tokens of each syntactic structure that can occur with the three GIVE LVs in the ToRCH 2009 Corpus are listed in Table 2. The corresponding instantiations of structures (a) to (e) in Table 2 were represented in examples (21a) to (21e), respectively. In Table 2, structures (a) and (b), occurring in IVCs, can only be found in the contemporary *jiyu*, whereas the two structures were readily available in Classical Chinese across all three verbs.

Table 2: Tokens of different syntactic structures concerning each GIVE verb in the ToRCH 2009 Corpus.

	a. IV+OBJ1+OBJ2	b. IV+OBJ2	c. LV+OBJ1+AN	d. OBL+LV+AN	e. LV+AN	Total
jiyu	15	17	13	34	30	109
yuyi	0	1	0	19	47	67
jiayi	0	0	0	23	45	68

(21) Instantiations (all retrieved from the ToRCH 2009 Corpus):
    a. Ta **jiyu**-le [wo]_OBJ1 [rensheng zhong gengwei baogui-de jingyan]_OBJ2
        he give-PRF me life in more precious experience
        'He gave me more precious life experience.'
    b. Guojia ji yao xiang minzu diqu touru gengduode zijin, you yao **jiyu** [geng youhuide zhengce]_OBJ2
        nation not.only need to ethnic area invest more money but.also need give more preferential policy
        'Our nation not only needs to make more investment in ethnic areas, but also needs to give more preferential policies (to them).'
    c. Ta zai shenghuoshang **jiyu** [ta]_OBJ1 [wuweibuzhide zhaogu]_AN.
        he on life LV her meticulous care
        'He cared for her meticulously in life.'
    d. Ta [dui zhe yi zuofa]_OBL **jiyu** [chongfen kending]_AN.
        he to this one practice LV adequate confirmation
        'He highly confirmed this practice.'
    e. Ri mei ye **jiyu**-le [zugou guanzhu]_AN.
        Japanese media also LV-PRF enough attention
        'Japanese media also paid enough attention (to this).']

Interestingly, structure (c) is closely connected to (a). As shown in Table 2, apart from the LV occupying the position that is normally used to accommodate an IV, the syntactic structures in (a) and (c) remain the same. Semantically, the meaning spreads from the central notion of physical transfer in (21a), corresponding to structure (a) in Table 2, to other types of transferring action in a more general sense, exemplified in (21b). This pattern nicely parallels with the model of extension (a context-induced reinterpretation of grammaticalisation) proposed in Heine and Kuteva (2007). The model suggests that the transition from a less grammatical meaning to a more grammatical meaning does not happen abruptly, but involves intermediate stages. According to Heine and Kuteva (2007), grammaticalisation usually occurs in four different stages: from the source stage (stage I), to a new context triggering a new meaning (stage II), then to the background of an existing meaning (stage III), and finally to be grammaticalised to the target manifest (Stage IV). As such, structure (c) in Table 2 can be seen as a new context that triggers new meanings (namely, the bleaching of *jiyu*).

Corpus data show that, in structure (c), only pronouns can fill in the OBJ1 position, see example (21c). This is because OBJ1 sits in the middle of the sentence (i.e., between the bleached *jiyu* and the AN), the structure of which is not suitable for newly-introduced information to get prominence (see the Chinese 'end-focus principle' in Ho (1993) and Zhang (1994)). Such incompatibility further motivates the re-structuring of the extant ditransitive LVC (i.e. structure c). Therefore, a peripheral argument—oblique—is introduced and placed in front of the verb *jiyu* to gain pragmatic prominence, thus giving rise to structure (d) in Table 2. This structure grew in popularity and, finally, in structure (e) of Table 2. The theme role is not obligatorily required in the LVC, which makes '*jiyu* + AN' behave more like a single constituent. The diagnostics in (22) demonstrates that the AN *guanzhu* 'pay attention to' cannot be separated from the LV *jiyu*.

(22) a. Faguo   meiti   dui   zhe-ci   huiyi   jiyu-le   guanzhu,
       French   media   to   this-CLF   conference   LV-PRF   care.about
       riben   meiti   ye   **jiyu**-le   *(guanzhu).
       Japanese   media   too   jiyu-PRF   care.about
       'French media have cared about this conference; Japanese media have cared about it too.'
    b. Faguo   meiti   dui   zhe-ci   huiyi   **jiyu**-le   guanzhu,
       French   media   to   this-CLF   conference   LV-PRF   care.about
       riben   meiti   ye   shi.
       Japanese   media   too   so
       'French media have cared about this conference, so have Japanese media.'

As we can see, the transition from (a) to (e) in Table 2 implies semantic generalisation, whereby a new context entails a more general meaning. This is, as observed in Heine and Kuteva (2007), one of the important factors responsible for grammaticalisation. However, the other two verbs, *juyi* and *jiayi*, have both lost lexical content to such a great extent that their contemporary syntactic context mostly favours the last two structures listed in Table 2. This implies that *yuyi* and *jiayi* are at a later stage of grammaticalisation compared to *jiyu*. In other words, *yuyi* and *jiayi* in particular are more grammaticalised than *jiyu*.

The percentage concerning the occurrences in IVCs and LVCs in Figure 1 lends further weight to the claim that *jiyu* is at an earlier stage of grammaticalisation than *yuyi*, and in particular than *jiayi*. Table 2 and Figure 1 demonstrate that the three GIVE verbs have diversified their uses due to their different grammatical status. This also shows the effects of the layering principle of grammaticalisation and the persistence effects put forward in Hopper (1991). It argues that new layers are continually emerging, whereas old layers, instead of being completely discarded, continue to coexist with the new ones and reflect the grammatical distribution from the lexical history.

Lexeme	IVC	LVC	Grammatical morpheme
jiyu	29.4%	70.6%	
yuyi	1.5%	98.5%	
jiayi	-	100%	

Figure 1: The percentage concerning the distribution of LVs and full verbs.

The earlier/later stages of grammaticalisation are, interestingly, compatible with the realisation/non-realisation of the perfective aspect marker *-le*. Following the ideas of constructional grammarians (such as Michaelis 2004 and Goldberg and Jackendoff 2004, see Section 2.2 for more), we believe that the perfective aspectual information is co-provided by the verb and the construction in all of the GIVE LVCs. We propose that perfective aspectual properties encoded in the construction of GIVE LVCs are represented in different degrees concerning the three GIVE verbs, depending on their grammaticalisation stages. Given that the usual grammaticalisation path is 'independent lexical verb>grammatical morpheme (i.e. aspectual marker in this case),' the more grammaticalised a GIVE verb is, the more enriched the aspectual meaning will be (grammaticalised from an IV), and the less likely it will resort to the verb to provide perfective aspect information.

The most grammaticalised *jiayi* can be used to exemplify the aforementioned idea. Since it is the closest to the end of grammaticalisation, we assume that the construction will include more aspectual information than other LVs in the GIVE group. In other words, the perfective meaning encoded in the construction of *jiayi* is sufficient to embody the perfective aspect. Therefore, the fixed aspectual value internally conveyed in the *jiayi*-LVC makes it incompatible with any perfective aspectual markers.

On the contrary, in less grammaticalised verbs such as *jiyu*, the perfective aspectual information is not sufficiently-encoded in the construction, thus leading it to resort to the verb to provide some more perfective aspectual values in order to embody perfective aspectual information when necessary. This will result in the morphological realisations, such as the presence of perfective markers *-le* and *-guo*, in *jiyu*-LVCs.

Thus far, we have provided some empirical evidence from corpora to support the hypothesis that perfective aspectual meaning is inherently encoded in the GIVE group LVCs according to the grammaticalisation stages of the verb.

5 Conclusion

This paper argues that the emergence of aspectual meaning is pertinent to LVCs from a diachronic perspective. Beginning with the distinct corpus observation of the three GIVE LVs in Mandarin Chinese, we propose that the GIVE verbs are at different stages of grammaticalisation, which parallels with the encoding of the perfective aspect of GIVE LVCs. More specifically, the verb *jiayi* is hypothesised to be the most grammaticalised amongst the three GIVE LVs, as evidenced by the corpus observation that all the instances of *jiayi* can only be used as LVs in Contemporary Mandarin. As grammaticalisation is typically understood as the movement from an IV to a grammatical morpheme, *jiayi*, as the most grammaticalised verb, is assumed to include more grammatical information than other LVs in the GIVE group. This also implies that the grammatical information, the perfective aspect in this case, encoded in the construction of *jiayi* is sufficient to embody perfectivity in its own right. Therefore, the perfective value internally conveyed in the *jiayi*-LVC makes it incompatible with any perfective aspect markers. On the contrary, in less grammaticalised verbs such as *jiyu*, the perfective aspectual information is not sufficiently-encoded in the construction, thus leading it to resort to the verb to provide some more aspectual values, in order to embody the aspectual information when necessary. This will result in the morphological realisations, such as the presence of the perfective markers *-le* and *-guo*, in *jiyu*-LVCs.

The findings in Chinese LVCs lend further weight to the possibility that LVs have been grammaticalised to encode aspectual meaning. In some earlier studies on English LVCs, Brinton and Traugott (2005), Rensky (1964), Stein (1991), and Prince (1972) found that the presence of the indefinite article (as in *take a bath*) contributes to the boundedness feature of the construction (cf. Sundquist 2018). Slightly different from the existing literature, our study shows that the Mandarin LVCs can encode aspectual information even without the help of the numeral-classifier structure,[15] which seems to imply that the construction encodes aspectuality itself. More interestingly, the observation and description throughout this paper seem to suggest that Mandarin LVCs are not light. Instead, they do contain some semantic and pragmatic content that is absent in their closely linked IV counterparts.

---

[15] Chinese does not have articles, but the numeral-classifier structure, such as *yi-ge* 'one-CLF', can in some cases be used to represent where English would have *a/an* article. For example, *yi-ge pingguo* is used to represent what in English would be expressed as 'an apple' in (a).

(a) wo   chi-le   yi-ge   pingguo.
     I   eat-ASP   one-CLF   apple
     'I had an apple.'

As revealed in our corpus study, the GIVE group LVCs denote a perfective aspect, viewing an event as a bounded unit. The aspect implied in the construction affects the morphosyntactic realisation of LVCs, such as the (non-)realisation of grammatical aspectual markers.

The findings of Mandarin LVCs complement the discussion of LVCs in many other languages. One of the fundamental questions asked cross-linguistically is what is light and what is heavy in LVCs. The introduction of LVCs in Section 1.1 shows that the meaning encoded in the LVs in languages such as Urdu, Irish, and English is not completely wiped out. LVCs are found to have some associations with aspectual system. In Nolan's (2014) study on Irish LVCs, he argues that LVs instantiate the change of phase (i.e. particular parts of an event construal) and the AN indicates boundedness or results. He further noticed that Irish LVCs affect the argument sharing of the complex predicates. A case in point is the Irish LV *thosaigh* 'start.' Example (23) shows that there is a change of a phase regarding the process of the moving event: the phase that is denoted by the LV is inception. The AN *bogadh* 'moving' implies the result of the LV: moving along a path forward. Also implied in the sentence is the sharing of arguments in the complex predicates. As indicated in the breakdown of the event in the last two lines following the free translation in example (23), the actor argument *antraein* 'the train,' although being inanimate, is shared over all the sub-events of moving.

(23) Thosaigh an traein ag bogadh ar
start-PST DET train:N at:PREP moving:VN on:PREP
adhaidh go mall
forward:ADV to:PREP slow:ADV
'The train started moving forward slowly.'
[**do** (train, [**start** (train, [**move** (train)] ^ **manner.of.motion.slowly** (train) ^ **path.forward** (train))])]   (Nolan 2014: 150)

In another study, Butt (1995) finds that the Urdu LV *ḍaal* 'put' is not light in semantics completely. It denotes a conscious choice of a given action, see (3a) and (3b) in Section 1.1, repeated as (24a) and (24b) below.

(24) a. vo ciik^h paṛ-aa
pron=NOM scream fall-PRF.M.SG
'He began screaming suddenly (despite himself).'
b. us=ne ciik^h ḍaal-aa
pron=ERG scream put-PRF.M.SG
'He screamed violently (on purpose).'   (Butt 1995: 110)

Similar findings can be found in the English LVC. Trousdale (2013) noted that the difference between *have a nibble* and its non-LVC counterpart *nibble* lies in the telic aspect encoded in the LVC. In LVCs with an AN complement, the action is conceptualised as 'things' that are in or come into the subject's possession, so *have a nibble* is telic whereas *nibble* is generally seen as atelic. This shows the inheritance of *have* as an IV in transitive constructions (e.g. *I had an apple*) to the *have* as an LV (e.g. *I had a nibble*).

The above examples, in a variety of languages, seem to suggest a cross-linguistic tendency in LVCs: LVCs are not completely light. To elaborate, they are light in the sense that they retain little, if any, verb sense of the corresponding independent variants of LVs. For example, *yuyi* has lost its original historical semantic content of giving. On the other hand, they are heavy in the sense that LVCs do encode aspectual information and/or have some consequential effects on their syntactic realisations. Therefore, a typological survey concerning the 'heavy' information contained in LVCs would potentially be interesting.

The hypothesis of this study, although supported by the GIVE LVCs, is mainly based on a one-million-word corpus, supplemented by some references to a larger corpus of 125 million characters. Although the sample of data is relatively small, it is sufficient to show a tendency or a preferred pattern of language use, especially when relative frequency is considered. For example, the use of the LV *yuyi* with *-le* has only one occurrence in the ToRCH 2009 corpus (see Table 1). This very low frequency may sound unreliable at first. However, a careful consideration of the relative frequency would support our interpretation (see Section 3 for detail). The relative frequency of *yuyi-le* in the ToRCH 2009 corpus is 0.2 occurrences per million characters, and its occurrence in the larger CCL corpus (absolute frequency: 119) is 0.59 per million characters. The two sets of data both demonstrate that *-le* rarely occurs in *yuyi*-LVCs. In addition, the relative frequency of *jiyu-le* amounts to 100 per million characters in the ToRCH 2009 corpus. This further reinforces our interpretation that *-le* rarely occurs in *yuyi*-LVCs, especially when compared with other LVs in the same group. Even so, it remains to be seen and would be of great value if such a hypothesis were to be attested in data from other varieties of Chinese and languages other than Chinese.

In essence, by rendering relevant semantic information as an inherent part of the construction, this study has sought to explain synchronic properties from the implications of diachronic features under the framework of Construction Grammar. In this way, we hope to encourage the investigation of underexplored areas in the study of Mandarin LVCs and to contribute to the emerging field of exploring Construction Grammar with a diachronic insight.

Abbreviations

3	third person
ACC	accusative
ADV	adverbial phrase
AN	action nominal
ASP	aspect marker
CLF	classifier
DE	pre-nominal modification marker, written as 的 in Chinese
DE₁	epistemic marker between a verb and its complement, written as 得 in Chinese
DET	determiner
ERG	ergative
EXP	experiential marker
INF	infinitive
LV	Light Verb
LVC	Light Verb Construction
M	masculine
N	noun
NOM	nominative
PL	plural
PREP	preposition
PRF	perfective marker
PROG	progressive
PST	past tense
PTC	particle
SG	singular
STAT	state
VN	verbal noun (equivalent to AN in this study)

References

Bader, Markus & Jana Häussler. 2010. Towards a model of grammaticality judgments. *Journal of Linguistics* 46(2). 273–330.

Bard, Ellen Gurman, Dan Robertson & Antonella Sorace. 1996. Magnitude estimation of linguistic acceptability. *Language* 72(1). 32–68.

Bauer, Laurie. 2014. Grammaticality, acceptability, possible words and large corpora. *Morphology* 24(2). 83–103.

Boas, Hans C. 2003. *A Constructional Approach to Resultatives*. Stanford: CSLI Publications.

Brinton, Laurel J. & Minoji Akimoto. 1999. Introduction. In Laurel J. Brinton & Minoji Akimoto (eds.), *Collocational and idiomatic aspects of composite predicates in the history of English*, 1–20. Amsterdam: Benjamins.

Brinton, Laurel J. & Elizabeth Traugott. 2005. *Lexicalization and Language Change*. Cambridge: Cambridge University Press.

Butt, Miriam. 1995. *The structure of complex predicates in Urdu*. Stanford: CSLI Publications.

Butt, Miriam. 2003. The light verb jungle. *Harvard Working Papers in Linguistics* 9. 1–49.
Butt, Miriam. 2010. The light verb jungle: still hacking away. In Mengistu Amberber, Mark Harvey & Brett Baker (eds.) *Complex predicates: Cross-linguistic Perspectives on Event Structure*, 48–78. Cambridge: Cambridge University Press.
Butt, Miriam & Aditi Lahiri. 2002. *Historical Stability vs. Historical Change*. http://ling.uni-konstanz.de/pages/home/butt/main/papers/stability.pdf (Accessed on 08-July-2015)
Bybee, Joan L. 1988. The diachronic dimension in explanation. In John Hawkins (ed.), *Explaining language universals*, 350–79. Oxford: Blackwell.
Bybee, Joan L. 1998. The emergent lexicon. *CLS 34: the panels*. 421–435.
Bybee, Joan L. 2006. From usage to grammar: The mind's response to repetition. *Language* 82(4). 711–733.
Bybee, Joan L. 2007. *Frequency of Use and the Organization of Language*. Oxford: Oxford University Press.
Bybee, Joan L. 2010. *Language, Usage, and Cognition*. Cambridge: Cambridge University Press.
Bybee, Joan L. 2013. Usage-based theory and exemplar representation in constructions. In Thomas Hoffmann & Graeme Trousdale (eds.), *The Oxford Handbook of Construction Grammar*, 49–69. Oxford: Oxford University Press.
Bybee, Joan L. 2015. *Language Change*. Cambridge: Cambridge University Press.
Bybee, Joan L. & Paul J. Hopper. 2001. Introduction to frequency and the emergence of linguistic structure. In Joan L. Bybee & Paul J. Hopper (eds.), *Frequency and the emergence of linguistic structure*, 1–26. Amsterdam: Benjamins.
Bybee, Joan L., Revere Perkins & William Pagliuca. 1994. *The Evolution of Grammar: Tense, Aspect and Modality in the Languages of the World*. Chicago: University of Chicago Press.
Comrie, Bernard. 1976. *Aspect: An Introduction to the Study of Verbal Aspect and Related Problems*. Cambridge: Cambridge University Press.
Croft, William. 2000. *Explaining Language Change*. Harlow: Longman Linguistic Library.
Croft, William. 2001. *Radical Construction Grammar: Syntactic theory in typological perspective*. Oxford: Oxford University Press.
Diao, Y. 2004. *Xiandai hanyu yuyi dongci yanjiu* [The research on weak verbs in contemporary Chinese]. Dalian: Liaoning Normal University Press.
Family, Neiloufar. 2014. *Semantic Spaces of Persian Light Verbs: A Constructionalist Account*. Brill: Leiden
Feng, Shengli. 2005. Qingdongci yiwei yu gujin de dongbin guanxi [Light verb movement in modern and classical Chinese]. *Yuyan Kexue* [Linguistic Sciences] 4(1). 3–16.
Francis, W. Nelson & Henry Kucera. 1979. *Brown Corpus Manual*. Providence, Rhode Island: Brown University Department of Linguistics.
Giry-Schneider, Jacqueline. 1978. *Les nominalisations en français: L'opérateur FAIRE dans le lexique*. Genève-Paris: Droz.
Goldberg, Adele E. 1995. *Constructions: A Construction Grammar Approach to Argument Structure*. Chicago: University of Chicago Press.
Goldberg, Adele E. 2005. Argument realization: The role of constructions, lexical semantics and discourse factors. In Jan-Ola Östman & Mirjam Fried (eds.), *Construction Grammars: Cognitive grounding and theoretical extensions*, 17–44. Amsterdam: Benjamins.
Goldberg, Adele E. 2006. *Constructions at Work: The Nature of Generalization in Language*. Oxford: Oxford University Press.
Goldberg, Adele E. & Farell Ackerman. 2001. The pragmatics of obligatory adjuncts. *Language* 77(4). 798–814.
Goldberg, Adele E. & Ray Jackendoff. 2004. The English resultative as a family of constructions. *Language* 80(3). 532–568.

Golshaie, Ramin. 2016. A corpus study on identification and semantic classification of light verb constructions in Persian: The case of light verb *xordan* 'to eat/collide'. *Language Sciences* 57. 21–33.

Grimshaw, Jane & Armin Mester. 1988. Light verbs and θ-marking. *Linguistic Inquiry* 19(2). 205–232.

Heine, Bernd & Tania Kuteva. 2002. On the evolution of grammatical forms. In Alison Wray (ed.), *The transition to language*, 376–397. Oxford: Oxford University Press.

Heine, Bernd & Tania Kuteva. 2007. *The Genesis of Grammar: A Reconstruction*. Oxford: Oxford University Press.

Heine, Bernd & Mechthild Reh. 1984. *Grammaticalization and Reanalysis in African Languages*. Hamburg: Buske.

Ho, Yong. 1993. *Aspects of Discourse Structure in Mandarin Chinese*. Lewiston: Mellen University Press.

Hook, Peter Edwin. 1991. The emergence of perfective aspect in Indo-Aryan languages. In Elizabeth Traugott & Bernd Heine (eds.), *Approaches to grammaticalization*. Vol. 2, 59–89. Amsterdam: Benjamins.

Hopper, Paul J. 1991. On some principles of grammaticalization. In Elizabeth Traugott & Bernd Heine (eds.), *Approaches to grammaticalization*. Vol. 1, 17–35. Amsterdam: Benjamins.

Hopper, Paul J. & Elizabeth Traugott. 1993. *Grammaticalization*. Cambridge: Cambridge University Press.

Hu, Yushu & Xiao Fan. 1995. *Dongci yanjiu* [The research on verbs]. Kaifeng: Henan University Press.

Jackendoff, Ray. 1990. *Semantic Structures*. Cambridge, MA: The MIT press.

Jayasselan, K. A. 1983. Case-marking and θ-marking in Malayalam: Implications for the Projection Principle. In Amy Dahlstrom, Claudia Brugman, Monica Macaulay, Inese Civkulis, Michele Emanatian, Donna Sakima & Raquel Teixeura (eds.), *Proceedings of the Ninth Annual Meeting of the Berkeley Linguistics Society*, 104–115. Berkeley: Berkeley Linguistics Society.

Jespersen, Otto. 1942. *A modern English grammar on historical principles*. Vol. 6: *Morphology*. London: George Allen and Unwin Ltd.

Kuo, Pei-Jung. 2011. A case study of obligatory object fronting in Mandarin Chinese. In *Online proceedings of glow in Asia workshop for young scholars*. http://faculty.human.mie-u.ac.jp/~glow_mie/Workshop_Proceedings/11Kuo.pdf (last accessed 15–Aug–2014).

Kuryłowicz, Jerzy. 1965. The Evolution of Grammatical Categories. *Diogenes* 13(51). 55–71.

Lakoff, George. 1987. *Women, Fire, and Dangerous Things*. Chicago: University of Chicago Press.

Lehmann, Christian. 1985. Grammaticalization: Synchronic variation and diachronic change. *Lingua e Stile* 20(3). 303–318.

Li, Charles N. & Sandra A. Thompson. 1989. *Mandarin Chinese: A Functional Reference grammar*. Berkley: University of California Press.

Li, Wendan. 2012. Temporal and aspectual references in Mandarin Chinese. *Journal of Pragmatics* 44(14). 2045–2066.

Liu, H. 2011. Jiayi de duoyuan cihuihua yu yufahua [The polylexicalization and polygrammaticalization of *jiayi*]. *Yuyan Kexue* [Language Science] 10(6). 629–639.

Lin, Jonah T.-H. 2001. Light verb syntax and the theory of phrase structure. PhD dissertation. Irvine: University of California.

Michaelis, Laura A. 1998. *Aspectual Grammar and Past-time Reference*. London: Routledge.

Michaelis, Laura A. 2004. Type shifting in Construction Grammar: An integrated approach to aspectual coercion. *Cognitive Linguistics* 15(1). 1–68.

Miyamoto, Tadao. 1997. The light verb construction in Japanese: The role of the verbal noun. PhD dissertation. Victoria: University of Victoria.

Mohanan, Tara. 1994. *Argument Structure in Hindi*. Stanford: CSLI Publications.

Nolan, Brian. 2014. Complex predicates and light verb constructions in Modern Irish. *Revista Española de Lingüística Aplicada* 27(1). 140–167.
Perek, Florent & Maarten Lemmens. 2010. Getting at the meaning of the English at-construction: the case of a constructional split. *Cognitextes* 5. https://journals.openedition.org/cognitextes/331 (last accessed on 08–Aug–2016)
Perek, Florent. 2009. Distributional characterization of constructional meaning. Talk presented at the Corpus Linguistics 2009, Liverpool, UK.
Petré, Peter. 2016. Grammaticalisation by changing co-text frequencies, or why [BE V*ing*] became the 'progressive'. *English Language and Linguistics* 20(1). 31–54.
Prince, Ellen F. & Senta Plötz. 1972. A note on aspect in English: The take a walk construction. In Senta Plötz (ed.), *Transformationelle Analyse*, 409–440. Frankfurt: Athenäum.
Renský, Miroslav. 1964. English verbo-nominal phrases. *Travaux Linguistique de Prague* 1. 289–299.
Schmid, Hans-Jörg. 2000. *English Abstract Nouns as Conceptual Shells: From Corpus to Cognition*. Berlin/New York: Mouton de Gruyter.
Smith, Carlota S. 1991. *The Parameter of Aspect*. Dordrecht: Kluwer.
Stein, Gabriele. 1991. The phrasal verb type to have a look in Modern English. *International Review of Applied Linguistics in Language Teaching* 29. 1–29.
Sun, Chaofen. 1996. *Word-order Change and Grammaticalization in the History of Chinese*. Stanford: Stanford University Press.
Sun, Chaofen. 2006. *Chinese: A Linguistic Introduction*. Cambridge: Cambridge University Press.
Sundquist, John D. 2018. A diachronic analysis of light verb constructions in Old Swedish. *Journal of Germanic Linguistics* 30(3). 260–306.
Thompson, Sandra A. 2002. Object complements and conversation: Towards a realistic account. *Studies in Language* 26(1). 125–163.
Tomasello, Michael. 2003. *Constructing a Language: A Usage-Based Theory of Language Acquisition*. Cambridge, MA: Harvard University Press.
Torrent, Tiago Timponi. 2015. On the relation between inheritance and change. In Johanna Barðdal, Elena Smirnova, Lotte Sommerer & Spike Gildea (eds.), *Diachronic Construction Grammar*, 173–211. Amsterdam: Benjamins.
Traugott, Elizabeth. 1989. On the rise of epistemic meanings in English: An example of subjectification in semantic change. *Language* 65(1). 31–55.
Traugott, Elizabeth & Ekkehard König. 1991. 'The semantics-pragmatics of grammaticalization revisited'. In Elizabeth Traugott & Bernd Heine (eds.), *Approaches to grammaticalization*. Vol. 1, 189–218. Amsterdam: Benjamins.
Trousdale, Graeme. 2013. Multiple inheritance and constructional change. *Studies in Language* 37(3). 491–514.
Xiao, Richard & Tony McEnery. 2004. *Aspect in Mandarin Chinese: A corpus-based study*. Amsterdam: Benjamins.
Xu, Hongzhi, Menghan Jiang, Jingxia Lin & Chu-Ren Huang. 2020. Light verb variations and varieties of Mandarin Chinese: Comparable corpus driven approaches to grammatical variations. *Corpus Linguistics and Linguistic Theory*. https://doi.org/10.1515/cllt-2019-0049.
Xu, Jiajin. 2014. "ToRCH2009 xiandai hanyu yuliaoku" jiancheng [The construction of the contemporary Mandarin Chinese ToRCH2009 corpus]. *Yuliaoku Yuyanxue* [Corpus Linguistics] 1(1). 103–104.
Zhan Weidong, Guo Rui, Chang Baobao, Chen Yirong & Chen Long. 2019. Beijing daxue CCL yuliaoku de yanzhi [The building of the CCL corpus: Its design and implementation]. *Yuliaoku Yuyanxue* [Corpus Linguistics] 6(1). 71–86.

Zhang, P. N. 1994. Word order variation and end focus in Chinese: Pragmatic functions. PhD dissertation. New York: Columbia University Teachers College.

Zhu, Dexi. 1982. *Yufa jiangyi* [Lecture notes on grammar]. Beijing: Commercial Press.

Zhu, Dexi. 1985. Xiandai shumian hanyu li de xuhua dongci he ming dongci [The weak verbs and nominalized verbs in modern Chinese written texts]. *Beijing Daxue Xuebao (zhe she ban)* [Journal of Peking University (philosophy and social sciences)] 5. 10–16.

Francesca Di Salvo
12 Light Verb Constructions in Latin
A study on (*in*) *memoria* and (*in*) *animo habeo*

Abstract: The aim of this study is to analyse two specific Latin constructions in which the verb *habeo* 'have' appears in combination with a Prepositional Phrase (PP), consisting of the preposition *in* 'in'+ a noun (*in memoria habeo* 'have in the memory' → 'remember' and *in animo habeo* 'having the intention to'), trying, through the application of some tests, to demonstrate that they are true Light Verb Constructions (LVC).

Keywords: Light Verb Constructions, Complex Predicates, Prepositional Phrase, Habeo, memoria, animo

1 Introduction

Light Verb Constructions (henceforth LVCs) are complex predicates consisting of a noun with a predicative value (G. Gross 1989: 39) and a semantically 'light' verb (henceforth LV) which encodes grammatical categories such as person, tense, mood, aspect, voice and *Aktionsart*.[1]

From the second half of the twentieth century, many scholars began to show interest in the description of LVCs in Latin. In particular, attention was focused on identifying and describing the most frequent LVCs in Latin ($N_{(ACC)}$ + V), i.e. those

---

[1] Other terminology that has been proposed to indicate LVCs are: *complex verbal structures* (Nickel, 1968), *phrasal verb patterns* (Live 1973), *periphrastic verbal constructions* (Wierzbicka 1982). The use of the term *support* (*verbes supports*) is due to Maurice Gross (1975), who used it for the first time in reference to those verbs which, in combination with predicative nouns, mostly realize the values of tense, aspect, mode and voice (Giry-Schneider 1987; Gross G. 1989; Langer 2004), which the noun alone could not express, thus performing a mere 'support' function. As far as the definition of complex predicates in concerned, according to Butt (2010: 49): "the term complex predicate designates a construction that involves two or more predicational elements (e.g. nouns, verbs and adjectives) which predicate as single unit, i.e., their arguments map onto a monoclausal syntactic structure."

Acknowledgements/Funding: This work is part of the research project "Interacción del léxico y la sintaxis en griego antiguo y en latín: construcciones con verbo soporte" (FFI2017-83319-C-3) financed by the Spanish Ministry of Science and Innovation and by "Diccionario de colocaciones latinas en la red (DiCoLat)", *Programa Logos*-Fundación BBVA".

https://doi.org/10.1515/9783110747997-013

in which the LV combines with a noun occupying the object position, as happens, for example, in *opem ferre* 'bring help' → 'help', *morem gerere* 'have availability (toward)...' (Marini 2000), *verba facere* 'make words', *verba habere* 'have words' → 'talk' (Roesch 2001), *ludos facere* 'celebrate games' or 'make fun of someone', *bellum gerere* 'war' (Baños 2012), *spem ponere* 'hope' (Jiménez Martínez 2011, 2016) and *poena afficere* 'punish' (Mendózar 2015). Pompei (2016) and Baños (2016) propose that LVCs should also be considered as constructions in which the LV is combined with nouns, in a case other than the accusative or with other parts of speech, such as adverbs and prepositional phrases (PP):[2]

> «The present study aims to extend the concept of light verb construction, including occurrences of Latin light verbs that do not co-occur with a noun in the accusative, but with something else, such as a noun in a different case to the accusative, a noun which is the complement of a prepositional case, or even an adverb (Pompei, 2016: 102)».

In this perspective we will try here to apply the concept of LVC to the co-occurrence of a verb with a PP or a noun in the ablative ($N_{(ABL)}$), a hypothesis according to which predicativeness can also be expressed by parts of speech in a different function than that of the direct object. In particular, the purpose of this work is (i) to analyze the constructions in which a verb, *habeo*[3] 'have', appears in combination with a PP composed of *in* 'in'+ ablative, such as *in memoria habeo* 'have in the memory' and *in animo habeo* 'having the intention of', and (ii) to verify, where possible, if there is a variant in which the verb appears simply in combination with a noun in the ablative.[4] The two constructions will be analyzed together since both are characterized by the presence of an abstract noun, i.e. *memoria* 'memory' and *animo* 'soul', which can be combined with the preposition *in* 'in' and with the verb *habeo* 'have' giving rise to constructions with a unitary meaning.[5] In particular, these two constructions realize experiential metaphors as noted by Fedriani (2011: 313):

---

[2] In particular Baños (2016) considers forms such as *in mentem venire, in morbum incidere* as LVCs combinations.
[3] The citation form for verbs in Latin generally corresponds to the first-person singular of the present indicative. This form will be used throughout the text.
[4] The corpus analyzed is that of *The Packhard Humanities Institute* (PHI), and the literary period examined ranges from the third century B.C. to the end of the 1st century A.D. All texts present in the *PHI* corpus have been analyzed by selecting the passages in which the PPs *in memoria / in animo* or the ablative nouns *memoria / animo* appear in combination not only with the verb *habeo*, but also with other LVs or with extensions of LV, namely + verbs that make the meaning of the construction more specific. The query was performed through *Diogenes*.
[5] In the constructions considered, only some of the semantic values present in the two abstract nouns *memoria* and *animo* are realized.

> «the verb *habeo*, jointly with a Prepositional Phrase metaphorically denoting a cognitive entity as a container, was used in Latin also to express the semantic field of remembering. This pattern was in use already from the second century BCE, with the meaning of 'remember' [*in memoria habeo*] as well as 'have in one's mind', also with the dynamic implication of 'recall'».

Fedriani (2011: 314) also observes that the construction *in memoria habeo*, but also *in animo habeo*, could have given way to an abstract interpretation of the verb *habeo* in combination with non-prototypical places and/or objects.

Therefore, the present work is aimed at demonstrating that the constructions under consideration are LVCs through the application of a set of syntactic and semantic tests for the identification of LVCs, which have been developed over the years. In particular, we will verify:
(a) the level of cohesion of the constructions and the possibility that they express a more or less abstract semantic value (section 2.1 and section 3.1);
(b) the predicativity of either the PP or $N_{(ABL)}$ (and the lightness of the verb), which can be proven by the co-occurrence with both other equally neutral or basic LVs (section 2.2 and section 3.2) and LV extensions (section 2.4 and section 3.3).

2 Light Verb Constructions with *memoria*

The Latin noun *memoria* can express different semantic values.[6] In this paper we will mainly consider the semantic values that the noun *memoria* can express in combination with the verb *habeo* and the preposition *in*, namely 'have in the memory → remember'. In addition, we will also (section 2.1) take into account the symmetrical forms, i.e. the constructions *in memoria sum* 'being in mind' (lit.) and *in mentem venio* 'coming to mind' (section 2.2), having the same meaning; the variant *memoria teneo* 'keep in memory' (section 2.3); and the LV extension of the construction (section 2.4).

---

[6] The *Oxford Latin Dictionary* collects different meanings of the noun *memoria*: "(s.v. *memoria*) the power or faculty of remembering, memory; to be able to recall, remember, also to keep in mind; the action or fact of remembering or thinking about, remembrance; that which is retained in the mind, memory, recollection, (spec.) the memory (of the dead); what is remembered of a person or thing, memory, repute; the period covered by one's recollection; the collective memory which men have of the past, tradition, history; the period known to history or tradition; tradition preserved in writing or other form, a memorial, record; a recording, mention; a reminder, memorial, monument."

2.1 *In memoria habeo*

Within the corpus of *Packhard Humanities Institute* (PHI), we have found the verb *habeo* 'have' co-occurring with the PP *in memoria* 'in memory' only in 6 occurrences (Table 1). On the other hand, in the whole period considered there are no cases with the noun expressing the semantic value of 'have in the memory' → 'remember'. In fact, there are no cases in which the verb *habeo* is combined with *memoria* in the ablative case without the preposition *in*, as shown in Table 1:

Table 1: (*in*) *memoria habeo*[7].

	Plautus	Terentius	Gellio	Tot.	%
N+V	0	0	0	0	0
PP+V	3	2	1	6	100
TOT.	3	2	1	6	100
%	50	33.33	16.67		

The fact that the LVC *in memoria habeo* has only 6 occurrences (3 in Plautus, 2 in Terentius and 1 in Gellius) is relevant from a diachronic point of view. In fact, Dolkowska[8] (2012: 37) observes that although the construction *in memoria habeo* is not representative in terms of frequency, it is important diachronically since it is attested, except for one occurrence in Gellius, only in early Latin, in Plautus and Terentius, and it is used to express analytically the meaning of "remember". The occurrences in the early Latin are the following:

(1) Habeo in memoria. Necessitate me
    have:1SG in memory:ABL.SG.F necessity:ABL.SG.F 1SG.ABL
    mala ut fiam facis.
    bad: ABL.SG.F CONJ happen:2SG make:2SG
    'Yes, I remember. Father, you are forcing me to be a bad woman'[9]
    (Plautus, *The Persian*, 381)

---

[7] Another occurrence of *in memoria* is recorded in coordination with the PP *in animo* (*postea totam Italiam fac ut in animo ac memoria tributim discriptam comprensamque habeas*, Cicero, *Handbook of Electioneering*, 30.5). Actually, in this case the PP *in animo* seems to be governed by *comprehensam*.

[8] Dolkowska (2012) specifically analyzes all occurrences of the noun *memoria* in combination with LVs.

[9] Translations are based on Loeb's Classical Library.

(2) *Facito* in memoria *habeas*
make:IMP.FUT:2SG *in* memory:ABL.SG.F have:SUBJ:2SG
'Mind you remember that' (Plautus, *The Little Carthaginian*, 1418)

(3) *Patrue,   facito*   in memoria   *habeas,*
uncle:VOC.SG make:IMP.FUT:2SG *in* memory:ABL.SG.F have:SUBJ:2SG
tuam   maiorem   filiam   mihi   te
your:ACC.SG.F mayor:ACC.SG.F daughter:ACC.SG.F me:DAT 2SG:ACC
despondisse[10]
to promise:INF.PERF
'Uncle, see you remember that you have promised me your older daughter'
(Plautus, *The Little Carthaginian*, 1278)

(4) {SO.} in memoria   *habeo*
       in memory:ABL.SG.F have:1SG
'I don't forget it, [Sir]' (Terence, *The woman of Andros*, 40)

(5) *tamen   contemptus abs te   haec habui   in*
Neverthless despise:PRT by 2SG:ACC this have:PERF:1SG in
memoria: *ob haec facta   abs te   spernor?*
memory:ABL.SG.F for this make:PRT by you:ACC.SG despise:PRES:1SG
'Jilted though I was by you, I didn't forget to do this for you, and for this
you – turn me off!' (Terence, *The Eunuch*, 170)

In all these occurrences the element costituting the construction, i.e. the preposition, the predicative noun and the verb, always appear adjacent, often with the order PP + V, except for examples (1) and (5) where the verb precedes the PP, without affecting the semantic value expressed by the construction. In this case the verb is stative, and it is sometimes constructed with an expressed pronominal object or propositional theme (ACC + infinitive), but often the object is implicit. In this case, we speak of an omitted object which is a very frequent type of omission in Latin (Luraghi 1997: 246).[11]

On a semantic level, the construction expresses the meaning of 'remember'. In particular, the noun *memoria* expresses a sort of abstract place where memories

---

[10] In the glosses, the masculine gender is not indicated because it is considered unmarked. For the same reason, for verbs the active diathesis, the indicative mode and the present tense are not specified.
[11] This is true especially when the omitted pronoun refers to a whole sentence and has, therefore, an anaphoric value.

are kept. From a syntactic point of view, the locative value is also conveyed by the PP introduced through the preposition *in*. If we consider that the semantic role of the possessor is put together with that of location, in the same place of the macro-roles hierarchy, according to Van Valin and Lapolla (1997: 127, 146), the function of the PP is to specify meronymically the place where the memories are located.

As can be seen from the Table 1, only one occurrence is attested in Late Latin, specifically in Gellius, (II sec. A.D.) shown in the following example:

(6) Habe   semper   in memoria   atque   in pectore   ut
    have:IMP.2SG always   in memory:ABL.SG.F and   in heart:ABL.SG.NCONJ
    tamquam   scopulum   sic fugias   inauditum   atque
    just as   rock:ACC.SGSO   avoid:SUBJ.PRES:2SG   new:ACC.SG.N   and
    insolens   verbum
    unusual:ACC.SG.N   word:ACC.SG.N
    'Always remember and take to heart: "avoid, as you would a rock, a strange and unfamiliar words"'   (Gellius, *Attic Nights*, 1, 10, 4)

In example (6), the construction has a less abstract semantic value than the constructions seen above (1–5), since the PP *in memoria* appears in coordination with the PP *in pectore*, which denotes less cohesion of the construction and more referentiality of the noun. Indeed, the degree of referentiality of the two nouns has to be the same according to the *zeugma test*, which prevents the coordination of two nouns which are different in predicative content.

Furthermore, it is interesting to note the use of the exhortative subjunctive in examples (2) and (3) and the imperative in (6). The verb *habeo*, in fact, is a stative verb and does not normally express control. The use of the imperative and the exhortative subjunctive, on the contrary, implies a certain degree of control of the action described by the construction.

2.2 Symmetrical form

The PP *in memoria* appears in the *PHI* corpus also in combination with another neutral LV, i.e. *sum* 'to be', another verb with a general meaning. The verb *sum*, as well as *habeo*, exhibits few occurrences in combination with *in memoria* – only two –, and it never appears in combination with the ablative alone, as shown in Table 2. In terms of absolute frequency, just two occurrences are too few to make generalizations, but the data becomes representative if it is observed in terms of relative frequency, since even the construction with *habeo* has only six attestations.

Table 2: *in memoria sum.*

	Cicero	Gellius	Tot.	%
N+V	0	0	0	0
P+V	1	1	2	100
Tot.	1	1	2	
%	50	50	100	

See the following examples:

(7) Nisi   forte   veri   simile est   P. Sullae   nomen
     CONJ   perhaps   true   like   be:3SG   of.P. Sullae:GEN.SG   name:NOM.SG
     in   memoria   Cassio   non   fuisse
     in   memory:ABL.SG.F   Cassius:DAT.SG   not   be:PRF
     'Perhaps you think it likely that the name of Publius Sulla had slipped Cassius'
     mind'   (Cicero, *for Sulla*, 37)

(8) Varro   rescripsit   in   memoria   sibi   esse,
     Varro   write:PF:3SG   *in* memory:ABL.SG.F   himself:DAT.SG   be:INF
     Q. Catulus   curator   restituendi   Capitolii   dixisset
     Catulus:NOM.SG   supervisor:NOM.SG   restore:GEN   Capitol:GEN   say:subj:PPF:3SG
     voluisse   se   aream   Capitolinam   deprimere
     desire:PRF   area:ACC.SG.F   Capitoline:ACC.SG.F   suppress:INF
     'Varro wrote in reply that he recalled that Quintus Catulus, when in charge of
     the restoration of the Capitol, he said that it had been his desire to lower the
     area Capitolina'   (Gellius, *Attic Nights*, 2, 10, 2)

In both examples, the construction with *sum* presents the syntactic order PP + N$_{(DAT)}$ + V and expresses the semantic value of 'being in memory (to someone)' > 'remember'. In this case the N$_{(DAT)}$ is the so-called dative of possession[12] (*dativus possessivus*) and indicates the owner 'of the memory', i.e. 'the one who possesses the memory': the subject of the construction with *habeo* in the construction with *sum* becomes a dative of possession. What is noteworthy is that there is a meronymic relation of the part to the whole: reference is made not so much to the one who possesses the memory, but to the fact that he possesses something in memory, a content expressed through a sentence. The LVC thus holds a propositional object. The construction with *sum* represents the symmetrical form of the construction

---

[12] For an extended discussion of the expression of possession in Latin see Baldi and Nuti (2010).

with *habeo*, since the construction with *sum* selects as its subject the argument that would be the object of the construction with *habeo*, thereby entering into a complementary diathetic relationship.[13]

The fact that this construction appears only twice in the entire corpus analyzed does not mean that it is not an LVC. Indeed, as Baños (2012: 40) observes, a low frequency sometimes hides a fully grammaticalized LVC. On the other hand, a construction with a high frequency, which also seems to carry out an argument alternation with regard to the construction *in memoria habeo*, is *in mentem venio* 'coming to mind', in which the verb represents a process and not a state; this construction is present in the corpus analyzed with 229 occurrences, shown in the following table:

Table 3: *in mentem venio.*

	Cato	Naev	Plaut	Ter	Caes	Cic	Lucr	Verg	Liv	Luc	Petr	Quint	Sen	Apul	Fron	Gell	Tot
PP+V	1	1	21	16	1	147	2	1	10	1	1	3	12	2	4	6	229
%	0.42	0.42	10.17	6.78	0.42	63.14	0.85	0.42	4.66	0.42	0.42	1.27	5.51	0.85	1.69	2.54	

Although structurally different from the constructions under examination (in this case the PP consists of *in* + $N_{(ACC)}$), it is interesting to highlight the existence of this further very productive strategy in Latin, in which the telic verb *venio* is used in the same way as the construction with *sum*. Only looking at Cicero, the LVC *in mentem venio* occurs very often, with 147 attestations.

As Baños (2018) observes, the high number of occurrences of the construction *in mentem venio* can be justified by the existence of the simple verb *memini* 'to remember': *in memoria habeo* (but also *memoria teneo*, see section 2.3) coincides with *memini* in that the first argument is the subject, i.e. the experiencer of the memory. In these cases, the simple verb is preferred to an LVC. On the other hand, for the reverse diathetic perspective (where the subject denotes the content of the recollection), there is no possibility of using the verb *memini* because it is

---

[13] As Benveniste (1966) notes, the constructions with 'to be' and 'to have' both express the notion of possession, but in the transition from one construction to the other the subject of the verb 'to be' is transformed into the grammatical object of the verb 'to have'. The two verbs are in a complementary situation: 'to be' expresses the state of "the one who is", while 'to have' expresses the state of "the one who has", i.e. "the one of whom something is". According to Benveniste (1966: 198-199), this clearly demonstrates the difference between the two constructions: on the one hand 'to be' establishes an intrinsic relationship of identity, while, on the other, 'to have' establishes an extrinsic relation with the possessee and the possessor, which are distinct and are linked by a relation of pertinence.

morphologically defective (nor other verbs such as *recordor* 'remember', which, being deponent, does not allow the diathetic alternance). Therefore, to say 'something is remembered' there is only the possibility of using *in mentem venio* (Baños 2018: 32–35): *aliquid in mentem (mihi) veni*, which would explain its high frequency.

From a syntactic point of view, the construction *in mentem venire* is very cohesive (in 82.2% of cases the PP and the verb are always contiguous, like in (9)) and expresses the semantic value of 'remembering', 'coming to mind'.

(9) *fac   tibi   paternae   legis*
    make:IMP:2SG you:DAT.SG paternal:GEN.SG.F law: GEN.SG.F
    Aciliae   veniat   in mentem
    Acilius: GEN.SG.F come:SUBJ:3.SG in mind:ACC.SG
    'Let the recollection of the Acilian law passed by your father come to your mind'   (Cicero, *Verrine Orations*, 1.1.51)

The equivalence between the constructions *in mentem venire* and *in memoria habeo* is also due to the semantic nature of the nouns: both *mentem* and *memoria* derive from the same root, i.e. **men-* 'thinking' which designates, in opposition to *corpus* 'body', 'the thinking principle', 'the activity of thinking' (Ernout and Meillet 2001). An important difference between the constructions *in memoria habeo* and *in mentem venire* lies in the different nature of the aspectual values they express: the first has a stative value, while the second has an eventive one.[14]

2.3 *Memoria teneo*

Before considering the effective LV extensions of *in memoria habeo* it is worth noting that the semantic value of 'remember' can also be expressed by the construction *memoria teneo*,[15] which seems to realize a similar semantic value to that

---

[14] As observed by Rosén (1981: 146) the alternation of contructions with *ad* or *in* + accusative must be interpreted in terms of aspectual value: "the *ad, in* + accusative periphrasis is at least very frequently interpretable in terms of aspectual content: *in mentem venire* 'to occur (to one's mind)', *incidere in mentem* (same meaning), *in timorem dare aliquem* 'to frighten', *adire ad pactionem* 'to come to an arrangement'".
[15] On this construction, see Ernout and Meillet (2001 [1932]): *s.v. habeo:* "Du sense de 'tenir' dérivent les sens de 'posséder, occuper', 'tenir immobile, arrêter, maintenir' et 'tenir dans son esprit' d'où 'se souvenir' (*memoriā tenēre*) ou 'comprendre, savoir' (*mente tenēre*)", which means that the meanings of 'to possess, to occupy', 'to hold still, to stop, to maintain' and 'to hold in one's mind'

expressed by the construction with *habeo*. Actually, as clearly shown by examples (9–10), the construction with *teneo* turns out to have a different semantic meaning from the construction with *habeo*. The latter, in fact, expresses a stative value, fitting the LV actionality and consistent with the locative value of the PP; *memoria teneo*, on the other hand, expresses – at least at its origin – a greater degree of agentivity, due to the selection of the verb *teneo* and also strengthened by the ablative case of *memoria*, which, in this case, could realize an instrumental.[16] In other words, memory would be the instrument used to keep in mind a certain circumstance or situation. The greater degree of agentivity that differentiates the two constructions is also evident from the numerous uses of imperative forms, which imply the presence of an animated subject and, consequently, an agentive one, endowed with the feature of control. This construction, with a total of 51 occurrences, is more productive than the construction with *habeo*:

Table 4: *Memoria teneo.*

	Caes	Cic	Asc	HygAstr	Sen	Svet	Tac	Tot
N+V	3	42	1	1	2	1	1	51
PP+V		1						1
%	5.77	82.69	1.92	1.92	3.85	1.92	1.92	

Furthermore, as can be seen from Table 4, unlike the construction with *habeo*, *memoria teneo* is absent in archaic Latin, while it is very productive in both classical and post-classical Latin, where *habeo* disappears. Therefore, a substitution of *habeo* by *teneo* has to be presumed. See the examples below:

(10) Memoria tenetis *Artemidorum Aetnensem,*
memory:ABL.SG.F keep:2PL Artemidorus:ACC of.Aetna:ACC
legationis eius principem, publice dicere
embassy:GEN.SG.F this:GEN.SG leader:ACC publicly say:INF
'You will remember the official statement made by Artemidorus of Aetna as the leader of its representatives [...]'   (Cicero, *Verrine Orations*, 2, 3, 105)

---

hence 'to remember' (*memoriā tenēre*) or 'to understand, to perceive (*mente tenēre*), are derived from the meaning of 'to hold'.
16 In the entire corpus there are no instances in which the verb *teneo* appears in combination with the PP *in memoria*. The hypothesis that the ablative *memoria* in *memoria teneo* has an instrumental value can be supported by the fact that the instrumental and the ablative share some semantic traits, including the local one (Fedriani 2011): the local feature is pertinent to the instrumental since instruments are often seen as containers.

(11) Vos,   quaeso,   memoria   teneatis   non   mihi
      you:NOM.PL   pray:1SG   memory:ABL.SG.F   keep:SUBJ.2PL   not   me:DAT.SG
      hoc   esse   propositum   ut   accusem
      this:ACC.N   be:INF   intention:ACC.SG.N   CONJ accuse:SUBJ:1SG
      Oppianicum   mortuum
      Oppianicus:ACC.SG   dead:ACC.SG
      'Pray bear in mind that though it is not my task to accuse the dead Oppianicus'
                                                (Cicero, *for Aulus Cluentius*, 30, 6)

In these examples, as well as in most of the other attestations, the two components of the construction are cohesive and contiguous with a syntactic order of the type N + V, except for 8 occurrences (equal to 15.68% of the total of occurrences), where the elements of the construction appear inverted without any influence on the semantic level.

It is also interesting to note that in most cases (62.74%) the construction holds an argument expressed by the infinitive. This shows that it is a real LVC, since neither the verb *teneo* nor the noun *memoria* alone could hold an argumental clause with the infinitive. As happens for *in memoria habeo* (8), *memoria teneo* also presents an occurrence in which the noun is coordinated with another noun, *animis* in this case, thus denoting a sort of metaphorical 'place', in which to preserve the memory of something, and hence maybe having a more referential and less abstract semantic value:

(12) omittam   igitur   Pompeium   iam   oratione
      Omit:FUT.1SG   therefore   Pompeius:ACC   now   speech:ABL.SG.F
      mea   reliqua,   sed   vos,   iudices,
      my:ABL.SG.F   rest:ABL.SG.F   but   you:PL   judge:VOC.PL
      animis   ac   memoria   tenetote.
      soul:ABL.PL   and   memory:ABL.SG.F   keep:FUT.IMP.2PL
      'I will therefore say no more of Pompeius in the rest of my speech, but do you, gentlemen, keep a recollection of him in your minds and memory'.
                                                (Cicero, *for Cornelius Balbus*, 17)

2.4 Light Verb extensions of the construction *in memoria habeo*

In the corpus there are also ccurrences of *memoria* in combination with other verbs than *habeo* and *teneo*, i.e. the so-called Light Verb extensions. LV extensions[17] make the meaning of the construction more specific. Indeed, in addition to providing grammatical information such as TAM and agreement features, they also supply information about the lexical aspect, act as intensifiers, or respond to socio-pragmatic needs (Cicalese 1999, Ježek 2004). With 11 occurrences (1 of *conservo* 'to conserve', 3 of *comprehendo* 'to enclose', 1 of *custodio* 'to keep', 5 of *retineo* 'to hold'), the presence of LV extensions, on the one hand, reinforces the idea that *in memoria habeo* can be considered an LVC, while, on the other, it testifies to the frequency of the predicative noun:

Table 5: Light Verb extensions of the construction (*in*) *memoria habeo*.

	conservo		*comprehendo*		*custodio*		*retineo*	
	N+V	PP+V	N+V	PP+V	N+V	PP+V	N+V	PP+V
Ennius	1							
Cicero			3		1		2	
Nepos							1	
Seneca								
ValeriusMaxiumus							1	
Fronto							1	
Tot.	1		3		1		5	

Let us consider the example in (13):

(13) *Et   quoniam   ad   externa   transgressi sumus,   quidam*
     and   since   to   external   cross:1PL   be:1PL   certain:NOM.SG
     Athenis   vir   eruditissimus,   cum   ictum
     Athens:ABL.SG man:NOM.SG   erudite:SUPER.NOM.SG   with hit:ACC.SG
     lapidis   capite   excepisset,   cetera
     stone:GEN.SG head:ABL.SG.N   receive:SUBJ:PPF.3SG   rest:ACC.PL.N
     omnia   tenacissima   memoria   retinens
     every:ACC.PL.N   tenacious:SUPER.ABL.SG.F   memory:ABL.SG.F   keep:PRT.NOM

---

[17] LV extensions correspond to those verbs that Gross (1996, 1998) defines as *verbes appropriés*. De Pontonx (2004), on the other hand, defines them as *verbes supports métaphoriques*.

litterarum	*tantummodo,*	*quibus*		*praecipue*	*inservierat,*
letter:GEN.PL.F	only	which:DAT.PL		specially	be.devote:PPF:3SG
oblitus		*est.*			
forget:PRT.NOM		be:3SG			

'And since we have passed to external items, a very learned man in Athens was hit in the head by a stone. He kept all else alive in a very retentive memory, forgetting only letters, to which he had been specially devoted'.

(Valerius Maximus, *Memorable Doings and Sayings*, 1, 8)

The construction with *memoria* maintains a fixed word order, i.e. N + V, also when the LV is an extension, and it is fairly cohesive (in 81.82% of cases): the $N_{(ABL)}$ and the verb appear contiguous in most cases, except in few examples in which between the verb and the noun there is a noun or a negation, as in the occurrence in (14), where the sequence is interrupted by *percepta*.

(14) *Idem   immortali   memoria   percepta*
     the.same   immortal:ABL.SG.F   memory:ABL.SG.F secure:ACC.PL.F
     retinebat   beneficia;   quae   autem   ipse
     retain:IMPF:3SG   benefit:ACC.PL.F who   but   himself
     tribuerat,   tam   diu   meminerat,   quo   ad
     bestow:PPF:3SG   so   for.long.time   remember:IMPF:3SG   which to
     ille   gratus   erat,   qui   acceperat.
     that   grateful:NOM.SG be:IMPF:3SG   REL.PRO   receive:PPF:3SG

'He had besides an unfailing memory for kindnesses received; but as for those which he himself bestowed, he remembered them only so long as the recipient was grateful'.

(Nepos, *Excerpt from the Book of Latin Historians. Atticus*, 11, 5)

Moreover, it is interesting to note that in (14) *memoria retinebat* is opposed to *meminerat*, which confirms, on the one hand, the unitary value of the LVC and, on the other, their semantic differences: in the first case it seems that the subject makes an effort to retain the received benefits in his memory, whereas with *meminerat* the situation is not controlled. Therefore, all of the LV extensions share the agentivity of the subject. This feature most closely associates these LVCs with that of *teneo*.

3 Light Verb Constructions with *animus*

The noun *animus* 'soul' also has different semantic values.[18]

In this paper we will mainly consider the semantic values that the noun *animus* can express in combination with the verb *habeo* and the preposition *in*, namely 'having the intention to' (section 3.1). In addition, we will also (section 3.2) take into account the symmetrical forms, i.e. the constructions *in animo sum* 'be in mind' (section 3.3); and the LV extensions of the construction (section 3.4).

3.1 *In animo habeo*

The noun *animus* 'soul' has different nuances of meaning depending on its occurrence in the simple ablative or *in* + ablative. In this case as well, the predicative noun that enters in the construction with *habeo* is an abstract noun, which refers to the intellectual and intentional sphere and expresses in most cases the semantic value of 'having the intention to'.[19] Table 6 shows all the occurrences recorded for this construction within the *PHI* corpus:

Table 6: *(in) animo habeo.*

	Cat	Lucil	Plaut	BellAfr	BellHisp	Caes	Cic	Sall	Varr	Liv	Quint	Front	Tac	Tot
N+V							1							1
PP+V	1	2	2	1	1	1	11	1	1	18	1	1	1	43
Tot	1	2	2	1	1	1	12	1	1	18	1	1	1	44
%	2.33	4.65	4.65	2.33	2.33	2.33	27.91	2.33	2.33	41.86	2.33	2.33	2.33	

With a total of 44 occurrences, *(in) animo habeo* turns out to be a very productive construction, in particular in the PP form (43 tokens), especially in Cicero (12 occur-

---

[18] The *Oxford Latin Dictionary* collects different meanings of the noun *animus*: s.v. *animus* "the mind as opposed to the body, the mind or soul ad constituting with the body the whole person (as including the *mens*); the element of air (as the principle of life); the mind as the seat of consciousness; consciousness, life, sense; the mind as the organ of thought; as the seat of memory; the mind as the originator of intentions; intend; the mind as the seat of desire or volition, of feelings and emotions; frame of mind, feelings, attitude; animosity; the mind as the seat of pride; the moral and mental constitution of a person, disposition, character".

[19] Baños (2021), who analyzes the PP *in animo*, observes that in combination with *habeo* or *sum* for the most part it realizes the semantic value of 'having the intention'. In other cases, they can also express the semantic value of 'having/being in the soul, in the mind'.

rences) and Livy (18 occurrences). Two examples from these authors are shown below:

(15) *accusatores   inimicosque   eius   habere   in   animo*
     persecutor:ACC.PL and.enemy:ACC.PL 3SG.GEN have:INF in soul:ABL.SG
     pecuniam   praetori   dare
     money:ACC.SG.F praetor:DAT.SG give:INF
     'his persecutors and enemies were proposing to offer the praetor money'
     (Cicero, Verrine Orations, 2.2.69)

(16) *deinde, ·ut   accepit   hunc   morem   esse*
     then   CONJ learn:PRF:3SG this:ACC.SG custom:ACC.SG be:INF
     Macedonum   tradentium   sese,   parcere
     the.Macedonians:GEN.PL surrender:GEN.PL RFL:ACC.3PL spare:INF
     victis   in   animo   habebat.
     vanquished:DAT.PL in soul:ABL.SG have:IMPF:3SG
     'Then, when he learned that it was the customary gesture of the Macedonians to indicate their surrender, it was in his mind to spare the vanquished'
     (Livy, History of Rome, 33.10.4)

This construction can follow the order or either V + PP, mostly in Cicero (8 occurrences out of a total of 11, i.e. 72.72%), or PP + V, mostly in Livy (100% occurrences equal to 41.86% of the total of constructions with the PP), without apparent semantic differences.

The LVC *in animo habeo* demonstrates very high syntactic cohesion (93.18%) which can be seen in the adjacency of the LVC components. In these conditions it mainly expresses an abstract semantic value ('to have the intention of', 'to have in mind, intend').[20] However, in some cases (6.82% of the occurrences) the LVC does not expresses this unitary meaning, the verb being less empty and the PP maintaining a locative value. Let us examine the example below:

---

[20] Pompei (2016a), analyzing the sentence *"hoc neque ipse transire habebat in animo neque hostes transituros existimabat* (Caesar, *The Gallic War* 6.7.6)", observes that *in animo habere* "becomes a sort of *verbum putandi*, in fact, it is coordinated with *existimabat* and it does not have an entity object (...), but a propositional theme expressed by an infinitive clause" (Pompei 2016a: 104).

(17) *Est   autem   consolatio   pervulgata*
     be:3SG moreover consolation:NOM.SG.F common:SUPER.NOM.SG.F
     quidem   illa   maxime,   quam   semper in
     certainly that:NOM.SG.F maximally REL.ACC.SG always in
     ore   atque in animo   habere   debemus [...]
     mouth:ABL.SG.N and   in soul:ABL.SG have:INF ought:1PL
     'Now there is a form of consolation, extremely common place, I grant you, which we ought always to have on our lips and in our hearts [...]'
     (Cicero, *Letters to friends*, 5.16.2)

In example (17) the noun is more referential, coordinating with *ore* 'mouth'.

In other cases, when the sequence PP+V is interrupted by another lexical element, the construction expresses a less abstract and more compositional semantic value, as in (18):

(18) *Hunc   tu   quas   conscientiae   labes*
     this:ACC.SG you.2SG REL:ACC.PL.F conscience:GEN.SG.F fault:ACC.PL.F
     in animo   censes   habuisse,   quae   vulnera?
     in soul:ABL.SG think:2SG have:INF.PERF REL.ACC.PL.N wound:ACC.PL.N
     'What stain of conscience do you think he had in his soul, what wounds?'
     (Cicero, *De Officiis* 3.85)

Therefore, a semantic continuum which goes from greater to lesser referentiality expressed by the predicative noun can be hypothesized, as well as a corresponding syntactic continuum that goes from lesser to greater syntactic cohesion. Such a continuum could be represented as follows:

+ referential		- referential
	semantic continuum	
-cohesion		+ cohesion
	syntactic continuum	

Schema 1: Semantic-syntactic continuum.

In the entire corpus there is only one occurrence of the variant $N_{(ABL)}$ + V, in (19):

(19) *Domum   Rabirianam   Neapoli,   quam   tu*
     house:ACC.SG Rabirian:ACC.SG.F Naples:ABL.SG rel:ACC.SG you.2SG
     iam   dimensam   et   exaedificatam   animo
     already   misured:Prt.ACC.SG.F and building:PRT.ACC.SG.F soul:ABL.SG

	habebas,	*M.Fonteius*	emit	HS CCCIƆƆ<XXX>.
	have:IMPF.2SG	M.Fontius:NOM	buy:PERF3SG	£1,150

'M. Fontius has bought Rabirius' house at Naples, which you had in your mind's eyes ready mapped out and finished for about £1,150'

(Cicero, Letters to Atticus, 1.6.1)

In this case, the semantic value expressed by the construction seems to be different, namely it does not express the semantic value of 'having the intention to', but rather that of a mental image[21].

3.2 *(in) animo sum*

The construction *in animo habeo* – like *in memoria habeo* – also has a symmetrical form, i.e. *(in) animo sum*, which realizes a diathetically opposite value. In the entire corpus investigated, 25 occurrences of the form with the verb *sum* 'be in mind' have been identified:

Table 7: *(in) animo sum.*

	Ter	Caes	Cic	Hirt	Liv	Sen	Quint	Tot	%
N+V	2	1	4	1				8	32
PP+V		2	5		7	1	2	17	68
Tot	2	3	9	1	7	1	2	25	
%	8	12	36	4	28	4	8		

Some examples are provided below:

(20) in animo   est,   quem   ad modum   ante
     in soul:ABL.SG   be:3SG   which:ACC.SG   in manner:ACC.SG   before
     dixi,   leviter transire   ac   tantum modo perstringere
     say:PRF:1SG   lightly pass.over:INF   and   only just   touch.upon:INF

---

[21] In other cases the construction is completely different, as happens in *"non est nobis committendum ut ad has XIII cohortis quas dubio animo habeo hostis accedere aut in itinere me consequi possit"* 'I must take steps that the enemy may not meet my fourteen doubtful cohorts or overtake me on the march' (Cicero, *Letters to Atticus*, 8.12A.3). In this context, *dubio animo habeo* effectively means 'to consider of dubious loyalty, unreliable'.

unam	quamque	rem,
one:ACC.SG	each:ACC.SG	matter:ACC.SG

'as I said before, it is my intention to pass lightly over and only touch upon each question' (Cicero, *for Sextus Roscius*, 91)

(21) Nunc   mihi   temporis   eius   quod   ad dicendum
     now   1sg:DAT   time:GEN.SG.N REL NOM.N   because   to speak:GER:ACC.SG
     datur,   quoniam   in   animo   est   causam   omnem
     give:3SG.PASS since   in   soul:ABL.SG be:3SG case:ACC.SG.F full:ACC
     exponere,   habenda   ratio   est   diligenter.
     set.forth:INF have:GERD:NOM.SG account:NOM.SG.F be:3SG carefully

'But, I must now take careful account of the time allowed me for my speech, since I intend to set forth the case in full'. (Cicero, *Verrine Orations*, 2.1.32)

The construction *in animo sum* also presents the variant N₍ABL₎ + V, which expresses a compositional semantic value, but different from that expressed by the construction with the PP. We can see this in the following example:

(22) quibus   autem   idcirco   negaris,   quod   te
     REL.DAT.PL however   for.this.reason deny:SUBJ:PERF.2SG   because   you
     impeditum   esse   dixeris   aut   amicorum
     hinder:PRT.ACC.SG be:INF say:SUBJ:PERF:2SG   or   friend:GEN.PL
     hominum   negotiis   aut   gravioribus   causis
     man:GEN.PL   affair:ABL.PL   or   more.important:ABL.PL.F reason:ABL.PL.F
     aut   ante   susceptis,   inimici   discedunt
     or   before   deeds:PRT.ABL.PL enemy:NOM.PL   go.away:3PL
     omnes-que   hoc   animo   sunt   ut   sibi   te
     all:NOM.PL-and   this   soul:ABL.SG be:3PL CONJ   REFL.DAT   you:ACC.SG
     mentiri   malint   quam   negare.
     lie:INF.DEP   prefer:SUBJ:PRES:3PL than   deny:INF

'but if you refuse because you are prevented (you say) by affairs of friends or by previous or more important reasons, they go away hating you; they are all in the mood that they had rather you lied to them than refused them'
(Cicero, *Handbook of Electioneering*, 46)

The variant N(abl)+*sum* has a semantic value different from that conveyed by PP+*sum*: it does not express an intention but refers to a state of mind. This would confirm the initial hypothesis according to which the preposition *in* contributes to the semantic value of the construction. In other words, the entire PP expresses a distinct predicative value with respect to the simple ablative noun. As also happens for *animo habeo*, in other cases *animo* in the pattern *animo sum* realizes an *ablativus qualitatis*.

3.3 Light Verb extensions

In addition to *habeo* and *sum*, other verbs can appear both with the PP *in animo* and the ablative noun *animo* giving rise to LV extensions. In the entire corpus analyzed, a total of 4 occurrences were recorded which testify to the productivity of LCV, although not representing a quantity that would allow for generalization:

Table 8: Light Verb extensions of the construction (*in*) *animo habeo*.

		N+V	PP+V	Tot	%
remaneo	Cicero		1	2	50
	Senecaw		1		
cogito	Terentius		1	1	25
sentio	Cicero	1		1	25
Tot		1	3	4	
%		25%	75%		100%

According to Table 8 the different nature of these extensions is immediately evident: they are represented by another verb with a stative and locative value (*remaneo* 'to remain' (23)), and two *verba putandi*, *cogito* 'to think' (24) and *sentio* 'to believe, to consider'(25), which intensify the notion of 'to have in mind'.

(23) ne in animo quidem igitur sensus
 not in soul:ABL.SG either therefore sensation:NOM.SG
 remanet; ipse enim nusquam est
 remain:3SG the same.NOM.SG for nowhere be:3SG
 'And so there is no sensation in the soul either, for the soul is nowhere'
 (Cicero, *Tusculan Disputations*, 1, 8)

(24) haec si voles in animo vere cogitare,
 this:ACC.PL.N if want:FUT:2SG in soul:ABL.SG really think:INF
 Demea, et mihi et tibi et illis
 Demea:VOC.SG and 1SG.DAT.SG and 2SG.DAT.SG and 3pl. DAT

> *dempseris molestiam*
> remove:FUT:PERF:2SG trouble:ACC.SG.F
> 'If you will think this over in a true light, Demea, you will find that you have relieved me and yourself and them of a world of trouble'
>
> (Terence, *The Brothers*, 818)

(25)   *hic, quod cum ceteris animo sentiebat,*
this:NOM.SG Which:ACC.SG.N with other:ABL.SG soul:ABL.SG feel:IMPF:3SG
id magis quam ceteri et voltu promptum
this:ACC.SG.N more than other:NOM.PL and face:ABL.SG clear:ACC.SG.N
habuit et lingua
have:PERF:3SG and tongue:ABL.SG.F
'[...] while Plancius, more than the rest, bore upon his countenance and upon his tongue, for all to see and hear, those feelings wich the rest shared with him'   (Cicero, *The Speech on behalf of Gnaeus Plancius*, 34, 9)

In (23) there is no cohesion between the LV extension *remanet* and the PP *in animo*; consistently, the meaning is compositional as the PP expresses an abstract location. On the other hand, the mention of this abstract place seems to be quite redundant in the presence of two real *verba putandi*.

4 Conclusions

In this work, two constructions of Latin have been examined (*in memoria habeo* and *in animo habeo*). The application of tests demonstrates that these constructions are actually LVCs: (i) (*in*) *animo* and (*in*) *memoria* can also co-occurr with another equally neutral LV (*sum*) and with LVs (extensions); (ii) both LVCs present cohesion to different degrees; (iii) congruently with the degree of cohesion, the meaning of *(in) animo habeo* can be more compositional or more abstract. In particular, both constructions express an abstract value when the noun is combined with the preposition *in*, designating an abstract place where memories are kept in the case of *in memoria habeo*, and intention or volition in the case of *in animo habeo*.

    The construction *in memoria habeo* is only attested in archaic Latin, while in later periods it is replaced by *memoria teneo*. In the latter LVC *memoria* has an instrumental value rather than a locative one, as also happens when co-occurring with LV extensions. On the other hand, the construction (*in*) *animo habeo* is attested throughout the evolution of the language, from archaic to post-classical Latin. When *animo* appears without the preposition, both in combination with *habeo* and with *sum*, it expresses a more referential value. In other cases, the ablative *animo* has a different meaning being an *ablativus qualitatis*.

Abbreviations

ABL	ablative
ACC	accusative
DAT	dative
DEO	deponent
FUT	future
GEN	genitive
GER	gerund
GERD	gerundive
IMP	imperative
IMPF	imperfect
INF	infinitive
PERF	perfect
PRT	participle
PP	past participle
PPF	pluperfect
PRT	participle
REL	relative
REFL	reflexive
SUBJ	subjunctive
SUPER	superlative
VOC	vocative

References

Baldi Philip & Andrea Nuti. 2010. Possession. In Philip Baldi & Pierluigi Cuzzolin (eds.), *New Perspectives on Historical Latin Syntax. Volume 3: Constituent Syntax: Quantification, Numerals, Possession, Anaphora*, 239–387. Berlin/New York: Mouton de Gruyter.

Baños, José Miguel. 2012. Verbos soporte e incorporación sintáctica en latín: el ejemplo de ludos facere. *Revista de Estudios Latinos* 12. 37–57.

Baños, José Miguel. 2016. *Cum in otium venimus (CIC. Att. 1, 7, 1):* inacusatividsad y colocaciones verbo-nominales en latín. Talk presented at VIII Congreso de la Sociedad de Estudios Latinos (León, June 29th–July 2nd 2016).

Baños, José Miguel. 2018. Las construcciones con verbo soporte en Latín: una perspectiva diacrónica. In Colette Bodelot & Olga Spevak (eds.), *Les constructions à verbe support en latin*, 21–51. Clermont-Ferrand: Presses Universitaires Blaise Pascal.

Baños, José Miguel. 2021. Estudio diacrónico de *animum inducere e in animum indicere*: convergencias y diferencias. *Emerita* 89(2). 279–307.

Bentley, Delia, Francesco Maria Ciconte & Silvio Cruschina. 2015. *Existentials and Locatives in Romance Dialects of Italy*. Oxford: Oxford University Press.

Benveniste, Émile. 1976 [1966]. *Problèmes de linguistique générale*. Parigi: Gallimard.

Bosque, Ignacio 2004. REDES. *Diccionario combinatorio del español contemporáneo. Las palabras en su contexto*. Madrid: Ediciones SM.

Butt, Miriam. 2010. The light verb jungle: still hacking away. In Mengistu Amberber, Mark Harvey & Brett Baker (eds.), *Complex Predicates: Cross-linguistic Perspectives on Event Structure*, 48–78. Cambridge: Cambridge University Press,

Cicalese, Anna 1999. Le estensioni di verbo supporto. Uno studio introduttivo. *Studi Italiani di Linguistica Teorica e Applicata* 28(3). 447–485.

Ernout, Alfred & Alfred Meillet. 2001[1932]. *Dictionnaire étimologique de la langue latine. Historie des mots*. 4th edn. Paris: Klincksieck.

De Pontonx, Sophie. 2004. Les verbes supportes métaphoriques. In Gaston Gross & Sophie De Pontonx (eds.), *Verbes supports. Nouvel état des lieux* 27(2). 265–281. [=Special issue of *Lingvisticae Investigationes*].

Dolkowska, Karolina. 2012. *Sintaxis y semántica de memoria en latín: empleos adverbales y colocacionales*. MA dissertation. Madrid: Universidad Autónoma de Madrid.

Fedriani, Chiara. 2011. Experiential metaphors in Latin: feelings were containers, movements and things possessed. *Transactions of the Philological Society* 109(3). 307–326.

Giry-Schneider, Jacqueline. 1987. *Les prédicats nominaux en français: les phrases à verbe support*. Genève/Paris: Droz.

Gross, Gaston. 1989. *Les constructions converses du français*. Genève/Paris: Droz.

Gross, Gaston. 1996. Prédicats nominaux et compatibilité aspectuelle. *Langages* 121. 54–72.

Gross, Gaston & Ference Kiefer. 1995. Les verbes supports: nouvel état des lieux. *Folia Linguistica* 29. 29–43.

Gross, Gaston. 1998. Pour une véritable fonction synonymie dans un traitement de texte. *Langages* 131(103). 114.

Gross, Maurice. 1975. *Méthodes en syntaxe: régime des constructions completives*. Paris: Hermann.

Jiménez Martínez, María Isabel. 2011. *Colocaciones lèxicas coon el verbo pono en prosa clásica*. MA dissertation. Madrid: Universidad Complutense de Madrid.

Jiménez Martínez, María Isabel. 2016. *Colocaciones y verbos soporte en latín: semántica y sintaxis del verbo pono*. PhD dissertation. Madrid: Universidad Complutense de Madrid.

Ježek, Elisabetta. 2004. Types et degrés de verbes supports en italien. In Gaston Gross & Sophie De Pontonx (eds.), *Verbes supports. Nouvel état des lieux* 27(2). 185–201. [=Special issue of *Lingvisticae Investigationes*].

Langer, Stefan. 2004. A linguistic test battery for support verb construction. In Gaston Gross & Sophie De Pontonx (eds.), *Verbes supports. Nouvel état des lieux* 27(2). 171–184. [=Special issue of *Lingvisticae Investigationes*].

Live, Anna H. 1973. The TAKE-HAVE phrasal in English. *Linguistics* 95. 31–56.

Lyons, John. 1977. *Semantics*. Vol. 2. Cambridge: Cambridge University Press.

Luraghi, Silvia. 1997. Omission of the direct object in Classical Latin. *Indogermanische Forschungen* 102. 239–257.

Marini, Elisabetta. 2000. Criteri di individuazione di una costruzione a verbo supporto: due esempi latini (*opem ferre* e *morem gerere*). *Studi e Saggi Linguistici* 38. 365–395.

Mendózar Cruz, Juan. 2015. Causatividad y construcciones con verbo soporte en latín: el ejemplo de poena afficere. *Cuadernos de Filología Clásica. Estudios Latinos* 35(1). 7–28.

Nickel, Gerhard. 1968. Complex verbal structures in English. *International Review of Applied Linguistics* 6. 1–21.

Pompei, Anna. 2016. Construction Grammar and Latin: the case of *habeo*. *PALLAS* 102. 98–108.

Roesch, Sophie. 2001. Les empois de verbum et sermo dans les expressions à verbe support *verba facere*, *verba habere* et *sermonem habere*. In Claude Moussy & Jacqueline Dangel (eds.), *De lingua Latina novae quaestiones*, 859–874. Louvain-la-Neuve: Peeters.

Rosén, Hannah. 1981. *Studies in the Syntax of the Verbal Noun in Early Latin*. München: Wilhelm Fink Verlag.

Sag, Ivan A., Timothy Baldwin, Francis Bond, Ann Copestake & Dan Flickinger. 2002. Multiword expressions: A pain in the neck for NLP. In Alexander Gelbukh (ed.), *Computational Linguistics and Intelligent Text Processing. Proceedings of CIC Ling 2002*, 1–15. Heidelberg/Berlin: Springer.

Simone, Raffaele. 2008a. Verbi sintagmatici come categoria e come costruzione. In Monica Cini (ed.), *I verbi sintagmatici in italiano e nelle varietà dialettali: stato dell'arte e prospettive di ricerca. Atti delle giornate di studio. Torino, 19-20 febbraio 2007*, 13–30. Frankfurt: Peter Lang,

Simone, Raffaele. 2008b. Coefficienti verbali nei nomi. In Pier Marco Bertinetto, Valentina Bambini, Cristina Bertoncin & Margherita Farina (eds.), *Categorie del verbo diacronia, teoria, tipologia. Atti del XXXI Convegno della Società Italiana di Glottologia*, 83–113. Roma: il Calamo.

Van Valin, Robert D. & Randy J. Lapolla. 1997. *Syntax. Structure, meaning and function*. Cambridge: Cambridge University Press.

Wierzbicka, Anna. 1982. Why you can *have a drink* when you can't **have a eat*? *Language* 58. 753–799.

Index

a avea (Romanian) 101, 107, 111, 113, 116, 117, 131, 132, 135, 140
acategorial root 75, 76, 80
accomplishment 91, 152, 170, 191, 192, 205, 213, 308
achievement 91, 108, 152, 170, 182, 184, 189–191, 193, 195, 205, 213, 241
actant 3, 21–24, 27
action 80–82, 89, 105, 112, 125, 126, 130, 131, 136, 138, 150, 152, 156, 159, 162, 172, 177, 191, 203, 206, 213, 227, 232, 233, 246, 259, 261, 263, 264, 267, 269, 281, 286, 306, 311, 321, 325, 329, 330, 339, 342
actional 9–11, 150, 160, 183, 267, 276
actionality 6, 9, 16, 99, 108, 149, 151, 156, 162, 163, 166, 169, 193, 216, 346
action nominal (AN) (see also action noun; predicative noun) 305, 308, 309, 321, 324–326, 329, 330
action noun (see also action nominal; *nomen actionis*) 225, 257, 258, 261, 264
active zone 164, 174, 175
activity 108, 121–124, 128, 133, 141, 151, 155, 167, 168, 170, 181, 187, 192, 205, 223, 226, 230, 234, 240, 243–246, 345
Actor (see semantic participant)
a da (Romanian) 101, 107, 111, 112, 115, 118, 121–124, 127, 131, 133, 136–138, 140, 157, 183
adicity 154, 155, 157, 158, 172, 176, 184, 195
a face (Romanian) 101, 102, 107, 115, 117, 120, 122–125, 127, 131, 133–135, 140, 157
a fi (Romanian) 105, 111, 113, 116–118, 131, 132, 134, 140, 142
Agent (see semantic participant)
agentivity 52, 162, 164, 173, 179, 185, 195, 346, 349
agreement 6, 102, 348
Aktionsart (see also lexical aspect) 9, 63, 64, 99, 103, 108, 110, 112, 138, 149–151, 153, 187, 191, 337
a lua (Romanian) 101, 107, 116, 117, 120, 123, 131, 137, 138, 141
analytic(al) construction 11, 13, 279–281, 283, 289, 293, 294, 340

analytic(al) predicate/predication 153, 222, 223, 285
analytic verb (form) 1, 121, 266, 291
animo (Latin) 12, 337–340, 350, 357
anticausative 11, 119, 138, 139, 141, 142, 291
apanhar (Portuguese) 105, 116, 117, 119, 120, 131
applicative 294, 298–300
a provoca (Romanian) 102, 111, 112, 116, 118, 134
argument
- external argument 77, 83, 85, 154, 156
- first argument 82, 112–114, 117, 118, 129, 151, 158, 344
- local argument 155
argument fusion 5
argument merger 5, 20
argument raising 155
argument structure 5–8, 11, 20, 62, 75, 113, 136, 137, 149–152, 154–156, 158, 163, 171, 172, 175, 179, 184, 185, 188, 194, 195, 206, 214, 305, 311
argument transfer 5, 20, 155, 172
argument variable 154, 155
aspect 2, 52, 68, 79, 80, 125, 151, 155, 175, 190, 205, 206, 209, 210, 215, 222, 258, 316, 327–330, 337
- lexical aspect (see also *Aktionsart*) 24, 150, 151, 201, 348
aspectoid 12, 275, 276, 281, 283, 286–290, 293
- aspectoid marker 12, 286, 287
aspect preservation hypothesis 167
aspectual class 82, 103, 112, 131, 152, 205
- aspectual classification 73, 75, 77, 83, 90, 91, 93, 158
aspectuality 12, 305, 309, 316, 328
aspectual marker 5, 12, 309, 316, 318, 327, 316, 329
- 'for-x-time' 155, 168, 210, 211
- 'in-x-time' 110, 155, 170, 211, 213, 214
- 'of-x-time' 110, 168
aspectual meaning 12, 305, 311, 318, 327, 328
aspectual properties 24, 74, 75, 121, 131, 314, 318, 324, 327
asyndetic 277
atelic (see telic) 108, 110, 121, 123, 128, 129, 133, 160, 170, 195, 330

atelicity (see telicity) 166, 169, 170
attraper (French) 117, 119
auxiliary 5, 6, 46, 79, 141, 161, 187, 224, 260, 277, 278, 307, 312
avere (Italian) 101, 105–107, 111, 112, 114–118, 126, 130–132, 137, 187, 224
avoir (French) 101, 103, 105–107, 111, 112, 116, 117, 131, 142, 152, 258

base (see also collocate) 2, 104, 156, 240
base verb 3, 27, 133, 136, 154, 170, 182, 184, 292
basic Light Verb (uses) 9, 11, 99, 103, 106, 112, 114, 119, 121, 125, 129, 132–134, 138, 139, 141, 142, 152, 157, 170, 176, 178, 266, 277, 339
basic verb meaning 9, 118, 158, 160, 232, 241, 242–247, 250–252, 305, 308
benefaction 162, 164
Beneficiary (see semantic participant)
bleaching 1, 5, 10, 105, 134, 150, 165, 194, 202, 204, 259, 306, 325
boundedness (see also unboundedness) 9, 11, 105, 108–110, 129, 137, 149, 150, 158, 160, 162–164, 166–169, 175, 181, 188, 189, 191–193, 195, 316, 328, 329
– boundedness constraint 150, 160, 163, 195
bounding 167, 168, 170, 193

capere (Latin) 139–141
carrier
– functional carrier 278, 279, 286, 287, 290, 292, 294, 295
– inflectional carrier 276, 282
– lexical carrier 275–280, 282, 284, 286, 287, 290, 292, 294, 295, 299
– lexical-semantic carrier 276
(Combinatory) Categorial Grammar 5, 61
categorizer 75, 76
causative Light Verb 25, 30, 35, 36, 135, 137
causativity 113, 138, 139, 142
change (aspect) 49, 77, 78, 80–82, 90–92, 160, 163, 183, 190, 226, 329
– change of location 78, 82, 83, 89, 161, 164, 165, 185, 186, 194
– change of possession 78, 87, 89, 161, 165
– change of state (see also state) 77, 78, 85, 190, 191, 193

children's corpus 247–249
classifier 12, 275, 276, 286, 294, 297, 299, 300, 317, 328
co-composition 153, 154, 160, 214, 216, 221–223, 227, 228, 232–237, 241, 251, 252
– co-compositional principle 4
coger (Spanish) 10, 105, 116, 117, 119, 120, 131, 138, 153, 239, 243, 245–248, 250, 251, 258
cognitive
– cognitive approach 171, 182, 183, 194, 195
– cognitive grammar 166, 179
– cognitive perspective 9, 159, 160, 163, 175, 223, 226
collocate (see also base) 2, 229, 240–242, 251
collocation 2, 3, 25, 205, 229, 239–242, 247, 249–252, 279
compatibility 12, 131, 160, 183, 191, 195, 288, 316
– aspectual compatibility 106, 132, 134, 188
– lexical compatibility 6
– meaning compatibility 49, 59, 60, 62
complex event nominal (see nominal)
complex predicate (see also multiword predicate) 4–6, 11, 19–31, 33–36, 38–41, 93, 149, 152, 154–156, 160, 163, 171, 194, 203, 221, 222, 234, 239, 257, 269, 305, 306, 308, 309, 329, 337
complex verb (form) 6, 11, 276, 277, 282, 297
complex verbal structure 337
computational grammar 8, 48, 68
construction
– Construction of Hitting Events 159
– Dative Construction 159, 171, 175, 184
– Imminent Time Construction 312, 313
– Modified Purpose Construction 312, 313
– Motion Construction 160
– nominal construction 26, 28, 29, 31–37
– oblique construction 309, 321, 323
– Physical Implication Construction 159, 171
– Transfer Construction 159
– valency-decreasing construction 159, 184
– valency-increasing construction 159
constructional meaning 309–311
Construction Grammar 7, 12, 305, 309, 310, 316, 330
– constructional framework 309
– Constructional view 75
– constructionist approach 159

- Constructivist view 73, 75, 76
- Neo-constructionalist framework 7, 8

continuative 205, 209–211, 215, 287
control (see also domain: control domain) 162, 164, 173, 177, 180, 186, 232, 306, 342, 346
control structure 4
control verbs 31
converb 277, 289
conversation 244, 245, 247, 248, 250–252
co-occurrence 8–10, 24, 99, 109, 110, 124, 129, 133, 135–143, 149, 154, 159, 160, 171, 184, 188, 191, 194, 224, 240, 241, 244, 251, 318, 338, 339
coreference (see also Light Verb Construction test) 2, 19, 30–33, 35, 36, 38, 40, 41, 112–114, 117, 118, 124, 129, 132, 134, 136–139, 141, 151, 177, 185
core meaning 10, 11, 231, 232, 239, 242, 250, 251
corpus analysis 230
- corpus annotation 8, 21, 23, 45, 52, 53, 68, 306
corpus-based 10, 12, 201, 215, 221, 242, 257, 305, 314
coverb 4, 277, 278

dar (Portuguese, Spanish) 100–107, 111, 112, 115, 116, 121–131, 133, 134, 136, 138, 140–143, 149, 153, 155, 157, 159, 160, 172, 176–177, 183, 192–195, 240, 246–247, 258
dare (Italian) 101–107, 111, 112, 114–119, 121–131, 137, 138, 141, 154–158, 176
dare (Latin) 9, 139, 140, 149, 150, 154, 170, 172–195, 345, 351
Dative Construction (see construction)
de (Urdu) 161
decoding process 251
decomposition model 76
deletion test (see Light Verb Construction test)
delexical sense 243, 250, 251
delexical verb 246, 251
deverbal noun 1, 10, 124, 127, 151, 155, 156, 201, 204, 215, 225, 265, 266, 269
- non-deverbal noun 151, 152, 269
diachrony 310, 312, 319
diathesis 113, 241
- active 8, 11, 263, 264
- middle 11, 124, 125, 136, 138, 139, 141, 191, 192, 195, 263–265, 269

- passive 8, 103, 106, 138
- reciprocal 103, 106, 128
- reflexive 124, 125, 128, 136, 183, 191
diathetic effect 9, 99, 113, 119, 131
discreteness 168, 175, 181, 187
Distributed Morphology 76
distributional model 244, 251, 252
distribution of valency complementations 19, 38, 41
dividness 168, 169
domain 52, 53, 64, 65, 67, 163, 260–262
- control domain 164, 165, 172–175, 179, 182, 185, 194
- domain of 'human interest' 164, 165, 173–175, 177, 179, 182, 185, 194
- domain matrix 172, 176, 179, 182, 185, 188, 191, 194, 195
- force-dynamics domain 164–166, 174, 175, 177, 180–182, 185, 187, 188, 190, 191, 192, 194, 195
- motion domain 260–262
- spatio-temporal domain 164, 165, 174, 175, 177, 180, 182, 185, 186, 190–192, 194, 195
- syntactic domain 4
donner (French) 100, 106, 107, 111, 112, 116, 121, 123, 127, 131, 140, 152, 157, 158, 176
duration 82, 91, 92, 108, 124–126, 132, 140, 152, 168, 169, 179, 181, 182, 188, 189, 190, 204
durative 53, 108, 109, 133, 156, 160, 167, 169, 170, 183, 210, 211, 290
durativity 8, 9, 108–110, 125, 129, 139
dynamic 64, 77, 78, 81–83, 90, 92, 108, 109, 120, 132, 139, 142, 151, 156, 160, 169, 170, 172, 205, 210, 288, 339
dynamicity 63, 82, 108, 109, 135, 169, 183, 191

echar (Spanish) 122, 125, 143, 246, 259
elaboration site (e-site) 166, 179, 186
emission (force of, sense of) 130, 136, 162, 164, 178, 180, 181
energy
- energy flow 165, 172, 174, 175, 181, 182, 185–187, 190, 191, 195
- energy sink 165, 166, 174, 175, 177, 181, 186, 193
- energy source 9, 165, 174, 175, 177, 181, 182, 185–187, 190, 193
- kinetic energy 77, 186
essere (Italian) 115, 118, 134, 187, 224, 225

estar (Portuguese) 116, 118, 134
event
- event augmentation 163, 193
- event modification 163, 193
- event summation 163
eventive 2, 9, 79, 151, 156, 201, 345
eventive Light Verbs 77–81, 90–94, 103, 106, 109
eventive noun (see also noun actionality: event-denoting noun) 9, 10, 102, 109, 112, 120, 121, 129, 133, 135, 139, 142, 149, 150, 159, 160, 172, 201, 204, 205, 210, 211, 214, 215
eventivity 78–80
event structure 8, 9, 11, 14, 73–76, 78, 82, 83, 89, 90, 92, 93, 108, 112, 149, 150, 158, 160, 171, 175, 181, 187, 188, 191, 194, 195, 214
eventuality 9, 75–82, 93, 222, 223, 225, 226, 230–236
event variable 75
evidentiality 295
Experiencer (see semantic participant)
extension (see also Light Verb extension) 12, 126, 130, 139, 140, 142, 159, 160, 307, 325, 355

faire (French) 1, 101–103, 105–107, 112, 116, 120, 122, 123, 125–127, 131, 133, 138, 140–142, 152, 157–159, 176, 183, 203, 257–258
fare (Italian) 1, 6, 10, 101, 102, 105, 107, 112, 114–116, 118, 120–126, 128, 130–134, 141–143, 153–157, 176, 183, 221–223, 229–235, 257–259
fazer (Portuguese) 101, 105, 107, 112, 116, 118, 120, 122–127, 131, 133, 140, 183
ficar (Portuguese) 117, 120
forcefulness 162, 164
formal grammar 48, 68, 242
full verb (see also heavy verb) 3, 5, 7–9, 11, 26, 27, 30, 135, 136, 141, 149, 152, 154, 158, 159, 163, 165, 171, 173, 179, 184, 188, 191, 195, 260, 281, 284, 285, 288, 307, 327
- full counterpart (see also heavy verb: heavy counterpart) 9, 11, 12, 112, 130, 136,137, 150, 155, 158, 161, 165, 172, 194
Functional Generative Description 20, 21

Generative Lexicon 2, 3, 7, 10, 103, 153, 160, 206
generic Light Verb 26, 103, 112, 152, 176
generic verb meaning 99, 112, 143, 232, 233, 258, 259
give (English) 161–163
Goal (see semantic participant; Motion component)
government 20, 65, 66, 86, 87, 91, 240
- government of preposition and noun by the verb 66
grammaticalization 1, 5, 11, 12, 135, 161, 260, 275, 276, 278, 279, 281, 282, 286–289, 292–294, 298–300, 305, 307, 312–314, 319, 324–328

habere 12, 13, 102, 117, 140, 141, 337, 338, 340–348, 350, 351, 353, 355–357
hacer (Spanish) 3, 101, 105, 107, 116, 120, 122–127, 131, 133, 134, 143, 159, 183, 240, 246, 247
Head-Driven Phrase Structure Grammar 5, 7, 8, 48, 60–62, 66
heavy verb (see also full verb) 73, 150, 161, 307
- heavy counterpart (see also full counterpart) 160–161

inchoative 9, 99, 103, 118, 119, 138, 139, 141, 142, 163, 193, 195, 205, 209, 213–215, 288, 290
incorporee 285, 297
incremental 9, 99, 105, 118, 119, 138, 139, 141, 142, 158, 312
inflectional 3, 56, 275–278, 282, 307
- inflectional language 38, 41
- inflectional paradigm 277, 278
- inflectional variant 245
inherent orientation 183, 190
Initiator (see semantic participant)
initiator-Predicat 6
initiatory phrase (initP) 74, 76, 77, 82–90, 94
initiatory subevent 76, 81–83, 85, 87–90, 92
insignificant verb 1, 7, 150, 156, 201
instrumental marker 174, 294, 296, 300
intentionality 172, 173, 179, 232
iterative 103, 169, 181, 205, 209, 211, 212, 215, 288
iterarativity 105

jiayi (Chinese) 12, 307–309, 315–320, 323, 324, 326–328
jiyu (Chinese) 12, 308, 309, 315–322, 324–328, 330

Index — 365

landmark 164, 175, 180, 186
late insertion 76
Lexical Conceptual Structure 75, 154
Lexical-Functional grammar 4, 5, 20, 152
lexicalization 11-13, 223, 258, 259, 275, 278, 279, 281, 282, 284-286, 294, 299, 300
lexical meaning 5, 22, 103, 134, 135, 149, 150, 151, 163, 194, 228, 308, 311, 313
lexical verb 9, 10, 91, 92, 159, 163, 201, 205, 215, 251, 260, 277, 278, 283, 288, 305, 314, 319, 327
Lexical view 75
Lexval 54-58
lightness 1, 2, 11, 12, 24, 90, 100, 102, 136, 150, 153, 154, 161, 201, 204, 206, 215, 305, 339
light noun 12, 275, 294-300
Light Verb Construction test
- clefting 25, 203, 215
- coreference 2, 112-114, 117, 118, 129, 132, 134, 136-139, 151, 177, 185
- deletion 24, 151, 153, 203, 215
- double syntactic analysis 154, 185
- passivization 25, 203, 215
- reduction 2, 132, 134-139, 151
- verb nominalization 25, 202, 203, 205, 215
- WH-question 202, 203, 215
Light Verb extension (see also support verb: support verb extension) 6, 9-11, 24, 103, 107, 115, 116, 118, 119, 121, 122, 126, 130, 133, 134, 136, 141-143, 157, 180, 201, 204, 215, 229, 338, 345, 348-350, 355, 356
Light Verb pattern
- [ideophone+V / V+ideophone] 11, 277, 280
- [V+Adj / Adj+V] 4, 7, 10, 11, 262, 277, 279
- [V+Adv] 7, 11, 258, 280
- [V+N / N+V] 4, 7, 9-12, 149, 150, 152, 158, 161, 163, 194, 202, 209, 215, 223, 258, 261, 279, 337, 343, 347, 349, 352, 354
- [V+PP / PP+N] 7, 8, 11, 258, 280, 341, 351
- [V+V] 4, 7, 11, 12, 152, 161-163, 277, 279, 281, 282
Library of Latin Texts 170
linguistic production 251
literal 163, 171, 172, 176, 177, 183, 232, 259, 307, 320
- literal meaning 163, 176, 202, 204, 227, 231, 232, 305

Little v 77, 82

manner verbs 266
Meaning-text theory 2, 3, 7, 10, 240
memoria 12, 337-349, 353, 356
meronymic relation 13, 175, 181, 185, 343
metonymy 172, 173, 178, 259
modal 12, 275, 286, 291-294, 300
modality 103, 206, 222, 226, 276, 291-293
monoclausal structure 4, 152, 203, 277, 278, 337
morphological type 275, 286
motion (see also noun semantic classification: motion noun) 7, 9-11, 122-125, 129, 133, 160, 164, 175, 183, 185-191, 193, 195, 257, 260-262, 265-267, 269, 281, 287, 289, 329
motion component
- Figure 164, 175, 180, 185, 186, 187, 260, 262, 266, 268
- Goal 159, 175, 179, 180, 186, 187, 191, 192, 195
- Ground 164, 175, 180, 186, 187, 191, 193, 195, 260
- Location 78, 82, 83, 161, 165, 175, 266, 342, 356
- Manner 9, 187, 189, 190, 192, 193, 194, 260, 266, 329
- Motion 175, 260, 262, 266, 329
- Path 11, 172, 175, 180, 189, 190, 193, 194, 260, 266, 268, 329
- Source 159, 175, 180, 181, 185, 186, 191, 262
motion event 124, 175, 186, 188, 191, 195, 266
motion verb
- basic motion verbs 266
- caused motion verbs 266
multiclausal structure 5, 277
multi-headed predicate 4, 152
multiword predicate (see also multi-headed predicate) 23, 24, 93, 203

nomen actionis (see also action nominal/noun) 201, 257, 259, 261, 263, 265, 269
nominal
- complex event nominal 155, 156
- simple event nominal 155, 156, 182
nominalization 25, 52, 53, 56, 63, 108, 151, 154-157, 167-170, 184, 188, 192, 202, 203, 205, 215
- bare nominalization 53, 56
non-root bound morpheme 274-276, 285

NorSource 8, 48, 66
NorVal 8, 48, 54
noun actionality 166
- event-denoting noun (see also eventive noun) 108, 162, 258
  - definite process noun (see also accomplishment) 108, 109, 120, 122, 125, 126, 129–133, 136, 138–141, 192–195
  - indefinite process noun (see also activity) 108, 109, 120–122, 130–132, 134, 135, 143, 194–195
  - punctual noun (see also achievement and noun of once) 105, 108, 109, 120, 126, 127, 129, 131–133, 136, 137, 139, 140, 150, 170, 182, 184, 191, 194, 195
  - stative noun (see also state) 9, 11, 113, 114, 116, 120, 132, 134, 135, 137–139, 142, 160
noun of once (see also single instance) 108, 128, 129
noun semantic classification
- articulate/non-articulate sound noun 176–179, 182, 195
- cause emotion noun 104
- hitting noun 157, 171–176, 179, 181, 182, 184, 186, 194, 195
- motion noun (MN) 9, 11, 104, 123, 124, 126, 133, 136, 137, 140, 141, 149, 150, 157–159, 163, 169–171, 183–186, 188, 189, 191–195
- noun of emotional state (see also state) 111–114, 132
- noun of verbal/non-verbal communication 126, 129, 132, 136, 137, 176
- physiological state noun (see also state) 111, 116, 117, 140
- psychological state noun (see also state) 102, 104, 111, 113, 115, 117, 119, 132
- (vocal) sound noun 126, 133, 136, 140, 150, 157, 159, 171, 176, 178, 179, 181, 182, 184–186, 194, 195
noun-verb-distinction 275

opaque 259, 278, 284, 300

particle 4, 11, 180, 280, 291
Path (see motion component)
Patient (see semantic participant)

pegar (Portuguese) 116, 119, 131
performative 78, 83, 125
periphrastic construction 4, 179, 184, 263, 269
perlocutive 129, 136, 137, 139, 142
Perseus 4.0 260
phase (aspect) 119, 125, 189, 190, 193, 204, 213, 214, 294, 295, 329
PHI Latin corpus 338, 340, 342, 350
plexity 168, 169
poiéo: 11, 261–265, 269
polarity 291
polysemous network 160
polysemy 5, 228, 241
polysynthetic language 7, 9, 11–13, 275–277, 279–287, 289–292, 294, 295, 299, 300
portion excerption/excerpting 123, 124, 129, 133, 136, 143, 167, 168, 192, 193, 195
postural verb 287, 288
predicate (see also complex predicate) 2–6, 20, 22–24, 73–75, 77, 79, 90, 91, 93, 103, 105, 151, 152, 156–158, 163–165, 170, 172, 179, 187, 192, 201–207, 214–216, 222, 224, 227, 234, 235, 237, 239, 241, 277, 278, 287, 305, 321
Predicate Composition 5, 155, 156
predicate noun (see also predicative noun) 239, 241
predication 1, 3–6, 8–10, 20, 82, 89, 90, 99, 105, 132, 150–154, 156, 203, 221–224, 226, 235, 236, 258, 321, 322
predicativeness 2, 100, 102, 103, 105, 151, 194, 195, 338
predicative noun (see also action nominal/noun; predicate noun) 1–3, 6, 10, 19, 21–31, 33–36, 38–41, 99, 100, 103, 104, 106, 108, 112, 118, 133, 138, 142, 150–156, 160, 166, 169, 170, 172, 179, 181, 183–185, 190, 191, 194, 195, 257, 259, 261–263, 269, 337, 341, 348, 350, 352
prendere (Italian) 10, 101, 105, 107, 116–120, 123, 125, 131, 137, 138, 141, 203, 222, 223, 229–236, 257–259
prendre (French) 3, 101, 103, 105, 107, 116, 119, 123, 124, 131, 133, 137, 138, 141, 142, 203
prepositional phrase (see also Light Verb pattern) 3, 8, 73, 175, 338, 339
preverbal element (PV) 73–75, 80, 82, 89, 90, 92, 278

process 8, 76, 77, 81–83, 90–92, 108, 110, 125, 134, 152, 169, 193, 204, 205, 212, 214, 251, 329, 344
process phrase (procP) 77, 82, 90–92, 94
profile entities of 'give'
- GIVER 164, 165, 171–174, 179–188, 190, 191, 193, 195
- RECIPIENT 164–166, 174, 175, 177, 179–182, 184–186, 188, 191, 195
- THING 164–166, 171, 172, 174–176, 184–186, 195
punctuality (see also noun actionality: punctual noun) 91, 92, 128, 137, 169

Qualia role 10, 227, 234, 236, 237
- agentive *quale* 214, 215, 234, 235, 237
- constitutive *quale* 214, 237
- formal *quale* 214, 237
- telic *quale* 214, 215, 237
Qualia structure 214
Qualia Unification 214

raising structure 4
Recipient (see semantic participant)
reduction test (see Light Verb Construction test)
referential 60, 99, 151, 162, 297, 347, 352, 357
referentiality 7, 11, 13, 259, 263, 342, 352
Relational Grammar 4–6, 152, 155, 263
relational marker 275
result 8, 74, 91, 105, 130, 132
resultativity 52
result nominal (see also result noun) 155, 182, 185
result noun (see also result nominal) 129, 243
result phrase (resP) 77, 79–81, 87, 92, 94
result state (see also state) 77, 92, 162
result subevent 76, 66, 81, 83, 91–93

selection of preposition and verb by the noun 66
semantic agreement 160, 241
semantic bleaching 105, 194, 259, 306
semantic coherence 103, 112
semantic compatibility (see also compatibility) 103, 112, 160
semantic configuration 10, 204, 214
semantic feature 103, 153, 161, 163, 241, 287, 297
semantic motivation 240, 241

semantic participant (see also semantic role) 20, 22, 23, 25, 26, 29–31, 33, 34, 40, 41
- Actor 22, 29–31, 33–39
- Addressee 22, 29–31, 33, 34, 36, 39, 157, 177
- Agent 8, 9, 46, 48–50, 77, 124, 125, 127–129, 135, 137, 138, 141, 151, 156, 158, 163, 172, 175, 183, 185, 232, 263, 266
- Benefactive 50, 174
- Beneficiary 124, 125, 138, 141, 159, 232
- Cause 50, 77, 82, 90, 156
- Causee 129, 134
- Causer 89, 129, 134, 136
- Donor 27, 30
- Effect 22, 36
- Effector 173, 179, 195
- Experiencer 26, 27, 34, 36, 37, 48, 50, 104, 113–115, 117–119, 132, 134, 138, 139, 142, 159, 179, 182, 184, 195, 232, 344
- Force 173, 179, 195
- Goal (see also Motion component) 159, 174, 179
- Initiator 50, 51, 74, 76, 77, 82, 156
- Instigator 25, 28, 30, 34, 36, 38, 40
- Instrument 174
- Locative 13, 22, 36, 39, 174, 191
- Malefactive 49, 50, 173
- Mover 50, 63, 64
- Origin 22, 36
- Patient 8, 22, 29–31, 33, 34, 36, 39, 46, 49, 50, 172–175, 183, 195, 246
- Possessor 113, 151, 173, 342, 344
- Recipient (see also profile entities of 'give') 8, 9, 27, 30–32, 49, 50, 121, 126–130, 133, 135–137, 139–140, 142, 158, 162, 175, 177, 179, 182, 184, 188, 195, 320
- Source (see also Motion component) 77, 159
- Stimulus 26, 27, 34, 48, 50, 114, 115, 117–119, 134, 140
- Theme 8, 9, 27, 30, 46, 49, 50, 64–67, 135, 158, 161, 163, 185, 195, 320–324, 326, 341, 351
- Undergoer 8, 49, 77, 82, 83, 90, 91, 308, 309, 321, 322, 324
semantic representation 10, 48, 221, 227, 320
semantic role (see also semantic participant; thematic role) 8, 19, 23, 27, 31–33, 35–36, 38–41, 113, 137, 156, 163, 171–173, 177, 179, 184, 185, 195, 342
- sharing of semantic roles 31, 33, 38, 40, 41

semelfactive (see also noun actionality: punctual noun) 108, 152, 168–170, 175, 181, 182, 184, 187–191, 195
semelfactivity 136
semi-lexical head 5, 161
simple event nominal (see nominal)
single instance noun (see also noun of once; semelfactive) 105, 108, 143, 150, 155, 156, 167–170, 182, 185
situation type 52, 63, 64
situational content 7, 8, 45–47, 57, 59, 60, 68
Sketch Engine 201, 207, 229, 230, 242
state 11, 26, 67, 76, 77, 78, 80–83, 85, 88, 90, 94, 102, 104, 105–109, 111–119, 129, 131, 132, 134, 135, 138–141, 152, 162, 167, 169, 170, 175, 190, 205, 212, 213, 222, 223, 225, 226, 259, 261, 289, 311, 344, 354
stative Light Verb 77–81, 90, 94, 118, 135, 137, 262
stative verb 13, 82, 88, 117, 132, 139, 142, 160, 246, 342
stativity 78–80, 130
Stimulus (see semantic participant)
subevent 9, 73, 76–78, 81–83, 89–91, 93, 94, 105, 167
- initiatory subevent 81–83, 87–90, 92
- process subevent 76, 81, 82, 90, 92
- result subevent 76, 77, 81, 83, 91–93
sumere (Latin) 139
support verb (see also *verbe support*) 1–3, 103, 106, 149, 151, 152, 239, 241–243, 245–247, 250–252, 260
- appropriate support verb 2, 103
- basic support verb 106, 152
- support verb extension (see also Light Verb extension) 1, 3, 152
support verb construction 2, 3, 151, 188, 239–243, 248, 251, 252
surface ellipsis 39, 41
surface position 20, 21, 25, 26
syntactic layer
- deep syntactic layer 8, 20–23
- surface syntactic layer 19, 20, 25
syntactic structure 4, 19, 21, 24, 28, 32, 33, 38–40, 76, 152, 153, 203, 222, 319, 321, 324, 325, 337
- deep syntactic structure 19, 28, 32, 33, 39, 40
- surface syntactic structure 19, 38

syntactic template 261, 268
syntagmatic level 206, 216, 228, 259
synthetic verb 1, 2, 6, 11, 100, 114–116, 119, 121, 124, 125, 128, 129, 133, 139–141, 143, 151, 153, 160, 172, 182, 184, 187–189, 210, 214, 269

TAM features 6, 150, 222, 258, 277, 278, 287
telic (see also atelic) 108, 110, 167, 169, 170, 187, 205, 212–215, 237, 330, 344
telicity (see also atelicity) 108–110, 166, 167, 170, 191, 192, 195
telos/*télos* 108, 167, 170, 190–192, 210, 211
temporal boundary 108, 110, 167
tener (Spanish) 101, 104–107, 111, 112, 116, 117, 123, 126, 131, 132, 141, 153, 243, 246, 247
tenere (Latin) 102, 140, 141, 345, 346
ter (Portuguese) 101, 105, 107, 111, 112, 116, 123, 124, 126, 131, 132, 141
thematic index 154, 155
thematic role (see also theta role; semantic role) 77, 185
thematic trace 156
Theme (see semantic participant)
Theta Criterion 155
theta role (see also thematic role) 27, 52
tomar (Portuguese, Spanish) 119, 141, 242, 243, 247–252
trajector 164, 175, 180, 185, 186
trajectory 9, 159, 164, 172, 175–177, 179–181, 185, 186, 188–190, 193, 266, 268
transfer (see also argument transfer) 127, 128, 135–137, 154, 158, 159, 161, 162, 172, 175–179, 182, 188, 246, 249, 325
- transfer of possession 9, 185, 195, 172, 179, 182, 184, 185, 194
transformative 205, 206, 209, 212, 215
Type Coercion 209
typed feature structures 48, 62, 65, 68

unboundedness (see also boundedness) 108, 135, 162, 167–170, 193
Undergoer (see semantic participant)
underspecification 241, 251–252, 257
unification 8, 45, 47, 59–62, 65, 236
unit excerption/excerpting 129, 133, 136, 143, 168, 181, 187
usage-based 10, 12, 309, 310, 312, 314, 316

valence 8, 45, 47, 52, 54, 56, 59, 61, 68
- valence catalogue 8, 48, 54, 68
- valence changing 12, 299, 300
- valence frame 54, 68
- valence satisfaction 60, 61
valency 12, 19–41, 46, 66, 159, 179, 184, 188, 191, 194, 195, 275, 276, 281, 283, 290, 291, 298, 300
valency coercion 159
valency complementation 19–23, 25, 29–32, 34–36, 38–41, 105
valency frame 23, 24, 28–31, 33–36, 38–40
valency structure 19, 23, 28, 40
Valpod 54, 57, 58
vector 10, 244–247, 278, 307

verb emptiness 10
verb lightness 2, 12, 150
verb root 277, 278, 281, 287, 289, 293
- verb root serialization 13, 277, 282, 284, 285, 287–289, 293
- verb serialization 4, 277, 278
verbe support (see also support verb) 1, 103, 150, 151, 257
volitionality 162, 164, 188, 195
V+V 'sum-of-parts' meaning 281

word-embedding 244, 245, 247, 248, 250

yuyi (Chinese) 12, 308, 315, 317–324, 326, 327, 330

Index of languages

Abkhaz 276
Ainu 7, 276, 280, 281, 283, 284
Ancient Greek 7, 10, 257–269
Arabana 279, 280, 283, 288

Basque 279, 280
Bininj Gun-wok 7, 279–281, 283, 291
Bulgarian 180

Caddo 276, 297, 298
Caddoan languages 276
Catalan 107, 129
Cayuga 284, 285
Chechen 279, 280, 283
(Mandarin) Chinese 7, 12, 277, 283, 305–330
Czech 19–41

Diyari 283
Dutch 252

English 1, 10, 58, 150, 161, 167, 169–172, 180, 201–216, 257, 279, 311, 312, 315, 321, 328–330
Eskimoan languages 276

Farsi (see also Persian) 277, 279–281, 283, 285
Fon 283
French 1–4, 9, 13, 99–108, 111–113, 115–117, 119–127, 129–131, 133, 134, 136, 140–142, 150–152, 157–159, 168, 171, 176, 183, 202–205, 257, 306

German 1–2, 104, 183, 191, 202, 258, 276, 279, 280, 283, 290, 294, 295
Gooniyandi 280, 283
Gunwinjgu 276, 282, 284, 297

Hindi 4, 279, 283, 306

Iberic languages 112, 117, 119, 126, 133, 136, 137, 141, 149, 157
Igbo 279, 283
Ik 183

Imonda 279
Irish 306, 329
Iroquoian languages 283
Italian 1, 4, 6, 9, 10, 15, 99–107, 111, 112, 114–123, 125–135, 137, 141, 142, 150, 153–157, 167, 169–171, 175, 176, 183, 187, 190, 202, 204–206, 221–236, 257–259,
– Old Italian 193

Jaminjung 280, 283, 287
Japanese 5, 6, 73, 202, 279–281, 283, 289, 292, 294, 295, 300, 306, 325, 326

Kalam 277, 279–281, 283, 285, 289
Ket 7, 276, 279–285, 287, 288, 290
Kiowa 7, 278–280, 283, 287, 288

Latin 7, 9, 12, 13, 16, 102, 112, 113, 117, 139–142, 149–196, 257, 261, 263, 337–356
Laz 278, 283

Malayalam 306
Marathi 283
Marrithiyel 279, 298, 299
Murrinhpatha 7, 279–283, 286, 287, 298, 299

Ngan'gityemerri 279, 283, 286–288, 298
Nivkh 276, 279, 283, 284, 289, 292, 293, 296, 297
Northern Australian 99, 277
Norwegian 8, 45–68

Panoan languages 276
Papuan languages 276
Persian (see also Farsi) 7, 8, 13, 47, 73–94, 99, 306, 307
Polish 177, 179
Portuguese 9, 99, 100, 102, 104, 105, 107, 111, 112, 115–127, 129–132, 134, 138, 140, 141, 157, 160, 171, 183, 312
Puluwat 283
Purepecha 276

https://doi.org/10.1515/9783110747997-015

Romance languages 9, 16, 47, 99–105, 107, 111, 112, 115, 118, 119, 121, 122, 124–136, 129–134, 136, 139–143, 149, 150, 152, 153, 157, 158, 160, 171, 176, 183, 184, 202
Romanian 9, 99–102, 104, 105, 107, 111–113, 115, 117–127, 129–142, 157, 183, 184

Sakao 283
Salishan languages 276
Sanskrit 263
Spanish 1, 3–4, 9, 10, 99, 100, 102, 104, 105, 107, 111, 112, 115–117, 119–125, 127, 129–131, 134, 136, 137, 141, 143, 150, 153, 157–160, 171, 172, 176, 179, 183, 192, 193, 202, 239–269
Swedish 306

Tamil 283
Thai 283
Tiwi 276
Tunica 282

Udi 279, 280, 283
Ulithian 283
Urdu 5, 152, 161–163, 306, 309, 329

Wakashan languages 276
Warlpiri 279, 280, 283
Wichita 278, 279, 283, 284, 288, 291

Yagua 283, 288, 289, 292
Yanomami 283
Yoruba 283

www.ingramcontent.com/pod-product-compliance
Lightning Source LLC
Chambersburg PA
CBHW031752220426
43662CB00007B/369